Alfa Romeo

all-alloy twin cam
companion 1954–1994

Four-cylinder History, Care and Restoration

Giulietta, Giulia and Alfetta Families

Pat Braden

www.
B BentleyPublishers™
.com

all-alloy twin cam companion 1954–1994

Chapter 2: McLure Halley's 8C2900 was displayed at the 1937 Milan auto show.

Chapter 7: More than any other feature, the all-alloy twin-cam engine defines the Alfa Romeo Giulia and Giulietta.

Chapter 8: When dismantling the engine, look closely at each bearing as it is removed.

Chapter 9: The standard Solex carburetor of the Giulietta mounts on a heated manifold and has two throats.

Contents

Chapter 12: With the case split, the shafts and gears of this 105-series transmission can be seen clearly.

Chapter 16: Anyone contemplating racing should start with a protective helmet, driver's suit and a full roll bar.

Chapter 17: If it weren't for its rarity and its desirability, this 1962 101-series Giulietta Sprint Speciale might not have been a candidate for restoration.

Appendix 1: Engineer Giuseppe Merosi (right) is with his colleagues in a Marchand automobile dating from 1899.

B BENTLEY PUBLISHERS™ | Automotive Books & Manuals

Bentley Publishers, a division of Robert Bentley, Inc.
1734 Massachusetts Avenue
Cambridge, MA 02138 USA
800-423-4595 / 617-547-4170

Information that makes
the difference®

www.
BentleyPublishers
.com

Copies of this book may be purchased from selected booksellers or directly from the publisher. The publisher encourages comments from the reader of this book. These communications have been and will be considered in the preparation of this and other books. Please write to Bentley Publishers at the address listed at the top of this page or e-mail us through our web site.

Since this page cannot legibly accommodate all the copyright notices, the credits listing the source of the photographs or illustrations used constitutes an extension of the copyright page.

Library of Congress Cataloging-in-Publication Data
Braden, Pat, 1934-2002
   Alfa Romeo all-alloy twin cam companion, 1954-1994 : four-cylinder
history, care, and restoration : Giulietta, Giulia, and Alfetta families
/ Pat Braden.
         p. cm.
Includes index.
   ISBN 0-8376-0275-0 (alk. paper)
   1. Alfa Romeo automobile. I. Title.
   TL215.A35B7297 2004
   629.222'2--dc22   2003026679

Bentley Stock No. GALG
ISBN 0-8376-0275-0
08 07 06 05 04   10 9 8 7 6 5 4 3 2 1

The paper used in this publication is acid free and meets the requirements of the National Standard for Information Sciences-Permanence of Paper for Printed Library Materials. ∞

Please read these Warnings and Cautions before proceeding with maintenance and repair work.

- Some repairs may be beyond your capability. If you lack the skills, tools and equipment, or a suitable workplace for any procedure described in this manual, we suggest you leave such repairs to a qualified shop.

- Disconnect the battery negative (–) terminal (ground strap) whenever you work on the fuel system or the electrical system. Do not smoke or work near heaters or other fire hazards. Keep an approved fire extinguisher handy.

- Always make sure ignition is off before disconnecting battery.

- If you are going to work under a car on the ground, make sure that the ground is level. Block the wheels to keep the car from rolling. Disconnect the battery negative (–) terminal (ground strap) to prevent others from starting the car while you are under it.

- Battery acid (electrolyte) can cause severe burns. Flush contact area with water, seek medical attention.

- Batteries give off explosive hydrogen gas during charging. Keep sparks, lighted matches and open flame away from the top of the battery. If hydrogen gas escaping from the cap vents is ignited, it will ignite gas trapped in the cells and cause the battery to explode.

- Connect and disconnect battery cables, jumper cables or a battery charger only with the ignition switched off. Do not disconnect the battery while the engine is running.

- Do not quick-charge the battery (for boost starting) for longer than one minute. Wait at least one minute before boosting the battery a second time.

- Do not allow battery charging voltage to exceed 16.5 volts. If the battery begins producing gas or boiling violently, reduce the charging rate. Boosting a sulfated battery at a high charging rate can cause an explosion.

- Do not reuse any fasteners that are worn or deformed in normal use. Many fasteners are designed to be used only once and become unreliable and may fail when used a second time. This includes, but is not limited to, nuts, bolts, washers, self-locking nuts or bolts, circlips and cotter pins. Always replace these fasteners with new parts.

- Never work under a lifted car unless it is solidly supported on stands designed for the purpose. Do not support a car on cinder blocks, hollow tiles or other props that may crumble under continuous load. Never work under a car that is supported solely by a jack. Never work under the car while the engine is running.

- Never run the engine unless the work area is well ventilated. Carbon monoxide kills.

- Rings, bracelets and other jewelry should be removed so that they cannot cause electrical shorts, get caught in running machinery, or be crushed by heavy parts.

- Tie long hair behind your head. Do not wear a necktie, a scarf, loose clothing, or a necklace when you work near machine tools or running engines. If your hair, clothing, or jewelry were to get caught in the machinery, severe injury could result.

- Do not attempt to work on your car if you do not feel well. You increase the danger of injury to yourself and others if you are tired, upset or have taken medication or any other substance that may keep you from being fully alert.

- Illuminate your work area adequately but safely. Use a portable safety light for working inside or under the car. Make sure the bulb is enclosed by a wire cage. The hot filament of an accidentally broken bulb can ignite spilled fuel, vapors or oil.

- Catch draining fuel, oil, or brake fluid in suitable containers. Do not use food or beverage containers that might mislead someone into drinking from them. Store flammable fluids away from fire hazards. Wipe up spills at once, but do not store the oily rags, which can ignite and burn spontaneously.

- Always observe good workshop practices. Wear goggles when you operate machine tools or work with battery acid. Gloves or other protective clothing should be worn whenever the job requires working with harmful substances.

- Greases, lubricants and other automotive chemicals contain toxic substances, many of which are absorbed directly through the skin. Read the manufacturer's instructions and warnings carefully. Use hand and eye protection. Avoid direct skin contact.

- Friction materials (such as brake pads or shoes or clutch discs) contain asbestos fibers or other friction materials. Do not create dust by grinding, sanding, or by cleaning with compressed air. Avoid breathing dust. Breathing any friction material dust can lead to serious diseases and may result in death.

- Some aerosol tire inflators are highly flammable. Be extremely cautious when repairing a tire that may have been inflated using an aerosol tire inflator. Keep sparks, open flame or other sources of ignition away from the tire repair area. Inflate and deflate the tire at least four times before breaking the bead from the rim. Completely remove the tire from the rim before attempting any repair.

- The ignition system produces high voltages that can be fatal. Avoid contact with exposed terminals and use extreme care when working on a car with the engine running or the ignition switched on.

- Aerosol cleaners and solvents may contain hazardous or deadly vapors and are highly flammable. Use only in a well-ventilated area. Do not use on hot surfaces (engines, brakes, etc.).

- Do not remove coolant reservoir or radiator cap with the engine hot. Doing so risks burns and engine damage.

- Before starting a job, make certain that you have all the necessary tools and parts on hand. Read all the instructions thoroughly, and do not attempt shortcuts. Use tools appropriate to the work and use only replacement parts meeting Alfa Romeo specifications. Makeshift tools, parts and procedures will not make good repairs.

- Use pneumatic and electric tools only to loosen threaded parts and fasteners. Never use these tools to tighten fasteners, especially on light alloy parts. Always use a torque wrench to tighten fasteners to the tightening torque specification listed.

- Be mindful of the environment and ecology. Before you drain the crankcase, find out the proper way to dispose of the oil. Do not pour oil onto the ground, down a drain or into a stream, pond or lake. Dispose of in accordance with federal, state and local laws.

Prologue

If we see Alfa as a living organism, its infancy spanned the time from its birth in 1910 to 1921. In 1922, it attained a brief puberty with a series of three-liter, six-cylinder cars. It became a young adult in 1925 when it won its first European Championship, and then went on to develop a series of sporting cars with twin overhead camshafts. Alfa's maturity came in 1951, when it withdrew from grand prix competition and turned its energies to the development of mass-produced cars. Alfa's purchase by Fiat in 1987 marks another chapter in the life of the unique organism. Alfa is now a badge on Fiat-engineered cars. Fiat is clearly too intelligent to squander Alfa's mystique, so there still persists a conviction among some that Alfa is still alive (much like Elvis).

The enthusiast viewpoint centers on whether or not the modern cars are real Alfas. This question is currently directed to the cars designed after the Fiat takeover: are they badge-engineered Fiats or true Alfas? The fact that Fiat has done so well with the marque tends to lower the level of concern, but it still exists. A similar question was asked of Hruska's front-drive AlfaSuds of 1972 and those assembly-line 1900 Sedans which broke with Alfa's tradition of hand craftsmanship in 1950. Equally arguable: true Alfas ceased to exist when the company became part of the Italian bureaucracy in 1931. But

then, perhaps there were no true Alfas after Vittorio Jano–or perhaps Giuseppe Merosi.

Viewed from a strictly business perspective, Alfa's history has four eras. The company was started in 1910 by a group of investors trying to make something of the failing Darracq manufacturing plant in Milan. Then, in 1918, the company was purchased by Niccola Romeo. In 1931 Alfa was taken over by the Italian Government. Then, it was reprivatized when it was sold to Fiat in 1987.

In 2000, General Motors agreed to swap stock with Fiat, giving it the ability to import Alfa Romeo to the United States again. The rumors circulating about the stock swap had Alfa reentering the United States in 2002 or 2003. Based on Alfa's experience at the hands of domestic Chrysler salespersons, the prospect of Fiat-designed Alfas decorating Buick salesrooms does not inspire great confidence in the marque's prospects in the United States. Considering Fiat's massive troubles and the fact that 2003 opened without Alfa's return to the market, GM dealers may or may not have to grapple with selling Italian cars in the future.

If one approaches Alfa's history according to its physical plants, then there are three eras. The longest part of its history centers on the original Darracq site on Portello road in Milan. In 1962, Alfa opened a research and manufacturing facility at Arese, a few miles from Milan. In 1972, AlfaSuds began rolling off an assembly line in the Pomigliano d'Arco plant near Naples. Viewed from a manufacturing standpoint, Alfa's history divides neatly in two: it was a hand-built car before 1950 and a mass-produced car thereafter.

None of these views reveals the source of Alfa Romeo's greatness, however. People made Alfa great. The individuals who designed Alfa Romeos and guided their construction loved high-performance cars and saw clearly what they must have to be outstanding. Automotive progress has consistently been advanced by individuals who are also enthusiasts: de Dion, Peugeot, Daimler, Benz, Bentley, Bugatti, Porsche, Lyons, Ferrari and Chapman. Committees just can't seem to get it together.

Those people in automotive history who have cared little for the cars they produced—the "bean counters"— consistently produce cars that are uninspiring. Production is so complex today that myriad skills are required to accomplish it. As a curious result, few in the modern automobile industry really seem to care anything about the cars they make: most engineers appear able to create ballpoint pens or cars with approximately equal enthusiasm.

Alfa Romeo, then, has been fortunate to have been shaped continuously by enthusiast engineers: made by enthusiasts for enthusiasts. If we consider Alfa's history in terms of its enthusiast engineers, we have three main eras: Merosi, Jano and Satta. Alfas designed by Giuseppe Merosi spanned the period between 1910 and 1924. Alfa's most glorious era lasted from 1925 to 1936 under Vittorio Jano. In 1946 Orazio Satta Puliga became the guiding engineer of Alfa's fortunes. His last effort for Alfa was the Type 33 race car of 1972, which appeared just two years prior to his death 1974.

To make the chronology of Alfa engineers complete, we must add other names. Engineer Bruno Trevisan shepherded the development of the 6C2300 and 6C2500 cars between 1937 and the end of the war in 1945. Rudolf Hruska helped develop the 1900 and subsequent models for mass production. As an organizational genius, Hruska forms a perfect bridge between the historic personality-driven Alfa Romeo and its current faceless identity under Fiat.

The people who founded Alfa Romeo and made it grow did not try consciously to create either patterns or a coherent history. They were just trying to make a living. In relating the heritage that lies behind the four-cylinder alloy-engined cars that this book covers, you may be startled by the number of Alfa designers whose lives were quite tragic. Alfa's first two engineers, Merosi and Jano, were both fired. Merosi probably died in poverty and Jano committed suicide. Trevisan was probably assassinated, as was Alfa's wartime president Ugo Gobbato. Colombo was discredited on almost every job he ever held. Yet every one of the engineers who designed and built Alfa Romeos had an abiding love of the marque and sporting cars.

To these names can be added a host of drivers, engineers and managers who contributed uniquely from their own enthusiasm. Enzo Ferrari's stewardship under Alfa is well known. Gioacchino Colombo, Wifredo Ricart and Carlo Chiti added to Alfa's fortunes. The engineers under Satta who were most responsible for the cars discussed in this book include Gian Paolo Garcea, Giuseppe Busso, Livio Nicolis and Ivo Colucci. All these individuals are discussed in Griffith Borgeson's fabulous book *The Alfa Romeo Tradition*.

I want to tell Alfa's history so it is most relevant for the new Alfa enthusiast. And, that means focusing primarily on the four-cylinder, alloy block, twin-cam engines that powered the vast majority of Alfa Romeos that were available to American owners when the cars were new. That means that this book will dwell on the Giuliettas and Giulias, Duettos, 1750s, 2000s and Alfettas that came to North America by the thousands.

— Pat Braden
Placentia, California
February 2002

Chapter 1

Alfa Romeo and the Modern Era

Alfa Romeo history may have started in the early days of the Twentieth Century, long before Orazio Satta Puliga joined the Milanese automaker. But it was during his tenure that Alfa Romeo left behind the mantle of limited-production automaker and became a modern mass-producer of automobiles. The 6C1750s of the late 1920s and the 8C2300 and 2900 Alfa Romeos of the 1930s, and the Tipo B and Alfetta race cars may be the most illustrious and famous of the marque's products, but the Giulietta and its successors reached far more people and in their own way made a far greater impact.

■ The Cars of Satta

An early title for this book was "The Cars of Orazio Satta." Although extremely accurate, it is hardly an inspiring title unless you know the man.

The cars of Orazio Satta Puliga span the years between the World Championship Alfetta race car of

1950 and 1951 to the Alfetta series production cars of 1972. Clearly, Hruska's and Satta's eras overlapped. Rudolf Hruska was a production genius; he managed the process of moving Satta's designs into production. However, it was Satta's crew that gave them the unique character which makes them all classic Alfa Romeos.

His 21 years at Alfa only hint at the importance of Satta's contribution. Beginning with the 1900, Alfa's first mass-produced car, Satta directed the design of the series about which this book is written: the Giulietta, Giulia, 1750, 2000 and Alfetta. His credits also include the Disco Volante, 2600 and Montreal. Satta's sure hand ushered Alfa into the modern era and guided the explosion of Alfa models. The Alfa Romeos we know best are all Satta's children, with Hruska's midwifery.

The craft of automaking has its share of egomaniacs. In marked contrast, Satta was an unassuming leader who deferred honors to his subordinates. Thus, he was meticulous in crediting Ivo Colucci with the design of the beautiful Giulietta Sprint, and Giuseppe Busso for its

This 1929 6C1750 Zagato roadster epitomizes the type of high-quality sports car Alfa Romeo built between the two World Wars. This example was once owned by the author.

Many consider the Alfa Romeo 8C2300 to be the finest road car the company ever built. This 1933 Monza was the racing version of the model.

With only approximately 40 examples built, the 8C2900 is one of the most coveted of all collector vehicles. With a supercharged straight-eight producing close to 200 horsepower and fully independent suspension, it was an extremely advanced design.

engine. Yet, as surely as it would have been Satta's head had the designs failed, it must remain to his credit alone that they have succeeded.

Satta was born in Turin on October 6, 1910. Turin has always been the automotive center of Italy, and it is an interesting coincidence that both he and Jano were born and studied there. Satta studied mechanical engineering at the Polytechnic and received his degree in aeronautical engineering in 1935. After a short stint in the military, he returned to teach aeronautical engineering at the Polytechnic until hiring on at Alfa in 1939.

Satta worked in the design department. After the war he was promoted to the overall management of design for the company. He continued to rise in the organization: in 1951 he was central director and in 1969, assistant general director of the company. In 1972, he left active employment with the company and in March 1974 he died after a protracted illness.

Satta's training as an aeronautical engineer positioned him perfectly to continue the work begun by Jano on the development of lightweight cars that attained high performance through a good power/weight ratio rather than raw displacement. One reflection of his training, no doubt, is the use of unit body construction, pioneered at Alfa with the 1900 series cars. His unique vision allowed him to

Immortalized by many victories by such driving giants and Nuvolari and Varzi, the Tipo B—also known as the P3—was one of Alfa's most successful racing cars.

concentrate on the car as a whole, rather than treating it as a collection of distinct elements. As a result, the Satta cars have distinct personalities, ranging from the solid masculinity of the 1900 to the feminine grace of the Giulietta.

Friendly and outgoing, he knew all of his subordinates by name and inspired great loyalty. Certainly he won the heart of Luigi Fusi, through whose eyes we have seen much of the Alfa organization. Fusi could not have created his museum at Arese without Satta's enthusiastic and unflagging support.

With a competitive life spanning both sides of World War II, the Alfetta Grand Prix car saw victories with drivers including Farina and Fangio (shown).

Orazio Satta Puliga was the engineer behind the design and development of the Giulietta.

Carlo Chiti (left) was a talented former Ferrari engineer responsible for running Autodelta, which raced Giuliettas and Giulias with much success.

During Satta's tenure at Alfa, racing successes continued, though somewhat sporadically. Some of the cars are covered in detail in this book because they are currently the most attractive "classic" Alfas available to the fervent collector, and many (such as the Giulia TI Super, GTA and GTAm) are closely related to the road-going cars. Strictly speaking, the pure-blood racing cars, such as the 1970 and 1971 Manufacturer's Championship cars and earlier Type 33 sport racers, are beyond the scope of this book, but the Giulietta- and Giulia-based coupes by Zagato are an important chapter in Alfa's racing history. Carlo Chiti guided Satta's sport cars to their racing successes, and his story is told in the chapter on the competition cars.

Satta's cars should remind us that there was once a time when craftsmen would stand at the table to draft a car, and then go into the shop to make it, employing skill and love in equal measure.

▪ The Alloy Fours: 2.0-Liter, 1750, Giulia and Giulietta

These engines, and the cars they powered, are the core of this book. Virtually every enthusiast between the 1950s and 1980s regarded Alfa as the premier producer of unit-body cars powered by small-displacement, high-performance four-cylinder twin-cam engines and driven through solid rear axles. It's defensible to argue that all the twin-cam fours since late 1959 are actually the same engine with only progressively larger displacements. That is not to say the various displacements are so identical that they are easily interchangeable. Detail changes over the years improved reliability or accommodated United States emissions laws, and it is never safe to assume that, say, a 1995 2.0-liter engine will drop right into a 1956 Giulietta chassis (it won't).

On the other hand, some essential manufacturing details are amazingly consistent: almost all these engines (excepting the early 750-series Giulietta) have the same main bearing diameter and cylinder spacing. This means that crankshafts from any model will fit in any other's block. Since the throws of the crank differ between displacements, the cranks won't bolt up to run, but the basic dimensions of the lower half of the Alfa block from 1959 through 1995 are the same, and the main bearing shells are interchangeable between engines.

The reader may marvel at the brilliance of a basic design that has remained competitive for so many years. From the standpoint of engineering and production convenience, Alfa's singularly long run of twin-cam fours makes a lot of sense. The long life of the design has let the machine tools pay for themselves many times over. MG did the same thing with its T-series engines, while Jaguar and Chevrolet did likewise with quite dissimilar sixes.

At first glance, such a long run of a single design would suggest a rather straightforward model history. To the contrary: this era is where Alfa has worked magic for its customers and disaster for its historians.

During the 1960s and 1970s, as the Giulia gave way to the Duetto and the 1750 and 2.0-liter models joined the lineup, Alfa managed to create a daunting model matrix. It attained total confusion by changing either the body or the engine but not both at the same time. Since the introduction of either a new body or a new engine really constitutes a model change, a simple recitation of Alfa models gives the impression of many different types of cars. In fact, the differences between many Alfa models are minor, bordering on the cosmetic. Finally, Alfa has further confused its own history by assigning the same name (e.g., Veloce) to cars of quite different specifications. To top it all off, the records of serial numbers, and therefore the total number of vehicles produced, have been somewhat garbled. This is to be expected in an organization which regularly changes bodies or engines in its racing cars with ultimate finesse, but it also results in predictable confusion when it's time to calculate taxes on earnings.

The Giulietta series consisted of a sedan, coupe and spider body, none of which saw significant changes for the ten years of their production (1954 to 1964). There were two series of engines (the change from 750 to 101

The Giulietta engine started in 750cc form, was developed into a 1100cc prototype (above) and first saw production as a 1300cc unit. Over a period of more than 40 years, this basic engine grew to 2000 cc.

came unannounced in 1959) and two stages of tune (the Veloce had twin Weber carburetors compared to the single Solex carburetor of the normal model). In addition to this trio, there were a few special-bodied coupes by Zagato (two styles—round-tail and cut-off, or Coda Tronca) and Bertone (the Sprint Speciale), a van (the Romeo) and onesey-twosey sedans from specialist bodybuilders like Zagato and Moretti.

The impact of the Giulietta is hard to understate: it put Alfa on the map as a producer of medium-priced sporting cars of very high performance. Giuliettas made the dream of Alfa ownership a reality for many young, under-funded enthusiasts. As a result of the Giulietta's success, which was continued by the Giulia, enthusiasts organized Alfa clubs and began to be interested in the history of the marque.

The Alfa Romeo product line for 1964 shows only one
Giulietta model (Berlina, far right).

This original build plate indicates that car 00007 is one of
the earliest 750 Giuliettas known to exist.

▪ Alfetta

Introduced in the United States in 1976, this all-new sedan body first appeared in 1975 with the 2.0-liter twin-cam engine that derived directly from the Giulietta. Its deDion transaxle reintroduced a sophisticated rear suspension to Alfa Romeo production cars.

The Alfetta was the first model to introduce the wedge-shape profile that has become so characteristic of the modern Alfa. The wedge was hardly noticeable when the car was introduced, but is more noticeable when compared to the models that succeeded it.

Imported into the United States until late 1979, the Alfetta was withdrawn from that market in an attempt to consolidate the Alfa lineup and make the company more profitable. The reason given at the time was that the sedan was not in keeping with the American perception of Alfa Romeo sporting vehicles. That claim, taken against the fact that the last surviving model in the United States was the 164 sedan, is another example of corporate marketing confusion.

In Europe, the Alfetta body style was available with engines displacing 1.6, 1.8 and 2.0 liters. A luxury version, the Quadrifoglio, was also offered, along with a 2.0- and 2.5-liter turbodiesel. The Alfetta was replaced by the 75, or Milano, which shared its unique driveline.

The name of the Alfetta model recalls the world-championship Formula 1 cars of the late 1940s and early 1950s.

Although the Alfetta was built from the mid-1970s through the early 1980s and featured a rear-mounted transaxle and a deDion rear suspension, it owed much to the original Giulietta.

▪ New Giulietta

In the 1970s Alfa began trying to enhance its fading appeal by recalling famous models of the past. The New Giulietta was introduced in 1977 in an attempt to offer a lower-priced Alfa and repeat the success of one of Alfa's greatest models.

The New Giulietta was a wedge-shaped sedan powered by an alloy, in-line, twin-cam four with displacements of 1570, 1779 and 1962 cc. Engines displacing 1.3 and 1.6 liters were added in 1980. The New Giulietta's transmission borrowed from the Alfetta. Two diesel Giulietta versions were available,

The Tipo 158 (with the author) was an extremely potent 1.5-liter supercharged Grand Prix car designed by Colombo at Scuderia Ferrari.

a Turbodelta with front wheel drive and Turbodiesel with rear-wheel drive. Basically an Alfetta with a new skin, the Giulietta was a very popular Alfa throughout Northern Europe.

▪ Family Tree

Close to ten years after Alfa Romeo withdrew from the United States market, the cars most people associate with the marque are the 2.0-liter Spiders sold from 1972 through 1994. With relatively minor alterations, such as the Kamm tail, that body design dated back to the Duetto Spider of 1966. Although the striking scalloped-sided, boat-tail body was new, the underpinnings were pure Giulia, and the all-alloy twin-cam engine was essentially a development the 101-series unit first seen in Giuliettas in 1959. As far-fetched as it sounds, the Giulietta of 1954 and the Spider of 1995 are very closely related. And without a doubt, this family of cars put Alfa Romeo on the automotive map in post-war Europe and America.

The New Giulietta was a largely unsuccessful attempt to recapture the charisma of the original and much-loved Giulietta.

When most Americans think of Alfa Romeo, they envision a spider like this 1973 2.0-liter model.

Chapter 2

Alfa in America

The fact of the matter, as revealed in the Prologue, is that the author's focus in this book is a view from the United States. That is probably not the optimal seating arrangement for the history of an Italian car. If I were an Italian citizen, my view would undoubtedly be more intimate.

On the other hand, we in the United States have seen both the best and worst of Alfa: the cars about which this book is written being the best; Alfa's failure in our market being the worst.

There are others who could write a much more coherent history of Alfa in America. A calculated, crafted, roseate view could be written by journalists and enthusiasts who have been fed claque press releases and luxurious long-lead introductions. Most striking to me, a story of intrigue, fear and despair would come from those within the company. Almost to a man, Alfa's American employees I have known have been so demoralized by their experience that they find it hard to discuss.

■ The Pre-War Era

There were Alfas in the United States before the outbreak of World War II. Ralph Stein has written the story of McClure Halley's wait for an 8C2900 roadster to be delivered to Zumbach's in New York City. The car's arrival was delayed for months, but when it finally appeared, there was a party to welcome a very significant Alfa to our shores.

According to Stein, pre-war Alfas were genuine bargains in the late 1940s. Since there were no import

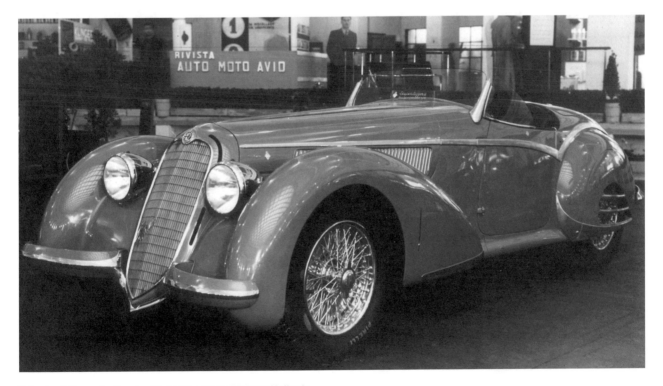

Prior to delivery to Zumbach's in New York, McLure Halley's 8C2900 was displayed at the 1937 Milan auto show.

restrictions as there are now, private individuals were free to bring European cars in. Surely the number must have been small, in spite of the fact that Stein told me used 1750 Alfas were easy to find in used-car lots and their average price was $750. He was offended that I had paid $1,500 for my Gran Sport Zagato, and feared that my extravagance would unrealistically drive up the price of these cars.

The West Coast had its own center of Alfa enthusiasm in Otto Zipper's Los Angeles store, where he kept his 8C2300 Alfa. There was also a contingent of Alfa owners in the Chicago area, and a small group of Detroit auto executives also enjoyed pre-war Alfas, including designer Dick Teague.

▪ The Glory Years: 1955–1967

Alfa's official presence in the United States began in 1955, but it was not until 1961 that it became an importer of cars. Before 1961, distribution was handled by Max Hoffman's offices in New York and Los Angeles.

Alfa's history in the United States can be divided into the following eras:

From 1956, when the first Alfas began appearing, through 1967, Alfa offered an unbeatable combination of Italian design and performance at a bargain price.

In the early 1960s Giulietta Spiders were the glamorous products that importer Max Hoffman promoted to the public.

Under the leadership of Arturo Reitz, Alfa Romeo Incorporated enjoyed prosperity, a cornucopia of desirable models, growing sales and a variety of activities which included very successful racing efforts.

1955: In 1955, Alfa Romeo Incorporated (ARI) was set up in New York City as a purchasing arm for Alfa Romeo Avio, the Finmeccanica group which manufactures aircraft engines.

In the late 1940s, British and Continental automakers began to understand that there was a market for their cars in the States. As noted in the biography of Max Hoffman, many companies, including Volkswagen, Mercedes-Benz, Jaguar and MG, initially sold cars in the United States without officially establishing their corporate presence in the country. Their cars were sold through distributors, who were responsible for developing the local market, establishing sales and service outlets and advertising the product.

You can't beat the "locals" at their own game. No one knows better than an Italian how to sell cars to Italians. The corollary of that is that no one knows better than an American how to sell cars to Americans (Southern and Northern distinctions apply). It also follows that a distributorship needs to be controlled by a "local," and those distributorships which are commanded by foreign staff are the equivalent of a champion sharpshooter who takes careful aim at the wrong target.

The advantage of using a local distributor to sell your cars, then, is that the distributor understands how to speak to the local market. The disadvantage is that distributors take some of the profit which could be made by the parent company. As a result, the life of a distributor is likely to be anxious and frequently short.

A second advantage of selling through a local distributorship is that it establishes an effective "firewall" for legal actions against the parent company. For a product liability claim to be lodged against a foreign company, the suit must be brought in an international court. And, since the distributor is characterized as only a sales organization and thus not responsible for design or manufacture, he can use his status to avoid product liability claims.

In the Midwest, S.H. "Wacky" Arnolt became famous (and wealthy) as the distributor for MG. On the East Coast, Luigi Chinetti proved hugely successful selling Ferraris, and the Max Hoffman Motor Corporation distributed Jaguar, BMW, Volkswagen and Alfa Romeo.

1956: Hoffman begins importation of the Giulietta. The Sprint has small headlamps for this year. Both Spiders and Sprints are imported. If any Berlinas were imported by Hoffman, the numbers were small.

1957: Importation begins in earnest and Hoffman ads begin to appear for both the Sprint and Spider.

The Veloce model carries Weber 40DCO3 carburetors.

1959: Without announcement, the dimensions of the Spider changed and the original "750" designation becomes significant. Veloces get 40DCOE carburetors.

These "transition" Alfas, which came along in 1959, featured larger dimensions in the engine, a relocated fuel pump, a completely new gearbox and a slightly longer Spider body with fixed side vent windows, all of which signaled a change to the "101" series cars.

The increasing number of sales in the United States caused some concern at Alfa SpA that the cars were not being maintained properly. To assure that they were, Maurizio Capeletti came from Fiat to check warrantee claims at Hoffman's facility. He was the first Alfa SpA employee in the United States, and also the oldest practicing Alfa mechanic in the country. Capeletti still runs an Alfa shop with his son (appropriately: Alfa West) in Long Beach, California.

1961: With the introduction of the Giulia in 1961, Arturo Reitz, a vice president of Alfa SpA, was sent to the Alfa Avio offices to organize Alfa Romeo International (ARI) and begin phasing Hoffman out. Temporary ARI offices were set up in Newark, New Jersey, to distribute cars and parts.

1962: In 1962, ARI moved to a permanent home at 231 Johnson Avenue in Newark and established a training center a few blocks away. Vern Bennett was ARI's sales manager and Don Black was in charge of service.

ARI also set up a branch in Long Beach, California, and took over distribution of Alfa Romeo cars and parts on the West Coast. The dealer network was gradually changed over from Hoffman to ARI during the 1961–63 period. Some stores were newly ARI-franchised dealers, and the remainder were converted Hoffman stores. During this time,

Alfa at a Glance				
President	Year	Sales	Dealers	Models and Sales Totals
Reitz	1961	387	n/a	Giulietta Spider & Sprint
	1962	749	n/a	
	1963	682	n/a	
	1964	919	n/a	**1961–1964 total (Giulietta): 2,737**
	1965	1,512	n/a	Giulia (sedan, Spider, Sprint, SS)
	1966	1,412	n/a	
	1967	1,552	n/a	
	1968	913	n/a	('67 model year vehicles) **1965–1968 total (Giulia): 5,389**
	1969	2,553	n/a	1750 Berlina, Spider Veloce & GTV
	1970	1,550	n/a	('69 model year vehicles)
	1971	2,552	n/a	**1969–1971 total (1750): 6,655**
	1972	2,347	n/a	Berlina, Spider Veloce & GTV
Ronchetti	1973	2,158	n/a	
	1974	3,139	n/a	**1972–1974 total (2.0-liter): 7,644**
	1975	5,418	n/a	Alfetta sedan & GT; Spider Veloce
Bozzi	1976	5,327	n/a	
	1977	5,426	n/a	
	1978	6,137	n/a	
	1979	4,011	n/a	**1975–1979 total (Alfetta and Spider): 26,319**
Dent	1980	2,997	141	Spider Veloce only
	1981	2,274	130	GTV-6 introduced in April
Zuchett	1982	2,193	117	
Vettore	1983	3,002	106	
	1984	3,102	120	
	1985	4,502	144	
	1986	8,201	153	Milano 2.5 introduced in April
Greco	1987	6,000	141	Milano 3.0 introduced
	1988	4,476	149	ARDONA formed with Chrysler
Davis	1989	2,912	132	164 introduced as 1990 model
	1990	3,482	193	Final Spider introduced in June as 1991 model
Vellano	1991	3,478	173	
	1992	2,828	135	
	1993	1,325	105	
	1994	565	94	
	1995	414	90	Leftover from 1994
		51,751		**1980–1995 total**
		100,495		**Grand Total**

Max Hoffman

After the war, it was Max Hoffman who was responsible for bringing Alfa Romeo to the United States.

The automotive world is filled with people who have cut a broad swath: Abarth, Bentley, Bugatti and Ferrari all come easily to mind. No less a swath was cut by Maxmillian Edwin Hoffman, the man responsible for introducing most of the famous European marques to the U.S. market.

Unlike the famous automobile designers and manufacturers, Max Hoffman was a distributor, an individual who buys cars from the manufacturer and then sells them to independent dealerships for ultimate sale to the customer. Distributorships were a perfect way for European manufacturers to tap into the infant North American market just after the Second World War. They did not have to learn how to sell to the locals, nor invest any money in infrastructure; both were the responsibility of the distributor. If the cars sold well, everyone was happy; if they did not, the manufacturers were out nothing and the distributor was free to try another marque.

The number of marques Max introduced to the United States is staggering: Jaguar, BMW, Fiat, Lancia, Mercedes-Benz, VW and Porsche. And the specific models he requested, and got, include the Giulietta Spider, Porsche Continental and BMW Bavaria.

Max was born just outside Vienna, Austria. His father owned a company that began manufacturing sewing machines, and ended up making bicycles. Max grew up with an interest in powering bicycles with small gasoline engines and raced motorcycles in his youth. Before long, he graduated to cars, eventually becoming a dealer in Grofri automobiles. His next step was to represent, as a distributor, a number of European makes including Rolls-Royce, Alfa Romeo, Talbot and Delahaye.

The French connection, perhaps, helped convince Max to move to France in the late 1930s, just before Europe was plunged into war. Then, in the face of an advancing German army, he left for the United States in 1941. At first, Max could not find work, but he realized that metal would be scarce during the war, so launched into the manufacture of plastic jewelry, plated to resemble metal. By war's end, he had made enough to be able to return to sale of automobiles.

On Max's first trip back to Europe, he ordered and paid for a shipment of Hotchkiss, Lancia and Alfa Romeo cars. Only a few of the Hotchkiss and Lancias were received, and none of the Alfas ever arrived. Undeterred, Max begain importing Allards and other British models, including HGR, Lancaster and Healey. He did manage to bring in some Cisitalias from Italy, and also imported a few Simcas from France. His first major marque contract was with Jaguar in 1948.

As with so many European cars, Max Hoffman was the man responsible for launching Alfa Romeo in the United States.

Readers will note that Hoffman's initial selection of cars was not exactly representative of the finest examples of the industry. In fact, he discovered that buyers of his 3.5-liter (Mark IV) Jaguar sedans were more likely to swear off European cars forever than return to buy another. Undeterred, Max enlarged his market base by appointing a Boston outlet, Ray Clark's Foreign Motors.

A potential big break came with an agreement to sell Volkswagen cars in 1950. Unfortunately, Americans were not yet ready for the car. Max gave up the distributorship and VW began setting up its own distribution network in 1954. During the same period, however, he developed a strong relationship with Porsche and that model did strike fire. The 1954 Porsche Speedster was the result of Hoffman's concern that the marque was too high-priced for the American market. With Porsche, Max was drawn back into racing, and imported a Glöckler-modified Porsche with which he won several races.

In 1951–52, he negotiated an arrangement by which he would be the East Coast distributor for Mercedes-Benz. Jaguar objected to this arrangement, and Max lost the Jaguar franchise in 1954. The final arrangement was not at all bad, however, because it included a premium payable to him for every Jaguar sold for the next few years. At about the same time, Mercedes management asked him to investigate their West Coast distributor. Max found the distributor in financial trouble and managed to take over the territory, becoming sole U.S. distributor for the marque.

Hoffman claimed to have been a major influence on the Stuttgart firm, insisting on light-colored sedans and urging the production of the 300SL and 190SL. His agreement with Mercedes, like Jaguar, eventually went sour. He negotiated an agreement that included a lump payment of $2 million.

In the early 1950s, Max received a call from the German agent for Alfa, asking if he would import some Alfas from Germany. This deal eventually engaged Alfa management

For more than ten years, beginning in 1961, Arturo Reitz (holding paper) led ARI during its most successful period in the United States. Vic Zafuto is to Reitz's right.

both ARI and Hoffman supplied parts to the entire dealer network, and some Hoffman parts and service employees were hired by ARI. Fred Bonzer was appointed by ARI as the first parts manager on the West Coast.

In 1962, a shipment of Alfas was submerged in salt water during a flood at the New Jersey port. About ten of these "salt-water cars" were sold by then-Alfa-dealer Chuck Stoddard and sold at reduced prices for racing use and others were broken for parts.

1963: Alfa ended the relationship with Hoffman at the end of 1963 and ARI became the official source of Alfas in the United States. That does not mean, however, that it was the only source: all Montreals and Junior Zagato coupes, for instance, were brought in by individuals.

Don Black was chief engineer for ARI.

in Milan, and they aggressively campaigned to make Max the U.S. importer. In sum, Max agreed, but only if a Spider were included in the model mix. Hoffman claims to have had a heavy hand in the design of the Spider, from its overall profile to its roll-up windows. During the discussion period, he also made contact with Fiat, and ended up being the importer for both Alfa and Fiat in the United States.

Hoffman's success with Alfa resulted in the factory's decision to take over importation. Once again, he was eased out of the picture: in 1963, Alfa became the single importer of its cars to the United States.

Undeterred, Max turned to BMW, which was offering the 502-series V-8 sedan. Max's preference for convertibles was demonstrated with the Giulietta, and he was able to convince BMW to create a roadster on the 502 chassis. The result was the Goertz-designed 507, certainly one of the most beautiful cars ever produced. Hoffman became the sole importer of BMW cars beginning in 1962, and it was through his distributorship that the four-cylinder sedans, including the 1600, 1800 and 2002 models, were sold. Once again, the deal unwound and BMW took over distribution of its cars in February 1975. An *Automotive News* article reported that according to the settlement, Max would be paid "more annual income through 1986 than the president and chairman of General Motors combined."

Max Hoffman died in 1981 at age 76.

Max Hoffman imported Giulietta Sprints (above) and Spiders (below) into the United States, but shied away from bringing in the Berlinas.

ARI service chief Don Black was so committed to Alfa Romeo that he even ran one of the all-alloy engines in his midget racer dubbed the Portello Special.

According to Dave Mericle, when ARI took over Max Hoffman's remaining stock of Alfas, they were directed by Alfa management in Italy to refurbish some cars to Giulia specifications. As a result, some 101-series Giuliettas ended up with Giulia gauges and hood scoops.

1965: The 105-series Giulia TI and Sprint GT appeared. Like the earlier models, the coupe was styled by Bertone and the sedan by Alfa's own styling office, Centro Stile.

1966: The Pininfarina-designed Duetto Spider was introduced on the *Rafaello* en route from Genoa to New York. Alfa SpA president Radelli participated. The GTA Alfa race car debuted at Sebring. In late 1966 the Giulia TI was withdrawn for the forthcoming introduction of the Giulia Super sedan.

1967: The Giulia Super is introduced, along with the Giulia GT Veloce. ATE brakes are adopted.

Alfa's V-8 Montreal supercar was a rare site in the United States, although a handful were privately imported.

■ The SPICA Era: 1968–1981

While other automakers resorted to air pumps and other power-sapping devices to reduce exhaust emissions, Alfa engineered a mechanical fuel-injection system which initially increased power when other car makers were experiencing drastically reduced horsepower ratings.

1968: There were no 1968 Alfa Romeos sold in the United States because of exhaust emission regulations. Some 1968 cars were brought in from Canada by individuals.

1969: The 1750-series was introduced with ads recalling the original 1750 model of 1929. The Berlina received an updated body which was less sculptured than the Giulia Super and featured a modern interior with separate "pods" for the speedometer and tachometer. The GTV was a facelift of the 1600 series, deleting the step nose for a smooth one.

The 1750 cars carried SPICA fuel injection for lower emissions and dual-boosters for the divided brake system mandated by law. The idle system for the 1750 used separate air bleed hoses, and there was no fuel cut-off solenoid. Mixture richness was adjusted with a locknut-captured screw on the body of the pump.

1970: There were no 1970 model year Alfas sold because of emissions regulations. Stocks of 1969 cars were cleaned out.

1971: A facelift to the Spider featured new interior treatments and a redesigned nose, and the tail was truncated as a "Kamm-Tail." The GTV and Berlina (sedan) remained basically unchanged with only detail refinements but a new injection system. A valve on a central plenum controlled the idle air, and the fuel cut-off solenoid served to adjust mixture richness. Up to this time, the brake and clutch pedals pivoted at floor level; beginning in 1971, all cars featured pendulum pedals.

The AlfaSud was certified for sale in the United States but Alfa management decided against its importation. When this car was first introduced in Europe, it was not well received for its Neapolitan workmanship. Indeed, Alfa management spent a lot of effort trying to get a regular workforce in an area where daily attendance was a novelty. A number of design changes were necessary before the 'Sud was widely accepted, but it became the favorite car for many Alfa enthusiasts, in spite of its propensity for rust.

The 'Sud's reception in the United States continues to be a topic of discussion. It still has a host of enthusiast owners, especially of the Sprint, which is a scaled-down version of the Alfetta coupe, but with a flat-four engine.

1972: The 2000 series was introduced with further facelifts and new interior appointments of all three cars. The larger displacement did little to stem the decline in overall performance caused by increasingly strict emission controls.

Alfa Romeo International moved from Newark, New Jersey, to new facilities in nearby Englewood Cliffs. The California office was moved from Long Beach to a new location in El Segundo, California.

In 1972, ARI moved into a new building in Englewood Cliffs, New Jersey.

Several Berlinas occupy the service reception area of the ARI facility in Englewood Cliffs.

1969–1971 Federal Regulations

Alfa did not sell any 1968 model cars, nor any in 1970 because of the new government regulations for emissions and safety. Rather than try to stretch the capability of the carburetor, Alfa was one of the first manufacturers in the world to adopt fuel injection for reduced emissions. However, the SPICA mechanical fuel-injection system left both dealers and mechanics puzzled.

With the SPICA system, Alfa tried to maintain its cars' performance against the increasing onslaught of safety and emission restrictions. In spite of their efforts, the SPICA-injected cars became increasingly heavier and slower, and developed a propensity for blowing head gaskets.

The Alfa Romeo double overhead camshaft engine, refined since 1923 in racing competition, where every element of an automotive power plant is tested to the ultimate. Engineers acknowledge this costly-to-build mechanism as the most desirable of all designs for internal combustion engines — no great Grand Prix car of *any* marque has ever been built around anything else. Output of the all-aluminum 4-cylinder D.O.H.C. engine in the 1971 Spider Veloce is 1.24 brake horsepower per cubic inch of displacement — testimony to its astonishing efficiency.

A 1971 American-market brochure featured a cutaway drawing of the 1750 engine. The copy cited the racing heritage of the power unit.

1974: The 1973 and 1974 cars were basically the same with refinement and specification changes to stay current with government regulations. Bumper over-riders with rubber pads were the most "outstanding" feature. Factory air conditioning was made available for the first time in 1974 (on Berlinas and GTVs only), as well as seatbelt interlock. The three-dimensional cam on the SPICA fuel pump of the 1974 cars gave the most horsepower of all models.

1975: The Alfetta GTV and Berlina featured a new deDion rear suspension but the same 2.0-liter alloy engine. The '75 models were the first all-new car since 1965, and introduced a driveline layout that would be used through 1989. The spider received new bumpers to meet government regulations, and all cars were equipped with air pumps for the emission-control system.

Beginning in 1975 Alfa, along with several other manufacturers, began using low-carbon steel supplied by countries behind the Iron Curtain. The joke of the time was that the steel came with rust built in. In addition, the Alfetta had a remarkable appetite for the rubber donuts which replaced the solid universal joints and helped absorb driveline shock. Between diminishing performance, rust, head gaskets and donuts, the desirability of the marque was waning. The Alfetta offered new styling to a line which was growing very old. However, a convertible based on the sophisticated driveline never appeared.

Alfa Romeo hosted 400 people for a dealer introduction in Italy with 200 cars driving in a police-escorted group all over Italy. The "Ciao trip" was a huge success with the dealers and press, in spite of the fact that one of the labor unions came in and broke up the drive-away section of the meeting.

There were no 1975 model year cars for the California market as Alfas were not yet equipped with catalytic converters. This was the first year for "California" and "49-state" cars offered for sale. Still, sales reached an all-time high.

1976: There were only minor cosmetic revisions to the 1976 model year cars. The Alfettas had quickly developed a reputation for a problematic driveshaft, and Alfa redesigned the rubber joints for the driveshaft three times.

1977: The year 1977 brought improved fuel calibration of the SPICA pump for more performance but the cars were otherwise basically unchanged.

Marketing materials for the Alfetta GT took advantage of the famous name first applied to the Tipo 158 and 159 Grand Prix cars from immediately before and after World War II.

From 1976 through 1979, Aldo Bozzi (in light suit) led ARI.

A fire in the hold of the *Taurinita* damaged both Fiats and Alfas on their way to the United States. To help dispose of the Alfas, ARI set up a race-car series and ran ads in *Competition Press* magazine. The cars were sold without titles for racing purposes only.

Alfa Romeo Canada ceased operations and an independent distributor took on Alfa Romeo distribution. In the United States, sales volume was maintained only by introducing heavy incentives.

1978: The Alfetta sedan was modified to be the Sport Sedan, a facelift which included new doors and interior. This was also the first model year that Alfa offered an automatic transmission. ARI management had insisted that the United States market demanded an automatic transmission in its sedans, and used this fact to help explain Alfa's continuing poor sales. ZF-equipped three-speed automatic transaxle Alfetta sedans are referred to as Alfamatics.

The cars in 1978 became "50-state cars" all equipped with catalytic converters, redesigned exhaust manifolds, upgraded interiors and minor changes to the Alfetta GT and Spider. The sedan received a major facelift for that year and an automatic transmission was made available for the first time. Good sales resulted as the United States market base widened.

1979: For 1979, the GT and Spider remained pretty much the same, but the sedan again received minor updates. A little-known fact: John DeLorean investigated the possibility of becoming the Alfa distributor for the United States in 1979.

1980–1994: Success and Disaster

In recognition that it needed local talent, ARI selected its first American president, Joe Dent, in 1980. Unfortunately, Dent developed cancer and had less than a year to reach the goals he was so clearly capable of accomplishing.

Luigi Zucchet served as ARI's president from 1982–83. He was replaced in 1983 by Ernesto Vettore, who had worked for Ford in Europe. Beginning in the fall of 1983, Joe Cooley filled the sales/marketing position and Jim Weber was put in charge of public relations.

In an attempt to increase sales, Cooley began awarding the Alfa franchise to dealerships with already existing franchises. These dual-franchise dealerships were an attempt to get away from the enthusiast dealers who, according to conventional wisdom, spent too much time enjoying the cars and their owners and not enough time developing the market. Cooley's efforts were continued by his successors and put Alfa into a flat spin from which it never recovered. Alfa lost its share-of-mind with its dealers, and became a second-class franchise.

This was a time of considerable public-relations activities, and it was during this period that Mario Andretti drove in Formula 1 for Alfa. ARI decided to launch the GTV-6 in Italy, and sent the automotive press there, with Andretti. A select group of California customers was invited to drive the cars at Sears Point and Carlsbad, under the supervision of the Bob Bondurant driving school. The launch of the Porsche 944 hurt Alfa sales: Porsche's coachwork and handling were better, but Alfa's twin-cam engine retained an aura which not even Porsche could equal.

Joe Dent's tenure as ARI president was curtailed due to illness.

Ernesto Vettore became president and CEO of ARI in 1983.

Joe Cooley joined ARI as sales and marketing chief in late 1983.

The Alfamatic sedan proved a marketing failure and was withdrawn from the market. Alfa returned a number of these fully optioned cars to Italy and re-badged them as "America" models. The novelty of the car, and its "American" associations proved a hit with the Italians, and Alfa actually went back in production to meet local demand.

1980: In spite of the fact that ARI management was still predicting sales of 10,000 cars a year, it was clear that Alfa was in decline in the United States. No sedans nor coupes were sold in 1980, and plans to introduce the new "Alfa 6" sedan were scrapped. As a final blow against its deteriorating performance image, Alfa tried to revitalize the aging spider with variable valve timing, a single throttle valve, 4.10:1 rear axle and a minor facelift.

In the last quarter of 1980, there was a major management consolidation at ARI. The West Coast had been operating for the most part as an independent distributor with a director, separate sales, parts and service managers and a warranty department. Alfa eliminated these positions, and control moved to New Jersey. Only middle managers for distribution and parts remained on the West Coast, and the management of the Western zone was shared with the Englewood Cliffs office.

1981: Sales were lethargic, and the stock of deteriorating spiders in the ports was a major problem throughout 1981, especially in the California markets. A large number of these unsold cars needed major refurbishment, including new tops, before being shipped to the dealers. The cost of reworking new cars to make them salable further eroded ARI's "profit" margins. To make matters worse, the 1981 emissions requirements necessitated exhaust gas recirculation for the venerable four-cylinder; the bottom of Alfa's performance slide had been reached.

When the GTV-6 was introduced in 1981, Alfa's hopes for the United States market were once again revitalized. Although the 1981 model line included only coupes and Spiders, both received rave reviews from the press. The new coupe was nominated for the best GT car for the 1980s by *Road & Track* magazine.

The GTV-6 coupe is outside the scope of this book, because it is powered by a 2.5-liter V-6 engine, even though its body is basically the Alfetta GT.

In the 1981–82 period, ARI employees were informed all Alfas would eventually be front-wheel-drive designs.

■ Alfa's Final Years in America

Hopes were high for the V-6 models that would reverse sliding Alfa sales in the United States. Rather than reverse the decline, that decline was merely slowed.

1982: Sometimes, you can't win for trying. In 1982 ARI decided to simplify stocking (and reduce inventory costs) of the new GTV-6 cars by offering only one interior color. Blue interiors were chosen for the expected red, silver and dark gray metallic exteriors. When it came time to order the cars, however, the only available exterior colors were silver, red and a metallic charcoal. The last two colors clashed with the blue

If an American bought a GTV-6 in 1982 it was destined to be finished in silver with a blue interior—unless the dealer had it repainted.

interiors, so only silver cars with blue interiors were ordered for the model year. Sales plummeted. Toward the end of 1982, a dealer cash incentive was offered on the cars, but many silver/blue GTV-6s remained in the ports well into 1983. To improve top speed figures, the final drive ratio was reduced from 4.10:1 to 3.42:1.

This year also saw the introduction of the "Graduate" Spider. This was a decontented Spider with steel instead of alloy wheels, a vinyl instead of leather interior and manual windows instead of power. It was available only in ivory.

The SPICA system had finally reached the limits of its design capacity, and the Spider received Bosch L-Jetronic electronic fuel injection. It also continued to develop a luxury, as opposed to a sporting image. New wheels and detail refinements enhanced sales, while leather interiors became standard Spider equipment.

The president and CEO, Joseph Dent, was diagnosed with throat cancer, and day-to-day operation was turned over to the CFO.

1983: The year began with a massive carry-over of silver/blue 1982 GTV-6s. California received an updated version of the 1983 GTV-6 with cosmetic changes and

Mario Andretti (left), ARI public relations man Craig Morningstar (middle) and CEO Joe Dent pose with an American-market Spider.

a new interior, but the "49-state cars" were still mostly silver with blue interiors.

Though the incentive program was clearing out the 1982 models, 1983 cars were arriving to swell port stocks. A major "clear the ports" program finally managed to clear the stale stock. Alfa's coupe sales had been hurt by the 280Z and feckless marketing on ARI's part, but the new Porsche 944 sealed the model's doom, a development Alfa management failed to foresee.

In April 1983, there was another management change. Ernesto Vettore, who had worked with Joe Dent on marketing projects in Italy, came over as a marketing consultant, and was then named president and CEO. He brought in a new director of sales and marketing, Joe Cooley. Another restructuring of management brought a number of field people into headquarters in Englewood Cliffs and reshuffled the field force.

1984: In 1984, the "49-state" GTV-6s received the same changes as the 1983 California cars. During 1984, much more emphasis was placed on promotions and public-relations activities than in the past. ARI began sponsorship of a bicycle racing team which used Alfas as tour cars.

1985: In 1985 there were minor changes to the GTV-6, and the most dramatic exterior change to the spider since 1975. The front and rear sheet metal was redesigned along with the interior.

Plans were now underway for the introduction of the Milano, which was introduced in Europe as the 75, to commemorate Alfa's 75th anniversary. Public-relations activities focused on the new model and ARI took a group of American journalists to Italy for a long-lead introduction. In anticipation of rising sales, the dealer network was enlarged.

1986: After some arm-wrestling with Ford, the Italian government (IRI) "negotiated" Alfa Romeo to Fiat. It is quite likely that no money actually changed hands in this deal. Fiat was expected to pay off Alfa's considerable debt by closing down unprofitable operations and selling others. Though Ford looked like the likely winner at the time, in retrospect, they hadn't a chance, and Italy's "jewel" remained a domestic product in what was an essentially political decision. Fiat's stewardship of Lancia caused real concern among Alfisti and the question "Is it a real Alfa?" began to be raised.

1986 was the last year the GTV-6 was imported to the United States. The 1986 model year cars were introduced in late 1985 and were expected to be sold off by the time the Milanos arrived in the spring of 1986. The United States name for the 75, "Milano," was coined by Don Black.

Hopes rose that the new Milano would revitalize sagging sales. Unfortunately, the introductory

The Milano, as the Alfa 75 was to be known, was a new
V-6-powered, rear-wheel-drive sedan intended to expand
Alfa Romeo's market share in the United States.

advertising campaign was not very well organized and
large shipments did not arrive until July, well past the
time prospective buyers had forgotton the positive
editorial comments which had appeared in the major
car magazines.

Even though it arrived late in the season, the Milano's
sales momentum started to build toward an all-time
sales record of 8,201 cars, spurred by Alfa's first national
TV campaign in the United States Three models were
offered: Silver, Gold and Platinum. The Platinum edition
was fully loaded, and included a leather interior, sun
roof and ABS brakes. However, its identifying medallion
was virtually indistinguishable from the Silver model,
and its sales were never good.

Though the Milano was responsible for Alfa's best sales
in the United States, the magic failed to stick, and Alfa's
exit from the market would come within eight years.

On the positive side, the Milano offered Alfa's
highest-technology engine in a four-passenger car which
would appeal to families as well as sooth the ego of the
diehard enthusiast. A tractable car even in heavy traffic,
it gave stunning performance. The cadre of Milano
enthusiasts, even now, is a singularly devoted group.
There is no question that the Milano had a lot to offer.

Yet the fire it struck sputtered quickly. In a turn-
around from the initially favorable reports, long-
term test results by the press criticized the Milano's
exterior appearance and ergonomics. As a result of
a disenchanted press and its unsolved mechanical
problems (cam belt detensioner, head gaskets, driveline

and power steering rack), the Milano market evaporated
almost overnight.

Alfa was in serious financial trouble in its home
market and could not afford to refine the United
States version of the car as much as was needed. For
one example, the Milano's wiring harness was
essentially the European harness with a few wires
added to accommodate mandatory components for
the United States.

Late in 1986, there were stories of Ford attempting to
buy the ailing Alfa Romeo to bolster its image in Europe
and to gain much-needed European production capacity
through the purchase. This was both good and bad news
to Vettore, who had come from Ford a few years before.

1987: ARI took over distribution of the Canadian
operation, further trimming jobs and overhead.

To stop the downslide in Milano sales, advertising
and public-relations efforts were stepped up. ARI's
market research continued to indicate that the public
really wanted an automatic transmission in their sedans
despite the failure of the Alfamatic Sport Sedans. While
Alfa enthusiasts in the United States were not concerned
by the lack of an automatic, the general public, the
people Alfa was trying to conquest, said they wanted
an automatic. Late in 1987, the first of the automatic
Milanos arrived—and, like the Alfamatic, died in a
largely disinterested market.

In spite of earlier denials that the V-6 would never
see increased displacement, the 3.0-liter Milano Verde
was introduced with 30 additional hp. A long lead press
introduction of the 3.0-liter Milano Verde was staged in
May so that editorials would appear in July and August
magazines. The 3.0-liter Milanos sold at a reasonably

good pace and their success may have further flattened sales of the 2.5-liter model.

In the last months of Vettore's command, all creative advertising work was halted and most money slated for advertising was redirected to incentive programs to liquidate the overstock of blue Milanos. Forty percent of the cars ordered were blue because only one person was left to make that choice.

In the third quarter of 1987, Fiat took over the day-to-day operations of ARI, and appointed Giuseppe Greco president and CEO. He immediately reauthorized dealer advertising as well as incentives to help move the cars in stock.

ARI sent a group of 26 American journalists to Milan for the international press introduction of the new 164 sport sedan. The car received a very good response from the journalists with very few suggested changes for the United States market.

1988: In 1988, Alfa entered into a distribution agreement with Chrysler, and Alfa Romeo Distributors of North America (ARDONA) was formed. There were two main reasons for doing this:

- It would supply the kind of domestic marketing acumen the company first sought in Joe Dent.
- It would immediately add dealer outlets and boost sales.

Neither hope was realized. Most tragically, the Chrysler sales force never understood what Alfa Romeo was, and the Alfas on Chrysler dealer floors were generally regarded as little more than traffic builders.

Fiat picked Giuseppe Greco to run ARI and appointed him president and CEO.

Further exacerbating the problem, the ignorance of the Chrysler salespersons offended the traditional base of Alfa enthusiasts.

Milano sales continued to drop in the face of chronic service/quality problems. Incentive programs helped move the overstock, and minor detail changes appeared on the 3.0-liter Milano. Stepped-up advertising and promotional efforts continued. Greco participated in the "One lap of America National Rally" in early April and received good press results. ARDONA stepped up the racing contingency program and constructed a new auto show display, the first since the late seventies.

1990: The 164 was finally introduced in United States, two-and-a-half years after its European introduction and after much of the excitement over the model had worn thin. Notwithstanding, the car received rave reviews by the press. By all accounts, the 164 was the best Alfa ever imported into the United States. With styling much less controversial than the Milano and improved ergonomics, it was actually competitive in the market. Within ARDONA, Alfa's fortunes seemed on the rise once more. The feeling, apparently, was shared by Fiat, who hinted at the direction Alfa was headed. Writing in *Quadrifoglio*, the company publication, Mike Hemsley reported that 1993 would bring an upscale 164, entirely restyled and with a new name, and a new front- or all-wheel-drive spider, coupe and Targa, possibly powered by a reed-valve engine (the laminar flow head).

1991: Both Chrysler and Alfa realized the mismatch between them, so the deal was dissolved, though the acronym ARDONA remained. Chrysler management left and 25 percent of ARDONA's employees were laid off. Sales volume dropped.

The Spider was restyled, with substantially revised front and rear treatments, and is generally regarded to be the most attractive Spider of them all, though clearly not the most sporting.

Mike Hemsley, one of the stalwarts of the Alfa club, reported that the 164 replacement model would appear in the United States during 1995.

1992: A simple summary: further layoffs and lower sales. The countdown had begun. Prices for Alfas, especially the 164, began creeping into the lower end of the luxury market. A loaded 164 brought nearly $30,000, while the Spider cost nearly $25,000.

1993: This was a year of mixed signals. Early in the year, dealers were notified that the new spider would not be introduced in the North American market, and rumors of an Alfa Romeo pull-out began to appear in the media. Sales volume of the soon-to-be-orphaned marque plummeted. On the other hand, the 164LS facelift, introduced in August, received positive reviews by the press, and dealer orders far outnumbered the planned sales volume.

1994: Two new models proved Alfa's last gasp in the United States. Signalling the approaching end of its presence, Alfa produced 190 Commemorative Edition Spiders, some of which were still unsold into 1995. A four-cam version of the venerable V-6 appeared as the 164Q model. Extra body cladding was added to increase the car's appeal, but by this time, it was too clear that Alfa was headed out of the market. That fact and high prices kept sales depressed.

Fiat is a privately held company not given to losing money. Though American enthusiasts still hoped that the new 164 would be desirable enough to keep the marque alive in this country, the continued decline in sales resulted in Fiat shutting the salesroom doors at the end of 1994.

2000: About mid-year, Fiat and General Motors announced an agreement that gave GM a ten-percent interest in Fiat and opened the possibility that Alfas would once again be imported into the United States. A persistent rumor is that the date for Alfa's reintroduction will be 2002 or 2003.

The 164 (LS model shown) featured the same basic 3.0-liter V-6 used in the Milano, but mated it to a new front-wheel-drive chassis.

Fitted with a four-cam version of the V-6, the 164 Quadrifoglio featured greater power, but greater sales never materialized.

▪ Seeds of Failure

The management of Alfa Romeo SpA never understood the American market: as a result, its marketing organizations in the United States, ARI and ARDONA, never really had a chance. This is unquestionably a harsh judgment about some reputable, hard-working executives, and certainly is fueled by a strong dose of hindsight, but I'm convinced the statement is true.

One of the main reasons Alfa never understood the United States is an impenetrable ethnocentrism. This insight grew out of a breakfast meeting I had with Ernesto Vettore, one of the most gracious gentlemen ever responsible for managing the Alfa operation in the United States. Vettore clearly tried to understand our market, and probably had a clearer view of it than many other ARI CEOs.

Vettore dismissed BMW as a pedestrian car. "The Germans make beer," Vettore compared: "The Italians make wine." Later in the conversation, he explained that Alfa's real role in the United States was to educate Americans to appreciate Italian products (and, by inference, their culture). In his view, low Alfa sales in the United States had nothing to do with the product or its marketing, but rather the average American's unwillingness to appreciate Things Italian.

National pride runs deep in all cultures. I lived in Naples, and know first-hand that Neapolitans are convinced their city is the center of the universe. Romans feel the same about Rome, Milanese feel the same about Milan, and New Yorkers feel the same about New York. I know better, of course, having grown up in Flint, Michigan, the *real* center of the universe (now, unfortunately the Black Hole of unemployment and dashed dreams).

Many of those who have criticized Alfa's management fall into the same trap, because they see the American market from an American perspective. To all those who feel the faults of Alfa's efforts in the United States were perfectly obvious, I can only answer that they were so only from an American perspective. From an Italian perspective, the United States market must seem a Shangri-La, both mysterious and tantalizingly unreachable.

The Italians never achieved the ability to set aside national prejudices as the only path to a clear view of foreign markets. In point of fact, the Americans have resisted the same truth: it was never intuitively evident that the world was waiting to buy the traditional American Barge. To their credit (and considerable profit), the Japanese simply made a better American car than the Americans. The best "American" cars are Camrys and Acuras: Neons, Cavaliers and Contours are lesser copies of them, as sales attest.

The second reason Alfa failed in the United States is that the managers were pressured to satisfy their superiors' desires to hear only good news. This is not an unknown phenomenon in any organization (good news travels up; bad news travels down), but the Italians are superb spinmasters, to put it as kindly as possible. We watched in amazement as each new Alfa CEO promised to reach a sales level of 10,000 units in X number of years in the United States. I had always assumed that 10,000 cars represented a break-even point for Alfa in our market, but I've recently been told that Alfa's real break-even volume was considerably higher. Apparently, 10,000 units/year was the acceptable pain level for SpA management. Soothed with that rosy prediction, management simply continued steering the ship towards the iceberg.

Essential to this somnambulism was the fact that Alfa Romeo SpA was totally submerged in the Italian bureaucracy. Alfa was taken over in 1931 by IRI (Institute for Italian Reconstruction) and was operated under Finmeccanica, a state-owned holding company. By the early 1990s, Alfa's economic position had deteriorated to the point that it was a significant drain on government finances. One reason for this is that Alfa did not lay off workers for whom there was no work; instead, they were paid full salaries simply to stay at home. Enough people were employed by the company that there was a real danger of toppling the government had it made the cuts necessary to put Alfa in the black.

Finally, Alfa had no experience marketing its products. It had always been a company which produced quality cars for a knowledgeable clientele. The need to search for buyers—to market the product—was totally foreign to Alfa's corporate culture. There is still a group of marketers within Alfa's organization that believe the "truly cultured" buyer will seek out an Alfa Romeo. This is clearly an ethnocentric philosophy, largely unsupported by the facts.

Truth will out. Finally, the government was faced with an impossible decision: cut its losses with Alfa or close the company down. The most palatable solution was to sell the corporate assets to a company which could then take the draconian measures necessary to pull out of the red. Ford stepped up, and for a while appeared to be a sure winner. But Fiat could not allow a foreign competitor to gain production capabilities in its home market, and so became the successful "bidder."

▪ Roads Not Traveled

What could Alfa have done to survive in the United States? The answer may have appeared obvious to Alfa enthusiasts and long-term dealers, but it clearly was not to Alfa, nor to Fiat management.

Alfa got its start in this country with enthusiast dealers who frequently cared more for the cars than their profit margin. The typical dealer would appear for Saturday-morning coffee sessions with his clientele, and sub-culture pockets of Alfa enthusiasts were formed around these dealers.

Since many of the dealers were not spectacularly profitable, ARI management concluded that they were holding down sales. What Alfa really needed, they reasoned, was a professional dealer body. This explains, in general terms, why the Chrysler association was probably inevitable. Alfa hoped that the successful mega-dealers would show the older enthusiast-dealers how it should be done.

Exactly the opposite happened. The new dealers were undertrained to sell the cars, while the parts and service departments treated their Alfa clientele with the same disdain as their own Chrysler customers. As a result, the core enthusiast body was disenfranchised and new customers were not prospected.

There were a few small voices within the organization arguing for a different approach. What was clear was that the company needed exciting new products to survive. Plans were developed to build the Micro spider on an AlfaSud platform.

An alternative product was a reworked prototype of the current Spider. Completed by Ron Mondrush's Synthetex company in Detroit with Don Black's involvement, the car was flown back to Italy and oblivion.

The performance GT would return some of the luster that years of progressive emission controls had erased. ARI knew that the parent company had a high-performance engine and had also developed a mid-engined car. Carlo Chiti put a V-6 in the back of an AlfaSud Sprint as a serious rear-wheel-drive prototype. This car, like the 'Sud Spider, was more than a prototype since it was finished off to a production-car level.

In addition to a line of antique designs, Alfa was plagued with quality problems which stemmed from years of benevolent government handling of the inefficient manufacturing organization. When there was no work, laborers were simply sent home—where they continued to draw their full salaries. Those who did work on the line had little incentive to perform. Many cars were not truly finished at the end of the assembly line, leaving the dealer to finish them during "pre-

One of many functions of the Alfa Romeo Owners Club was to organize track days.

delivery." Clearly, the impact of semi-finished cars on the "professional" Chrysler dealers had a lot to do with their attitude towards the marque.

Many of the problems which plagued the American operation also applied in Europe as well. Both the AlfaSud and ARNA were plagued with quality and rust problems.

Ultimately, Alfa Romeo had a lot of technology, but no marketing knowledge. In a maddening twist of fate, convertibles—especially the Mazda Miata and the Porsche Boxster—became hot commodities not long after Alfa left the United States market.

Given the complete incompetence of Alfa SpA to survive in a world market, the purchase by Fiat has been a distinct improvement. While Fiat has done remarkably well with the Alfa badge, it is important to emphasize that the Alfa organization—indeed, all the people who made Alfa what it was—has been completely submerged, and slowly replaced, by Fiat management.

That does not mean that the current Alfas are bad cars, only that the institution which dates back to Merosi and Jano has been irretrievably dismembered.

■ The Alfa Romeo Owners Club in the United States

The Alfa Romeo Owners Club (AROC) has been the primary locus of Alfa enthusiasm in the United States. The club was founded by a small group of Chicago enthusiasts in early 1958. In 1959, the group wrote a letter to *Road & Track* magazine, advising Alfa owners of the club's existence. Membership skyrocketed, and the club became a viable proposition.

Founding members included Bruce Young, Dic Van der Feen and Paul Tenney. Bruce was the first editor of the club's newsletter, *The Alfa Owner,* and both Dic and Paul assumed that post in subsequent years. Paul was the first technical editor of the magazine, and I was its vintage editor.

The club, with Scog Gilmore as its treasurer, centered on the Lake Forest dealership of Bill Knauz. Annual conventions were held in the basement of Bill's dealership and the club was essentially an extended, but Chicago-based, family.

As the club grew, it established local chapters which met monthly and, in most cases, published a local newsletter. In some cases, as with the Detroit chapter, AROC absorbed groups which had existed before it was formed. As the membership became national, the importance of the *Owner* grew, and for those not within commuting distance of a chapter meeting, it became the only real benefit of club membership. To counter this trend, the AROC established four regional "technical hot lines" to help answer immediate maintenance problems for nominal telephone charges.

A series of volunteer editors discovered that producing a regular "kitchen-table" publication was a daunting task, and late issues were common. Finally, the lack of a regular publication made the directors decide to hand the magazine over to a Chicago-based printer/publisher, who could assure the publication's regularity.

Inevitably, some of the local chapters began to disagree with club management. The club had established strict safety regulations for chapter speed events in order to keep its insurance costs as low as possible. Disagreement with the restrictive provisions caused the San Francisco group to break away and form the Alfa Romeo Association (ARA). The ARA has become the "alternate club" nation-wide for some Alfa enthusiasts. Other chapters, while not breaking away from the club, have distanced themselves from the national group and operate quite independently. The growth of Alfa information on the Internet has furthered the diffusion of Alfa interest away from the club.

By the late 1970s, the publication of the magazine was again becoming irregular, and the board decided to seek another publisher. A West Coast firm was selected, and this time it was made responsible for retaining a professional editor to assure the magazine's regularity. Since the club's new secretary was also a West Coast resident, focus of the club changed from Chicago to Southern California, the area of largest Alfa ownership.

In the 1980s, the club ran into a financial crisis after its operating balance was suddenly almost wiped out by a large tax bill. In response, it raised dues to a level which caused considerable objection from some members. The dues increase eventuated a bank balance in excess of $100,000 which has not been converted into member benefits.

In 1998 the AROC celebrated its 40th birthday. With the growth of independent chapters, interest groups formed by aftermarket parts suppliers and the meteoric rise of information on the Internet, its position as the center of enthusiast attention had been largely diluted and the management of the club has become largely a closed society, unresponsive to the needs of its membership. Special interest groups have grown up to become formal registers (so named because they maintain a registry of serial numbers). Most of the registers are truly international, and many communicate using the Internet. A notable few publish newsletters, among them the 1900 Register (Peter Marshall in England and Joost Gompels in the United States), the 2500 Register (Malcom Harris in Seattle), the Berlina Register (Andrew Watry in Berkeley) and the Giulia Berlina Register (Barry Edmonds in Australia, Dave Mericle in the United States and Charlotte Van Coolen in Europe). On the other hand, because all these registers are volunteer efforts, they have a tendency to come and go, and any listing of them is likely to be outdated very quickly.

The *Alfa Digest* on the Internet (a service donated by Richard Welty) has become the most important just-in-time source of technical Alfa information. Finally, there are very informal groups of enthusiasts who hang together, driven by their mutual enthusiasm for the cars themselves.

▪ Alfa-AROC Relations

In spite of the fact that it contributed money to the club annually, some of the management of ARI underestimated the value of an enthusiast group, in just the same way it underappreciated its enthusiast dealers. The relation between the club and ARI was further damaged by a few AROC members who felt their position gave them special access to ARI management. In fact, it should have, but the interests of both sides tended to be self-serving and some prominent AROC members were held in open contempt by ARI managers.

Probably the most acerbic exchange between the club and ARI occurred over the technical details of the SPICA system. ARI management refused to release design information about the system for fear it would appear to the government that it was in collusion to permit owners to disable the emission controls built into the system. This would have been an extremely serious breach of law, and ARI's service manager, Roberto Francioni, was diligent in trying to maintain the cars in absolutely factory-stock tune. In point of fact, the SPICA pump was not considered serviceable in the field and all units were returned to the distributor for repair. As a result, as soon as any difficulty with the pump was suspected by an owner, the entire system was discarded in favor of Weber carburetors (which were more serviceable but also more polluting).

In the early 1970s, the technical editor of the *Owner* was Joe Benson, then an engineer at Chrysler Corporation's proving grounds in Chelsea, Michigan. Joe published a technical analysis of the SPICA system which included details on its modification for improved performance (and higher emissions). To make matters worse, the editor of the *Owner* excerpted some of Joe's comments as an "open letter" to ARI mangement, pleading for a free exchange of technical information. The series brought the relations between the two organizations to an all-time low and sacrificed Joe's continued participation in the club.

While this brief review of the AROC may seem unrelentingly critical, the fact remains that Alfa failed in the United States because it could not sell enough cars, and the single largest interest group, the AROC, did virtually nothing to relieve the situation. For example, the need to clear the ports of models in the 1980s—and the discounts available from dealer incentives—went unreported in the pages of the *Owner*, in part because the distributor felt it was none of the club's business.

In retrospect it was, and both organizations failed each other in fatal ways.

Over the years, many Alfa Romeos have ended their lives in American scrap yards like Tom Zat's Alfa Heaven.

■ Where Have They Gone?

In the years I've been associated with Alfa, I've had opportunity to watch a lot of things go away. A car has a predictable life. Driven off the showroom floor, its value can immediately fall as much as 25 percent, depending on model. The car's value continues to fall for 10–15 years, by which time it has reached its least valuable state. About 20 years after it was produced, the car begins a comeback as a collectible. Then, some 30 years or so after it first appeared, it may rise to the status of "classic." There is no good definition of a classic car: some old cars, such as Chevrolet Vegas or Henry Js, will never make that distinction. They are old collectibles: the distinction between collectible and classic is certainly in the eye of the beholder and has more to do with price than inherent value.

A majority of cars, of course, are junked out. Some break, some are rusted out and others are wrecked. These cars are picked apart in the junk yards until nothing but a shell remains, and they are crushed, their metal seeding a new generation of models. Perhaps half of all cars end like this. The least desirable models go first, providing parts for the more desirable ones. Giulietta and Giulia Berlinas have been among the most vulnerable of models, with the spiders being most resistant

A significant percentage of cars are parted out prematurely. This phenomenon is the result of over-enthusiastic owners who plan to do a major restoration of a vehicle, the ultimate value of which will be less than the cost of the restoration. A general rule (in the late 1990s, at least) is that the cost of restoring any car approaches $20,000, almost regardless of make. One should not try to restore a car which is not worth that price unless there are powerful reasons for doing so. Saving money by doing the work yourself is not one of those reasons. Restoration for the experience or for other emotional reasons is defensible, but no one should think that he will make money from a do-it-yourself restoration. What happens to these cars is that they are permanently disassembled by their enthusiastic owners, but never put back together, from lack of skill, time or money. My most-favorite 1900 CSS Zagato languished for several decades in a disassembled condition until it became so valuable that its reassembly made economic sense.

A similar fate awaits the information about these cars: shop manuals, brochures, magazine reports and similar literature are harder to find the older they are. One of the reasons for this book is to try to capture much of the information about a significant line of cars before that information is lost. Collections burn or are floated away in floods; people die, leaving unrecorded much of the practical information about a car's

Many American Alfa owners have multiple examples of their beloved marque. The 1965 Giulia Spider Veloce (left) is owned by Felix Chiu, who also has a TZ, a Sprint Speciale and a Junior Zagato 1600. Michele Muller, owner of the 974 GTV (right) also has a Giulietta Sprint and her husband has a Giulia TI.

maintenance. The loss of literature about the old cars is almost as critical a matter as the cars themselves.

Curiously, enthusiast collectors themselves can contribute significantly to the loss. In my own case, in the 1970s I traded away several issues of *Alfa Corse* magazines from the late 1930s and suspect that these have now completely disappeared in the hands of owners who were less cognizant of their ultimate value than I. In the case of the magazines, I photographed each page before letting them go, but then loaned the negatives to another enthusiast who lost them.

Hard parts are no less vulnerable than soft ones. I have been personally involved in a good example of how valuable old cars are lost. After purchasing my Gran Sport Zagato, I was able to obtain the front half of a Castagna-bodied 1750 Turismo drophead coupe. The car had been located in England and was intended by its new American owners to be a "shipping crate" for a supercharged Gran Sport engine. The English broker was directed to remove the original engine and replace it with the more powerful one, then ship the car to the United States. The idea was that this approach would save the cost of crating the good engine and also provide some spare parts for the cars already owned by the buyer. Unfortunately, the engine swap was never made and the car arrived in the United States intact. Now, understand that a single-cam Castagna-bodied 1750 in the early 1960s was a most undesirable car: the supercharged Gran Sports were going for less than $2,000, and the Castagna would have hardly brought a

few hundred dollars. The American owners were so infuriated with this that they cut the car in half, selling off a few unneeded parts before offering me the front half of the car for a couple of hundred dollars.

Certainly the largest collection of old Alfa parts in the United States was assembled by an enthusiast living in the Midwest. As his business developed, this individual began to buy lots of parts from smaller collections at prices unavailable to the individual enthusiast. The lower prices were a definite business advantage, but I think that they also diminished the perceived value of the collection in the owner's eyes. After a number of years building his business, this person began to tire of his vocation and sold off all the older (and more valuable) parts of his business as a lump sale. These parts are still supplying restorers from their new resting place in southern California.

One other anecdote illustrative of how we lose things: a well-known West Coast collector decided to create the ultimate library of Alfa material. Wealthy enough to bring it off, this individual amassed a collection of virtually every Alfa document since the end of the Second World War. In addition to all the published materials, this collection also included privately circulated Alfa items which were gifts to those within the organization. His collection grew through donations as well as the outright purchase of smaller collections. Only a few of the duplicate items in his collection were used in trade for missing materials. This individual amassed a similarly complete collection of Alfa tools, buying from individuals as well as dealerships going out of business. This individual passed away and, some ten years after his passing, the collection remains intact but unavailable. No one, including the person's widow, quite knows what to do with it. The collection of literature alone more than fills a house. No one else, it is probable, has room for such a mass of paper, and the libraries contacted feel that the collection is too large and specialized to be accepted. The fate of this fabulous collection is still undetermined, but it is feared that it will be sold in bulk to a dealer who will parcel out the most valuable items and simply dispose of the rest for its scrap-paper value.

Times, as well as interests, change. That is what creates something rare and precious. If we could travel backward in time, or see the future clearly, nothing would be rare, nor even collectible.

Chapter 3

Sprints and Other Coupes

Thanks to Dave Mericle, I can report Gian Paolo Garcea's account of how the Giulietta name came about:

After a particularly thorough and exhausting set of trials, the prototype engine was approved for production in early 1954. I and seven other engineers went out on the town to celebrate the occasion. While at dinner that evening, we were entertained by an exiled Russian Prince, who made his living by entertaining people in that fashion. When he heard of our new project, and we described the passion we had expended on it, the Russian remarked: 'Ah, you are eight Romeos without a single Giulietta!' The classical Shakespearean allusion was immediately apparent to all of us, and from that moment on we lobbied to name the new tipo the Giulietta. The rest is history.

The generic term for an Alfa Romeo coupe (that is, a close-coupled, closed, two-door car with occasional rear seats) is Sprint. Though plans were to introduce the Giulietta in its sedan configuration, the first model to appear was the Sprint, and for that reason, the Sprint comes first in this book.

Alfa has a tendency to play fast and loose with its model designations. *Sprint* is a generic term for a two-door, two- or four-place coupe, suggesting high performance over a short distance. Alfa has managed to confuse the term with GT (*Gran Turismo*, or grand touring), a coupe capable of maintaining extremely high performance over extremely long distances. If you think of the Alfa coupe as a *sprint*, and a Ferrari coupe as a *Gran Turismo*, then you have some idea of the distinction the two terms should convey. This is clearly the kind of distinction a salesman would never abide.

In the classic past, Alfa used *Gran Turismo* to indicate a mid-range state of tune for its cars. Turismo referred to the single-cam version of the 6C1750 engine, while Gran Turismo referred to the twin-cam version, and Gran Sport meant the engine was supercharged. The

The Sprint was the first of Giulietta models to reach the public. Sleek and beautiful, it was designed by Bertone.

issue is completely confused with the Giulia line, which includes both a Sprint and a GT, as well as a Sprint GT.

In a similar vein, Alfa has used *veloce* as a kind of oil to add luster to its sporting models. Originally, Veloce (*fast*, in Italian, with the implication of velocity, as opposed to meter, as in *presto*) was a Giulietta with higher compression, dual Weber carburetors, etc. The term carried over to the Giulia models along with the Weber carburetors. "Veloce" is what the V in GTV stands for (*Gran Turismo Veloce*, or Fast Grand Touring). The word has taken on a life of its own, however, and is applied to SPICA-injected cars and later Spiders with performance that is, arguably, far from "veloce."

Alfa is virtually alone among European manufacturers to practice the infuriating habit of awarding the same name to two distinct models that are separated by at least a génération. This becomes a challenge to writers, who have to be more specific, say, in identifying a 1750 or an Alfetta, than should be necessary. But then, Alfa is the only car maker to have permitted the manufacture of a retro-car, the Quattroruote Zagato, which is a modern-day interpretation of the 1750—that would be the 1929 model, not the one first introduced in 1966.

Enthusiasts have further exacerbated Alfa's terminology by assigning their own set of names. They have retro-named the Giulia Tubolare Zagato, or TZ. After the TZ2 appeared in 1967, the original model began to be called the TZ1, even in Fusi's benchmark book. To clarify: there is a TZ and a TZ2, but the term TZ1 was never applied to the car when it was current. Similarly, the early "low-nose" Sprint Speciale, devoid of bumpers, is distinguished from the "high-nose," production model, terms the factory never acknowledged.

There is, unfortunately, some precedence for retro-naming Alfa models. When it first appeared, the eight-cylinder twin-supercharged grand prix Alfa of 1924

was the Tipo B. It was not long before the fantastically successful car was being referred to as the P3, honoring Jano's P2 masterpiece of 1925. The terms Tipo B and P3 are now interchangeable, even within Alfa.

Perhaps the most annoying invention for me is the use of "normale" to indicate the alternate state of tune to "Veloce," which is a genuine Alfa designation (no matter how loosely applied). There was an RL Normale in 1921, an RM Normale in 1925 and even a 6C1500 Normale in 1927. Since then, however, "normale" has not been applied to a model except by owners who want to distinguish their Solex-aspirated Giuliettas from the Veloce version. Even the Kelley Blue Book now refers to Giulietta Normale as if it were a factory designation. The practice has become so widespread that this little diatribe will not stop it, so the reader needs to know that, outside of this book, there are TZ1s and Normale means a Giulietta with a single Solex carburetor. Here, however, TZs are TZs, Giuliettas are Giuliettas (with Solex carburetors) and Veloces are Veloces (with Weber carburetors and a host of other modifications—until Alfa started using the term for SPICA-injected cars).

In this chapter, it will be especially important to keep track of the subtle differences between the names Alfa has applied to its Sprints. The original Giulietta Sprint is a fastback with the standard Solex-carbureted engine, while the Giulietta Sprint Veloce had dual 40DCO3 Weber carburetors and a host of engine modifications. Both the Sprint and Sprint Veloce were identical, externally, with the exception of Veloce badging on the faster car and the use of aluminum external trim pieces. The Giulietta Sprint and Giulia 1600 Sprint are similarly identical from the outside and carry series number 101.12.

The 1963 Giulia Sprint GT, also by Bertone, introduced "notchback" styling and carried the series designation of 105.nn. This model is easily distinguished by eight horizontal grille bars. The same body was re-introduced in March 1966 as the Giulia Sprint GT Veloce: this model is generally referred to as the GTV and has three horizontal grille bars. The earlier version is distinguished by the slender scoop formed by the leading edge of the hood; the hood is flush with the body in the 1750 GT Veloces beginning in 1970. Early Giulia Sprint GT 105-series cars have been generally referred to as "step-nose" GTVs, and the latter model as "smooth nose." The GTV body survived until the introduction of

Introduced in 1963, the Giulia Sprint GT was essentially a 101 Sprint with fresh coachwork by Bertone's Giorgio Giugiaro.

the Alfetta Sprint in 1975 (which is also a GTV if it has the 2.0-liter engine). Thus:

Series	Years	Description
750B	1954–59	Giulietta Sprint fastback
750E	1956–57	Giulietta Sprint Veloce fastback
101.02	1959–65	Giulietta Sprint fastback
101.06	1960–62	Giulietta Sprint Veloce fastback
101.12	1962–63	Giulia 1600 Sprint fastback
105.02	1963–66	Giulia Sprint GT notchback
101.02	1964–65	Giulia Sprint 1300 fastback
105.31	1972–75	GT 1300 Junior RHD
105.36	1966–68	Giulia Sprint GT Veloce notchback
105.44	1967–72	1750 GT Veloce
105.51	1968–73	1750 GT Veloce (United States specification)
115.01	1972–75	2000 GT Veloce (United States specification)
115.03	1972–75	GT 1600 Junior
115.05	1972–75	GT 1600 Junior RHD
115.31	1967–71	GT 1300 Junior RHD
116.10	1974–75	Alfetta GT
116.02	1975–77	Alfetta GT 1.6 RHD
116.04	1976–80	Alfetta 1.6 GT fastback
116.09	1972–78	Alfetta 1.8 RHD
116.11	1975–76	Alfetta GT 1.8 RHD
116.36	1976–85	Alfetta 2000 GTV (includes 116.36 A, B & C)
116.37	1976–78	Alfetta 2000 GTV RHD
116.29	1975	Alfetta 2000 GTV (United States specification)
116.15	1975–79	Alfetta 2000 GTV (United States specification)

■ The Genre

The Touring-bodied 8C2900 coupe of the late 1930s is considered the seminal Gran Turismo (GT) coupe, from which all other GT coupes have evolved. Other prewar Alfa GT coupes were offered on the 6C2300 and 6C2500 chassis. The definition of the GT coupe is that it is a car designed to carry two passengers and their luggage in comfort at high average speeds over long distances.

After the war, Touring and Farina GTs on the 1900 pan were extremely popular. The three-window Touring-bodied 1900 GT coupe is arguably one of the most beautiful GT coupes of all time. That model, not incidentally, is also the direct inspiration for the Giulietta Sprint Coupe.

The Alfa Sprint Coupes virtually define the diminutive end of the Gran Turismo genre, while Ferrari defines the larger GTs. Considering the fact that the first Giulietta Sprint appeared over 40 years ago, many readers may not be able to appreciate the impact it had on the small—but growing—sports-car market.

The bulk of sports cars in the United States at the end of the 1940s came from England. The significance of this is that, with the exception of the XK120 coupe, all the "real" sports cars were open. For a British car of the period, open described the weather protection whether or not the top and side-curtains were erected. This is based on first-hand knowledge: I owned a pair of MGs and a Triumph TR2 before the Giulietta became a practical possibility for my pocketbook; the Porsche was priced so much higher that it was not a consideration.

The Giulietta Spider was famous for having a tight-fitting top and roll-up windows. There is no doubt that the Giulietta Spider was the more sought-after model, but the fact that the Sprint was an enclosed car gave it a special appeal, especially for Michigan winters, and in spite of the fact that Giulietta heaters were famous for their incapacity.

The other appeals of the Giulietta were its shiny alloy twin-cam engine, its undoubted performance (not as fast as the XK, certainly, but better than the MGs) and the cachet of its Italian heritage. Its styling was understated Italian, with a hint of the tumble-home that made Ferrari coupes so dramatic. The Giulietta's uniqueness may be hard to appreciate in today's market, which is flooded with "me-too" designs. The Giulietta really had no other competitors. Max Hoffman (the car's original importer) was no dummy.

The Giulietta Sprint was immediately recognized as a benchmark design, an accolade which has been amply verified with the passage of time. The body toured with the Carrozzeria Italiana show in 1980, accompanied by the original wooden buck over which its panels were first formed.

sports car
sleek-lined
agile
speedy

coupé
2+2 seats

The lovely Sprint was marketed as a sports car that was sleek, agile and speedy.

The reason the Sprint is such a benchmark design is that it combines the best design techniques of its era into a definitive statement of the genre. In his hurry to get something out for the Turin show, Bertone's stylist Franco Scaglione kept the basic concept simple. The distillation, however, produced a unique design, the features of which cannot be traced to a previous model. It is unusual to have a design which cannot be traced to a progenitor. For instance, elements of the Giulietta Spider are visible in the Lancia Aurelia Spider and even the Fiat 1100 TV. Bertone's earlier BAT series of cars clearly define the Sprint Speciale, but not the Sprint. The nearest model to the Sprint is Bertone's Alfa 2000 prototype, designed in the same year as the Sprint.

After years of trying to identify exactly what makes a Sprint so desirable, I've finally concluded that its attraction is the sum of many small pluses and no significant minuses. Like the Cisitalia coupe, the Sprint is notable for its unadorned simplicity and unity of design. All the parts fit together extremely well and none stands out as being added at the last minute. A minimal use of chrome trim allows the purity of the

design to speak for itself. A Sprint looks great with no chrome at all, and the little which is added (the hood spear and the strip below the doors) do not modify the elegance of the basic shape. There is little overhang front and rear and the fastback gives an aerodynamic look. Over the years, stylists have made cars look lower, and the Sprint may appear slab-sided now, but for its day, it was sleekness personified.

Some things about the Sprint need getting used to. The driving position is the first and most critical: arms outstretched and knees akimbo as if the steering wheel and accelerator pedal are almost on the same plane. The seat is not very high off the floor and the roof line is low, yet outward vision is not hindered. Although the seats may appear flat, lateral support is quite good.

There are some mechanical characteristics that also require acclimation. The engine is quite busy at highway speeds and it takes a while to be reassured that a steady 4,000 rpm is a survivable proposition. The Solex-carbureted version has adequate torque, but the Veloce is the all-time textbook example of the difference between torque and horsepower (you drop the clutch at 3,000 rpm to get underway). Fair warning: as desirable as a Veloce may seem, it is not a car for heavy traffic.

Those who own 115- and 116-series 2.0-liter Alfas will be pleased to know that Giuliettas —and Giulias— do not blow head gaskets. They do rust when driven over winter salt-covered roads. The warning sign is a small bubble beneath the paint just above the rear wheel arch. Originally, the chrome grille eyebrows had an annoying tendency of falling off, but that shortcoming has probably been repaired on any surviving models. The Sprint had very weak seatbacks, and they would tear loose from the seat bottom if you habitually used them as a fulcrum when lifting something from the rear parcel shelf. The doors were large and could sag after years of use, but a strategically placed section of two-by-four, wedged between the top hinge, could bend things back into place quickly when assisted with a solid upward pull on the door bottom.

The Sprint, although closed, is not a spectacular cold-weather car. The heater is a cruel joke. The best you can do is shut its doors and hope that enough heat rises by convection to defrost the windshield. If you have a Veloce, then you subtract the ambient temperature from 100 to get the number of times to pump the accelerator before trying to start. And, you must run the largest wire you can find between the battery ground in the trunk and a starter attaching bolt.

There are a number of endearing features of the Sprint, also shared by the Spider. The first is the model's cold-bloodedness. The coolant temperature never gives pause even in the heaviest traffic, and you rely on the oil temperature gauge to know when it is safe to use full throttle. The steering and gearbox are joys, and the headlight flasher ring around the horn is a feature which never should have been dropped. The instrument cluster, shift lever position and general interior trim clearly put the driver's comfort and safety first and styling second. The Giulietta Sprint is a purpose-built car designed by those who knew what a car was supposed to—and could—do. That simple truth illuminates it still.

■ The Birth

Beginning with the introduction of the 6C2300 in 1934, Alfa offered progressively less expensive cars to the benchmark 6C1750 and 8C2300 models. The post-war 1900 represented a major attempt to capture the burgeoning family-sedan market. The 1900's success as the first-ever sports sedan emboldened Alfa to try another step downscale with a smaller car which could be owned by the average worker with an only slightly above-average income.

The overall design of the Giulietta borrowed heavily from the 1900 series. The engine was traditional

What's in a Name?

The idea of naming the new Alfa after a Shakespearean character was undoubtedly an attempt to embellish the "Romeo" connection. "Giulietta" is the diminutive of Juliet (Giulia) in Italian and can be roughly translated "little Juliet," though the form suggests an endearment more appropriate to "sweetie." The name applies remarkably well to the qualities of the Giulietta, but makes the root word "Giulia" sound more like a Wagnerian heroine (big Juliet) to American ears. Giulia is also commonly used as a reference to "maid." Names aside, both models share the endearing qualities of diminutive size, sleek styling, exceptional responsiveness and satisfying performance.

The Giulietta Sprints wore this elegant script.

Alfa, with twin overhead camshafts and hemispheric combustion chambers. Its composition was a dramatic departure from the 1900, however, with all-alloy construction, cast-iron wet cylinders and a fully balanced five-main-bearing crankshaft. The gearbox and differential housing were also of alloy. As a result, the car promised sporting performance from only 1290 cc.

There was hardly an Italian who didn't anticipate the appearance of the new Alfa sedan. That was because Alfa organized a lottery for those who bought its stock. One thousand certificate holders would receive one of the sedans. As a marketing ploy, the offer was outstandingly successful. The problem was that the date of the lottery came and went without a drawing or a winner.

Things were just proceeding normally: everything was behind schedule. Since Alfa was government-owned, rumors began to circulate mentioning fraud. There was considerable pressure to introduce the new sedan and award the thousand lucky winners.

Necessity being the mother of invention, Alfa came up with a remarkable solution: create a one-off show car, based on the sedan's components. The car debuted at the 1954 Turin show and reassured the public that the production car was almost ready. Bertone's shop was small and efficient, and he had the additional advantage of knowing what Alfa executives liked. The coupe Franco Scaglione designed for Bertone borrowed heavily from a 1900 coupe from Touring, and it was completed only days before the Turin show opened.

The diminutive coupe was a star of the show, and Alfa struck on the idea of having Bertone build 1,000 coupes to satisfy the lottery. Thus was born the Giulietta Sprint Coupe.

Bertone was not large enough to satisfy such an order easily, but an order for 1,000 cars was not to be ignored. As a result of the Alfa order, his company grew dramatically and become the preferred supplier for Alfa's coupe bodies. Pininfarina was selected to supply the convertibles, while Alfa used its own designers for the sedans, an arrangement which continued, generally, until the Fiat buy-out.

■ Prototype Giulietta Sprints

The archive at Arese contains several photos of prototype Sprint Coupes. The earliest model carried the general configuration of the production model, but had rear taillamps which protruded to the rear in a rather exaggerated fashion. A second version continued the overall design, but shortened the taillamp extension and added a hatchback. These "mules" have probably long disappeared, and only their photos remain to give us a glimpse of the car's development.

▪ Production 750 Sprints

For almost ten years, that is from 1946 to 1956, there was no sporting closed car worthy of the name which was also affordable by the young enthusiast. Porsche was simply too expensive. The Triumph-based Peerless was a good try, but the first post-war car to hit the mark squarely was the Giulietta Sprint. This is a purely American view which ignores cars like the Lancia Aurelia because they weren't imported in any numbers and they were substantially more expensive.

The Italian version of the Giulietta Sprint's debut is a much more interesting story. Alfa was rescued after the war by the Marshall Plan, which financed the production of the 1900-series cars. In a move to build additional sales, Alfa designed a smaller sedan which would appeal to a much larger market than the still slightly exotic 1900. As an advertising ploy, and largely to deflect attention from the fact that the new Giulietta sedan's introduction was running far behind schedule, Alfa decided to build a small run of coupes based on the

The Giulietta Sprint offers a simple and uncluttered design that has aged beautifully in the almost 50 years since it was first unveiled.

new platform and raffle one off to the person who could give the car a name. The coupe broke no new styling ground, but it was a wonderfully engaging car, executed in impeccable taste. Though the sedan never made it to the States, the Spider and Coupe set a benchmark which few marques have ever bettered.

Some cars, like some people, are irresistibly lovable. The Giulietta Sprint is one of the most affection-attracting cars of all time. It is not just its diminutive size: if small were the measure of desirability, the Fiat Abarth Zagato would be the world's favorite car. The fact is that the Giulietta Sprint also quickly proved that it was a very capable car, every bit the Gran Turismo which could traverse countries as easily as lesser cars cross counties. Though you sit rather high in the Sprint's cabin, with legs stretched almost straight in front of you, there's ample wiggle-room and enough in the way of amenities to make the trip truly comfortable. As a confirmation of the Sprint's desirability, it became a favorite way for the Italian Mafia to reward good deeds.

Thus, a Giulietta Sprint in Italy became endowed with a special kind of *machismo*.

▪ Styling

In evaluating the Sprint's styling, it's important to remember that we're looking at it through eyes schooled on Ferrari F40s and Acura NSXs. In comparison to the modern car, the Sprint seems bulbous and uninteresting, with large expanses of side panels unrelieved by styling lines. The dash is spare, devoid of cup holders, air-conditioning controls or 2-DIN cutouts for megawatt stereo systems. But to the contemporary, and especially in comparison with the 1900 and 6C2500, the Giulietta Sprint was a trim little machine. Every line on the car reflected the best styling of the era. To those who are old enough to have seen it new, the Sprint's body is one of the most beautiful ever crafted.

A Sprint is busy at speed, and the fact that you're in a closed body helps intensify the impression. I remember a trip back to Detroit from Chicago with a British vintage-Alfa enthusiast in my '57 Sprint, holding a steady 4,000 rpm. "Don't

The interior of the Giulietta Sprint was elegant and light, more in keeping with an expensive grand tourer than a small sports car.

The simple grille and sliding windows reveal this as one of the lightweight Giulietta Sprints.

you get nervous," he asked, "holding such a high engine speed for so long?" I understood his concern, having recently personally demolished the engine of my MG-TF trying to hold expressway speeds without giving the valves a chance to cool. But the Giulietta was good for a steady 4,000 rpm for as long as you cared, and the Veloce's 7,000-rpm redline—not to mention the twin Webers—was the stuff that dreams were made of.

The Sprint wasn't cheap, but it was a lot less than a Jaguar and a whole lot less than a Ferrari or Maserati. And, when you lifted the hood, you saw the twin-cam covers which announced that this engine was a serious exercise in power production which did not resort to the crudity of cubic inches. In an era of incredible Detroit claque, there was something transcendentally believable

about the Giulietta. It was evidence that a few dedicated artisans could make a car which was nimble and comfortable at the same time.

In spite of its considerable competition successes, I was never impressed with the Giulietta as a race car. Those Giuliettas which were really competitive were typically heavily modified, using traditional hot-rod techniques. Trained on MGs and Triumphs to equate handling with lack of body roll, I found the Giulietta's willingness to wallow outward in a turn especially disconcerting. The Giulietta's limit straps, however, served a real function, allowing a supple ride while reining in weight transfer at a precisely determined loading. And, it was true that a stock Veloce could be driven to the local track, collect trophies and then motor home without changing anything. Its brave 1.3-liter engine was the match of virtually any 2.0-liter the Brits could offer. We used to say that the Italians built larger cubic inches than the English.

It's hard now to say whether it was the Giulietta which endowed Alfa with the respect I hold for the marque or vice-versa. What I do know is that the Giulietta Sprint was a pinnacle of styling and engineering at a time when a few people in the United States were discovering that there was life outside Detroit. The Giulietta gave an unmatched combination of performance and comfort without compromising either. And, it was one of the trend-setting bodies of its time. It can honestly be said that the success of the Giulietta in America gave Alfa a marketing impetus that carried it through until it withdrew from the market in 1995.

■ Lightweight Special

There were a few purpose-built racing Giulietta coupes with lightened bodywork. These cars are immediately identifiable by their sliding side windows. Opening panels—the hood, doors and trunk—were aluminum, as were all external trim pieces. The seats were tube-frame construction, and there was minimal interior trim. The reason for the sliding windows was that the winding mechanism was removed, some indication of the extent to which the car was lightened.

Because of their small production numbers, Giulietta lightweight specials are among the most collectible of all Alfas, and they bring extremely high prices on the market.

▪ 101 Giulietta Sprints

The introduction of the 101-series and engine in 1958 was reflected in the Sprint body, which gained stamped, egg-crate grillework, a slightly upscale interior trim and larger taillamps. The 101 series retained the triangular gauge layout on the instrument panel: this would become horizontal, with newer gauges on the Giulia 1600 Sprint. As mentioned elsewhere, 1958 was a transitional year, during which 750 and 101 parts were mixed and matched freely. There was no change in performance between the earlier 750 and later 101 cars, even though the later engine was much more robust.

The 101 series Giulietta featured a more robust 1300cc engine and a revised, heavier grille. This 1962 Sprint Veloce features Borrani wire wheels, which, while not a catalogued option, were fitted to a small number of Giuliettas by the time they were delivered to their first owners.

The Giulia Sprint featured the taller tallights of the 101 Giuliettas, as well as the bigger 1600cc engine.

▪ Giulia Sprint

The original Giulia Sprint was little more than a Giulia engine (1570 cc) in a 101-series Giulietta Sprint body with small interior detail differences, most notably a horizontal instrument display and padded dash. The model was introduced at Monza on June 27, 1962, with great success. A total of 21,542 Giulia Sprints was produced until 1963, when the model was dropped for the Giulia Sprint GT.

As rare as they are, Giulia 1600 Sprints are not especially collectible. They were a more robust car than the Giulietta Sprint, and their 1600 engine with a single Solex carburetor gave almost the same performance as the Giulietta Veloce, with significantly better driveability. A five-speed gearbox was standard. The cars were distinguished by a "1600" badge located just aft of the Bertone "nut" on the front fenders, and a similar badge on the trunk lid. The car had large three-function taillamps with a back-up light at the bottom. Circular reflectors were added below the taillamps.

Because a completely new sedan was introduced at the same time as the Giulia Sprint, it was clear that the Giulietta-bodied coupe and spider were both interim solutions and that an entirely new configuration was expected. At the time, enthusiasts also looked forward to "Veloce" versions of the Giulia, for they would clearly be outstanding performers.

▪ Giulia Sprint GT

The Giulia Sprint GT, introduced on September 9, 1963, is the first of the notchback Bertone coupes. This shape would remain Alfa's coupe style until the introduction of the Alfetta in 1975. The Giulia Sprint GT was discontinued when the Giulia Sprint GT Veloce was introduced in 1966. Distinguishing characteristics of the several coupe bodies are:

Sprint GT: Sprint GT script on the rear deck. No emblems on the C-pillar. Scoop nose with two headlamps. A gray dash face.

Sprint GT Veloce: Sprint GT script on the rear deck and Veloce script between passenger-side taillight and license plate. "Alfa Romeo" on the rear license plate light. Green four-leaf clover (Quadrifoglio) on C-pillar. A snake instead of the Quadrifoglio on 2.0-liter cars.

GTA: The GTA is distinguished by a smaller front radiator grille with mesh backing. There are two oval openings for additional cooling air below the grille. The door handles are to the GTA. In addition, it was fitted with 6 X 14 Campagnolo alloy wheels.

The new 105-series coupe body was designed by a young Giorgietto Giugiaro for Bertone. Following the lead of the Giulia sedan, the coupe was much more squared-off than its predecessor, and was distinguished by its notched back. It was the first coupe to be produced at Alfa's new facility at Arese.

Enthusiasts realized that the Giulietta Sprint Coupe was going to be a hard act to follow. There is no doubt that Alfa Romeo had developed a favorite car in the Giulietta. The Giulietta Sprint coupe was especially loved, a fastback car of minimum displacement and maximum enjoyment. In practical terms, the odds of bettering the success of the Giulietta were poor, since the Giulietta had launched Alfa Romeo into successful serial production. The Giulietta had made the Alfa affordable for others than kings and movie stars. It had to be with some trepidation that after almost ten years, Alfa prepared to introduce the Giulietta's replacement.

The real objection to the new GT was that the profile of the new coupe did not continue the smooth fastback lines of the Giulietta Sprint. Certainly, my own reaction to the new coupe style was one of disappointment.

When I recalled this fact many years later in the club magazine, I received a heated response from a vociferous Alfa historian asserting that the new body style was most certainly an instant hit.

How time does cloud our perceptions: in the magazine *Classic and Sportscar* for June 1982, John Dooley wrote a retrospective of the Bertone coupes with the observation "It must be said that at the time (of its introduction) enthusiasts thought it would never be a successful classic like the Giulietta Sprint!" And, in *Autocar*'s February 3, 1979, issue Roger Bell noted: "A Latin gem of an earlier era, the delectable Giulietta Sprint sired the Bertone-styled Sprint GT 1600, the more angular lines of which were not initially greeted with universal acclaim after the gracefully curvaceous Giulietta, though you may find few styling critics today." But when introduced, the new coupe style was considered less attractive than its Giulietta precedent. The turn-around in appreciating this body style is remarkable.

Remembering its doubtful acceptance, it's especially instructive to read contemporary road tests of the Sprint GT. *Road & Track*, in December 1964, established a genteel approach: rave about the car's handling, its engine and transmission, but give only a factual description of the bodywork. Even through 1966 this formula was followed. *Motor*'s July 13 review of the new 1750 coupe did not even mention styling, concentrating instead on the car's superb mechanics, which were, after all, what was new.

Certainly, first-year production figures show that the old-style coupe attracted many more buyers than the

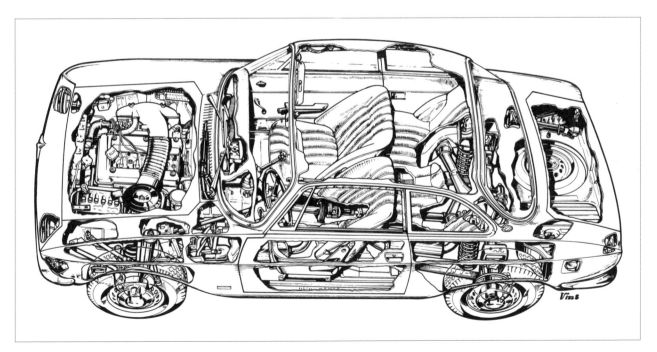

This cutaway of the Sprint GT shows engine and suspension layouts as well as interior accommodations.

newer one: 3,388 Giulia 1600 Sprints were produced in 1963, compared to only 842 Sprint GTs.

When did we learn to love Giugiaro's coupe? Just as soon as the Alfetta coupe was introduced in 1975. There's a working, if unspoken rule, that any new Alfa is considered devolutionary by most Alfa enthusiasts. While I can't quote any reviews to support the proposition, I suspect that the 6C1500 Alfa of 1927 was derided as a toy compared to the eminently reliable RL series it replaced. I first ran up against this type of prejudice many years ago when a fellow enthusiast lamented the Touring bodywork on the 8C2900 spider of 1937: he would have preferred to have seen that magnificent engine clothed in the classic Zagato body of the earlier 8C2300 and 6C1750 cars.

Though it is true we love all but the newest Alfa, the other side of the rule is that only a single intervening model is required to elevate an Alfa to the status of a beloved classic. Because another model (the Giugiaro fastback) has since intervened, we are now free to consider the Giulia Sprint GT more lovely than the Giulietta.

In fact, the body is now considered by some as one of the most beautiful cars ever produced by any maker. The Giulia Sprint GT is a true grand touring car, with a twin-cam 1600cc engine carrying dual side-draft Weber carburetors and giving the capability of traversing very long trips at very high speeds in absolute confidence and comfort.

▪ GTA

Introduced in 1965, the GTA was a lightweight competition version of the new Giulia Sprint GT. Although the shape and dimensions were shared with the road-going version, the body panels were stamped from aluminum on the same tooling used for the production steel bodies. The inner structure, however, remained of steel. Another clear way to identify a GTA is by the rivets attaching the alloy roof panel to the body pillars. Further weight savings came from plexiglass side and rear quarter windows, lighter door latches and handles and a total absence of sound-deadening materials. The road-going version of the GTA, the Normale, cost $5,550 POE and weighed 1,639 pounds—a full 450 pounds lighter than a GTV—with bumpers. Race-prepared, a GTA Corsa ($7,550 POE) registered 1,540 pounds.

The heart of the GTA was the twin-plug cylinder head and 45DCOE14 Weber Carburetors. All GTAs came with a lightened flywheel, headers, dual electric fuel pumps and dual distributor and coils, while the Corsa version sported a magnesium sump, bell housing, remote housing and a lightweight gearbox with close

"O rapture unbearable"

alfa romeo
Giulia Sprint GT

The public's rapture at seeing the new shape of the Giulia Sprint GT was not immediate. In time, the shape was well-accepted and today Sprint GTs and GTVs are highly coveted.

The GTA Normale was the roadgoing version of Alfa's racing GT.

ration gears. The Normale version was rated at 133 bhp, while the Corsa came with a dyno sheet showing between 150 and 160 bhp.

First introduced with a 1600 version of the twin plug engine in 1968, the GTA Junior was introduced with a short stroke 1300cc version of the twin plug engine. Even with the reduced displacement, power output was still rated at between 96 and 150 hp depending upon state of tune.

The suspension of the Normale GTA was similar to that of the Sprint GT and GTV, but used different springs and shock absorbers and added a rear anti-roll bar and alloy rear reaction triangle. The Corsa, however, was fitted with a sliding block to improve the lateral location of the rear axle and lower the roll center of the car. While the Normale GTA used 14 X 6 wheels, the Corsa was fitted with wider 14 X 7 rims.

The GTA Corsa (GTA Junior shown) was raced successfully and extensively in Europe and the American Trans-Am series.

GTA engines were identified by two plugs per cylinder. The Normale version (shown) was rated at 133 hp; the Corsa version was rated at 150–160 bhp.

Inside, the GTA was fitted with lightweight seats and interior trim and a special wood and alloy steering wheel. Instrumentation and basic layout remained similar to the Sprint GT, but the redline on the tachometer was raised.

■ 1300 Sprint

Because of the negative response to the new notchback GT body style, the fastback Sprint was reintroduced as the Giulia 1300 Sprint in March 1964. This car was essentially a 101-series Giulietta with improvements to the head and block from the 105-series engine. The official reason for this model's reintroduction was "In order to satisfy clients' requests." Two months later, the same downsized Giulia engine appeared in the new Giulia sedan body as the 1300 Giulia. The 1300 Sprint

and 1300 Giulia were the progenitors of the "Junior" series cars, and began a proliferation of engine sizes which reached its extreme in 1974, when Alfa offered the coupe in 2.0-, 1.6- and 1.3-liter displacements.

To keep the new body style before the enthusiast, in 1965 Alfa began campaigning GTA racing versions of the Giulia Sprint GT throughout Europe. The racing successes of the new body style helped build public acceptance, as did the GTC. Both of these variations on the Giulia Sprint GT are covered in Chapter 5.

The early sales fiasco of the Giulia Sprint GT coupe is a curious detail in the history of what has proved to be an overwhelmingly successful design. The compact body tucks in both fore and aft while a sharp crease runs along the side of the body adding both grace and lightness to the design. The greenhouse has a significantly greater glass area than the Giulietta coupe and helps provide a much more comfortable driving experience.

The seats of the Giulia coupe are deeply contoured and the dash is cleanly and efficiently laid out. Like the Giulietta coupe, the driver sits close to the floor with his legs stretched forward, and there is a somewhat unnerving sense of sitting high in the car.

The Giulietta coupe was a breakthrough design in that it was the first car to offer true, low-cost Gran Turismo capabilities. The grand touring car was intended to carry two people cross-country over a variety of roads with high average speeds, survivable comforts and good reliability. GT cars contemporary with the Giulietta included Lancia, Maserati, Ferrari, Porsche and Aston Martin. These early GT cars were far from ideal: Ferrari tended to stress higher speeds than comfort, while Aston proved slightly longer on comfort than reliability.

While the Giulietta coupe was clearly a significant step toward a low-cost GT, the Giulia added a significant gain in reliability and performance while offering creature comforts superior to almost any other true GT. It lacked only the absolute top speed of the much more expensive grand touring cars.

Like its Giulietta forebear, Giulia Sprint GT's diminutive size was part of its charm (especially since the 2000 and 2600 coupes are an almost identical design done larger). It was nimble on the road and encouraged a sense of oneness between driver and car: you truly "put it on" like a glove, and the fit was very comfortable. The large expanse of leg room in the pre-1969 coupes was a

Shown here is the willing 1300cc twin-cam-powered "Junior" variant of the second-generation Sprint and GTV coupes, as well as Spiders.

novelty for the era and contributed to long-trip comfort for the passenger.

Unlike the Giulietta Sprint, the Giulia version was a true 2+2, meaning that there was a pair of seats at the rear which could be used (in an emergency). Because the coupe was (theoretically) capable of seating four it raced in the sedan class in the United States. Thus, we watched GTVs and GTAs warring with BRE Datsun 510 sedans on tracks all over the United States. The fact that the Datsuns tended to win is a tribute to team leader Pete Brock's determination (well, it *was* a nifty basic design, too).

The Giulia coupes continued the Alfa tradition of an arms-out, legs-up approach. The new coupe was even more demanding in this respect than its Giulietta predecessor. Michael Scarlett, in an *Autocar* article dated October 9, 1960, comments on the position relative to "Willum," a GT 1300 with British plates (WLM39G): "Willum…had been made for a particularly deformed specimen of the Darwinian ape who is Italian Standard Man for most Latin car interior designers…. (he) has very short legs, a stocky trunk and long arms. (In the GT 1300 he has) the right leg considerably shorter than his left; the accelerator pedal is therefore some way back from the brake and clutch. He is a strong enough fellow however, happily applying nearly 50 lb. of pedal effort over 6 in. every time he de-clutches. Not being as healthy, I found this tiring in traffic. Not being the same shape, my right leg had to remain partly unsupported and there wasn't enough rearward seat movement by about 2 in. My head brushed the roof. If I reclined the seat enough to clear, then I could hardly reach the wheel or gearlever."

A similar comment popped up in *Road & Track*'s August 1972 test of the 2000 GTV: "Other long-standing faults of the GTV's people accommodations are not corrected. The driver position, for instance, is something

not a single staff member finds comfortable, and the trouble stems from the relation of seat, steering wheel and pedals as we have often pointed out."

Somehow, we all seem to have survived the contortions required of the Alfa coupe driver, and the car performs well enough to make adjusting to its ergonomics worth while. In a road test of the 1750 GTV published in *Autocar* for June 17, 1971, Ray Hutton observes: "Motoring writers, myself included, are often unduly cynical about the cars that they drive. I suppose it is a side-effect of sampling so many different types, only a few of which can ever really appeal to any one person. It is not often that one appreciates a car so much that it seems worth positively striving to own one, even if it is outside the realistic price bracket. For me, the Alfa Romeo 1750 GTV is that sort of car. It is not the ultimate (what is?), but it is a car that I have enjoyed more than any other I have used regularly."

The stock configuration for all of the early Giulias was a Solex twin-throat downdraft carburetor and five-speed transmission. The five-speed Giulia transmission was especially appreciated and a lot of Giulia transmissions have since been retrofitted to the Giulietta, which had only four forward speeds. Virtually all the Giulias imported to the United States were equipped with twin Weber DCOE carburetors, the same basic setup which graced the Veloce Giuliettas.

The Giulia 1600 Sprint suspension, like the body, was identical to the 101-series Giulietta. However, with the new 105-series body style, both front and rear suspensions were revised.

The 105-series Giulia GT front suspension had a lower A-arm, with trailing and transverse links locating the top of the suspension. At the rear, a large T-shaped member controlled the side-to-side motion of the solid axle. While early Giulias had three-shoe drum front brakes (with 2¾-inch-wide shoes), models built from late 1963 featured disc brakes on all four wheels. In 1967, the brake system was changed from Dunlop to the much more refined ATE system.

Lubricated suspension points were eliminated in favor of permanently-lubricated fittings and rubber bushings. Early failures of some sealed joints prompted brave owners to add grease fittings, hoping to relieve squeaks and seizures. If you own a Giulia which has grease fittings added, it's important to maintain them regularly. You may wish also to dismantle the joint at some time to verify that the spindle on which the bush fits was not damaged by the drill bit when the fitting was added. The most failure-prone suspension link is the forward joint located near the headlamps in the fender well. Rough roads will cause this joint to fail rather quickly. Fortunately, its replacement is very simple.

For 1967, the Giulia Sprint GT evolved into the GT Veloce, or GTV as it was commonly known. Distinguished by a different grille treatment, it came equipped with the 1600cc twin cam fitted with twin Webers. Performance was strong and the body style began to overcome the initial resistance to the shape.

■ Giulia Sprint GT Veloce

Although initially, the Giulia Sprint GT was a marketing failure, Alfa's decision to campaign a lookalike car in the GTA did turn the public's perception of the body style. Primarily as a result of the GTA's successes on the track, in 1966 Alfa felt that it was opportune to reintroduce the Sprint GT. It offered a virtually identical "new" model, the Giulia Sprint GT Veloce, now known universally as the GTV. This time, the magic worked: 6,128 were produced in the first year and the body style became widely accepted.

The GTV developed 109 hp compared to the 106 hp of the Sprint GT. Part of the horsepower increase can be attributed to some basic research into the gas flow dynamics of the head. Alfa had been experimenting with various port sizes and found that a slightly smaller port increased fuel mixing because higher velocities were involved. As a result, the 1967 GTV has smaller inlet ports than the previous model.

The GTV featured comfortable accommodations for two, but leg room was severely limited for passengers in the rear.

In its February 24, 1967, issue, *Autosport* magazine compared the new Sprint GT Veloce to the Giulia GT: "The GTV employs the same body shell, suspension and transmission as the Giulia GT, but the power output has been increased by three bhp (theoretically—it certainly feels more). Yet surprisingly there is simply no comparison between the GT and the GTV, for the very minor alterations make the Veloce a much better car. Around Lake Garda the improvements were not that noticeable but the cars were brand new. The GTV is the latest and the best of the current range of Alfa Romeos I have driven, the Giulia TI Super being my previous favorite."

The original GTV had a simple grille with single headlights.

The GT Junior used a simplified version of the GTV's grille.

The 1750 GTV used a four-lamp version of the original GTV grille. This example has received a set of Cromadora alloy wheels.

Handling has always been one of Alfa's strengths, and the GTV offered exceptional handling. In the *Road & Track* test of July 1967 we read that "…even a Porsche owner ungrudgingly approved the entire Alfa gestalt, and spoke highly of its quick, precise handling and instant recovery through a badly chuck-holed stretch of dirt road. And a former Chrysler engineer tried a brief test ride, returned wondering 'how the devil do they do that with a live rear axle,' then forthwith demanded more time for a really thorough examination."

▪ 1750 GTV

Alfa had done the right thing by waiting patiently for its customers' tastes to mature: the 1967 GTV was received well enough to establish it as the standard Alfa coupe. In January 1968 it received a larger engine (introduced in the United States in 1969 with SPICA fuel injection). The bore and stroke of the new engine were 80 x 88.5 mm and the total displacement, at 1779 cc, qualified the car to be called an 1800. Instead, recalling Jano's masterpiece, the car was retro-named 1750. Since very few owners will have both vehicles, there was little danger of confusion. *Autosport* magazine, in its August 16, 1968, issue did pause to compare the old and new 1750s: "…the greatest change is ease of handling. The old supercharged car had to be steered with sensitive fingers and the gear-change demanded extreme precision. The latest model, in spite of having one carburetor choke per cylinder, is quite remarkably flexible and will pull hard at very low speeds. For this reason, it is an ideal dual-purpose car…."

Horsepower for the 1750 engine was up to 132 at 5,500 rpm and there was a significant increase in torque

The 1750 engine used SPICA injection to produce 132 hp for the American market.

(134 pound feet at 3,000 rpm compared to 103 pound feet at the same revs for the Giulia). A hydraulically operated clutch replaced the mechanically actuated unit of the Giulia and the pedals became pendant rather than floor-mounted (right-hand-drive coupes retained floor-mounted pedals). A rear anti-roll bar was also new. In the middle of the production run, the crank bearing journals were tuftrided to increase durability.

Continuing with *Autosport* magazine's evaluation of the 1750: "The new engine gives a lot more performance, with improved acceleration right through the range and a maximum speed within two mph of the magic 120. The longer stroke is noticeable, the unit being obviously busy at 6,000 rpm, and one would certainly not attempt to emulate the 8,000 rpm of the early Giulietta. The extra punch is so great that this is a much better engine

for touring, though it would be sacrilege not to make proper use of the delectable five-speed gearbox."

While the leading edge of the GTV hood had been raised above the plane of the nose, the 1750s were distinguished by a flat hood line. A wire-mesh grille with a single chrome bar carried four headlamps, and a different dash featured a large speedometer and tachometer carried in their own pods, while the water temperature and fuel level gauges were located in a center console which also carried the shift lever and accessory switches.

The seats of the 1969 1750 GTV were perhaps the best—or at least the most attractive—of any fitted to the coupe. They were deeply contoured, and solid vinyl inserts formed heavy bolsters which allowed some air circulation while seated.

■ 2.0-Liter GTV

In mid-1971, the four-cylinder engine was enlarged still further to almost 2.0 liters. The bore and stroke became 84 x 88.5, which was achieved by modifying the centerlines of the cylinders within the block. At the same time the head received larger valves. The new engine was fitted to the spider, sedan and GTV. To signal the 2.0-liter version, the grille on the GTV became a series of horizontal bars from which the Alfa grille outline was embossed. A restyled interior featured different seats and a dash layout which put the smaller fuel level and coolant temperature gauges in their own pods between the tachometer and speedometer.

The 2.0-liter developed 131 hp at 5,500 rpm and 134 pound feet of torque at 3,000 rpm. You will note that, initially, the larger 1962cc engine developed one hp less than the 1779cc predecessor. That is a nod to engine exhaust emissions which were beginning to bedevil even Alfa. The series reached its nadir with the 1980–81 spiders which, in the United States, were so heavily emission-controlled that they became docile touring cars with an emphasis on comfort rather than performance. The performance deficit was largely rectified by the introduction of Bosch Electronic Fuel Injection (EFI) in 1982 on the four-cylinder spider and in 1981 on the new GTV-6 coupe.

By the time the body style was retired, the GTV was growing very long in the tooth. Even in 1972,

Horizontal bars contributed to the final iteration of the GTV grille for the 2000 version of the Bertone coupe. This European model was built in 1972.

The interior of the 2000 GTV featured vinyl bucket seats and a beautiful wood-rimmed steering wheel.

▪ Alfetta GT

The GTV was replaced by the Alfetta GT in 1975, a change lamented at the time by all true Alfa enthusiasts. The GTV continued to be marketed, however, until 1977 by which time the production total for the 2.0-liter model had reached 37,459.

In 1975, Alfa introduced a new body style for its sedan and coupe. The coupe, styled again by Giugiaro, returned to the fastback styling of the original Giulietta, but had a very modern, aerodynamic profile, which resembled an airfoil with a front notch formed by the windshield. As mentioned just above, the new style seemed bloated and awkward to those accustomed to the tight profile of the GTV and it was not uniformly well- received. In the United States, the model further suffered from anemic performance; sales were just as anemic.

Modern Motor magazine observed of the 2.0-liter GTV: "the Alfa Romeo 2000 GTV is a very good 1964 grand touring car—produced in 1972. In the old days, it surprised the world with (for then) revolutionary handling, with good ride, sensitive steering isolated from road shock and a remarkably clean, crisp, body style.

"Today it is the same as it was in 1964. Certainly it has more power than its 1600 great grand-pappy and it has a few more refinements and creature comforts. But only a few more."

Though not appreciated at the time, the Alfetta GT began a styling approach which has characterized Alfa Romeo's products ever since. The Giulietta, and to a lesser extent the Giulia, was a benchmark statement of the GT coupe drawn using a classic vocabulary. In the early 1970s, when Alfa finally formed a marketing department, it was decided that future models would have to be distinguished by styling which was strikingly different from virtually everything else. Beginning with the Alfetta GT, Alfa adopted styling which "hit you in the stomach," to use the words of Ernesto Vettore.

The Alfetta GT was designed by Giugiaro and showed a pronounced wedge shape. This red coupe was built in 1976.

The Alfetta GT was the progenitor of a styling theme Alfa called *la linea* (the line). More prosaically, *la linea* is a wedge, characterized by a slender nose tapering upward to a high trunk area which cuts off sharply. The profile of the Alfetta, with its slender grille and fat midsection, was saved from *la linea* by a rather awkward taper away from the midship bloat. It is *la linea* which is responsible for the "hit-from-behind" profile of the Milano sedan, surely one of the most controversial profiles of any production Alfa. The company's in-your-face approach reached its most extreme expression in the ES30 Zagato sprint and has been progressively toned down from the 164 to the current family of Fiat models, including the 155 and 156, which are more characterized by the unabashedly phallic motif of the hood and grille than a wedge-shaped profile.

Inside, the Alfetta GT continued its "thinking-out-of-the-box" design, with the tachometer and oil pressure gauge placed directly before the driver but the remaining instruments arrayed out of the driver's line of sight in the center console. Presumably, the passenger could keep herself amused by watching those instruments. Controversial styling aside, the Alfetta GT is a wonderfully comfortable and capable car, providing you don't expect the kind of performance its styling suggests. Creature comforts inlcude a height-adjustable steering column, reclining seatbacks and air conditioning. You seem to sit much lower in the Alfetta than in previous Alfa coupes, primarily because the door sill is higher. The coupe is spacious inside for the front-seat passengers, though there is inadequate leg room and limited head room for adult rear-seat passengers.

The Alfetta is remarkable for a rust rate which far exceeds all previous models. At about the time the Alfetta was introduced, Italian manufacturers began buying steel from the Iron Curtain countries. This lower-priced sheet steel also came with "rust built-in." Alfettas rust at unusual places for an Alfa. Most critical is a tendency to rust around the front shock absorber towers. If allowed to rust to the limit, the tower will collapse, taking the suspension with it. For marginal cars, a sturdy cross brace, running over the engine and between the two towers, will keep things in alignment temporarily. I have seen an Alfetta coupe in which this cross brace was welded in, making the engine non-removable. The owner excused the modification by explaining that, by the time rust had destroyed the integrity of the brace, the car itself would be worthless and could be

The Alfetta GT and the later Alfetta GTV were the last Alfa Romeo coupes to use the venerable all-alloy twin-cam four. Here it is in its 2.0-liter, SPICA-injected form.

Former racer John Fitch with the "Mille Miglia" version of the Alfetta GTV.

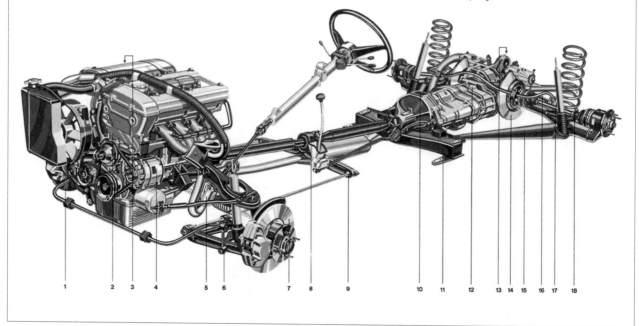

1. Front disc brakes
2. All-aluminum engine, 4 cylinders, dual overhead camshafts; light alloy oil sump
3. Spica fuel injection system
4. Alternator
5. Rack-and-pinion steering
6. Front suspension with stabilizer bar
7. Front wheel disc brake
8. Two-part drive shaft with flexible joints
9. Torsion bar (2) and cross-member
10. Flywheel and clutch
11. Rear cross-member connected to body. Accepts rear axle and Watts linkage connections
12. Gearbox/differential unit connected directly to body
13. Watts linkage
14. Rear disc brakes mounted inboard on differential output shaft
15. Triangulated DeDion rear axle
16. Rear stabilizer bar
17. Half shafts with two constant-velocity joints and tapered ends
18. Coil springs

With the alloy twin-cam four up front and the transaxle in the rear, the Alfetta GT offered ideal weight balance.

thrown away. Other popular rust points for the Alfetta include the surrounds of both the front and rear glass.

Further exacerbating the Alfetta's poor quality image, the interior of the early cars was both cheap and fragile. The door panels warped quickly and the quality of the upholstery was poor.

Alfetta coupes were available from 1975 through 1979 in the United States. There were no coupes imported in 1980, and the V-6-engined version of the Alfetta appeared in 1981 as the GTV-6. While the more powerful V-6 engine and its more robust driveline would appear to be perfect retro-fits for the Alfetta, this has not been a popular modification, probably because so few of the four-cylinder cars have survived in the first place. In the mid-to late-1980s, ten-year-old Alfettas were virtually worthless. Several of the Alfetta sedans and coupes in my back yard were given to me, and I have offered several for free, but have been unable to find a taker.

The Alfetta's ultimate appeal may be that it is the last coupe to carry the all-alloy, all-Alfa four-cylinder engine which had so much to do with Alfa's post-war success. And, since it was the last of that line, it also becomes the last of the coupes surveyed in this book.

The four-cylinder Alfetta coupe remained in production until 1985, even though a V-6 engine in the same basic body was introduced in 1980. Both models were revised in 1983 with tinted glass, dark side moldings, revised front seats with a mesh headrest and improved sound insulation.

In order to encourage sales, a "limited edition" Mario Andretti version of the coupe was introduced with unique trim details, including exterior striping, a rear wing and identifying dash plaque. Since these items were "tacked on," they, and the cars on which they were mounted, have largely disappeared.

Alfetta enthusiasts should not despair, however. History teaches that value, if not virtue, will eventually out. I was an Alfa enthusiast when you couldn't give Castagna-bodied 6C1750 dropheads away. Those once-denigrated 6C1750s are now quite valuable, as are the once-dismissed 6C2500 cars. My personal opinion is that the Alfetta will become a valuable collector car. Unfortunately, that time may come long after the current crop of enthusiasts has died off.

Chapter 4

Berlinas

*B*erlina is the Italian term for a closed car with seating for at least four people. That definition would include roll-up windows and a fully furnished interior. American enthusiasts held little interest in the Giulietta Berlina when it was introduced, thanks in part to the fact that Max Hoffman thought it couldn't compete in the American market. As a result, Americans tend to undervalue the Giulietta Berlina in spite of its all-alloy twin-cam engine and comfortable interior. In retrospect, the Berlina is an underpowered, minimally furnished and noisy car with enough outright charm to win over all but the most diehard curmudgeon.

All this changed with the introduction of the Giulia sedan, which offered greater comfort and performance. Arguably, the Giulia Super is one of the all-time great Alfa Romeos, an exclusive group that includes the great Jano cars and many of the Zagato-bodied race cars. Even in the late 1990s, Giulia sedans are practical transportation, offering the relative simplicity of carburetion and points, plugs and condenser ignition.

Giulietta is a play on Niccola Romeo's name in a Shakespearean context. Alfa held a party for the new Giulietta Sprint and Berlina at the Portello factory, complete with a "Romeo and Juliet" dressed in Elizabethan costumes. Alfa's marketing sense grew with the Giulietta, and it was more heavily advertised than the 1900. The Giulietta was an enormous success, in part because it hit its market squarely as a lower-priced car that appealed to a larger market than the 1900. While the 1900 was designed as the mass-produced car which would assure Alfa's success in the post-war market, it was the Giulietta which actually achieved this goal.

Alfa intended to introduce the Giulietta Berlina before the Sprint or Spider. The fact that the Berlina's schedule was falling so far behind prompted Alfa management to rush the Sprint into limited production. One of the earliest mechanical drawings of the Berlina is dated September 10, 1952, indicating that Alfa had begun planning the smaller Giulietta series only two years after the introduction of the 1900. Twelve Berlina prototypes were produced in 1954, a short development time for a new model even by modern standards. The Sprint was

The Berlina was the Giulietta most Italians knew best. It offered good performance and accommodated four adults. This 1956 Giulietta TI is one of the few in the United States.

introduced at the Turin show in 1954 and the Berlina was first presented at Turin in 1955.

Because of Max Hoffman, there are very few Giulietta Berlinas in the United States. In 1961, Alfa produced 35,711 Giuliettas. Of that number, 25,147 were Berlinas, suggesting just how lopsided is the American view of Alfa's product mix. Reflecting the model's popularity (it was referred to as *Mama Giulietta* by the Italians), there were a number of special-bodied Berlinas from firms such as Moretti, Colli, Vignale, Zagato and Pininfarina.

The Giulietta was styled very much along the lines of the 1900 sedan and, like the 1900, was available in standard and a higher-powered TI configuration. The Giulietta Berlina retained its basic body style throughout its production life, but underwent three minor variations. At the time of its introduction, enthusiasts

Although thousands of Europeans bought Giulietta TI Berlinas, few of the model were sold in the United States.

The interior of the Giulietta was simply designed and well-appointed.

understood only that the Berlina was styled "in-house," without having a very good idea of what "in-house" meant. The "in-house" styling department of Alfa Romeo is *Centro Stile*, which was headed by Professor Scarnatti during the Giulietta-Giulia era.

The initial Berlina featured grillework stamped into the front body panel, with a chrome eyebrow like the Sprint and Spider, and a simple, center chrome strip ending outboard in the parking lamp. At the rear, the taillamps were relatively small and set off with a narrow chrome trim. Inside, the driver manipulated a four-speed column shift and gazed at an oval instrument cluster with a speedometer describing an arc of almost 180°. There was no tachometer, and many enthusiast owners simply ran the engine up to valve float, or something on the order of 8,000 rpm! The engine tolerated this amazingly well, but later versions included a tachometer with a visible redline. The base car had a body designation of 750C and produced 53 CUNA horsepower at 5,500 rpm, while the model 753 TI gave 65 hp at 6,150 rpm. The extra horsepower came mostly from the use of a dual-throat Solex 32PBIC carburetor and 8.5:1 compression ratio, compared to the single-throat Solex 32BIC carburetor and 7.5:1 compression ratio. To the basic dash layout, the TI added a round tachometer mounted to the left of the speedometer pod and a matching combination oil/water gauge set on the right of the pod.

The Weber-carbureted Veloce version of the 750 and 101 engines never appeared in the Berlina. The cars featured a mechanically actuated Lucas starter until mid-1957, when a solenoid-equipped unit was fitted. With its 1300cc alloy twin-cam engine, the Berlina was capable of about 90 mph and the TI, about 95. In 1959, the grillework on the Berlina was upgraded to a chrome assembly, nestled where the stamped-steel grille originally appeared. The dash was revised to a horizontal layout with a ribbon speedometer.

The Berlina and TI were upgraded in 1961 with 101-series mechanicals and new front and rear trim, indicated by the 101-series body number. The grille became a more aggressive chrome latticework, completely covering the sheet metal. The Berlina engine developed 62 hp and the TI's hp rose to 74.

The performance of the Berlina is certainly modest by modern standards, but it performed quite adequately against its contemporaries. The bench-seat interior is spare but functional and there is little trim, especially on the first models. The four-speed column-shift transmission is precise and entertaining, as is the mechanically engaged starter on the early cars. If you're willing to wait, the Berlina can cruise at quite acceptable speeds, but getting there is something less than half the fun.

■ Tipo 103

Thanks in large part to the success of the Giulietta Berlina, Alfa was growing rapidly in the early 1960s. Alfa's management wanted to keep the sales momentum going, and was convinced that the marque's future lay in the volume production of affordable vehicles. In 1959 Alfa's design department began working on a 103-series 896cc front-wheel-drive car (the cast-iron 2.0-liter was series 102). Had the development schedule of the Giulietta been duplicated for the 103, the car would have appeared in 1961 or 1962. The 103, however, was

stillborn. Alfa's next step down-scale in the automotive market would not be realized until the introduction of the AlfaSud in 1971.

At the same time it was working on the 103, Alfa Romeo had an agreement with Renault to assemble Dauphines in Italy (they were Alfa's series 104), where they were called "Ondines." The Dauphines were originally assembled at Portello, but were soon moved south to a new facility built by Alfa Avio at Pomigliano d'Arco, an industrial suburb of Naples. This was a time of heated discussion about where the driving wheels of a car should be. Renault's advertising made much of the Dauphine's rear-engine/rear-drive configuration, and the French company claimed that the front-wheel-drive design of cars such as Saab and DKW was less stable. How Renault would have been embarrassed had the public known that its Italian companion was developing a front-drive car!

The front/rear-drive contention would not be decided by the technical details so much as public acceptance. Ultimately, the public was convinced that front-wheel drive was the better configuration, thanks in part to the Corvair and Mr. Nader. The matter had been settled for almost a decade by the time Alfa introduced its front-drive AlfaSud, which was also manufactured at the Pomigliano d'Arco plant.

The front-wheel-drive Tipo 103 sedan was never produced.

The 896cc engine of the Tipo 103 was mounted transversely and drove the front wheels.

Stillborn 103

Alfa's 103-series transverse twin-cam engine was unusual in several respects: it had no intermediate sprocket to halve the speed of the cam chain. Instead, double-size pulleys were fitted to the ends of the twin overhead camshafts. A single-throat downdraft carburetor sat behind the engine while the exhaust manifold sat up front, next to the radiator. The engine had an extremely deep block that also served as a sturdy mount for the transaxle unit. Driveshafts to the front wheels were located behind the engine/transaxle assembly. In overall layout, the 103 anticipated closely the configuration of the modern front-wheel-drive vehicle.

An entirely new body clothed the 103 mechanicals. It was much more squared-off than the current Giulietta sedan, and the front hood line featured a shallow V to improve forward visibility. Strikingly similar lines can be seen in the production Renault 8, a further reflection of the close working relationship between the Italian and French firms. Even more striking is the similarity of the 103's design to the final Giulia sedan. From a styling standpoint, the Type 103 proved to be a prototype for the Giulia.

Although the 103 was ready for testing in 1960, plans for its production were set aside to permit engineers to concentrate on refining the new Giulia engine. The 103 was once again reevaluated for production in the mid-1960s, but again rejected in favor of the design that eventually became the Alfasud.

In hindsight, the front-drive 103 of 1959–60 is an important car because it foreshadowed the configuration which would finally become "industry standard." Rumors of a move to front-drive circulated quietly among Alfa management for decades, but their products continued to cling doggedly to a chassis layout dating back to before the Second World War.

▪ Introducing the Giulia

The successor to the Giulietta line was the Giulia. In Italian, this is a play on words: *Giulietta* is the diminutive of *Giulia*. In retrospect, therefore, the Giulietta is a "little Giulia."

Alfa introduced the Giulia TI at the Monza racetrack on June 27, 1962. The production sedan carried a 105-series designation, and featured a slight scallop running along the side of the car just under the window line and another smaller scallop running along the top of the car just above the rain gutter. The hood depression of the prototype 103 was eliminated, and the front grillework of the 2600 sedan was adapted to the smaller car. The gearbox was similar to the 101-series Giulietta, but now carried a fifth gear, as the larger cast-iron-engined 2000 cars had since 1958. The Giulietta was available with a column shift (model 105.14) or a floor shift (model 105.08).

The Giulia engine was essentially a 101-series Giulietta unit with its bore and stroke changed to 78 x 82 mm for a displacement of 1570 cc. To accommodate the longer stroke, the height of the block was increased, but the bore centers were unchanged. Sodium-cooled exhaust valves were standard. The engine offered 92 hp with the single Solex carburetor and a compression ratio of 9:1 (compared to the Giulietta's 53 hp and 7.5:1 compression ratio). The Giulia TI's larger engine gave it almost the same performance as the Giulietta Veloce spiders and coupes and also made it much more tractable.

The engine, however, was not the highlight of the Monza introduction in 1962: the body was. The Giulia is one of the most-loved models because of its superior strength, comfort, excellent accommodations

This Giulia 1600TI dates from the model's introductory year of 1962 and shows lines that are more squared off and modern than the Giulietta it eventually superceded.

and driving position. No other model Alfa has had more permutations than the Giulia sedan. There are ten major variations from the initial TI of 1962 to the Giulia Diesel of 1976. It was a favorite car of the Italian "freeway police" in both its sedan and station-wagon form. In Super tune (with dual Weber carbs) the Giulia was able to catch all but the most exotic speeders. While enthusiasts are most interested in the sporting coupes and spiders, the Giulia sedan is in many ways their equal in performance and undoubtedly their superior in comfort and accommodation. It is easy for enthusiasts to overlook a sedan when voluptuous coupes and spiders abound, but the charm of the Giulia sedan, once tasted, is not easily forgotten.

Dave Mericle has translated a 1966 interview in which Orazio Satta talks about the design of the Giulia Berlina:

Alfa Romeo is not merely a maker of automobiles; it truly is something more than a conventionally built car. There are many automotive makes, among which Alfa Romeo stands apart. It is a kind of affliction, an enthusiasm for a means of transport. It is a way of living, a very special way of perceiving the motor vehicle. What it is resists definition. Its elements are like those irrational character traits of the human spirit which cannot be explained in logical terms. They are sensations, passions, things that have much more to do with man's heart than with his brain.

Of course some of the elements are purely mechanical and are easy enough to identify. They are concepts which arise from the questions posed by motor racing, where their sort of excellence is necessary. We have always held it to be necessary that they should be transmitted, in the best way, to the cars that we sell—braking, roadholding, steering, the feel of the car in the hands of he who drives it. Those things always have been a tradition with us, a thing that we always have sought to provide in our cars.

Mericle notes that Alfa has a long history building airplane engines. During World War II Satta and his design team at Alfa Romeo helped design and build some engines for the best Italian fighter plane in existence, the Macchi Folgore C.202. After the war the company was at the forefront of aircraft engine design, but of course could not build fighter planes.

Satta and his staff applied everything they had learned about aircraft to the automobile:

Aeronautical technology had, over automotive technology, the great superiority of the necessity of absolute reliability and thus the need for much greater planning and application. It required concepts of a much more developed and sophisticated technical character because, naturally, the reliability and therefore the safety of an aircraft

The airy cockpit of the Giulia (1300 model shown) provided excellent accommodations for driver and passenger.

should be as absolute as possible. Beyond that, all of the branches of science and technology which were necessary for keeping abreast in aero engines were, for me and all of us, a very important school. This is why, when we had finished with aero engines at the end of the war, we were able to transfer all those systems to the design of new automobiles. I think that it was done at just the right time.

This explains how Satta was able to design small, efficient cars like no others in the world. The interview continues:

The major imprint of our design center (Centro Stile) on automotive models and the Giulia in particular is really quite simple: safe and fast cars. Large inside and small outside, with light and sturdy structures, roomy trunks and precise aerodynamics united to both high-speed driving and low fuel consumption.

The leading principle for a serious design studio is usually only one, but the clues to these principles range from tens to hundreds. The style of any new car is modified by evolution. For instance, look at the incomparable speed with which graphic art fashion—and many other facets of our everyday

life not directly related to the automobile—evolve. Everything around us changes its aspect, line and character. The consumer is now, and will be increasingly, forced to change his car. But the fashion of new cars is proving very expensive for both manufacturers and customers. The Americans set the best example I can think of in this respect; Mr. Jones changes his just-run-in car because Mr. Smith already has a new model, and if Jones doesn't do the same it will appear that his business is not doing so well.

Well all right then, let Mr. Jones and Mr. Smith change their cars. But how can we Italians do this when our income is nine times inferior to theirs? Instead, we must build cars that are a leap beyond the norm for today, so that in ten years our automobiles will still be competitive.

Safety was our first priority in designing Giulia. Ours are sports cars in which, due to their power and mechanical ability, the safety of the driver and passenger comes before anything else. Besides this, there is the necessity to harmonize the finish and comfort with the increased performance of our sporting cars. In other words, to render a car silent you have got to increase its weight. Some foreign

According to Ing. Satta, safety was more important during the design process of the Giulia than the performance and comfort for which it is best known.

cars have many hundreds of kilos of sound-deadening material. So we think, okay, let us put it in our cars. But what will the client say if he doesn't succeed any longer in reaching 100 km/h in that brief matter of seconds? He will say to himself that we have compromised wrongly, and he would be right. In addition, certain other compromises involve other factors and higher costs: for instance, if we design the brakes beyond their already spectacular ability, and then we increase the engine's state of tune to the range of the incredible, etc., let's add 10,000 lira here and 20,000 lira there and so on, and at the end where will the price go? Beyond the range of the client.

Now with the Giulia Super, for example, all these factors have been taken into account and the result is a car which features the best of all worlds; the engine always guarantees the famous Alfa Romeo performance and the car boasts a finish that fully meets the requirements of safety and comfort. The primary feature I was concerned about was without doubt the excellent road holding, this involves the suspension, visibility and handling. It doesn't matter if the new Giulia owner engages in dangerous and racing type driving. The basic problem comes down to a wet road, an inattentive lady, a young man too sure of himself. The driver is an electronic system who, at every instant of his journey, stores data and processes it more or less rapidly. The reaction to an external impulse can be quick or slow, right or wrong. In these cases what counts most is the capability of the car to forgive mistakes, and that it can undergo a too violent motion of the steering wheel and still remain on the road, besides responding with swift composure to braking which is a few seconds too late. This is what the Alfa Romeo character is all about, and this is also why the Giulia Super is a direct descendant of this grand tradition.

No one who has owned a Giulia Super could disagree with Satta's evaluation of the car.

The first news American enthusiasts had of the Monza introduction ignored the sedan almost entirely, centering instead on the Spider and its engine. *The Alfa Owner* of July, 1962, reported: "On June 28, a new 1570cc Alfa Romeo called the Giulia was introduced at Monza. According to *Motoring News, Competition Press*,

Giulias proved remarkably fast and rugged in competition. This Giulia TI Super was sponsored by Knauz Continental Motors outside of Chicago and driven by Horst Kwech.

and Commandante Morrone of Alfa Romeo (South Africa), the Giulia appears to be identical in outward appearance to the Giulietta, except for a false air intake on the hood. Berlina TI, Spider, and Sprint versions will be produced."

Details of the new body were added in the August issue of *The Alfa Owner*, when a small photograph of the new Giulia sedan was reproduced. Additional details of the car were listed:

"In addition to information carried in the July issue of the *Owner*, we can now add the following, applicable to the TI only: triple-shoe front drum brakes; ball-jointed A-arm front suspension; rubber bumpers inside the front coil springs and shock absorbers now between the springs and wheels at the apex of the "A"; at the rear, rigid axle and radius rods are retained; rear coils are lower mounted not on the axle but on the trailing radius rods; radius arms are fabricated angle pieces; (the) base on the torque reaction triangle is almost the width of the car; all grease nipples except two at universals on the drive shaft have been eliminated."

The triple-shoe front drum brakes were fitted only to the first 2,000 cars. Otherwise, the American summary nicely characterizes the significant changes between the Giulietta and Giulia mechanicals. The new chassis, introduced on the Giulia TI in 1962 as the type 105, would become the standard configuration until the introduction of the Alfetta in 1972; this suspension would remain on the spider until its demise in 1994.

▪ Giulia Press Reactions

In its review of the Giulia TI, *Road & Track* magazine reconfirmed its well-known Alfa enthusiasm. The review began: "If there's another car that offers more for the same price, we can't think what it is," and concluded: "We could get hooked on the Alfa TI. In fact we are."

In spite of their enthusiasm, the reviewers at *Road & Track* had some misgivings about the car's appearance:

The editors of *Road & Track* enjoyed the Giulia Super but they didn't particularly appreciate the work of the Alfa stylists. This 1967 Giulia Super is in original and unrestored condition.

The spacious interior of the Giulia Super offered good seats and clear instrumentation.

"…the TI won't win any beauty prizes. It is boxy, square at all corners and it has more of the looks of one of the workaday medium-size Fiats than the sleek sexiness we ordinarily expect attached to the Alfa emblem."

The squareness of the new car (the Giulietta sedan was round in comparison) had utility, for it provided interior room and seating that was hard to match. According to *Road & Track*: "The seating position is high, the steering wheel is located at just the right angle and in just the right place, and the vision is excellent in all directions. It is a car that encourages vigorous driving and everything conspires to it being conducted allegro con brio."

While its engine had only a single Solex carburetor, the TI offered a drivetrain which was remarkably sophisticated for a sedan in 1962, and *Road & Track* gave it due mention: "Underneath that unprepossessing exterior, however, there is as fine a set of 1600 internals as you'll find anywhere. This engine…is attached to that fine all-synchro 5-speed gearbox…and a better combination can hardly be imagined."

Several months later, *Road & Track* tested the dual-Weber-carburetor version of the sedan, called the Super. The Super, introduced at the 1965 Geneva motor show, had a more highly tuned engine and a more sporting interior, with separate front bucket seats and equal-size speedometer and tachometer on the dash. A Nardi-inspired steering wheel was standard. *Road & Track* loved the details of the Super, but not the basic sedan body. The review's headline was: "A sporting sedan with almost everything but beauty."

Lest the casual reader miss the aesthetic verdict, the editors underlined their coolness for the sedan's styling in the opening paragraph: "It's nothing much in the way of pretty, what with slab sides and boxy lines, but it sure is everything else a car of this type ought to be." Neither did *Road & Track* like some of the interior details, most noticeably the heater: "One of the standard Alfa jokes concerns their use of a heater indicator light— a very practical accessory because otherwise you'd probably never be able to tell whether the heater was on or not."

Such are the judgments of what was to become the single most popular sedan in Alfa history and, arguably, one of the greatest sedans of all time. True, it was slab-sided and vertical in a tradition one usually associates with Triumph Mayflower sedans. The virtue of the slab-sidedness, however, has already been suggested: ample interior room (though the Super was found to be short in driver leg-room by *Road & Track*, perhaps because the editors had not yet discovered the typical Alfa arms-extended driving position). There were other advantages: the sedan was surprisingly aerodynamic though its Cd of 0.34 was probably only a coincidence of its design. In comparison, the Cd of a Maserati Ghibli is 0.35 and the Porsche 911 is 0.34. As a result of the very low turbulence, at speed the Giulia sedan is remarkably quiet and stable.

The seating position in the sedan is certainly upright, providing superb comfort and visibility. The seats in the Super are adjustable for rake, allowing the American driver to have the steering wheel a bit closer to his chest than typical Italian (arms extended) driving position permits. The TI dashboard has a round tachometer integrated into a bar-type speedometer, bench seats and either floor or column shift, though the column shift is more common. A plastic, two-spoke steering wheel is standard. The Super's dash has two very large instruments positioned in front of the driver: a speedometer on the right with a fuel gauge in its lower segment, and a tachometer with water temperature and oil pressure gauges around the bottom.

In spite of the joke about the heater light, ventilation and heating on the Giulia was light years ahead of the Giulietta unit, which also had a light to tell you it was on. However, since the Giulietta's heater motor had a tendency to seize, the Giulietta owner could always tell that his heater was on by the piercing howls made as the heater motor bearings tried to free themselves to turn

A bevy of Giulia engines awaits installation into Berlinas on the assembly line.

the fan. The author's original Super was quite competent to keep him warm in high-speed sub-zero dashes to the upper reaches of Michigan for an entire winter. The secret is to use cardboard to completely block off the front of the radiator.

▪ TI

There is a curious twist in nomenclature between the Giulietta and Giulia Berlinas. Recall that the Giulietta was available in two versions: a single-throat Solex version, and the higher-performance TI. The basic Giulia Berlina, however, was the TI, with a dual-throat 32PAIA Solex carburetor. The Giulia TI engine produced 92 hp at 6,200 rpm, and vehicle dry weight was 2,200 pounds (1,000 kg).

Like the 101-series Giulietta Berlina, the Giulia TI was available with a ribbon speedometer and instrument cluster, and bench-type seats front and rear with vinyl covering. Cars built for export had a painted, anti-glare, wrinkle-finish dash. A steering column shifter was available, though floor shift was an option. Externally, the TI was identifiable by the transverse air inlets just below the windshield, and the chrome Giulia TI badge on the trunk and chrome taillight surrounds.

The TI series remained pretty much unchanged from the 1962 models, with the exception of a right-hand-drive model being produced for export to Great Britain, Australia, and New Zealand. In addition, all Giulia Berlinas were built at Arese.

▪ The 1300 Series

On May 11, 1964, a 1300cc version of the Giulia TI, the Giulia 1300 Berlina, was introduced at Monza. This model is distinguished by its busy, latticework bars in the grille, dual headlamps with no fog lights, minimal external trim and lack of bumper overriders. The 1300 Berlina had the two-spoke steering wheel and ribbon-type speedometer/round tachometer instrumentation of the TI, but featured a floor shift and developed 78 hp from its twin-throat Solex carburetor.

All 1300 Giulias were floor shift and their transmissions had a closer-ratio fourth and fifth gear to help take advantage of the engine's ability to rev. Interior trim stayed very plain with vinyl seats and rubber floor mats. The 1300 Berlina remained the most spartan of Berlinas and was discontinued in 1971.

The 1300TI was introduced at St. Felice Cicero, near Rome, on February 4, 1966. Ate brakes replaced Dunlop units. Other improvements included stainless steel bumpers front and rear, a new grille with the top portion of the Alfa heart attached beneath the front edge of the hood, a pair of chrome trim strips running underneath the doors, a nice C-pillar cross and serpent emblem plate and a switch from horizontal to vertical inlets at the base of the windshield.

The Giulia TI 1600 was withdrawn for 1967. The Giulia 1300 and TI received the wood dash and plush seats of the Super, along with

The author's all-time favorite publicity photo from Alfa shows a Giulia 1300TI.

a new three-spoke steering wheel. The 1300 grille had three thinner chrome bars leading to a stamped, one-piece Alfa heart on a black mesh background. This model ended production in 1972, along with the 1300 Super.

■ TI Super

In March 1963 Alfa upgraded the Giulietta Sprint Speciale to Giulia status by giving it the larger engine with dual Weber carburetors and a compression ratio of 9.7:1. The larger Giulia engine then developed 112 hp, compared to the 92 hp of the Giulia TI or the 100 hp of the Giulietta SS.

On April 24, 1963, Alfa invited the press to Monza to introduce the TI Super, a race/rally version of the Giulia TI powered by the Giulia Sprint Speciale engine. While the TI's gear change was typically located on the steering column (floor shift was an option), TI Super put it on the floor where it belonged in a proper race car. The TI Super also had lightweight Zagato-designed tube-frame front seats, rubber floor mats, round gauges and a three-spoke steering wheel (as would appear later in the Giulia Super). From the outside, the TI Super could be identified by the air intake grilles that replaced the inboard headlamps, and alloy wheels.

This description may make the TI Super sound like a superb road-going car for the hard-core enthusiast.

The 1969 Giulia 1300TI interior offered rubber floor mats instead of the Super's fabric fitment. Note the later-style instruments.

The Giulia TI Super was a stripped-down factory racer. They can be identified by the lack of a rear seat and mesh grilles in place of the inboard headlamps. Here Horst Kwech drives the car owned by Knauz Continental Motors.

Its state of tune and interior appointments, however, are too stark for everyday comfort. The TI Super uses slightly thinner sheet metal and has a total lack of any felted sound-deadening material under hood, trunk, floor pans and doors. As a result of these weight-saving measures, the car weighs 2,002 pounds (910 kg) dry compared to 2,178 pounds (990 kg) for the production Super. It was homologated under license IGM 3374 OM, and while it proved very successful in races, it is not an appropriate car to be driven on the street.

The model was originally conceived as a rolling test bed and entrant in the Touring Car championship series. During the 1963 and 1964 race seasons, it provided a lot of data which eventually benefited the GTA coupe. The TI Super was discontinued as a successful experiment in 1964. Because of its development work with the TI Super, Alfa got a significant head start on the design of its new GTA coupe.

The Guilia Super was the Berlina model which sold the best in the United States. Before the heyday of the BMW 2002, the Giulia Super was *the* sports sedan.

The Giulia Super converted many a driver to Alfa ownership.

Present-day TI Supers are all likely to have been extensively raced and so it is impossible to generalize on what kind of equipment or modifications a buyer is likely to find. The cars are very collectible and a TI Super with documented history is a blue-chip investment even though it may look very tatty. Only 500 chassis numbers were allocated for homologation purposes, and probably fewer than 20 TI Supers survive today.

▪ Giulia Super

This is the Giulia sedan most frequently found in the United States, primarily as 1966 and 1967 models.

The Super was introduced in 1965 at the Geneva motor show. It was distinguished from the TI by longitudinal air inlets just below the windshield, a three-spoke Nardi-like wheel, a distinctive instrument panel with two large circular instruments, bucket seats and a chrome strip under the door sills. Though its engine was externally identical to the 1964 112-hp Giulia Spider Veloce, the Super developed only 98 hp from its twin-Weber-carbureted engine. The reduction was due in part to a lower compression ratio of 9.0:1 instead of the Spider Veloce's 9.7:1.

Of all the Alfas I've owned, the Giulia Super vies with the 6C1750 Gran Sport Zagato for my second-place affection (first place is the 1900 CSS Zagato). If you want to know what really made the post-war Alfa great, drive a Giulia Super. It still remains the quintessential definition of the sport sedan. While the Sprint and Spider are presumably more sporty, the Super gives up nothing in performance or sheer exhilaration. Over the years, I've puzzled over the Super's appeal. Nothing stands out to suggest its remarkable attraction. Rather, I think, it is the lack of negatives which makes the Super so desirable. It does everything right, and its performance and amenities exceed expectations. After all, it was an all-alloy twin-cam, five-speed sedan of the mid-1960s.

You sit upright in the Super because there is a significant drop between the top of the seat cushion and the floor. The thick seats cradle you in a comfort largely unknown in other Alfas and the reach combination between pedals and steering wheel—so often criticized in the Sprints and Spiders—is quite normal. The controls are easily reached and logically arranged. Even the heater worked: I used a Super to commute between Mancelona, Michigan, and Ann Arbor in sub-zero temperatures. With the radiator fully blocked by a cardboard square, I was able to maintain a comfortable interior temperature even at 70 mph.

The Super was a fast car, capable of holding very high speeds over very long distances. One factor contributing to this is the car's astounding coefficient of drag of only 0.34. Since there are photos of the body being tested in Alfa's wind tunnel, the figure was not an accident, though it seems incredible to those who equate low drag with gumball shapes. Coming back to Los Angeles from the Monterey weekend (nominally, a six- to seven-hour trip), I was asleep in the back seat of Dave Mericle's immaculate Super. Dave woke me to say that we were doing an indicated 120 mph on the speedometer—I then promptly fell back to sleep, the car was so comfortable. Dave held this speed for several miles, and the trip was accomplished in four hours.

In 1968, the Super was updated with some details from the 1750 Berlina. The dash was revised slightly. The front grille retained its five horizontal bars, but they now led to a one-piece Alfa heart on a black mesh background. Velour and cloth materials were offered for the first time and a dished wooden-rim steering wheel

was added. The Alfa Romeo and Giulia Super scripts were in capital letters.

The Giulia Super ceased production after 1972, as did the 1300 TI and 1300 Super.

■ The Colli Wagons

In 1967 Don Black, chief engineer of ARI, ordered five Supers to be converted to station wagons (*Promiscua*) for use as mobile service school vehicles in the United States. These custom-built vehicles were sent to Alfa distributorships around the world. Alfa picked Colli to do the modifications, which were totally handmade from the C-pillar back. Colli added steel side panels or glass side rear windows depending on the customer's wishes, a rear hatch that opened up all the way from the top of the roof line down to the bumper, and a flat bed floor inside with fold-down rear seats that necessitated redesigning access to the spare tire from underneath the car. They are among some of the niftier Giulias, and a very few have survived intact to the present day. Three Colli wagons are known in Australia, three in America and one in the UK.

■ Other Giulia Berlinas

The Giulia series was both successful and long-lived. So long, in fact, that by the time it was phased out it had become quite dated. These later Giulia models picked

Only a very few of these Giulia Supers were converted to wagons by coachbuilder Colli.

The short-lived Giulia 1600S was a down-market version of
the Giulia Super.

The Giulia Nuova Super was available in 1300 (shown) and
1600 versions; they were externally similar.

up some of the trim details of Alfa's main line 1750 and
2000 Berlinas, including a hydraulically actuated clutch.

A cheapened version of the Giulia Super, the 1600S,
was introduced at the 1970 Turin show. It was advertised
as the "long-distance Giulia," and developed 95 hp from
an engine which was virtually identical to the TI. Like
the TI, it had three chrome strips on the grille. The car
was not successful and was withdrawn after about a year
and a total production of 2,212.

The Giulia 1300 Super also
appeared at the Turin show in 1970.
It featured some of the refinements
of the 1750 series sedans that had
been introduced in 1967. The
1300 Super, like the Giulia Super,
offered dual Weber carburetors,
but produced only 89 hp because
of its smaller displacement. It was
withdrawn in 1972.

For 1976, the well-aged Giulia
body received a British Perkins
diesel engine that displaced 1760 cc
and produced 55 hp at 4,000 rpm.
To make the interior habitable,
the engine bay received almost
11 pounds of sound-deadening
material. The model was withdrawn
the following year.

▪ Giulia Nuova Super

The last of the line, the Giulia
Nuova Super, appeared in 1974 but
remained available until about 1978.
It was offered in both 1300 and
1600 versions. The 1290cc version
developed 103 hp while the 1570cc
model turned out 116 hp. Both had
a single chrome spear on the grille,
four headlights and a very rounded
Alfa "heart," similar to that on the
Alfettas. Like many of the later
Giulias, it shared many components
with the 1750 and 2000 sedans.

Since all the Giulia sedan bodies
carried identical sheet metal,
grillework was used to set apart
the various models. To summarize:
the grille of the 1600 TI had eight
horizontal chrome strips and four
headlamps. The grille of the Giulia
TI Super replaced the inner small headlamps of the stock
TI grille with mesh-covered air intakes for the engine.
The Giulia Super had three horizontal chrome strips and
four headlamps. The Junior-series Giulia 1300 sedans
had only two headlamps and a stamped-mesh grille. The
Nuova Super's grillework copied the 1750 sedan.

As significant as the Giulia sedan is to Alfa history,
most enthusiasts pay scant attention to it, preferring
instead to concentrate on the spider and coupe. It
is their loss. To quote one owner, "True Alfisti drive
sedans." And, I can assure you, the happiest of them all
are in Giulia Supers.

Although the 1750 Berlina is often perceived as a new automobile, underneath the crisp new suit the car is very much a Giulia.

■ New Clothes for Giulia

The proliferation of Giulia models indicates just how determined Alfa was to keep its bread-and-butter sedan appealing. In January 1968 Alfa introduced the 1750 to the press at a scenic site near Salerno, just south of Naples. The exterior sheet metal was all new, as was the interior. However, these changes should not cloud the fact that the car was still very Giulia-like. The greater wheelbase of the 1750 Berlina (2,570 mm compared to 2,510 mm of the Giulia) gave it a longer, more limousine-like appearance and, in the United States, the engine was fueled by the mechanical SPICA system to accommodate emissions regulations.

In spite of the fact that it represented only minor changes over the Giulia series, somehow the 1750 lost a lot of the Giulia's charm. The modernized exterior styling had less character and the seats were slightly less well padded. The controls seemed less intuitive and the prominent "bullet" instrument pods were an awkward preview of the 1971 1750 Spider Veloce dash treatment, which was much more successful. From a driver's standpoint, the new Berlina seemed less powerful and responsive. As a result, many in the United States concluded that the SPICA system was a power-robber, and Weber conversions were popular.

Perhaps the Giulia was an impossible act for any car to follow; perhaps in hindsight the slightly more powerful 2000 Berlina overshadowed the 1750. For

Giulia Model Designations

Series	Years	Description
105.14	1962–64	Giulia TI column shift
105.16	1963–64	Giulia TI Super
105.09	1963–65	Giulia TI right-hand drive, knocked-down for export
105.08	1964–67	Giulia TI floor shift
105.06	1964–71	Giulia 1300
105.26	1965–68	Giulia Super (1965-68, 1969-71 & Nuova Super 1.6 models)
105.39	1965–72	Giulia 1300TI
105.40	1966–70	Giulia 1300TI right-hand drive, knocked-down for export
105.85	1968–70	Giulia 1600S
105.87	1969	Giulia 1600S right hand drive
115.09	1970–72	Giulia 1300 Super
115.10	1972–73, 1974	Giulia Super 1.3 (1972–73) & Nuova Super 1.3 (1974) right-hand drive
105.28	1972–76	Giulia Super right-hand drive, knocked-down for export
115.09S	1974–77	Nuova Super 1.3
115.40	1976	Nuova Super diesel

whatever reason, the 1750 Berlina is among the least desirable of Alfa sedans. There was nothing inherent in the mechanicals to make this so. In fact, the 1750 coupe is more highly prized than its 2.0-liter successor. It's just that all the 1750 Berlina pieces didn't go together as seamlessly as the Giulia. That is a distinctly personal opinion: 101,879 examples of the 1750 Berlina were produced in just five years, compared to the 196,239 Giulia sedans produced over 12 years.

Alfa deleted the strange dual-pod instrumentation layout of the 1750 when it introduced the 2000 Berlina in 1971. The body shell of the two cars was identical and there was only enough change in the interior to suggest that this was a new model. Along with the other sedans, the 2000 Berlina got a bigger, heart-shaped grille. White instruments were featured and this model was the first of the Alfa fours to receive an optional three-speed automatic transmission, which proved most popular in Australia.

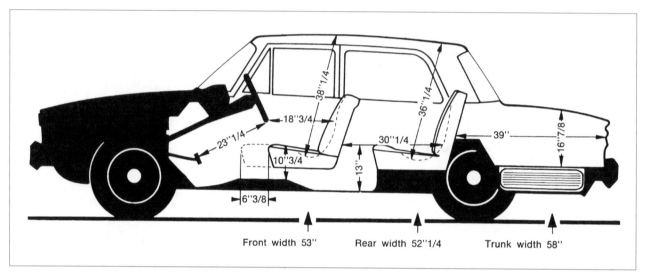

The 1750 (and later 2000) Berlina offered surprisingly roomy accommodation for passengers and baggage.

Although the grille was simpler and the interior revised, except for the bigger engine, the 2000 Berlina was very similar to its 1750 predecessor.

■ Alfetta

I need to preface my comments on the Alfetta with an explanation. One of my beliefs is that the Giulia represented the pinnacle of Alfa's post-war designs. It follows, if this is true, that the subsequent models were less desirable. One may draw his own conclusions as to the reason, but Alfa's departure from the United States and Australia indicates that something went very wrong. Clearly, Alfa's purchase by Fiat is an unequivocal indication that its problems were not limited to one or two markets.

One of the possible reasons for Alfa's difficulties may lie in the product itself, but that is only one of several possibilities. Shifting preferences in the market, inappropriate pricing, incompetent advertising, poor customer relations, bureaucratic inefficiency and an adversarial relationship with the dealer body can all be contributing factors. One of my premises is that all of the above contributed to Alfa's failure and its consequent purchase by Fiat.

It's easy enough to blame organizations and strategies for the failure, but when it comes to knocking the product, owners get very defensive. I've yet to identify an Alfa model that some owner didn't love almost more than life itself. Relative to other marques, Alfas may all be exquisite, but within the Alfa pantheon, there are certainly greater and lesser gods. The Alfetta sedan is clearly a lesser god than the 8C2900. Exactly

how much less is very hard to say, especially when a car is 30 years old and at the nadir of its value. My evaluation of the Alfetta is based on first-hand experience: I'll admit to owning six of them, and that's not counting several parts cars.

For a number of years, Alfa was under increasing pressure to update its model line. The Spider was unchanged from 1965 through Alfa's departure from the United States. The Spider was never a hot seller outside the United States, and the decision not to import the new Spider into the United States foretold unmistakably Alfa's departure from our market.

One of the most pressing needs, if Alfa were to retain any aura of technological leadership, was to adopt independent rear suspension. At a time when Alfa's four-cylinder alloy engine was reaching middle age, contemporary Toyota sedans were offering four-valve-per-cylinder engines of greater sophistication—and power.

Alfa simply didn't have the money to develop its new V-6 and a revised four-cylinder engine at the same time, and the V-6 won. It's notable that an upgraded four had to await Fiat's cast-iron block before the four-valve head found a home on a production Alfa. Moreover, it's clear that Alfa, in the years just before its purchase, was stringing out the technical developments as much as possible. The V-6 grew from 2.5 to 3.0 liters in spite of the fact I was assured by ARDONA that such enlargement

The wheels and other trim items reveal this late Alfetta Berlina as a European model.

was "impossible." The four-valve head featured on some of the last 164s would have been a welcome addition in the United States some years earlier than it actually appeared, and certainly not as a tragic last gasp.

This is the background (and a little foreground) behind the appearance of the Alfetta in the United States during 1975. In fact, the only question stateside was when the car would actually appear on our shores. Alfa announced the Alfetta in 1971 and the model went on sale in Italy in early 1972. Initially, the car was powered by the 1600 or 1750 alloy fours. In 1975, the body was lightly restyled and the Alfetta Berlina was finally imported to the United States, powered by the 2.0-liter engine (the 2.0-liter Italian version did not appear until 1977). In 1977, the body was again restyled. The vent windows were deleted and flush, plastic door releases replaced the chrome-metal handles of the earlier model. This model appeared in the United States in 1978 as the Sport Sedan. Although the overall appearance was hardly changed, almost none of the exterior sheet metal of the earlier Alfetta will fit the later Sport Sedan.

Almost everyone reading this book will know that the original Alfa Romeo Alfetta took the World Championship in 1950 and 1951. For those new to

the marque (or very forgetful) Alfa hammered the connection in its Alfetta advertising, setting new records for presumption. Just as no one seriously thinks a LeMans Pontiac would be capable of competing at that famous venue, no one was fooled into thinking that the new Alfa Alfetta was really a thinly disguised grand prix car.

The key to the Alfetta conceit was the model's deDion rear suspension (see Chapter 13), a feature shared (though reversed in plan view) with the world-championship car. To its critics, who looked with pride at the independent rear suspensions of many other sporty cars, Alfa answered with another solid rear axle; at least, there would be no untoward camber changes under hard cornering! The deDion advantage of lower unsprung weight was realized in the Alfetta, as was the potential for a true 50/50 weight distribution (*Road & Track* reported 51/49 f/r), thanks to the use of a transaxle. Especially when cornering hard on rough roads, the Alfetta had no peer.

Giuseppe Busso was responsible for the design of the Alfetta transaxle arrangement, so it is no surprise that it emulates the design of the 158/9 grand prix cars with which he was involved. Dave Mericle interviewed Busso in 1998 and learned he was given "a clean sheet of paper" to design the car in 1968. Satta asked him for three approaches to the new car's suspension: a low-cost option, a more technical solution to represent a trade-off between cost and complexity, and finally a cost-no-object, technically superb design. His first effort was a front-drive design, presaging the current crop of Fiat-designed cars. The second design featured independent rear suspension along the lines of Jaguar and the TZ. His third design, as you may already have guessed, emulated the layout of the grand prix 158/9 cars he had worked on in the late 1940s and early 1950s. On paper, at least, the Alfetta is the pinnacle of Alfa Romeo's post-war designs.

Busso stated that all three designs were first submitted to Alfa's "bean counters" and then to the company's board of directors. After many delays, the decision was made to proceed with the most expensive option because it offered a degree of sophistication and performance unmatched by any other car in production. The distinction still

This European Alfetta Berlina features a speedometer calibrated up to 220 km/h.

holds true, even in 2000. Busso concludes: "When the decision was made to proceed with the very best design, I realized I had worked for many decades for the very best automobile manufacturer in the world."

By the time of its introduction in the United States, however, the Alfetta's poor build quality and propensity to rust were well known. The car's overblown advertising further dampened the enthusiast market for the Alfetta. The Alfetta was further bedeviled with poor performance, thanks to increasing emission controls and safety regulations. The bumpers on United States-specification Alfettas are worthy of a world-class weight lifter. Further negatives included an engine output for the 2.0-liter engine of only 111 hp (SAE), compared to 122 hp (CUNA) for the European carbureted model. Owners soon discovered the car's propensity for blowing head gaskets and tearing the rubber donuts that were used both to dampen oscillations and provide flexible couplings for the driveline. One pasttime was trying to estimate the number of driveline donuts that could be replaced before the body rusted itself beyond redemption.

To broaden the model's market appeal, 1978 models offered automatic transaxles. This probably did more to depress sales among enthusiasts than to convert those intenders who had never manually shifted a gear.

Finally, increasing smog regulations and marginally worn emissions equipment, including catalytic converters and SPICA pumps, have conspired to make the Alfetta virtually unlicenseable in the most strict smog-control states. Several full-time Alfa specialist mechanics report that two to three days' work is required to get the car near smog limits, with no assurance of meeting them at the testing station. Parts replacement will be also be a burden: aftermarket catalytic converters are about $150, and a rebuilt SPICA injection pump will be about $750 on an exchange basis. Put the two items together and you've exceeded the value of the car without even considering labor charges for installation.

Hopefully, Alfetta owners reading this will have a broad smile on their face. While my criticism is not in jest, mine have been the kind of negative comments that have made the Alfetta the absolute best value in used Alfas. During the late 1990s, running Alfetta sedans could be had for as little as $500, and I have even been given several. You can't buy more fun for the money, even if the near-term fate of the car is the junkyard. Personally, the most annoying fault in my Alfettas has been the fragile nature of the ignition switch, and its reluctance to complete the starter circuit.

By the time this 1979 model was released, it was dubbed the "Sports Sedan." Due to rust problems, very few have survived.

With its plush brown velour interior, this sports sedan is clearly a product of the 1970s.

When you think about it, it's incredible that a comfortable four-door sedan with handsome styling, a twin-cam alloy engine, torsion-bar front suspension and a deDion transaxle at the rear should be regarded so poorly. During 1997–98, both my wife and I drove matched 1978 Alfetta sedans—with automatic transaxles—for daily transportation. There's a reason: the auto-transaxle version does not eat donuts. As long as my wife drove our manual-transaxle 1979 Sport Sedan as a beater, I replaced one or two driveline donuts, on the average, about every six months. Here-a-lurch,

there-a-lurch driving subjects the driveline donuts to fatal loads. With the smooth-shifting ZF automatic transaxle, however, the Alfetta driveline donuts will live forever.

The ergonomics of the Alfetta are not quite perfect, but almost: the radio is too low in the instrument stack and the steering effort is excessively high at very low speeds. If you feel that these are survivable faults, then it'll be easy to love the Alfetta on its merits. Most United States models are air-conditioned by a dealer-installed Behr unit. The tilt steering wheel is a nice feature, as are the reclining front seatbacks, and interior space is commodious.

Because of their faults, Alfettas are being scrapped out at a high rate. Just wait: in 20 more years, your Alfetta sedan will be a rare and valuable classic.

The Alfetta's last year in the United States was 1979. For the rest of the world, Alfa offered a restyled version in late 1981 and again in 1983. The Australian version was called the "Sportiva," and remained popular into the mid-1980s. Progressive modernization included optional headlamp wipers and washers, rear headrests and, in 1983, power windows and power door locks. Four engines for the Alfetta were offered: 1.6-, 1.8- and 2.0-liter gasoline and a 2.0-liter turbo diesel. In 1985 the model was finally withdrawn.

Chapter 5

Spiders

Just as *Sprint* is the proper designation for the Alfa coupes and *Berlina* means sedan, *Spider* applies to the convertibles.

Spider is an old term, originally describing a high-wheeled, lightweight horse-drawn carriage with a sporty, high-performance image. *Spyder* is the German spelling, and incorrect when referring to an Italian car.

Bertone had saved Alfa from considerable embarrassment by hurrying the Giulietta Sprint into production, and hoped to do the same for a companion Spider. The Bertone prototype Spider is an interesting styling exercise, more aggressive than the Pininfarina design. The nose of the Bertone spider droops downward at a sharp angle, giving a sense of taughtness missing in the Pininfarina design. From the windshield back, however, the design is more conservative, reflecting the lines of both Touring and Pininfarina.

The Bertone version of the prototype Spider carried some styling cues from the Arnolt Bristol. Two cars were made and both have survived: one in the United States and the other in Europe. When this design was rejected by Alfa, Bertone came back with still another design, essentially a Sprint with its roof cut off. This model, too, failed to impress Alfa management and the Pininfarina design was chosen. The Bertone "chop top" is currently under restoration in Europe.

Superleggera Touring was not in this competition, in spite of the fact that it had done so many handsome bodies for the 1900 chassis. In fact, the styling that would be seen on both the Giulietta Sprint and Spider was inspired by the 1954–55 Touring-bodied 1900 Sprint. One of the reasons for Alfa's decision not to let Bertone build the Spider may be the fact that Bertone was so overwhelmed with orders for the Sprint that it

In the United States the mention of Alfa Romeo invariably conjured visions of small open sports cars such as this 1750 Duetto from 1969.

Bertone submitted this Franco Scaglione design for the new
Giulietta spider, although the contract was subsequently
awarded to Pininfarina.

This early Giulietta dates from 1956 and lacks the quarter
windows of later Giuliettas and Giulias.

The author's Lancia Aurelia Superamerica convertible,
which was also styled by Pininfarina, shows many
similarities to the Giulietta.

could not possibly have been able to build the Spiders. With Touring not in the competition and Bertone busy with the Sprint, design of the Spider went to Pininfarina.

The Giulietta Spider was introduced in a rather low-key manner in Milan early in 1955, and formally at the Paris show a few months later.

■ 750-Series

Initially, this model was called the Giulietta Spider. There was no need for special identification until 1959 Spiders began appearing with the more robust 101-series engines and gearboxes, and a longer wheelbase. The 750 designation is Alfa's internal identifier, and the parts manual uses 750 as a prefix for this model (actual parts are numbered 13nn). You can tell a 750-series Spider by the series plaque on the firewall: 750D is a Spider and 750F is a Spider Veloce. This is a handy way to distinguish between real Veloces and those Spiders that have had Weber carburetors hung on them. Another good test for a real Veloce is whether or not the wiring harness contains a wire for the electric fuel pump, a feature unique to the Veloce.

The earliest surviving Giulietta Spider, on display at the Arese museum, has side curtains, a curved windshield reminiscent of the Lancia Aurelia Superamerica convertible, and a three-pod instrument cluster located immediately in front of the driver. The oldest Giulietta in the United States, chassis number 007, carries an obviously handmade windshield assembly that matches the later production models in configuration, has roll-up windows, but retains the three-pod design of the instrument panel. For the production version a unified instrument cluster was adopted. Very early production cars featured a gearshift lever that curved upward to give the final several inches of the lever an almost vertical position. Later versions of the lever were straight.

Americans were generally less interested in the Sprint, so the Spider became the standard mid-priced sports car in the 1960s, competing with Triumph and

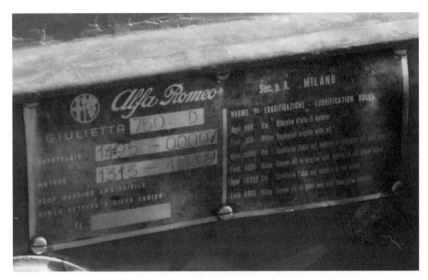

This very early Giulietta still carries its original build plate, although the original attaching rivets have given way to screws.

This early Spider owned by Tom Zat shows the three-instrument layout of the dashboard. Later Spider taillights have been fitted.

Austin-Healey for the enthusiast's heart. Alfas were rare enough that most people didn't know what to make of them. They were clearly a cut above the MG because they had roll-up windows and a snug top. This was a matter of some embarrassment to those of us whose first cars were MGs. We felt that the true sports car had to exhibit the bone-jarring ride and wind-in-the-teeth standard set by the roadsters. The Alfa was a much more refined car, not cobbled together from the parts bins of other manufacturers. Its undeniable roadability kept

Pininfarina—or Pinin Farina as the company was then
known—won the contract to design and build the Giulietta
Spider. This Spider Veloce was built in 1958.

it from being in the same rank as the 190SL Mercedes,
which was not considered a sports car. The only
competing car from Germany was the Porsche, and it
was significantly more expensive.

Max Hoffman is responsible for bringing Spiders
into the United States market. During repeated visits
to Italy in the early 1950s, he was shown progressively
detailed designs of the car. According to Busso (in an
interview with Dave Mericle) Max would typically

The interior and instruments of this 1958 Spider Veloce are
completely stock except for the period cord-wrapping on the
steering wheel and a rear-view mirror that has been moved
to the windshield to reduce vibration.

make acerbic comments like: "Americans want creature
comforts like real side windows and easily erected
tops." Each comment produced a redesign of the Spider
until, late in 1954, Max could no longer find anything
objectionable. The Alfa's price put it within the reach of
most enthusiasts, and its heritage made it a much more
desirable car than, say, the Austin-Healey. In a very real
sense, the Alfa had no competition in its market niche. If
you wanted a true sports car with comfort features you
could live with, the Alfa Spider was the clear choice.

▪ 101-Series

In 1959, Alfa Spiders began appearing unannounced
with bodies, gearboxes and engines which were slightly
different from the 750 series. The key lay in the new
101-series designation. Prior to 1959 the only Giulietta
to bear the type number 101 was the Giulietta Sprint
Speciale. Because the new spiders and coupes also
carried the 101 designation, it was then simple enough to
begin calling the original models 750 and the new, 101.

Except that it was not quite so simple. During
1959, some short-wheelbase 750-series spiders and
coupes were delivered with the newer 101-series
engines and transmissions, while some 101 cars used
750 transmissions with 101 engines. In spite of the
brave attempt by Evan Wilson (*Alfa Romeo Giulietta*,
published by Osprey in 1983) to sort out the changeover,
a satisfactory accounting has never been given of exactly
which cars, by serial number, carried what mixture of
engines and transmissions. Part of the confusion is no
doubt due to the fact that Alfa did not keep meticulous
records of its own production. Many Alfas show serial
numbers which cannot be accounted for using Fusi's

The Giulietta 101-series featured a fixed side quarter window and a more robust gearbox. This example has covered about 250,000 miles and remains with its original owner.

book *Tutte le Vetture Alfa Romeo dal 1910*. Probably, the unpredictable mix of assemblies stemmed from parts availability at the factory. The supply of 750 engines and transmissions was apparently greater than the supply of bodies, so it was common to find the older running gear fitted to the newer body. Similarly, there appear to have been more engines than transmissions, because 750 engines were often mated to 101 transmissions.

The situation has become further confused over the years, as owners have discarded the earlier engines for the more robust 101-series. This is, in fact, not an easy retrofit. The transmissions differ in their length, their mountings, the location of the shift lever, the length of the front propeller shaft section and the flywheel weights. The details of the conversion are outside the scope of this book, but the author can personally attest to the fact that it is not an easy job.

An obvious change was in the body's wheelbase, which had grown from 2,200 mm to 2,250 mm. For several decades, we felt that these "long-wheelbase" cars were unmistakably distinguished from the earlier models by the fixed vent window in the door. Recently, however, some 750 spiders have appeared with the longer wheelbase and fixed vent window, so the distinction is not at all clear, in spite of the fact that it has seemed so for so many years. The Giorgio Nada

two-volume set *Alfa Romeo Production Cars* states that the fixed vent window was introduced in 1957, and both styles were produced until the 101-series cars appeared in 1959. We now know that short-wheelbase cars with vent windows were sold in Europe, but not the United States. In the United States, at least, the fixed vent window signals a long-wheelbase, 101-series Spider.

Equally distinctive from the 750, the 101's shift lever telescoped slightly when you pressed down on it to overcome the reverse-gear lock-out. The original gearbox was notable for its solid lever, which looked sturdy enough to be a lift-point for the entire car. This original Giulietta gearbox, called the "tunnel case," was assembled into a cylindrical alloy casting, and a special puller was required to draw the gear sets into the case.

The new transmission case was split longitudinally into two halves and was almost identical to the five-speed unit fitted to the 2000 cars that had been introduced in 1958. Its outer case differed only in that the front bell housing was smaller to accommodate the Giulietta engine, while the tail casting on the 2000 was longer to accommodate a fifth gear. It was not long before five-speed Giuliettas were running around with transmission parts pirated from the larger cars. Not a cheap conversion, it was an exceedingly satisfactory one, especially on the Veloce.

The earliest Giulietta transmissions needed a low-pressure lubricant (Dentax) to function correctly. Since Dentax was available only in 55-gallon drums, small groups of owners banded together to buy proper lubricant for their new transmissions. The alternate solution was to use 40- or 50-weight engine oil with a dose of molybdenum disulfide. It took Alfa several years to release 101-style synchronizers that worked with standard EP-type gear oil, and few 101 transmissions survive now with the original non-EP-type synchronizers. On the other hand, 750 "tunnel case" transmissions never had non-EP replacement parts, so they must always use motor oil fortified with molybdenum, or one of the modern substitutes from Redline or Swepco.

So far as the engine was concerned, the differences were almost all dimensional. While the bore and stroke remained the same, the newer engines had larger-diameter main bearings, camshaft bearings and valve stem. The camshaft lobe width was also increased

Alfa Spider Designations		
Series	Years	Description
750D	1955–59	Giulietta Spider
750F	1956–60	Giulietta Spider Veloce
750G	1956	Giulietta Spider Monoposto
101.03	1960–62	Giulietta Spider
101.07	1960–62	Giulietta Spider Veloce
101.18	1964–65	Giulia Spider Veloce
101.19	1963–64	Giulia Spider RHD
101.23	1962–65	Giulia Spider
105.03	1966–67	Duetto
105.05	1966–67	Duetto RHD
105.57	1967–71	1750 Spider
105.58	1968–71	1750 Spider Veloce RHD
105.24	1971–74	2000 Spider Veloce
105.62	1968–71	1750 Spider Veloce U.S.-specification
105.91	1968–77	1300 Spider Junior (105.91S is 1974–77)
105.92	1968–69	1300 Spider Junior RHD
115.02	1972–77	2000 Spider Veloce U.S.-specification
115.07	1972–75	1600 Spider Junior
115.35	1974–89	1600 Spider Junior, 1600 Spider Veloce
115.41	1977–89	2000 Spider Veloce U.S.-specification
115.38	1975–85	2000 Spider Veloce, Quadrifoglio Verde

to improve load-bearing capacity. The head was redesigned to the extent that 750 and 101 heads are not interchangeable. A steel crank pulley was fitted and the generator mount strengthened. In addition, the fuel pump was relocated low on the engine where it could be driven off a cam on the crankshaft which drove both the distributor and the oil pump.

The changeover in drivetrains and wheelbases, unannounced and unexplained, caused total confusion among enthusiasts and there was a great effort to make some logic of the situation. The model confusion was finally ended by the appearance of a new Giulietta parts catalog for 1960, which showed all the new parts numbers beginning with 101 (the Giulietta TI body was still number 753 in 1960). By 1961, all new Alfas were 100 percent 101-series.

At the time, the purpose of these larger bearings and valve stems was not fully appreciated. In fact, what had happened was that Alfa Romeo had created the basis for the Giulia engine, and was "field-testing" a small-displacement version of it in the 101-series Giuliettas made from 1959 to the introduction of the Giulia in 1962.

▪ Giulia Spiders

As noted in the previous chapter, the Giulia 1600 Spider was introduced—with the TI and Sprint—at Monza on June 27, 1962. The car was virtually a 101-series Giulietta, with a slightly larger engine and the addition of a false hood scoop, larger taillights and revised instrument faces.

One of the earliest road tests of the new Spider in the United States was written by Bob Taylor for the May 19, 1963, issue of the *Newark Sunday News*. It's worth noting that Alfa's United States headquarters were in Newark, New Jersey, at the time.

Bob got to the increased performance early in his review: "Rated by the manufacturer as capable of 107 miles an hour, it turned in a speed of 112 miles an hour. It also got 27 miles to the gallon of gas during four turns of the track, although Alfa Romeo says only that it will get 25.2 in average usage."

The review continues in an almost requisite praise by the reviewer of Alfa handling: "The car…turned out to be one of the most capable sports cars tested in this long series. It was magnificently efficient on curves, rounding them as if they were straight. There was little lean of the body nor any heavy wheel-jumping apparent to the driver, and the steering was neutral from 30 miles an hour up to that 112." Similarly, reviewers seem obliged to praise the Alfa gearbox: "The five-speed shift on the Alfa, synchronized on every gear, is a marvel. Operation is smooth and the synchro mechanisms always efficient. Fifth gear is an overdrive and fourth is direct."

The Spider body was remarkably comfortable for a convertible, especially to enthusiasts who thought that sports cars had to have side-curtains and tops that flapped like sails. "The Maryland run showed the Giulia to be a comfortable cruiser," Bob reported. "It has the longest seat adjustment of any sports car…. The top on the test car was completely waterproof in a rain storm if the car's occupants took pains to make sure a cloth drip panel was outside the top of each side window." Bob concluded his report: "This road tester rates it as one of the world's really fine automobiles."

Car and Driver magazine summed up the differences between the Giulietta and new Giulia in its road test: "The differences amount to various subtle changes

that have proved most effective. The new model is about two inches longer, both in wheelbase and over-all length, and its front track is slightly wider…. The Giulia has a new ball-bearing worm and roller steering box…." Unfortunately, all those "differences" did not exist, since the Giulia used the Giulietta body and most mechanicals: there are several morals here, none of which have to do with the car.

Nevertheless, *Car and Driver* was appreciative of the car's handling: "The Giulia's unhesitant steering response surpasses what is ordinarily described as quick and precise—it has these qualities to a degree that calls for new adjectives. There is absolutely no trace of the Giulietta understeer, the car remaining perfectly controllable up to the point of breakaway.

"The suspension seems taut and works noiselessly even when observation tells you that considerable wheel travel is occurring. The rear suspension… remains one of today's best arguments against accepting the additional cost of independent rear suspension."

There was some feeling, when the Giulia was introduced, that Alfa should have adopted independent rear suspension (IRS) to compete with Porsche. After all, the reasoning went, Alfa had produced a very successful IRS with its 2.5-liter cars, and to be competitive in the current market, should have provided the enthusiast with a fully independent suspension. Most road tests touched on the controversy obliquely, as did the *Car and Driver* test. In a *Cars Illustrated* test of June 1964, the same subject was approached: "The Alfa Romeo Giulia does not feature independent all-round suspension, and if all rigid axle systems were as good as this, there would have been no need for independence to have been invented in the first place."

Thus, two basic arguments in favor of Alfa's traditional solid-axle rear suspension emerged: it was less expensive and worked as well as the more exotic IRS. The point has been evident for years; no one, not even in the final year of 1994, lamented the lack of IRS on the Spider.

The Giulia rolled on a longer wheelbase and featured a 1600 engine and a five-speed transmission. It was readily distinguished by the false scoop on the hood.

Pininfarina designed and produced an attractive removable hardtop that turned the Giulietta and later Giulia (shown) into a snug coupe. Several companies offered aftermarket hardtops, but none were as desirable as the factory version.

Spider Interior

The seats of the Giulia spider received mixed reviews. *Cars Illustrated* declared that the spider "features two of the best bucket seats for driver and passenger we have ever encountered. More than adequate support for the thighs and shoulders is provided, and despite some fairly hard driving at no time did passengers feel the need to hang on to a grab handle to prevent themselves from sliding about." *Car and Driver* called them "…relatively inexpensive. Both offer backrest adjustments which give such good support in any position that non-stop all-day drives are quite pleasant." However, Bob Taylor found that "There was a little ache induced at the base of the driver's spine for the first 100 miles…," and *Road & Track* observed that "the side pads were fundamentally deadening over a long trip, and definitely were not designed for the broad of beam."

It appears that, while Alfa never changed the basic configuration of the spider seat, there were at least two different degrees of padding used. The author's own Giulia Veloce seats definitely matched the *Road & Track* description, being two of the deepest buckets I've ever experienced. On the other hand, the typical spider has a very shallow bucket which is much more comfortable for "broad-beamed" enthusiasts. There is no documentation that Alfa changed the contour of the seats for the Veloce, but personal experience suggests that they did.

While reviews of the Giulia spider were uniformly positive, there was still a growing sense that the basic body had been around overly long. In its review of the Giulia Spider Veloce, *Road & Track* observed of the Giulietta, Giulia and Giulia Veloce spiders: "These three models are markedly similar to the eye. In fact, one observer asked, 'When are they going to change that design? I thought it was a '59 with a new paint job.' This canard will be instantly rejected by Alfisti as both irrelevant and irreverent, but it is nevertheless true that Bertone's original Sprint lines, modified by Pininfarina into the svelte Spider version, have been with us without significant change for nearly a decade. And, just as true, the lines are as clean, honest and pleasing to the eye today as they were in the prototype."

For all its aesthetic qualities, the Giulia spider was nevertheless dated by 1965, and even the appearance of the Veloce version could not hide the fact. Alfa had not been idle, however, and had been preparing for a new body to grace the Giulia mechanicals.

The Spider's Market Position

By the time of the Giulia's appearance, Max Hoffman no longer played a significant role in marketing Alfa in the United States, and Alfa Romeo International (ARI) had been set up in New Jersey as the official factory importer.

The Giulia's market position was evaluated in a *Cars Illustrated* road test, providing the modern reader with a reminder of Alfa's competition in 1964: "Why did Alfa Romeo decide on 1600 cc for the upgraded version of its best-selling open two-seater? Why not 1,800 cc as MG has done (and Sunbeam can be expected to do)? The question is easily answered…its 1.6 liters give performance comparable with that of the 2.2-liter Triumph TR-4 and the fuel economy of some 1100cc cars."

The road test concludes: "Few cars can rival the 1600 Alfa for sheer driving enjoyment…the car does everything so effortlessly, with proper use of the five-speed gearbox, that one gets the feeling of commanding much more power than it actually puts out. And as for fatigue, it just seems never to set in—this car's all fun."

The Giulia Spider and Spider Veloce (shown) were very desirable sports cars held back in the American market only by their relatively high price when compared to British offerings such as MG, Triumph, Sunbeam and Austin-Healey.

At $3,400 for the Spider and $3,700 for the Veloce, the Alfa filled a marketing niche almost by itself, being more expensive than the MGB or Fiat and significantly less than the Jaguar E-Type or Porsche Cabriolet. Yet, so far as quality of ride and level of trim, the Alfa was closer to the higher-priced cars.

In 1964, the standard sports car was still the MG. If one had very limited resources then the Midget (or Austin-Healey Sprite) was the only choice. Slight affluence qualified one to consider the Triumph Spitfire, or, for just a bit more, the MGB. All these British cars were very traditional in concept (the IRS of the Spitfire being a notable exception), and came with the generally harsh ride, spartan interior and good road holding the enthusiast equated with a "real" sports car. British tops leaked much more than was really necessary, and contributed to the image that the true enthusiast drove top-down, even in the rain.

The Sunbeam Alpine was a more refined car in ride, but it was not taken seriously by the enthusiast because of its more supple suspension and refined character. The Jaguar, always its own standard, cost significantly more than the Alfa, but the eager Alfa enthusiast imagined his car almost as fast as the Jaguar—or the Corvette—though both those cars were really in another league. The only other competitor in this group was the Datsun roadster, which had only limited distribution and even fewer fans.

For a premium of $300, the Giulia Spider Veloce offered a 20-percent increase in performance. Other than badging and a different induction system, the standard and Veloce versions were visually similar. This Veloce dates from 1965.

The interior of the Giulia Spider was as attractive and carefully thought through as the exterior.

Fiat has always been careful to provide serious domestic competition for Alfa Romeo, and is large enough to bracket whatever market Alfa chooses. The inexpensive 850 (introduced in 1966), rear-engined and very sporty, was really more of a competitor to the Spitfire and Midget than the Alfa. The 1100 TV roadster was cheaper than the Alfa, slightly less luxurious and less powerful. Its replacement, the 1200 roadster, continued to undercut the price of the Alfa convertibles and offer a more modern body style to boot. The 124 Spider was direct competition for Alfa, with a twin-cam engine,

fine appointments and almost equivalent performance. The 124—and Fiat in general—was derided by most enthusiasts as inferior. In fact, it was a fine car but its factory support in the United States was abysmal. It might have survived its propensity to rust had the North American Fiat organization been more committed to customer service.

Alfa enthusiasts considered Porsche the only true competition, even though it was significantly more expensive. The 356-series was a benchmark car, and the rivalry between Alfa and Porsche was as much social as mechanical. The Porsche enthusiast, every bit as fanatic as his Alfa counterpart, was somewhat more elitist and certainly less able to tinker with the mechanical aspects of his car. The Porschephile would quickly explain that, being better engineered, the cars required less tinkering than the Alfa.

Both cars gave very civilized interiors, protection from the elements and superior roadholding. Porsche was the reason Alfa had to live with the frequent criticism that its solid rear axle was really antique. Alfa owners could only respond that the solid rear axle was less expensive (hardly a convincing retort) and was much more forgiving as one approached the limits of adhesion. The arrival of the 912 and 911 cars left the rivalry unchanged.

No one really took the 190SL Mercedes roadster seriously as a sports car, though a few of them did race. In fact, the Alfa approached the 190 in comfort and quiet more closely than enthusiasts cared to admit. In retrospect, the Alfa was much closer in character to the 190 than the other sports cars it competed against at the time. However, by 1964 the 190SL had been discontinued and the more upmarket 230SL had joined the Mercedes-Benz lineup at a significantly higher price.

Which explains the fact that, stock, the Alfa wasn't really that competitive a sports car on a twisty course. A bit too soft and heavy, it could be made a winner only with some significant modifications. In fact, the spider is not a true racing car—Alfa assigned that duty to its line of coupes from Zagato and Autodelta.

▪ Duetto

By the mid-1960s, it was very clear that the original Giulietta Spider body style would have to be upgraded or Alfa would find increasing resistance to its obsolescent line of convertibles.

Introduced at the 36th Geneva auto show in the bitter spring of 1966, Alfa Romeo's Spider 1600 (the "Duetto" name would come months later) was a smash hit. The combination of reliable Giulia-derived mechanicals and pretty Pininfarina body proved to be irresistible.

It is typical that Alfa would leave the development work for a new body to the carrozzerie. Both Pininfarina and Bertone had worked closely with Alfa over the years, and both names were carried on current production cars (Bertone coupes and Pininfarina spiders). A number of concept cars were produced in the 1950s which, in retrospect, had much to do with the appearance of the new spider. Several idea cars built on the Giulietta chassis are notable, for elements of those cars appeared on the new Spider, introduced at the Geneva auto show in March 1966.

Probably the earliest one-off of any significance is the Giulietta Sportiva prototype, which introduced the flowing lines that would finally distinguish the

In 1966 the Duetto was introduced to replace the aging Giulia, even though under the sculptured new skin it was basically a Giulia. This example is from that first year of production.

new Giulia spider. Relevant details include the slightly sloping nose with a bulge for the grille, covered headlamps and generally smooth execution.

A much more seminal development was the 1957 Disco Volante with "Superflow" bodywork by Pininfarina. This car continued the theme of smooth, flowing lines and covered headlights, but also introduced a striking—and large—"blood trough" along the side of the car. This Pininfarina motif was carried on many of his subsequent cars, including the Daytona Ferrari and the Rover 3500 sedan.

At the 1959 Geneva Salon, Pininfarina introduced another Alfa prototype on the Giulietta chassis. This model was almost a dead ringer for the new spider. This car had a symmetry unmatched by any other modern car: the pointed lines of the nose were almost duplicated at the long overhang which was the tail. The resulting profile was ultimately aerodynamic.

When the new spider appeared on the Alfa Romeo stand at the March 1966 Geneva auto sow, it was an instant hit, being the last design credited to Battista Pininfarina, who died April 3, 1966. The first three United States-market Spiders arrived in New York in May, and a love affair was begun.

Road & Track summed up the development of the Duetto in its July 1966 announcement story: "The new body is also by Pininfarina, and it is as different from the old as ravioli from antipasto. It is fresh and bullet-like, not like anything else on the road but not exactly radical either. Like many new models, it is essentially a version of an earlier show car theme—in this case a Pininfarina design from the 1961 Turin salon. Unlike

The Spider Super Sport shown at Geneva in 1959 displayed many styling features later seen in the Duetto.

The Super Sport Speciale coupe of 1960 also had a strong family resemblance to the later Duetto.

most production adaptations of show designs, this one is almost a literal translation, save for the headlights and the top."

Introduction on the *Raffaello*

The May 1966 review in *The Alfa Owner* serves as a general introduction of the Duetto to the United States. Alfa had taken care to build excitement before the introduction of its new spider. In Italy, it had created a contest to name the car (the winning name was submitted by Guidobaldo Trionfi of Brescia, Italy), and for the United States market, it threw a shipside party on the SS *Raffaello*. *The Alfa Owner* reported: "Star of the whole show was the new 1600 Spider, with three examples on display. Two of the cars were on the top deck available for driving and being driven occasionally by members of the Factory Racing team who were on hand, resplendent in blue blazers.

"The pictures in this issue of the *Owner* do not do even 50 percent justice to the tremendous attractiveness of the new Spider. The car is simply overwhelming when actually inspected. Among the more interesting features are:

- Fully-ducted cooling to the oil pump
- Battery in the engine compartment
- Near-complete underpanning
- 4-wheel disc brakes
- Very large, very legible instruments
- Velcro closure around the rear of the top
- Useful area behind the seats (almost 2 plus 1)
- Vast trunk volume
- Reutter-type seat recliners
- Inside deck lid release
- Functional quarter windows
- Completely new suspension design"

The rear boattail of the Duetto is just as striking as the sleek nose.

Enthusiasm aside, the "completely new suspension" was really an adaptation of the 105 Giulia Berlina's front suspension. This fact was hinted at later in the *Owner* review: "Construction costs and stocking requirements have been reduced by using identical modules wherever possible. Excepting the GTA, all models use the same basic driveline components, suspension, etc. PLEASE NOTE THAT ALL 1600's NOW HAVE WEBERS."

The *Owner* review concludes: "Consensus of the old-time Alfa types assembled at the party was that the new Spider was the most exciting Alfa production model they had yet seen. To quote one knowledgeable type, 'It sure makes the competition look antiquated.'"

Antiquated, indeed. As the years have passed, the Duetto has become a much more familiar car, and we have now passed well into the time when they are recognized collector cars. In the late 1990s, Duettos commanded between $9,000 and $15,000, depending on condition. Compared to the newer cars, at least in the United States, they have the advantage of carburetion with which the owner can fiddle, while the SPICA fuel injection of the later cars is more intimidating.

In character, the Duetto was only a slightly refined Giulietta: that is, in fact, a high compliment. There were some notable improvements: the instruments were larger and more dramatic, the seats reclined, the top was more easily handled, the heating was superior and the bumpers were a rust-free stainless steel. Mechanically, the car had everything that made Alfa desirable: four-wheel disc brakes, twin overhead cams, two twin-throat Weber carburetors and a fully synchronized five-speed gearbox. Seating position was still high and, reviews notwithstanding, visibility was most acceptable.

The tires on the new car were 14 inches in diameter, down from the 15-inch rims used on the Giulia/Giulietta cars. Since the rims on the new cars were wider, it became common for enthusiasts to switch rims from the Duetto to the disc-braked 1600 spiders. The 14-inch rims, however, won't clear the Alfin drums of the Giulietta cars. The car carried the same suspension introduced on the Giulia TI, and so had a lubrication-free chassis (the driveshaft still required grease) and a series designation 105. To summarize the various Spider models:

Alfa marketed the Duetto from 1966 to 1969, years which saw enthusiasm build only slowly for the car. Alfa records show that 6,325 Spider 1600s were produced in 1966 through 1967. Performance data for the '67 car in *Road & Track* showed 0–60 time of 11.3 seconds, a quarter-mile time of 18.5 seconds, a top speed of 113 mph and overall fuel economy that averaged 23 mpg.

For 1969 Alfa introduced the 1750 mechanicals to the Duetto. In the United States market, the new cars were fuel-injected, and received minor trim changes, but otherwise continued unchanged.

In June 1968 Alfa released a 1300cc version of the Duetto Spider called the Spider Junior. This car was not imported into the United States, nor were any new Alfas in 1968, but was intended to round out Alfa's lower-displacement line, which offered tax advantages in Italy. In 1974 and corresponding with the introduction of the Giulia Nuova sedan and GT Junior coupe, it released an updated Kamm-tailed 1300 version of the Junior which was also available with a 1600 engine. Thus, in 1974, one could purchase Alfa spiders with displacements of 1.3, 1.6 and 2.0 liters.

Press reports indicated that many critics thought the Duetto looked awkward, even after several years' opportunity to become used to the shape. In retrospect, the Giulietta spider body was a really tough act to follow, and the Duetto had a bit too much avant-garde styling to overcome the classic appeal of its predecessor. Most criticism of the Duetto centered on the tail of the car. It may have been a logical design, but it was considered ugly for a very long time. Of course, the reviewers could wax eloquent about the Alfa mechanicals, and revel

The steering wheel offered a clear view of the comprehensive instrumentation that was standard equipment on every Duetto.

in the fact that the new Duetto sported dual Weber carburetors as standard equipment (the term *Veloce* had became a marketing, not technical designation) and four-wheel disc brakes. But even *Road & Track* had to admit: "We found almost no disagreement among members of our staff about the appearance of the new model—no one liked it as well as the Giulietta or the Giulia. One condemned it as a contrived design with meaningless styling gimmicks. Another said, 'I think

The Spider Junior was outwardly identical to a Duetto Spider, but was powered by a 1.3-liter version of the twin-cam engine.

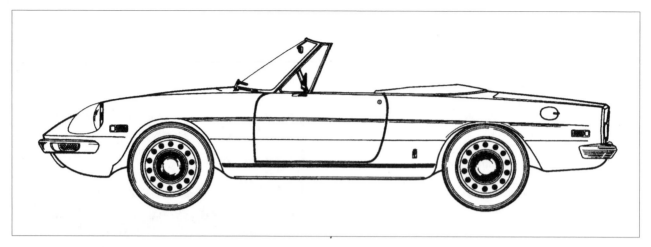

For 1970 the tail of the Duetto was cropped in a move to freshen the car's look and provide mounting for a more robust bumper for the 1750 Spider Veloce. The black trim on the hubcap was a trim feature of all 1750s.

Pininfarina missed the ball this time.' Somebody else commented, 'They did this shape five years ago on a show car and it isn't any better now.'"

Other critical comments regarded the seating position (*Road & Track*: "It was difficult to find a position where the lower rim of the steering wheel did not interfere with the legs….") and the painted fascia (*Motor Sport*). *Car and Driver*, in its May 1967 review, was most negative. It faulted the Duetto's motor noise: "A prospective owner starting the Duetto for the first time might well be severely disappointed. Due, perhaps, to the extensive use of light alloy in the engine, there is a good deal of clatter…." In addition, the staff found a slipping clutch, disappointing fuel economy, unsatisfactory visibility and too much wind noise: "The car's most serious fault was excessive wind noise: at speeds above about 70 mph. in top, wind roar began to drown the engine until at high speeds the engine was barely audible at all."

For counterpoint, *Road Test* magazine in August 1967 observed: "With the windows up, wind noise is quite moderate for a car of this type."

Kamm-Tail

Finally, for the 1970 model year, Alfa simply chopped the tail off, producing the "Kamm-tail" spider. The squared-off rear provided a much more robust mounting arrangement for a functional bumper, and the Kamm-tail is a much better choice if the spider is to be used in traffic. Once again, due to Alfa's inability to comply with federal regulations, there were no new cars imported into the United States for 1970.

The squared-off tail was more of a practical than aesthetic move, then, and marked the first of a long

line of modifications designed to answer owner concerns and keep the model fresh. Max Hoffman's vision of an American market for the spider has been amply validated. The rest of the world had tired of the evergreen spider, and changes to it late in its career added novelty but not utility and certainly not performance. Alfa's neoclassic spider quietly slipped out of production with Alfa's withdrawal from the United States in December 1994.

▪ A Spider Chronology

The earliest cars in this chronology will be older than many readers of this book. Over a series of owners, it's normal for a car to take on some modifications, either out of preference or necessity. One of the results of this natural evolution is for individual cars to become unique, and this can cause some unexpected results. New owners may be told that their cars are "special editions" because of different trim or other fitments. In the overwhelming majority of cases, this is not the case, simply the result of age. Alfa did indeed, later, offer limited-number special editions of its cars, but not until the late 1970s and into the 1980s.

1955: The first Giulietta Spiders appeared. The very earliest 750-series car (specifically, 1495.00007, which is not listed in Fusi) had many detail differences from the later "production" models. This included a three-pod instrument panel layout and large "Dagmar" front bumper overriders. The most notable character of the early Giulietta Spiders was their spareness: they were devoid of excess. The design of the engine and bodywork was focused on efficiency and utility. As a result, the cars achieved superior performance from a diminutive displacement. They are unquestioned artistic masterpieces. The taillights on these first cars were oval and a single color.

1959: A longer-wheelbase (2.25 meters) 101-series model began appearing in the United States, most easily identified by its fixed vent windows on the doors. At the same time, the engine was modified in preparation for a larger displacement, and the "tunnel" transmission was changed to the "split-case" design of the 2000 model. Taillights became squared off at the bottom with a yellow-colored turn indicator.

1962: The promise of the more robust 101-series engine was fulfilled with the 1570cc Giulia engine. The Spider's hood gained a fake air scoop, an alloy steering wheel and a modernized instrument set resembling the 2600. A large chrome trim piece faired the taillights into the body. Roughly speaking, the increased displacement gave the Giulia equal performance to the Giulietta Veloce, with an additional virtue of more low-end torque. The

From the rear, a 750 Giulietta could be distinguished by the small single-color taillights.

The fixed side windows and revised taillights of this 1962 spider are the hallmark of the 101 Giulietta.

Giulia Veloce set new standards of performance for a post-war production Alfa, being the first with a top speed approaching that of the 8C2900B. Because of its elegant style and superior performance, the Giulia Veloce Spider is a favorite collectible.

1966: The Spider 1600 Duetto appeared. Built on Alfa's new Type 105 chassis, the car featured a Weber carbureted "Veloce" version of Alfa's enduring DOHC 1570cc four, rated at 125 hp SAE at 6000 rpm.

1968: In January, at the Brussels show, Alfa Romeo introduced the Spider 1750. In June, Alfa brought out the affordable Spider 1300 Junior. No matter: Americans could only wait, for while the new Spiders complied fully with the tough federal Motor Vehicle Safety Act of 1966, their carbureted high-performance 1779cc fours choked on the Clean Air Act of 1968. There were no Alfas imported officially in 1968.

1969: A new number on the trunk lid for the Spider—"1750"—celebrated the larger engine. The bored and stroked 1600 yielded a new displacement of 1779 cc, close enough to 1750 that Alfa decided to invoke the memories of that classic Jano car. The 1969 American Spider 1750s featured SPICA mechanical fuel injection,

The lack of the longitudinal trim strip on the hood in favor of the false scoop marks this 1965 Spider Veloce as a Giulia.

a new *Iniezione* badge, side marker lights and a new grille bar. The price was $4,333.

The 1750 SPICA injection system was different from the later 2000-series system in two important ways. The idle circuit for each cylinder fed directly into the manifold (later style had a small manifold on the intake manifold with five rubber hoses attached to it—four for the intake paths and another feeding the filtered

Quick and distinctive, it took a while for the looks of the Duetto to catch on.

This European 1973 spider has covered headlights, no side marker lights and a Weber-carbureted engine.

air source). On the 1969 model, fuel mixture was set using a screw and locknut, while the later style added a fuel cut-off solenoid that was also used to adjust the fuel mixture. Also, the protrusion of the thermostatic actuator was different between the two: 27 mm for the earlier and 29.5 for the later.

1970: In Europe the 1750 Spiders proved to be quite popular. The horsepower increase from 125 to 132 was minor, but the torque increase—from 115 pound feet at 2,800 rpm to 137 pound feet at 2,900 rpm—gave the 1750s a slightly different feel than their 1600 predecessors, though they were still "high-revvers." In America, we could only ruminate over this: No 1970 Spiders were imported into the United States because of increasingly tougher emission laws.

1971: Even though the Duetto's symmetrical profile made a lot of aesthetic sense, it proved to be an overly fragile design for the real world. To strengthen the car's protection, especially when parallel parked, the Pininfarina "boattail" was lopped off, shortening the car six inches (from 167.3 inches to 161.1 inches) and reducing trunk capacity from 7.5 cubic feet to 6.9 cubic feet. In addition, the windshield was raked more, the front grille widened and lowered, the bumpers restyled, the door handles flushed in and the instrument panel

changed. More importantly, alterations to the SPICA fuel injection system let the car meet U.S. emission standards.

1972: The first Spider 2000 was shown to the press in June 1971, and the first examples appeared in the United States during the spring of 1972. A bore increase from 80 mm to 84 mm bumped the 1779cc four-cylinder engine's displacement up a notch-and-a-half to 1962 cc. The result? A horsepower increase from 132 hp to 150 at 5,500 rpm, and a similar torque increase, from 137 pound feet at 2,900 rpm to 153 at 3,500. Though the SPICA fuel injection system remained, the cars had a very, very different character which would become increasingly softer as the model aged. Minor trim changes included a new badge, new bolt-on hubcaps and a wood-grain steering wheel.

1973: There were few changes to the U.S. Spider for the 1973 model year: license plate lights moved from the bumper to the back panel, the bumpers got "nubs" and alloy wheels were added to the option list. Incredibly, those wonderfully reliable 2.0-liter engines had started life in the 1950s as 1290cc fours with "square" cylinders—bore and stroke dimensions were 74 mm and 75 mm respectively. Nearly two decades later, the capacity had been pushed upward over 50 percent to 1962 cc. Bore and stroke was now 84 mm and 88.5 mm with no change in crankshaft journal diameters since 1959. Both the intake and exhaust manifolds for a '59 will bolt right up to an '86 model.

1974: Alloy wheels were made standard equipment and the 1974 Spiders received handsome wood-rimmed steering wheels. This model year represents the pinnacle of performance for the increasingly smog-restricted engines. Alfa would be forced now to give up its performance image and chase a luxury market it was ill equipped to attract.

1975: Heavy new black rubber bumpers made '75 Spider-spotting easy. But not out west: despite new air pumps and single-outlet exhaust manifolds, the 2.0-liter engines did not comply with California's suddenly unique exhaust emission laws. The '75s were 49-state cars only.

1976: The addition of catalytic converters let Spiders return to the California marketplace.

1977: Alfa's concentration on meeting emission regulations forced another change to the exhaust manifold and improved catalytic converters.

1978: Catalytic converters were now standard equipment on all Alfa Spider models, not just the California cars.

1979: The emphasis on creature comforts and a de-emphasis on performance continued. For 1979, the Spiders got upgraded interiors, and leather trim became an option.

1980: Emissions add-ons hurt the 1980 models' performance: a new EGR system sapped the engine of power, and new options such as chromed electric mirrors and power windows added weight. To overcome the further power loss, Alfa introduced a variable valve timing system and electronic ignitions. The engine was left gasping.

1981: There were no important changes to the Spiders for the 1981 model year, though the exterior mirrors were body color again. The 1981 Spider is a nadir for Alfa. EGR dictated a large alloy intake plenum with a single-throttle plate. This design made it virtually impossible to service the SPICA fuel injection pump or distributor. The large bumper and its supporting structure restricted air flow to the radiator and the cars were prone to overheating.

1982: After 13 years of service, the SPICA mechanical fuel injection system was replaced by the new Bosch

The heavy black bumpers were grafted on to allow the Spiders to meet American crash standards.

L-Jetronic system. Of equal importance though much less noticeable, the Spider chassis was stiffened considerably. There were two Spider models offered for the first time: the familiar Veloce and a less expensive "Graduate" model which came only in ivory with steel wheels, manual windows and vinyl interior.

1983: The Veloce and Graduate received a rubber rear spoiler and front air dam to go with its restyled bumpers, grille and taillights. The variable valve timing system was now electronically controlled.

1985: There were no changes to the Veloce or Graduate. By this time, Alfa's sales were so poor that rumors of Alfa's sale began circulating, and the emphasis on styling became even stronger. Unfortunately, though there were new body styles waiting in the wings, there were no funds for a model change. Alfa was stuck with a design first introduced in 1966, and was destined to ride it into the ground, gimmicks and all.

1986: Trim changes were minor for 1986. The Veloce was given a new rear spoiler with a federally mandated Center High-Mounted Stop Light (CHMSL) in the middle. The spoiler, it should be noted, was very much in line with the design theory of the Kamm tail. Its addition, however, remains a styling embarrassment, though very few owners ever considered removing it. All the Spiders received functional new instrument panels. The big news was yet another addition to the model lineup: the upscale "Quadrifoglio." With 15-inch

The ALFA ROMEO Niki Lauda Spider

Introducing... a special edition of Alfa Romeo's Spider Veloce convertible honoring Formula One World Driving Champion Niki Lauda

In an attempt to encourage slumping sales, Alfa turned to add-on trim and graphics for models such as the Niki Lauda Spider.

alloy wheels, a revised interior, plastic spoilers and side skirts and an optional hardtop, this model was somewhat controversial: traditional *Alfisti* were (and remain) in shock over its styling excess. Happily for Alfa, the marketplace loved it despite a suggested price of $19,750. The Quadrifoglio is the most "optioned" Alfa ever and the furthest from a no-frills sports car.

1988: Graduates received plastic wheel covers.

1990: Mechanical changes included Motronic engine controls and a new electric fan. Performance was improved with a change back to the 1974-era "Tri-Y" exhaust manifold.

1991: With rumors of a completely new spider abounding, this last-of-breed model offers new, rounded front and rear sheet metal, a new dash and interior—and an optional automatic transmission. This restyle was intended as a three-year interim model until the appearance of a new front-drive spider

The 1991 models were introduced to America at the January 1990 Detroit and Los Angeles auto shows.

This 1987 Graduate Spider is fitted with the optional factory hardtop.

For 1994, the Spider body was freshened up with new front and rear fascias that integrated their bumpers much more successfully.

Alfa's sales in the United States now depended more on the fact that it was the only affordable European two-seat sports car on the market.

1994: In 1994 Alfa Romeo offered the Commemorative Edition Spider, which was part of the company's exit strategy for the United States. Mechanically unchanged, it featured a suede and walnut interior and was available with an optional automatic transmission.

This chronology has made clear the fact that the newer Spiders became increasingly less sporty and more luxurious in their character. This was due to Alfa's attempt, in the mid-1980s, to change the appeal of the car without changing the car itself. Emission rules were robbing the model of its performance, and Alfa further diminished the Spider's power-to-weight ratio by adding accessories such as power windows and rear-view mirrors. The later Spiders are closer to the Mercedes 190 roadster in character than the Duetto spider from which they derived.

One example of Alfa's ill-conceived luxury transition was the "need" for an automatic transmission. It was clear that most American sedans were equipped with automatic transmissions. Since those cars were selling well, it followed that an automatic-transmission-equipped spider would sell equally well. Only those totally innocent of the market could have believed this: thus, the notion gained wide acceptance within Alfa. The automatic spider (and, later, Alfetta sedans) died an early death.

Chapter 6

Other Giulietta- and Giulia-Based Alfas

Because this chapter deals with the "others," we approach the very center of Alfadom, and its rarest, most fabled cars. Even Luigi Fusi's encyclopedic treatment has discrepancies (most typically revealed when some enthusiast observes that so-and-so's engine number isn't covered by the book). I know too much to pretend that anyone, including myself, could have access to more information than Sig. Fusi. As a result, one must approach descriptions of any Alfa model with a grain of skepticism. It is this persistent degree of uncertainty that makes Alfa scholarship both frustrating and exhilarating at the same time.

For most of its history, by modern standards Alfa was a prototype shop. If the variety of Alfas is utterly amazing on the macro scale, it is absolutely stultifying on the micro. Alfa would make component changes on little more than a whim:

- The original 6C1750 engine went through a number of series, the third, fifth and sixth being the three most common. Later cars had a different kind of transmission case, and the distance between the tower shaft and cylinder block changes depending upon whether the engine has one or two cams. The supercharged twin-cam Gran Sport engine was also available "senza compressore" to distinguish it from the Gran Turismo twin-cam unsupercharged engine.

- There were three series of the 8C2300, two displacements of the 8C2600 (one by Scuderia Ferrari and another by Alfa itself) and two different 4C1900 engines (camshaft rotation was reversed and the location of the oil pump changed). By the way, a correct 8C Monza had a magneto driven off the geartrain, and never had a distributor mounted on the head.

The TZ was a very successful racing variant of the Giulia.

This variety continues: three different, non-interchangeable front rubber donuts were fitted to the 1977 Alfetta driveshafts.

As a final observation: parts manuals are not infallible sources of correct information. A prominent Alfista uses his collection of parts manuals to reach occasionally sweeping conclusions. In one instance, he assured me that the seats from the Alfetta sedan could not fit in the Sport Sedan. This was after I had succeeded, with little effort, in making the seats fit. The source of the confusion is that parts are frequently assigned new numbers for comparatively trivial reasons. Two different part numbers may be interchangeable. This fact is especially important to the restorer who fails to secure a rare part simply because its part number differs from the part he's replacing.

The almost-infinite permutations of the four-cylinder engine come to light only when you try to mix and match used parts. I recently assembled an engine for an Alfetta sedan from used parts. During the years of its production, the Alfetta's dipstick was located on either the sump or the block (depending on Lord knows what) and the block and sump castings I had selected both presumed that the dipstick was located on the other piece. As a result, I was able to assemble an engine only to discover, just before dropping it in the body, that there was no way to check the oil. While this is probably not the best story to tell when you're trying to sound like an expert, it nicely illustrates how Alfa ownership keeps you humble.

Because of its surprising diversity, the Giulia is perhaps the most humility-inducing subject in all of Alfadom. Fusi lists 49 models in the Giulia line, with a total production of 265,877. The model line includes right- and left-hand-drive cars, knock-down (CKD) cars shipped disassembled to countries where domestic assembly has tax advantages, and six models with production under 100 units (the most rare, the 1600S with right-hand drive, had a production of three; the most popular, the Giulia 1300 TI, had a production of 140,684).

In this chapter I want to examine some pieces of the Giulia story that do not conveniently fit in any of the other chapters of the book. I do this with the trepidation that comes from not having personally owned all the examples I'm about to discuss. If you are fortunate to own one, remember that owners over the years may have worked changes that you might consider original. Not only is there no definitive source to satisfy conflicting claims of original specification, but Alfa itself may have changed the design just after publishing its specification.

▪ Touring Alfas

GTC

When the Giulietta was first planned in the early 1950s, Alfa asked both Bertone and Pininfarina to submit competing designs. The prototype Bertone Giulietta Spider survives in the United States, and there are several Farina coupes on the 1900 chassis to suggest what the losing coupe design might have looked like. Thus, we can imagine what Alfas would have looked like if Alfa had reversed the awards.

But Alfa settled for letting Bertone build its coupes and Farina its spiders. The GTC, a thousand examples of which were produced between 1965 and 1966, is

The elegant 1965 GTC was built in very limited numbers and was one of the few post-war Alfas from Touring.

an exception to this rule and shows us how neatly the Bertone coupe could be converted to a ragtop. The car was introduced at the 1965 Geneva show and is basically a strengthened Sprint GT coupe chassis with its fixed top exchanged for a soft top.

The same technique has been used successfully by the American ASC firm in converting Toyota Celica, Ford and Chevrolet coupes to convertibles. The curious thing about the conversion, however, is that it was given to Touring, and not Bertone.

Touring had been a favorite bodybuilder for Alfa up to the 1900 but had failed to enter the competition for the Giulietta or its descendants. In spite of the fact that

Touring did not have a hand in Giulietta production, I must observe that the Touring-bodied 1900 Super Sprint coupe of 1955 certainly anticipated the slender nose treatment of the Giulietta Farina convertible.

In the early 1960s, all of Italy suffered from worker strikes and Touring was stuck with an 80 percent walkout. Its inability to meet existing orders led to cancellations and eventual receivership for the company. In 1965, Touring's total work force was 263, compared to 403 only a year earlier. Production continued at surprisingly high levels during receivership, but the company was finally closed on January 31, 1967. Some of Touring's assets were purchased by Alfa Romeo.

One of the most desirable limited-production Alfa road cars of the post-war period is the GTC, which is a strengthened Sprint GT coupe converted to a cabriolet by Touring of Milan.

The Giulietta Sprint Speciale prototype had no front bumpers and a slender grille. Its superb aerodynamics allowed it to reach unsusually high speeds considering it was powered by a 1300cc engine.

■ Bertone Alfas

Sprint Speciale

The success of the Zagato Giulietta SVZ made Alfa realize that there was a viable market for an image car built on production components. Now, both Bertone and Farina had much closer working relations with Alfa than Zagato, so it is not surprising that Alfa allowed Bertone to design a limited-production dream car on Giulietta mechanicals.

Nuccio Bertone and his designer Franco Scaglione, of course, had designed the Giulietta Sprint in a very short time and under trying circumstances. The success of that car thrust Alfa into six-digit production figures for the first time in its history.

Prior to the Giulietta Sprint, Bertone had created a series of three aerodynamic studies on the 1900 chassis known as the BAT cars (Bertone Aerodynamica Technica). These three cars were numbered 5, 7 and 9.

BAT 9 had a drag coefficient (Cd) of only 0.19, compared to 0.34 for the Giulia Super and about 0.35 for sporty coupes like the Toyota Supra. The prototype Sprint Speciale had a Cd of 0.28. The BAT series of cars were a sensation. Not beautiful in any classic sense, the cars seem wildly disproportionate. Yet their flowing lines and large finwork nevertheless have a strong attraction,

BAT 9, 7 and 5—all designed by Bertone's Scaglione—foreshadowed several styling cues that later surfaced in the Giulietta SS.

for they are clearly single-minded in their search for aerodynamic efficiency.

Many presume that the Giulietta Sprint Speciale proceeded directly from the well-known BATs. That is not precisely the case, though like the BATs, the Sprint Speciale gives away some beauty to aerodynamic efficiency, and the greenhouses of the BAT 9 and Sprint Speciale are very similar. The true inspiration of the Sprint Speciale is the Alfa-Abarth 1000 GT which was shown, along with the prototype Sprint Speciale, at Turin in 1958 and mentioned in Chapter 8. This car was a true lightweight (indeed, "Abarth" and "lightweight" are synonymous), with aluminum bodywork designed

by Franco Scaglione and a tubular space frame with a heat-bonded plastic sheet for the floor pan. It is generally assumed that this Alfa-Abarth, though intended for serial production, was abandoned in favor of the Sprint Speciale.

It's not clear exactly how sporting Alfa expected Bertone's design to be. In the literature on Zagato, one gets the feeling that Alfa may have wanted to quash the Zagato effort by offering a similar car itself at a lower cost. That would have been an easy assignment, for Zagato was having to buy complete cars to disassemble before starting his own bodywork. Evidence that this may have been Alfa's intent are the facts that a number of aluminum-bodied Giulietta Sprint Speciales were built, and the Weber-carbureted Veloce versions of the Giulia engine were first introduced in the Sprint Speciale bodywork (at Geneva in March 1963).

If the plan were to outdo Zagato in the production of a light racecar, Bertone certainly missed the mark. Although the Sprint Speciale has been raced, it is rather like the 190SL Mercedes in having more sporting appearance than capability. What Bertone did succeed in creating was the ultimate small GT. I've been fortunate enough to take a 100-plus-mile freeway trip in a Giulia Sprint Speciale and can say the sensation of traveling near 100 mph for mile after mile in quiet and comfort is memorable. There is almost no wind noise, and the seating position, large glass area and

Bertone and Alfa countered Zagato's SV with the sleek, Scaglione-designed Giulietta SS.

The SS proved overly heavy for successful competition use and as this photo of a Giulia SS from a 1967 race in Morocco shows, the suspension was also too soft.

leather-trimmed appointments make traveling in an SS a journey in luxury.

Before offering a critical examination of its styling, I want to remind the reader that the Sprint Speciale is one of the hottest collectible Alfas going. Indeed, there is a kind of feeding frenzy as speculators gobble up every Sprint Speciale they can find. For years, a very good friend of mine had a junked Sprint Speciale in his back yard. The car was used as a source of parts for his concours-quality Sprint Speciale. It had been hit both front and back, the floor pan was rusty and all opening panels had been removed. My friend is now beginning to get calls—and being offered large sums of money—for the "restorable SS" he has been hoarding in his back yard.

Having given a nod to the undoubted collectability of the Sprint Speciale, I can now suggest that it is perhaps a less successful design than the Giulietta Sprint. The Sprint Speciale follows the classic approach to aerodynamics: get good penetration from a pointed front and back so that the laminar flow stays with the car as long as possible. The result is excessive overhang and a front and rear which do little more than just start and end. Its greenhouse seems disproportionately tall and peaks too early along the profile view. The high greenhouse is a result of having to maintain adequate headroom within a shortened wheelbase because of the excessive overhang. The tail treatment seems especially weak. Its tentative, squared-off configuration is a concession to practicality, not aerodynamics: the prototype tail tapered to a small-radius curve. In contrast, Zagato, with the SZ Coda

The distinctive styling of the Sprint Speciale, its suitability for touring and its reliable Giulietta or Giulia underpinnings make it a very desirable car today. This is a 1964 Giulia SS.

Tronca, used Kamm's aerodynamics more boldly to produce, arguably, a prettier car. In addition, the styled flare over the front wheels seems contrived.

If I am somewhat mean-spirited over the Sprint Speciale's styling, I need to reassert that the basic concept is unarguably voluptuous. Individual components have a stunning fluid beauty, but the total effect is less than the sum of the parts.

Tom Zat has created a one-off "shaved" version of the Sprint Speciale which displays the car's basic lines much more successfully, in my opinion, than the production version. He has eliminated many of the styling details so that the flow of the body seems much less compromised. The net effect of Zat's modifications is a vision of the concept's essential elegance.

In March 1963 Alfa introduced the Giulia SS, with only minor detail changes over the Giulietta version. Even with a larger engine, higher compression, wider camshafts and dual side-draft Weber carburetors, changed gear ratios gave the Giulia the same top speed as the Giulietta Sprint Speciale.

Details of the Sprint Speciale were immediately familiar to Alfa owners, for there was extensive use of production components throughout. A unique radiator was required to accommodate the lowered hood line, but the instruments and most of the interior furnishings were regular production items.

The 1600 badge on the tail is the easiest way to identify this SS as a Giulia.

Canguro

In 1964, Bertone requested a TZ chassis to build a show car for the Paris show. Busso sent a TZ2 (No. 101) and Bertone had Giugiaro, then working as head of his design office, create a body. Alfa decided against production.

The Canguro (Kangaroo, in Italian), from a design standpoint, was a much more successful effort than Bertone's Sprint Speciale body. It shares the same wonderful fluidity but is not marred by a too-short wheelbase, awkward passenger compartment nor compromised tail. Like the Sprint Speciale, its glass area is beautifully integrated into the lines of the body.

In retrospect, the Canguro probably suggests a direction Alfa should have taken. Giugiaro's design for the Alfetta coupe is much less aesthetic though, unquestionably, more practical: on the other hand, practicality has never been Alfa's long suit anyway. The sensuous, flowing lines of the Canguro make it a masterpiece of design.

The Canguro kicked around Bertone's facility for a number of years and was finally "officially lost." After its show-car duty, the Canguro

Using a TZ chassis, Giugiaro developed the Bertone Canguro, which was a visually striking and very attractive small coupe.

Undeniably beautiful, the Canguro never reached production.

was being driven around the Bertone facility when it was damaged in a wreck with a Corvair-based show car. It finally ended up, minus running gear, outside the shop in something of a designer trash-heap. Those who questioned its whereabouts were told that it had been destroyed. In a sense, that was true: when it was discovered by American Gary Schmidt, it was missing its hood and most of its mechanical parts. Gary had the car under restoration for a long period, even asking for contributions from other enthusiasts to assist in completing the work. The car has been sold to a Japanese collector.

Montreal

Most Alfa enthusiasts know the story about how the hit of the 1967 World's Fair in Montreal became a regular production vehicle in 1970. That it took Alfa almost four years to capitalize on a sensation is one measure of the firm's bureaucracy.

It was still worth the wait. The Montreal was another Bertone design, but executed by Marcello Gandini, instead of Giugiaro, who had gone to Ghia. Even in its prototype form for the World's Fair, the Montreal was much more real-world than the BATs or, even, the Sprint Speciale. As a consequence, the production version differed only slightly from the show car.

I think the Montreal is wonderfully underappreciated. Wonderful, because it is still affordable. It carries a unique V-8 engine derived from the Type 33 race cars in a show-car body, and had a production run of only 3,925: powerful, beautiful and

rare. Yet, only a few years ago I turned down a good example for $12,500 and even today they bring little over $20,000. When one considers that he could spend the same for a Giulietta Veloce spider, or many times that for a Sprint Speciale or TZ, the Montreal must be the bargain of the century. A momentary bargain, perhaps, since published comments such as this can have a dramatic effect on the market. Since I do not currently own, nor plan to own, a Montreal, these comments should be taken as both objective and heartfelt.

Some caveats, of course. Montreal ownership is likely to be stressful, for few mechanics will recognize the car, let alone be competent to work on it. And most will probably be comfortable increasing their rates to Ferrari scale for any work on the car. Like all Alfas of the era, Montreals rust. Like many high-speed tourers, the steering is heavy at low speeds.

There are some distinct advantages, however, to owning a Montreal over similar head-turners with Ferrari or Maserati badges. Many stock Alfa parts can be made to work (note: I did not say "fit"). The SPICA fuel injection system is really little more than two 1750 pumps bolted together with a single logic unit. The eight-plug Marelli distributor seems adapted from the twin-plug GTAs. The rear axle appears to be a stock Giulia unit with an extra sump bolted on for additional cooling.

You'll note that I'm hedging: instead of "fits," I'm saying "seems," or "appears to fit." That is because I know of no one who has verified conclusively any of the similarities between the Montreal and its 105-series stablemates. Knowing Alfa's ability to make up unique parts on a moment's notice, I'm especially wary of

The Montreal prototype was flown to Expo 1967 in Canada where it debuted. Three years later it reached production. Those sail panel vents are reminiscent of the front quarter vents used on the Canguro several years earlier.

assuring anyone that the Montreal shares a single bolt with the Giulia. But it sure looks like it does.

The most encouraging fact about Montreal ownership is that most of its parts are in the 105-series, which is the same series as the Giulia and the reason why I'm including the car in this book: in spite of its V-8 engine, the Montreal is a 105-series Alfa.

While the block is a derivation of the V-8, Type 33 sport car engine, Montreal heads appear to be derived from the 1750. There was a series of letters in the Alfa club magazine on just how 1750-like the Montreal heads were. One accomplished Alfa mechanic (he served as a technical advisor for many years) who had worked on many Montreals claimed they were 1750 knock-offs. Not so, claimed Alfa's chief engineer in the United States when the Montreal was current: he stated that the Montreal heads were unique, with no relationship to the 1750.

It's fun to trace the derivation of a style. The Montreal had features that Bertone used in other cars. But there are no other Bertone cars which looked exactly like the Montreal, either: it was a surprisingly unique design. The prominent slats on the sail panel (eight on a prototype, seven on the show car, six on the production model) had a forebear in Bertone's 1963 Iso Grifo coupe, and the prominent sail panel on a fastback was also found on the 1964 prototype coupe Bertone designed for Alfa. The idea of using the sail panel as an air duct was also tried on the 1963 Corvair Testudo. The undulating fender line was found in the 1964 Canguro as well as a 1966 special built on a Porsche 911 chassis.

The NACA duct on the hood was added to the production car. The prototype had a series of slats across the hood, similar in execution to the slats on the sail panel.

The slatted headlamp covers were an attempt to do something interesting with the traditional round headlamps. A more successful, if involved, approach has been found with pop-up headlamps, but the Montreal's front remains certainly distinctive.

I've used "slatted" to refer to three items on the Montreal's exterior: the sail panel, headlight covers and hood openings. If the design of the Montreal is to be faulted, it is that it came perilously close to gadgetry: all the vents and slats detracted from its basic form (the same criticism is leveled at the Sprint Speciale).

The interior of the Montreal was show-car to the core. Two large pods carried the speedometer and tachometer and a high tunnel separated driver from passenger. A short gearshift lever connected to the five-speed transmission. You sat low in the Montreal. Heavy low-speed steering lightened considerably at road speeds and the car really came into its own just above legal cruising limits.

In a sense, the Montreal continued a line established by the 2.0-liter and 2600 Bertone coupes. All were intended to be luxurious, high-speed tourers. With 2.6 liters giving 200 hp at 6,500 rpm (compared to 145 hp for the 2600), the Montreal offered a top speed of 135 mph compared to 120 mph for the 2600.

It is a shame the Montreal did not sire a line of high-performance coupes based on the V-8 engine. I have always felt that the Montreal could have been easily refined into a line of sports cars of outstanding character. In a sense it had one child: the sensuous Stradale, which was also Type 33-based. Only a very few Stradales were produced, a fact sorely lamented by all Alfa enthusiasts.

■ Zagato-Bodied Alfas

Like Gilbert and Sullivan, Alfa and Zagato are a team with a magic that is unsurpassed. The relationship between the two companies is old and close: the most famous and desirable Alfas dating back to the mid-1920s have bodies by Zagato. Indeed, the simple conjunction of Alfa and Zagato means a car of great distinction and value.

The most recent efforts of Zagato have proved most controversial. Stylists are still learning to cope with the science of aerodynamics and have not really achieved a good balance between art and science. At the same time, Zagato has been urged near the edge by Alfa's apparent insistence on a striking, if not jarring approach to styling. If one is to use the ES30 as the rule, then it would be appropriate to say that the Zagato/Alfa collaboration produces cars that are interesting, even striking, but not beautiful.

The very definition of the classic roadster derives from the ultimately

beautiful Zagato bodies fitted to Alfas designed by Vittorio Jano between 1926 and 1935. Those cars are unmatched for their flowing lines and sheer animal magnetism. More recently, the Alfa Romeo Giulia has benefited especially from Zagato's best work: the Tubolare Zagato Giulia coupes are certainly among the most beautiful cars ever created.

Sprint Veloce Zagato (SVZ)

The opportunity to create something on the Giulietta floor pan—it was a unit construction without a conventional frame—came when Dore Leto di Priolo crashed his Alfa Sprint during the Mille Miglia. A famous gentleman motorist, Priolo was dedicated to winning, and so asked Elio Zagato to rebuild the Giulietta to make it as light as possible. Of course, Zagato would use aluminum body panels, but the fact that the car already had a steel body manufactured in unit with the floor pan meant that the bodywork had to be cut away and a completely new shell fabricated around a steel substructure.

Priolo's car became the Alfa SVZ prototype. In styling, it shared much with Zagato's other work of the era. Like the Fiat Abarths he was bodying, this SVZ had a double-bubble roof. Other touches echoed Zagato's Alfa 1900 CSSZ, especially around the greenhouse. Many styling cues came from the production Bertone coupe. From the front, at a glance, the SVZ might be mistaken for a stock Alfa; but only at a glance, for the grille sat quite low, allowing the hood line to slope more

Phil Hill drives the quintessential marriage of Alfa Romeo and Zagato—a 6C1750 spider.

Ugo Zagato

Ugo Zagato was born June 25, 1890, at Gavello in the province of Rovigo. His father died before he was born and his mother never remarried.

It was a time of grinding poverty in the Italian countryside and the only escape available to a young man was to enter a seminary. Thus, Ugo received his basic education at the Seminary at Rovigo. He was 14 when he left, so he had the equivalent of a classic ninth-grade education. (Take in context: that probably made him more widely read in science and the arts than most modern college graduates.) Immediately on his graduation from Rovigo, Ugo left to find work in Germany. He worked as an apprentice in Cologne for four years only to be recalled by his mother to Italy to answer military conscription. Some basic flaw in the system allowed him to serve about 40 days in the military with the Third Bersaglieri of Livorno and then be discharged.

Ugo decided to remain in Italy and seek employment in the auto industry. This was in 1909—the same year the French firm Darracq decided to build a version of its car for the Italian market: the following year, the Milan factory was bought by Italian businessmen to build the A.L.F.A.

Ugo didn't hire into the upstart firm, however. He chose to work in Varese for Carrozzeria Varesina, a company founded in 1845 to build horse-drawn carriages. The company was expanding into bodywork for automobiles and had a few clients in France and Switzerland.

To improve his skills, Ugo began part-time studies at the Santa Marta School for Designers in Milano. One should not get the idea that Zagato found himself in the mainstream of the Italian automobile industry: that locus was most definitely with Fiat in Torino. One should not denigrate Milano, however, where Isotta Fraschini was located. It was, in 1909, the second-largest Italian car maker after Fiat.

As the Great War approached, Ugo moved to Torino where he worked for Pomilio di Torino designing airplanes. It was there that he learned the lightweight construction techniques he would later apply to automobile bodies. In February 1919, at the end of the war, he returned to Milano to open his own body shop in Via Francesco Ferrer.

In the early part of the automobile's development in Italy, it was hard enough designing a running engine and a chassis to carry it: fitting a body was typically left to another firm. Manufacturers were quite accustomed to delivering running chassis to outside firms, which were usually retained by private customers to create customized bodywork for the chassis they had bought.

In 1919 Ugo Zagato founded the coachbuilding company that crafted so many sublime bodies for Alfa Romeo.

So it was that Ugo Zagato of Milano received his first commission to body a Fiat 501.

In 1920, Ugo married Amelia Bressello, whom he had met some ten years earlier. On February 27, 1921, a son, Elio, was born. Another son, Gianni, was born on August 17, 1929.

Zagato's lightweight bodies became fashionable and his work prospered. In 1923 his company moved to larger quarters at Viale Brianza 10 in Milano. His work had come to the attention of Niccola Romeo through Vittorio Jano, an Alfa new-hire from Fiat. At Fiat, Giovanni Agnelli regarded Zagato as a kind of Michelangelo of bodybuilding and the favorable reputation followed when Jano went to Alfa. Zagato was selected to build a body for Jano's first effort for Alfa, the P2.

For Fiat, Zagato was accustomed to laying his aluminum bodywork over wood, a classic approach used by the British even many decades later. From his work on airplanes, Zagato realized that a lighter and stronger approach would be to lay aluminum over steel framing.

The outstanding success of the Zagato-bodied Alfa Romeo P2 Grand Prix racer opened the door for much greater collaboration between the two companies.

aerodynamically than the stock car. But Zagato's efforts were only incidentally a styling exercise. The completed car weighed 750 kg compared to the 895 kg of the stock coupe, advantage enough for Massimo (Dore's brother) to win the Coppa Intereuropa at Monza Sept 2, 1956.

Nothing attracts attention like a winner. Soon, Zagato was besieged with requests for lightweight cars like the Priolo's. As great as these cars were on the track, they could never be competitive in the marketplace because the conversion work had to begin with the disassembly of a completed Bertone coupe. Because he did not need to remove an existing body before constructing his own, Bertone's product was created with much less labor and at a much lower cost.

The SVZ, however, became a focus of Alfa racing attention. It received the attention of the great Italian tuners: Vicchi and Stefanelli at Milano, and Conrero and Bosato in Torino.

The successes of the SVZ clouded the reputation of the first Sprint Veloces, which were lightweight cars with aluminum panels and sliding plexiglas door windows. In a kind of retaliation against Zagato's success with the SVZ, Alfa asked Bertone to design a competing car. The resulting Sprint Speciale was designed by Scaglione while he was at Bertone. Somehow, the design goal escaped Bertone. The SS was a wonderfully aerodynamic car but it was fully appointed and steel-bodied. As a result it never equaled the racing success of Zagato's cars.

It was this technique which he first used on the P2 Alfa, which won the championship in 1925, and remained competitive well into the 1930s. A derivation of this approach, laying aluminum over a network of steel tubes formed to the shape of the body, was later adapted by Carrozzeria Touring for its Superleggera construction.

Of course, the success of the P2 prompted Jano to select Zagato to build sporting bodies for his first passenger car, the 6C1500. Similar Zagato bodies were constructed for the 6C1750 and 8C2300 chassis. As briefly as this era is told here, it is still important to emphasize that Zagato's work on Jano's chassis formed a golden age of automobile history.

In the latter part of the 1930s, Zagato built sporting bodies for a number of clients, but he did not hold the dominant position at Alfa, which was now using the work of Castagna, Touring and Farina for many of its production cars. It's ironic that much of Alfa's production efforts during the war were to build aero engines, which virtually eliminated any need for Zagato's services. During the war, Zagato built truck bodies for Isotta Fraschini. His factory was demolished by bombs in August 1943.

At the end of the war, Zagato opened a new plant at Via Giorgini 16, Milano, to produce the Panoramic series of cars for Fiat. These cars featured rounded styling and a large glass area for excellent visibility. By 1949, he had added Maserati and Ferrari to his list of clients for Panoramic-bodied cars. Most of his production capacity, however, was taken up by Fiat for the mass-produced Topolino.

Beginning with the 1950s, Zagato's name was again linked intimately to Alfa. It was Zagato who constructed the bodywork for the world-championship 1951 Type 159 Alfa.

Zagato was at hand to provide styling exercise for Alfa's first series-produced car, the 1900. In 1952 he created a prototype spider body for the 1900 and in the following year, the 1900 Super Sprint Zagato (SSZ) coupe, which went into production in 1954. Zagato's elegant fastback design for the 1900 did not remain exclusively Alfa's. Similar bodies were constructed for the Fiat 8V in 1953, the Maserati A6G and 212 Ferrari in 1954.

In 1956, Zagato began production of the Fiat-Abarth series of cars and did no further work for Alfa until 1958, when a down-sized version of the 1900 SSZ body was created for the Giulietta.

The 1900 SSC (at right, with the 8C2300 Castagna at left) was the first post-war Alfa Romeo undertaken by Zagato.

Giulietta Sprint Zagato

It could never be economically viable to dismantle a perfectly good car just to make another. In 1959, Zagato signed an agreement with Alfa that allowed him to purchase unfinished Giulietta Spider Veloce chassis from Farina, making his manufacturing costs competitive with Bertone. The new car, called simply the Sprint Zagato, was derived especially from two of the last SVZs owned by Miro Toselli and Ada Pace. It was introduced March 3, 1960, at the Geneva motor show. Zagato's labor cost was still enormous: 300 hours were required to build one.

For the Giulietta SZ, Zagato carefully reconsidered the direction in which he had taken the 1900 CSSZ. The basic driveline dimensions of the 1900 demanded a rather vertical body: the tall engine forced the envelope to be both high and narrow. The Giulietta, on the other hand, was the first Alfa to offer a design that was clearly wider than it was high. As a result, the Zagato SZ bodywork looks still very modern, while the 1900 SSZ is definitely of the classic mold.

Because the Giulietta's engine sits so low in the basic shell, the nose of the car can be a dramatic taper rising up to the windshield frame. Zagato made poetic sense of the possibility and added faired-in headlamps enclosed in plastic shells which followed the flowing lines of the fenders. Softly rounded lines gave the impression of great aerodynamic efficiency. In the first of the Giulietta Zagatos, the rounded lines were repeated at the rear. The rounded front and rear, combined with a dramatic "tumble-home" roof line gave the sheetmetal a feeling of great taughtness—and a rather football-like appearance.

The SZ was a fast and very competitive entry in the smaller displacements of the great open road races. Here, the D'Amica Giulietta SZ shows its speed in the 1961 Targa Florio.

The SZ or Sprint Zagato was lighter and significantly more competitive than the Sprint or Sprint Speciale.

Coda Tronca

The SZ Alfas were being hard pressed on the racetrack by the new Lotus Elite coupe from Colin Chapman. The Giulietta engine had been developed to its virtual limits by Conrero and his competitors. As a result, if extra performance was to be obtained, it was clear that it would have to come from aerodynamic improvements.

Track tests proved that the SZ was too short: to get better penetration (laminar airflow control), the nose and tail needed to be lengthened. Early tests revealed that a very long tail, however, caused steering difficulties on twisting roads.

Zagato decided to employ the revolutionary aerodynamic theories of Professor Kamm. The classic aerodynamic approach was the teardrop, in which the tail of the car tapered gradually to maintain a layered flow of air over the body for as long as possible. Kamm realized that this extended contact

between the body and the air
actually increased drag, and
proposed that a chopped-off tail,
though it would cause a more
turbulent termination of the flow,
would provide less overall drag
because the turbulence would affect
a smaller area of the vehicle.

The final configuration was
determined during a series of
trial-and-error tests. Ercole Spada
designed bodies with progressively
longer tails that were evaluated
during high-speed runs. The most
successful configuration proved
to be both narrower and lower
than the SZ. The Coda Tronca

To improve the aerodynamics of the SV, the body was
lengthened and the tail abruptly chopped off to yield the
SV Coda Tronca, of which 30 were built.

had only a slightly more sleek front and virtually the
same greenhouse as the SZ, but its tail was chopped
off abruptly, following Kamm's theory. In order to
maintain aerodynamic penetration, and also to avoid
sheer ugliness, Zagato provided a substantial rear fender
overhang, making the Coda Tronca also longer than
the SZ. With this configuration, Spada and Elio Zagato
reached 227 km/h on the Milan Bergamo road—a truly
remarkable speed for a car of 1300cc displacement.

A total of 30 SV Coda Tronca cars was produced,
though some owners modified their early SZs to the
Coda Tronca configuration.

Tubolare Zagato (TZ)

The ultimate Kamm application appeared on the
Giulia-based Zagato coupe, which carried a large,

indented flat panel at its tail. The basic lines of the SZ
Coda Tronca were continued though the greenhouse
gained some sheet metal and therefore seemed much
heavier. The Tubolare Zagato, however, was actually not
a development of the SZ, having been conceived within
Alfa Romeo (as project 105.11) at about the same time
Zagato was rebodying Priolo's crashed Sprint Veloce.

In 1955, Carlo Abarth was working on the
development of a box-type sheetmetal chassis which
would provide superior strength and outstanding
lightness. His idea was to create a light, Alfa-engined
Abarth of 750cc displacement. He actually built a
chassis and presented it to Alfa for testing, according to

In prototype form, the TZ featured a rounded tail
and rectangular headlights in a nose that owed
much to that of the SZ.

Giuseppe Busso. The chassis proved too flexible, and it was reinforced at Alfa with a tube perimeter frame. This is the chassis on which Boano built the 750 competition prototype roadster.

Early in 1958, Abarth once again proposed an Alfa-Abarth, this time with a 1.0-liter Abarth derivative of the Giulietta engine and a tubular chassis designed by Alfa. The chassis work was carried out at Alfa by Colucci, under Busso's direction. The collaboration produced the Alfa-Abarth which was shown at the 1958 Turin motor show. Production costs of the exotic car would have been too great, and Abarth asked permission to use a stock 1300 Veloce engine to lower costs. His request was refused. Perhaps in retribution, Abarth hired Colucci. With Colucci's departure from Alfa, chassis development was assigned to Zava, who almost immediately left with Villa, an engine designer, to do consulting work for Autodelta and Euroracing.

At the end of 1959 Satta proposed a lightweight race car to be built using the mechanicals of the as-yet unannounced Giulia. Based on Colucci's work for Abarth, Busso recommended tubular chassis construction. Zagato was the obvious choice to do the work, not only because he worked fast and reliably, but also because he had demonstrated with the SVZ that he had mastered working with a network of small tubes.

The Tubolare Zagato (TZ) was completely designed by the end of 1960. The engine configuration was basically worked out by Conrero on a third prototype engine. He fitted Borgo pistons, changed the carburetion to 45DCOE Webers (1964 Sebring cars had 50DCOE3 Webers), modified the cam timing and spark advance profile, ported the head and increased its compression ratio to 10:1. A seven-liter sump was obtained by fitting a 45mm spacer between the stock sump and the block. The cars had limited-slip differentials and their front and rear transmission castings were in magnesium.

The car did not use the basic body pan of the unit-bodied parent. Instead, a true multi-tube space frame was constructed, giving the car its name of Tubolare Zagato (TZ). Only 112 of these cars were built from 1963 to 1967. They are certainly among the most desirable and the most valuable post-war production Alfas.

The entire front of the TZ tilted forward to provide ample access to the suspension and the power plant. The intake to the dual Weber carburetors was a ram system which increased manifold pressure as road speed increased. A true header exhaust featured four independent tubes that snaked around the chassis tubes. The rear suspension was independent with top and bottom A-arms and coil springs. It was certainly the least-developed part of the car. TZs are not known for their ultimate roadholding capabilities, though the number of racing wins shows that the cars demanded great respect. I have always suspected that the reputation of the TZ rear suspension suffers, like the SPICA fuel injection, from inept adjustment rather than poor basic design.

The first two chassis were delivered to Zagato in January 1961 for the construction of two prototype spiders. The body was unusual: though the top was removable, the rear window was fixed, a design which anticipated cars such as the Lancia Zagato and the Toyota Supra. The result was too aerodynamically inefficient, and the hard top was never removed during testing. The prototype was outstandingly light: the bare space frame weighed only 62 kg, and with the top

Although the TZ is one of the most distinctive and attractive of all Zagato-bodied Alfas, it is a true race car that earned much success. This 1964 TZ still competes in historic races.

off, the entire car weighed less than 600 kg. The most troublesome unit proved to be the new rear suspension, which endowed the prototype with excessive understeer.

Poor handling and unrefined aerodynamics kept the top speeds of the prototype to only 208 km/h. The spider bodies were scrapped in favor of a coupe following the general lines of the Giulietta SZ Coda Tronca, which was introduced at just the time the prototypes were under test. Dramatic, rectangular headlights were a striking front-end feature of this first coupe. Speeds immediately rose to 215 km/h.

Development of the TZ coupe continued during the early months of 1962. Although the rectangular headlamps were retained, the nose was lengthened and the rear inset of the Kamm tail was recessed even more deeply than on the Coda Tronca. A lip was added to improve the Kamm effect. The final configuration was achieved in early 1963, after nine different prototype noses were tested for the car. Round headlamps were part of the final design.

After all the work, Alfa realized that it had no production capacity for the TZ. As a result, the TZ was completely sublet: the chassis was constructed by Ambrosini at Passignano sul Trasimeno; assembly of the mechanical components and suspension went to Autodelta, Udine (founded by Carlo Chiti), and the body, of course, was constructed by Zagato. The final configuration of the TZ was shown in March 1963 at Geneva.

Make no mistake about it, the TZ is a race car through and through. Alfa's racing team, Autodelta, campaigned the cars with great success. Yet, it is quite capable of being driven for everyday transportation. The seats are very comfortable, though the heat and noise of the interior is much greater than on a passenger car. In an attempt to improve performance further, the last three TZs carried plastic bodywork by Balzaretti and Modigliani of Milano. The plastic body was cast using a production aluminum TZ as a pattern, and so was identical, but it was both lighter (62 kg vs 92 kg) and stronger.

TZ2

Studies for a follow-on car to the TZ began early in 1964. Busso wanted some modifications to the TZ chassis to get a lower roof line but still retain the independent rear suspension which had finally been refined so that it contributed to the car's performance. Like the last three

TZs, the new body was fiberglass-reinforced plastic. The wheelbase of the new model was unchanged from the TZ but the rear window was a single piece of plastic, compared to the three-piece backlight of the TZ. The lower profile mandated a dry-sump engine (with a seven-liter tank capacity). To gain more power from the Giulia engine, a dual ignition head was fitted with larger valves and changed cam timing to give 165 hp at 7,000 rpm.

In order to make a lower roof line, reclining seats were used and the driver assumed a slightly reclining position. Its low roof line gives it a menacing stance and it is clear that this is a car which is intended to go very fast. The total weight of the car was between 620–630 kg, and it was called TZ2.

The first TZ2 was presented at the Torino show on October 16, 1964. In a press release for the show, Zagato enthused that the body was so efficient that a 1300cc engine would be a perfect power plant. Alfa would have none of it and insisted that the current Giulia 1600 engine be used.

While TZ2 is the proper name for this car, the earlier TZ does not, therefore, become the TZ1. The TZ2 is the most collectable Giulia-based Alfa. Only twelve were produced, and none were sold to private owners. As a result, with the exception of the Type 158/159 and possibly the Disco Volante, it is also the most valuable post-war Alfa. Clearly, the TZ2 has now found its way into private hands, but the rarity of the car makes a market value almost impossible to establish. Such cars are almost always traded privately, but a million dollars (in 1999) would be a starting point.

It is sad that the most rare and desirable of all post-war Alfas should be so stillborn. Alfa did not develop the car, preferring instead to devote its efforts to the GTA.

No TZ2 fronts are identical due to their one-off construction and decades of racing adventures.

Pininfarina bodied a single example of the TZ2. From the front, the rising fenders and roof shape suggest the Ferrari Dino 206, which was also bodied by Pininfarina.

Pininfarina TZ2

Pininfarina also asked for a TZ2 chassis and asked for permission to construct a show car which would follow the basic lines of the TZ2. Unlike the Bertone Canguro (described earlier in this chapter), the Pininfarina design was strictly for show. This car has suffered a much more happy fate than the Canguro and has always been well cared for. For years, it was in the Matsuda collection in Japan, but it has since changed hands.

■ The Juniors

At a time when Alfa Romeo's new Bertone-designed 1600cc Giulia coupe was meeting with a cool reception, Alfa realized it could not afford to abandon the Giulietta contingent entirely, so a 1290cc "Junior" sedan was introduced at Monza in May 1964. At the same time, to keep the Giulia Sprint GT as desirable as possible, the fastback Giulia 1600 Sprint was dropped so that the only way to obtain a 1600cc coupe was to opt for the new notchback body which carried the 1600cc engine.

In September 1966, Alfa invited the motoring press to its test track at Balocco to try the new 1300 GT Junior. This car carried the GTV body but its grille featured a single chrome spear. Its engine had a bore and stroke of 74 x 75 mm and developed 89 hp at 6,000 rpm. The GT Junior appeared in GTA racing form in 1968.

About a year later, *Motor* magazine did a road test and found that "The 1300 is a light and easy car to drive, and fun too. If you want to keep ahead of the larger cars you have to use the gearbox, but mostly the engine pulls sufficiently well throughout its wide range to keep going at a very respectable rate; good roadholding keeps average speeds up on cross-country trips.

"In performance the GT 1300 is about as fast as the Giulia TI saloon…. Very few 1300cc production cars can top 100 mph — the Lotus Elite and Renault Gordini being two that spring to mind—and it is quite a tribute to the Alfa, which is essentially a fast tourer, that it can do this quite easily. On motorways the comfortable cruising speed is around 85–90 mph which can be maintained up hill and down dale all day without the oil temperature rising further than 170 degrees F."

Autocar, in its April 10, 1969, issue, found that "The GT Junior returned a mean maximum speed of 102 mph, compared with 113 and 116 mph for the 1600 and 1750 equivalents. Its best one-way was 104 mph…. As frequently happens, the use of a smaller engine does not result in significant gains in economy. The overall figure of 24.4 mpg, although good in relation to the car's performance and the way we drove it, is little better than the 23.9 mpg of the 1750 GT Veloce."

A Spider 1300 Junior was introduced in 1968 and produced until 1972. In 1974, when the current engine for the sprint was the 2.0-liter, Alfa introduced GT Juniors with 1.3- and 1.6-liter engines, thus (as noted above) reprising almost the entire Giulia line in a single model year.

The 1.3-liter Juniors were 105-series bodies powered by engines with 101-series Giulietta displacement (the bores and strokes were identical). These later engines were not exact replicas of the 101, however. They carried 105-series numbering and incorporated the design improvements of the later series engines, including smaller ports and camshafts from the 1600-series cars.

They were junior in trim level as well as in displacement. In a February 1973 road test of the 1600 Junior, *Sports Car World* found: "Interior fittings have been kept quite spartan—for instance, there is no console, and the fuel and temperature gauges are merely tacked on under the dashboard instead of being worked into it. Trim is also at a lower level than in the

GTV, and the seats aren't so lavishly styled. Nor do you get that superb woodrim wheel."

These Juniors, however spartan, were very popular since the lower displacement meant a lower tax in Italy and other countries that tax a car based on its displacement. Further, they filled a void for many enthusiasts who were not willing to see the beloved Giulietta replaced even by a slightly more appealing product. From a performance standpoint, they gave away little to the Solex-carbureted 1600 engine up to about 90 mph. Quite a few Junior coupes made it to the United States.

The Junior Zagato

When Alfa released the Giulia 1600cc engine in 1963, Alfisti landed in the next higher "circulation" tax bracket. To soothe those who enjoyed the smaller-displacement engine (and lower annual tax), Alfa introduced the 1300 Sedan and Sprint in 1964, using the new Giulia sedan body but the old Giulietta/Giulia fastback sprint body. When the 1300 engine finally appeared in the notchback Bertone coupe in 1966, it was called the GT 1300 Junior coupe. So far as I can tell, this is the first instance of the use of the Junior title for the

The primary identifying feature of the GT 1300 Junior was the single horizontal grille bar. The smaller engine kept the little coupe in a lower tax bracket, but still developed 89 hp.

1300-series engine. The Junior has a 74 x 75 mm bore x stroke, identical to the Giulietta. I have never been clear on the exact differences between this "new" 1300 Junior engine and the 101-series Giulietta power plant. My direct questions to Alfa personnel in Arese only elicited the response that the Junior engine benefited from "all the advances of the 1600 engine."

Juniors may have had smaller engines and lesser levels of trim, but the same engineering, design and underpinnings were used as on the more senior members of the range.

This Zagato rendering shows the proposed shape for the concept that became the Junior Z.

The Junior line became a virtual duplicate of the Giulia series, with Junior sedans, spiders, coupes and competition coupes. The GTA Junior, in fact, was a wonderfully successful competition car. Like its larger brother, it sported a dual-plug head which helped wring 110 SAE hp from its 1290cc displacement.

The lovely Zagato Junior, produced between 1972 and 1975, is doomed to be regarded as a prototype Honda CRX, perhaps just as the Lotus Elan has become a proto-Miata. With the SVZ, SZ and TZ cars, Zagato had established a good working relation with Alfa. The company wanted to trade on this relationship to get the contract for a series production car which would place Zagato in the same league as Bertone and Pininfarina.

Just after the war, the Zagato factory survived by building Topolino Fiats. This brush with the security of a serial production agreement was not forgotten. In 1966, Zagato reorganized and opened a new factory at Terrazzano di Rho. Ugo Zagato was 76 years old and had just signed an agreement with Lancia for the serial production of the Fulvia Sport, a touring, not a racing car (the Fulvia HF was handling that assignment). The agreement to build 92 Quattroruote 4R replicas of the Alfa 1750 Gran Sport Zagato foreshadowed Zagato's decision to get out of racing and concentrate on building high-volume passenger cars. Thus, the decision was made to build the Junior Zagato as a steel-bodied road car. It was the last car Ugo Zagato

would supervise, and he died in 1968, almost a year before the Junior Zagato went into production.

This goal was almost met in 1963 with the 2600 SZ, but it had been plagued with difficulties. The 1965 Quattroruote 4R Zagato, which proved trouble-free, still suffered from the economics of small-batch construction since it was never intended to be anything but a low-volume item.

With the Zagato Junior, Zagato's wish came true: some 1,500 of these lovely, steel-bodied cars were produced between 1969 and 1975. The initial run featured the 1300cc Junior engine. Beginning in 1972, the 1600cc engine was used. It is a measure of Zagato's limited capacity that in 1974 the total production of his factory was devoted to the Junior Zagato.

The production orientation of the Junior Z means that it is a comfortable, fully equipped car quite capable of being driven every day. Its styling is attractive without being either cute or outlandish, its aerodynamics superior and its drivetrain outstandingly reliable.

Occasionally, driving along the freeway to work, I look at a car (since I live in Los Angeles, it is most frequently a Japanese car) and wonder how I would regard it if it had been produced by Alfa. In many cases, I'm disappointed that Alfa didn't create cars styled more closely along the lines of the best contemporary work: an Alfa along the lines of the 240Z, for instance, would have been irresistible (and, perhaps, called a Montreal 2). Think, however, how we would have regarded Alfa had it produced the Maxima or the Cressida, the RX7 or MR2. It's popular to lament the fact that the Miata closed off the entry-level ragtop market which had been available to Alfa for literally decades (not many know that a Micro Spider for just such a market had been considered for the United States). In the case of the Junior Zagato, Alfa not only hit the target, but did it several years ahead of its time. That is a testimony to the potential of the Alfa-Zagato team. The sorry fact is that Alfa did not have the capacity to capitalize on its success.

Zagato continued its association with Alfa in fits and starts. Between 1976 through 1978, there was no Alfa work in-house. In 1978 Zagato got the contract to build Alfetta armored cars. In the following year it produced a one-off Giulietta (new model) designed by Fiorucci. In 1980, V-6 Zagato-armored Alfa sedans began production and in 1983, Zagato produced the Alfa Zeta 6 show car, as well as an Autodelta mid-engined V-6. In 1984 Zagato designed the Free Time, a modular Alfa 33 with removable body parts that allowed conversion from sedan to station wagon or sportster.

The Junior Zagato was so successful as a limited-production passenger car that, beginning in 1973, Alfa upped its displacement to 1600 cc. Fusi shows a production run of 1108 GT Juniors, certainly few enough to qualify it as a true collectible. ARI did not import the cars into the United States, though there are quite a few here which were imported by private parties.

The drivetrain of the Junior Zagato is all stock 105 stuff, with a solid rear axle, five-speed gearbox and unmodified DCOE-carbureted engine. Fit and finish on the car are top-notch, and it provides truly comfortable touring for two. Its wedge shape gives it low wind noise, good mileage and a top speed of just under 110 mph.

The styling is designed to turn heads, and the car would succeed wonderfully in this respect if it weren't for the fact that the Honda CRX stylists must have all taken test drives in a Junior just before penning the lines of Honda's sporty two-seat coupe. While some Junior owners may enjoy driving a "funny-looking CRX," the similarities are frustrating to most. In this litigious era, it's surprising there have been no lawsuits over the design's expropriation by Honda.

Its low production volume assures that the Junior Zagato will remain a valued collectible, while its steel body means that it will resist the everyday door dings alloy-bodied cars must avoid at all costs. A Junior Zagato can still be a distinctive daily driver. This augers well: historically, the most enjoyable collectibles were the most useable examples of their era.

Stylish, small and in demand, Zagato built 1,500 of the endearing Zagato Juniors.

It may have been diminutive in size, but with the bigger 1600cc engine, the Junior Zagato could be extremely quick. This 1600 Junior Z rolls on Cromadura wheels.

Although production was limited, there is no question that the Junior Zagato is a highly coveted cult-Alfa Romeo, as demonstrated by the little enclave at an Alfa Romeo Owners Club convention in 1984.

▪ Quattroruote Zagato

In the 1960s it was popular to build imitation classic cars based on modern running gear. This was the era of the Volkswagen-based Bugatti and the Excalibur, which was essentially a V-8-powered, automatic-transmissioned SS Mercedes. These replicars and "neoclassics" (one sees mind-boggling ads: "1927 Bugatti, VW running gear…") shared neither the roadholding nor the beauty of their namesakes; indeed, the most outstanding feature of most of the retro-cars is their ugliness. Even Siata got into the game, with an 850-based, shoebox-shaped retro-car called the Spring.

Quattroruote (Four Wheels) is the premiere Italian car magazine. It is perhaps not surprising that its passions run high: it has disassembled cars for road tests, and it is not unusual for one road test to occupy almost as many pages as the entire editorial content of United States enthusiast magazines.

As a primary medium for advertisers, it's also not surprising that *Quattroruote* carries a lot of weight with Italian car companies. Thus, *Quattroruote*'s suggestion to Alfa management that it should create a modern imitation of the 1750 Zagato was taken quite seriously.

The challenges for such an undertaking are daunting. The chassis of the 1750 was a thin, spare construction which provided, by twisting and flexing, much of the car's ride comfort. In contrast, the Giulia carried unit-body construction, and its coil-spring suspension virtually dictated a wide, low body outline: the 1750's was neither. Finally, the 1750 was right-hand drive, and the retro-car would have to be left-handed if it were to sell in the United States.

At 750 kg, the car was significantly lighter than the Duetto (at 990 kg), but its top speed was limited by its poorer aerodynamics to only 95 mph, compared to about 110 mph for the modern roadster.

It is easy not to take the 4R Zagato seriously, lumping it together with the plastic-bodied jokes of the era. Nothing could be further from the truth. Until Shelby resumed Cobra production, the 4R Zagato was the only replicar created by the manufacturer of the original product. And, since only 92 were produced, it is a collectible of considerable virtue. It is not nearly so beautiful as the 1929 6C1750 Zagato on which it was modeled, but few other contemporaneous cars ever were.

▪ Colli Wagon

The Giulia sedan was a superbly reliable car, ideally suited for family use. I am very sorry that Alfa did not import the station wagon to the United States. It would

As the view of the front suspension illustrates, the Quattroruote Zagato is built using Giulia components.

have offered all the Giulia advantages of performance, comfort and reliability with additional cargo capacity.

The "Promiscua," or Giulia Wagon was created when Don Black ordered five Supers to be used as mobile service school vehicles. Alfa picked Colli to do the modifications, which were totally handmade from the C-pillar back. The wagons were extensively used by the highway police in Italy and some ambulances were also fashioned from them.

There are a very few which found their way over here. I know of one decrepit Colli in San Francisco and another under restoration in the same city. A third Colli wagon with no rear side windows is currently owned by Giulia guru Dave Mericle.

Colli modified stock sedans, rather than fabricating the entire body from scratch. The one Colli I have examined seems to have been entirely stock Alfa excepting the rear bodywork. Indeed, it would be easy for any panel-beater to fabricate a wagon from the sedan, but I've never read anything about exactly how the conversions were accomplished. Because of the basic strength of the body and the fact that the new construction would probably add strength, no additional reinforcing should be required to create a sturdy and serviceable wagon.

■ OSI Scarabeo

For some time, Alfa had been experimenting with the idea that driver position could significantly affect vehicle performance. It's easy to imagine racing a Type 159 Alfetta, for it offers many passenger-car analogs, which is where we all learned to drive. On the other hand, the experience of just sitting in the 512 is fearful, for you feel as if you were on the end of a very blunt battering ram with little more than sheet aluminum and a few tubes between you and oblivion. Moreover, you're very aware that the bulk of the car's mass is behind you, waiting to squash you like a grape in a head-on. Add the undoubted fact that the rear end is more than willing to pass you in a curve and you have a machine capable of providing protracted terror if not outright catatonia as soon as you release the clutch.

In 1954, Alfa experimented with a configuration of the 159 (called the 160) which placed the driver at the very rear of the car, similar to a contemporary dragster. The purpose of the placement was to improve the driver's sense of where the car was on the track without also inducing undue terror. It was felt that, if the driver had a better sense of control, he could be more aggressive in his driving and the net result would be a faster car.

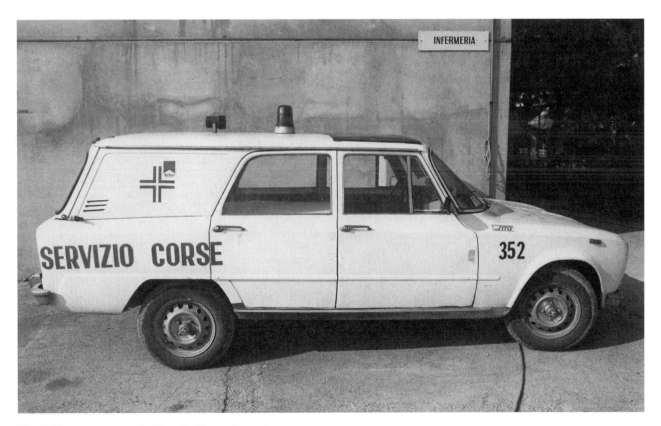

The Colli wagon was perfectly suited for police and ambulance duties. Very few made it to the United States.

A single Scarabeo spider was built as part of an exercise that ultimately produced an additional pair of coupes.

One of the two Scarabeo prototypes has been preserved in the Alfa Romeo Museum.

The Scarabeo of the mid-1960s recalled the experiment with the type 160 in that it attempted to place the driver as far back in the car as the mechanicals would permit. Curiously, given this goal, the GTA engine was placed transversely behind the driver with the transmission attached conventionally in line with the crankshaft. At the end of the transmission, a conical gear was used to drive a short shaft diagonally to the rear to the pinion gear of the differential. Independent rear suspension was used. In side view, the driver appears to sit no further back than in a conventional layout.

A spider prototype was constructed along with two coupe prototypes and a short production run was planned. Subsequently, those production plans were cancelled. The second Scarabeo coupe remains with Alfa

Romeo and is stored in the museum at Arese. Another Scarabeo survives and is in private hands.

I do not want to leave the Scarabeo without a final suggestion of a road not taken. Like the Montreal, the Scarabeo had a fastback design with a heavy mass of body behind the door jam. If you can imagine a cross between a Montreal and Scarabeo, then refine that vision along the svelte lines of the Canguro and Stradale, you begin to understand a styling direction that Alfa could easily have taken with a mid-engined coupe powered by the 33 engine. Such a car might well have rivaled the 8C2900B in beauty and excitement.

▪ Giulietta Turbodelta

When I visited the Alfa factory for the long-lead introduction of the Milano, I saw racks of turbocharged engines, waiting for installation into production Alfas. The 1983–84 Giulietta 2.0 Turbodelta was also turbocharged, but with an Alfa Avio compressor. It produced 170 hp at 5,000 rpm.

▪ Special Edition Alfas

Several times in this book (and elsewhere) I've tried to define Alfa's mystique. My words have closely paralleled those of other writers about other marques: they all praise a purity of design, joined with a mechanical responsiveness cloaked by a svelte body. The most favored terms (an extension of your will, ergonomic interior, wind-swept design, etc.) are applied equally to Ferraris and Toyotas. The degree of prejudice this fact reflects is forgivable, for all enthusiasts need something to enthuse over.

We still need to extract something from this mire of claque that is unique about Alfa, in order to understand why it ended up a division of Fiat. From 1910 to the early 1970s, Alfa had no marketing department to produce images designed to fire the imagination. The only product was the car. As the owner of three BMW Bavarias and a once-owner of a 328 Rennsport, I do not think BMW is now, nor ever has been, the "ultimate driving machine," except in the imaginations of its ad agency creatives.

In the 1930s, Alfa held unquestioned claim to just that title: it was, incontestably, the ultimate driving machine. Its nearest competitor for that title, Bugatti, was a much more fussy conveyance. An Alfa in the 1930s was fabulously expensive. It was also fabulously successful as a race car and similarly fabulously beautiful, especially when bodied by Zagato, Farina or Touring. In sum, the position Alfa held was based on real accomplishments in engineering, design and competitive performance. This is an honesty which has been completely lost in the modern era of "LeMans" Pontiacs and "Monte Carlo" Chevrolets.

When Alfa entered serial production with the 1900, it inadvertently sold its soul to the sales god. The Giulietta and its descendants were products designed to build sales. As a result, they became progressively less engineering exercises and increasingly marketing exercises. It is in that slow metamorphosis that Alfa lost its way, and finally failed.

In the 1970s and 1980s, the public was not generally aware that Alfa was offering heavy dealer incentives. Lower pricing was unable to move Alfas off the showroom floor. ARI was hard pressed to meet its own optimistic sales projections, and therefore resorted to some definitely American techniques to try to move product.

By and large, the special edition Alfas sold in the United States were the work of Aldo Bozzi. They were his effort to market an increasingly unmarketable product. This fact will hurt the proud owners of Mario Andretti Spiders and Maratonas, but it is the honest truth. If you think this is harsh, I need to add that disdain for these models was more intense within the organization that without. Long-term employees who grew up with the simple elegance of the Giulietta and Giulia were offended by stick-on and bolt-on accessories that tried to obfuscate an obsolete design and sagging performance. The cardinal sin of these cars is that their special additions had nothing to do with Alfa's essential nature. They did not increase performance, and the only comfort they enhanced was the ego of the owner. Design has proved to be a much more durable quality than a few decals.

So, apologies in advance to those few owners who prize their Special Edition Alfas. For these folk, eager to learn exactly how rare their cars are, I need to state that I do not have production figures for these cars. In all probability, more were produced than were sold, and the Alfa executives I've spoken to about the cars have a strong aversion to discussing them.

1976 Alfetta GT Mario Andretti edition

- Striping and decals, including a Mario Andretti signature
- Momo Prototipo steering wheel
- Koni shock absorbers
- Silver paint
- Alloy wheels

1978 Sprint Veloce Mille Miglia

- Lower rear hatch spoiler
- Mille Miglia badges on exterior
- Mille Miglia badge on dash
- Alloy wheels

1978 Spider Niki Lauda

- Blue/white decals similar to Brabham/Alfa Formula 1 graphics
- Rear spoiler
- Autodelta badge at rear

1978 America

This European version was the result of the marketing disaster in the United States of the Alfamatic sedan. Units of the automatic-transaxle version which could not be sold in the United States were returned to Italy and renamed "America." The automatic transaxle, air conditioning and well-appointed interior, as well as

One of many special editions used to add interest to the aging spider was this Niki Lauda Special Edition.

some aura of "American Iron," was enough to make this model surprisingly popular. A short run of new Americas was necessary to fill demand.

1979 Sprint Veloce Velocissima

- Front- and rear-wheel arch flares
- Boundary layer air fence on top of rear hatch
- Quadrifoglio badging
- Black paint
- Alloy wheels

1979 GTV 2.0 Turbodelta

This European variant was carbureted with dual Solex or Dellorto carburetors, pressurized by a KKK turbocharger to give 150 hp at 5500 rpm.

A similar turbocharged engine was used in Formula 3 cars between 1979–92.

1981 GTV Grand Prix

This was a Europe-only version which previewed changes to the GTV appearing in 1983.

- Red paint only
- Redesigned dash, reflecting the instrument layout of the GTV-6.
- Black/grey velvet seat inserts
- Grand Prix plaque on dash
- Front air dam
- Enlarged rear spoiler
- Special wheels and side trim
- Reduction of chrome trim

1994 Commemorative Edition Spider

Refer to the Spider chapter for a full description of this last "special." Badging aside, this is certainly the most comfortable of the later Alfas, achieving some of the "slickness" to which styling-driven cars aspire.

Technically, because of their V-6 engines, the two models following are beyond the scope of this chapter.

On the 1979 Alfetta GT, the buttressed rear spoiler was more a marketing add-on intended to increase desirability than it was a functional tool to add rear downforce.

But because they share the body that originally-housed the twin-cam engine derived from that of the Giulia, these two special GTV-6 models are included.

1982 GTV-6 Balocco

- Special interior with leather-wrapped steering wheel
- Red paint
- Special badging with black striping

1984 GTV-6 Maratona

- Silver paint
- TRX tires on alloy rims
- Wheel flares and rocker molding cladding
- Special steering wheel
- Rear license plate housing

Most of these special additions are largely forgotten. But due to the incredible popularity of the Giulietta, Giulia and later derivatives of these cars, the four-cylinder, twin-cam-engined cars have achieved immortality.

Chapter 7

Alfa's Alloy Four

This book centers on the Giulietta engine and its descendants. Alfa's association with the twin-cam engine since 1926 is an industry legend and one of the important sources of the Alfa mystique. The Giulietta alloy four is a classic engine, and its design dates back to Ernest Henry's seminal 1912 Peugeot Grand Prix car.

The Peugeot engine featured hemispheric combustion chambers with dual overhead camshafts. Although both features had appeared on other engines by themselves, Henry was the first to design an engine which combined them. The 1912 design also featured four valves per cylinder.

In 1914, Merosi tried unsuccessfully to copy Henry's design. Jano adopted it successfully and used it exclusively, as did all of Alfa's designers after him until Hruska sketched the AlfaSud.

In order to appreciate why the twin-cam design is so good, a little information about the internal combustion engine is necessary.

■ Making the Most of a Bad Idea

If the world had never heard of the internal combustion engine and you walked into the United States patent office with one today, you'd be laughed out of the place.

To be brutal, the internal combustion engine is an incredibly feckless design that has been patched up over several generations into a barely workable compromise. First, you need some kind of external power to start the thing. Much of the mass of the engine is taken up with turning unusable up-and-down motion to twisting motion which can be used to turn the wheels. Only one stroke out of four—25 percent—of all that motion is devoted to the actual production of power. And, most of the energy that *is* produced passes out the exhaust pipe.

Combustible mixture gets into the chamber through an exceedingly primitive valve arrangement which blocks the passage significantly when open and is prone to leakage when closed.

The internal combustion engine is most efficient running at a single speed, yet we demand that it produce power over a range of speeds—usually between 1,000 and 6,000 rpm.

Finally, the internal combustion engine may prove to be to our society what lead water pipes were

More than any other feature, the all-alloy twin-cam engine defines the Alfa Romeo Giulia and Giulietta, like this example from a 101-series Giulietta Sprint Speciale.

The 1750 engine (left) is one of the most famous of Jano's twin-cam designs, while the Giulietta twin cam (right) spawned the company's most prolific engine line.

to the Romans: fatally polluting. I could go on, but you get the idea.

Why does such perversity flourish? In part because we have devoted the better part of a century to perfecting it. Having grown up around Detroit, I can testify that an entire culture has been built around the automobile (they feel the same way in parts of Japan, Korea—and northern Italy). The internal combustion engine has probably been refined more than any artifact man has ever conceived. Once set on the course, we have been unable, largely, to take a wiser path.

Such wiser paths certainly exist, as Professor Wankel has demonstrated. The Sterling engine is another path. And, had we spent only a fraction of our efforts perfecting ways of storing electricity, we could all be humming along quietly in our electrics. Finally, if we could discover a way (other than blowing things up) of harnessing the energy suggested by $e=mc^2$, no one would ever have to worry about power sources again.

Of course, many of the faults of the internal combustion engine can be directly traced to its steam-engine parentage. In order to harness steam, its energy (expressed as a need to expand) was used to force a piston down a cylinder and then, by sliding a valve which redirected the steam, to force the piston back up again. A rod connected to the piston turned a wheel, in the case of a locomotive, or a crank in the case of a stationary engine. The crank is a primitive, massive

device that turns reciprocating motion into rotary motion.

Sterling and steam engines use external combustion: the energy source is located outside the engine. The internal combustion engine puts the fire inside the cylinder so you don't need anyone to shovel coal all the time. Instead, you just squirt some "liquid coal" in the cylinder, then light it off.

Well, not exactly. You need some path into the cylinder and then some way of closing it off—that job is handled by the valves, which are a functional analog of the steam engine's sliding valve. You need a way of squirting the fuel so it will burn: that's the carburetor's job (or, nowadays, fuel injection). And, lighting everything off is the job of the ignition system, which uses a low-voltage power source working through a coil to throw a spark across a gap at just the right time. ("Honestly, Mr. Otto, we've seen some crackpot ideas here at the patent office, but….")

My derision of the genre has a serious point. The internal combustion engine is a design which needs all the refinement it can get. And, over the 100 years it's been with us, it's had a lot of refinement. The net result is that, while the concept is straightforward, very little of its execution is simple.

▪ Twin-Cam Advantages

The main purpose of the twin-cam design is to improve the engine's efficiency by providing the lowest possible restriction to gasses flowing through it. While the dynamics of gas flow were not fully understood in the early Twentieth Century, it was clear that by placing the valves at an angle to each other, you could eliminate turns in the intake path and improve the engine's ability to breathe. That is, you improve the engine's volumetric efficiency.

The design offers other advantages. A straight-through path reduces the opportunity for atomized fuel to pool out into unburnable puddles in the corners of a curved path. Moreover, whenever the path of the gas is obstructed by a turn, the gasses compress against the wall, then bounce back, creating back pressures which reduce volumetric efficiency.

Most twin-cam engines have their valves set at almost a right angle to each other. This allows a hemispheric combustion chamber and a centrally located spark plug, the best possible configuration for completely burning the gasses in the combustion chamber in a smooth flame front which propagates from the central spark plug outward to the circumference of the cylinder.

▪ Fading Interest

The engines that power our cars are all exceedingly subtle designs which develop gobs of reliable power. Adjustments to fuel and ignition, for instance, are now sciences that deal with micro-values to extract the maximum possible performance. With the introduction of emission-limited and computer-controlled engines, it's been estimated that the average (successful) mechanic requires the equivalent of at least two years' college just to understand exactly what he's doing.

In contrast, the modern owner has been largely isolated from design concerns by no-maintenance cars. Components requiring regular maintenance have disappeared, along with interest in their design. Points, condensers, distributor caps and rotors—even valve adjustments— were routine maintenance for the Giulietta and usually performed by the owner. The same held true for the suspension, which required regular doses of grease. The timing chain needed regular tensioning, and that was also a good time to check valve clearances.

Thanks to electronic engine controls, rubber-bushed suspensions and inextensible fabric timing belts, the first "major" maintenance interval for modern cars is 60,000 miles. Further, emission regulations have frustrated traditional hot-rod modifications to the engine, so the average "modified" car of 1997 has a lowered suspension, special wheels, stick-on "aerodynamic enhancements," a custom interior and paint job, but an absolutely box-stock drivetrain. A growing number of owners have no idea of how many cylinders their car has, let alone the shape of its combustion chambers.

Since the modern automobile encourages the owner to ignore its mechanical nature, the excellence of Alfa's alloy four is likely to be lost on modern Alfisti. In lieu of a hands-on familiarity with things such as thrust washers and valve keepers, I can offer some background information which may help explain what a neat little package it really is, and why Alfa's alloy four is such a benchmark of automotive design.

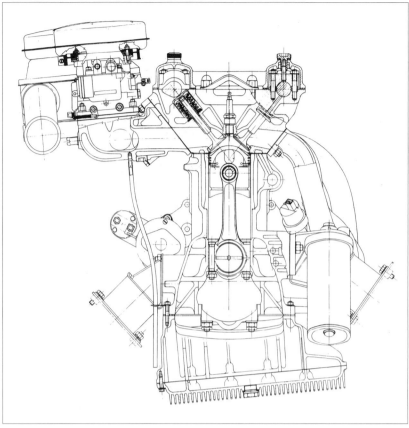

In cross-section, the Giulia engine retains the basic twin-cam design first penned by Ernest Henry for the 1912 Peugeot Grand Prix power plant.

Some inside-the-engine experience—as well as the mechanic's same two years of college—seems a prerequisite to appreciate Alfa's alloy four. Hopefully, a careful reading of this chapter will substitute.

▪ Four-Cylinder Alloy Engine Design

In 1968 Luigi Fusi showed me a prototype Giulietta engine that displaced 750 cc. That engine was clearly a prototype, and lacked a boss for the chain tensioner. Since the earliest Giuliettas have a 750-series designation, it seems clear that the Giulietta was originally intended to have a displacement of 750 cc.

This 750cc engine has become a mystery, for when I revisited the factory in 1985, no one remembered it, and I was told that no such engine ever existed. The factory archives contain a photograph of the engine Fusi showed me. But the photograph is labeled as an 1100cc prototype. There certainly was an 1100cc prototype, but I maintain that the first prototype displaced 750 cc. The only person I have found to reassure me of the existence of the smaller engine served as the chief engineer for Alfa Romeo in the United States.

Dating from 1955, this competition protoype bodied by Bertone evoked the Abarth 207A clothed by Boano.

The significance of the small displacement is that there was a 750cc supercharged formula class in the early 1950s, so the small prototype engine suggests that there was an Alfa racing endeavor which never quite made it beyond the planning stage. Alfa's plans for a 750cc supercharged car have never been documented, and no mention of it occurs in the literature, with the possible exception of the 750 Competition Prototype car of 1955. This car was originally designed along the same lines as the Abarth 207A with Boano body (including external Abarth exhaust) but was fitted with a 1488cc engine with a bore x stroke of 77 x 82, presumably Giulietta-based, but with the same stroke as the Giulia.

Alfa could have planned to market a normally aspirated version of the racing 750cc engine, with slightly larger displacement, in a passenger car. Thus, the real source of the Giulietta series may have been to create a normally aspirated road-going version of a supercharged formula car. Shades of Jano's P2 and its relationship to the 6C1750.

The Block

The Giulietta engine is cast aluminum with wet-sleeve cast-iron cylinders. I need to distinguish this design from those engines that use dry iron liners that are cast or pressed into the alloy block. Dry liners are not washed directly by coolant, and heat must dissipate from the

liner, past any gap between it and the surrounding alloy and then to the coolant. With cast- or pressed-in liners, heat dissipation suffers.

In contrast, the Giulietta has free-standing cylinders which are bathed directly by coolant, and so the sleeves are "wet."

The advantage of the Alfa wet-sleeve design is not only that it gives superior cylinder cooling, but also easy cylinder replacement when a rebuild is necessary. The Alfa engine is infinitely rebuildable because all its most significant wearing surfaces, including the cylinders and bearings, are replaceable. In contrast, dry cylinders can only be resurfaced once or twice before the block is scrap.

The reason manufacturers do not flock to the wet-sleeve engine is that the design requires superb engineering to maintain the seals at both the top and bottom of the free-standing cylinder. There are inherent dangers in the design when the block and head are aluminum, and the cylinders steel, because the expansion rates of the two metals differ. As things heat up and cool off, the dimensions of the major components change significantly, and at different rates. During expansion and contraction, only a very slight amount of movement of the cylinder against the head gasket will cause the gasket seal to fail. Finally, there is a tendency for the dissimilar metals to cause electrolysis, which corrodes the softer aluminum.

It is a measure of Alfa's engineering excellence that all the potential problems associated with the wet-sleeve design are unknown to Giulietta and Giulia owners. The engines are remarkably reliable and able to absorb punishment which would destroy less sophisticated designs. The larger-displacement 2.0-liter engine suggests that the limit of the design has been reached at 500 cc per cylinder, for failed head gaskets are more common on that model than in the cases of the earlier, smaller-displacement versions of the design.

Many thoughtful details contribute to the engine's durability. Five main bearings support the crankshaft, while most four-cylinder engines of the era had only three. Another contributor to long engine life is the large finned oil sump which helps reduce heat and maintains proper oil viscosity. Other small details contribute to the engine's robustness. For example, the coolant flows first to the metal around the exhaust valve seats, so the coolest water available is applied to the hottest part of the engine. All Giulietta spiders and coupes were equipped with an oil temperature gauge, which served as the best indicator of when the engine was ready for you to put your foot in it.

There were some less-than-durable components. The early Giulietta crankshaft and generator pulleys were aluminum, and given to rapid wear. The generator was originally bolted to a single boss on the timing cover, and when the generator mounting bolt loosened, as it always did, the aluminum mounting boss wore very quickly. The typical repair was to press in a steel sleeve for the mounting bolt. The Veloce added a rear bracket for the Marelli generator that helped secure it.

The block is divided halfway down by a sturdy partition that is holed to accept the wet cylinder sleeves. Beneath the partition is a network of braces that help contain the stresses of the crankshaft and improve its load-bearing capabilities. It is an interesting study in the use of curved surfaces to improve rigidity. There are very few truly plane surfaces in spite of the fact that the design could be very slab-sided, indeed.

Most blocks split the main bearing on the same plane as the gasketed surface where the block and pan

The top of the Giulietta block shows the four cylinders, which are washed directly by the coolant, thus dissipating heat.

2.0-liter engines like the one in this 1991 Spider experienced more head gasket failures than the smaller versions of the venerable twin cam, suggesting that the engine had reached its upper limit of displacement.

mate. This is an economical arrangement because a single pass of a mill will finish a lot of surfaces that need machining. The drawback of this arrangement is that it puts the weakest joint of the block in the plane (the main bearing cap) of highest stress, and the bearing support by the block is limited to a radius of 180°.

The Giulietta takes the more-costly approach of putting the main bearing cap split deep into the block so that ample supporting webs can be cast into the block. The result is that the periphery of the block forms a

The light alloy pistons use a pair of compression rings and a single one for oil control.

The short and sturdy Alfa rod uses remarkably large big end and small end bearings for its size.

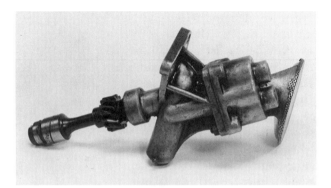

The oil pump pickup (top) reaches into the deep finned alloy sump (bottom).

sturdy "skirt" around the crankshaft and the bearing support radius exceeds 200 degrees.

The cylinders are a slip-fit into the bores of the block and are sealed at their bottom by a slender rubber band. It has always amazed me how trouble-free this seal is. I have never had an Alfa which leaked coolant into the sump, and I have heard of only one in my 30 years of Alfa experience.

Alfa pistons are made of a light alloy and have two compression rings and one oil control ring. For racing, Alfa supplies a higher-compression piston with thinner compression rings. Under normal use, the stock pistons are more than adequate and will safely withstand higher

compression ratios obtained by milling the head. The piston pins are free-floating and are secured with small circlips on either end. The pin is splash-lubricated by oil in the sump.

The rods are short and very sturdy. Giulietta rods have a slight offset between the center plane of the rod and the big-end bearing. During reassembly of an engine, it's important to observe the offset. The rod is properly assembled if it is centered on the piston pin with equal gaps between the rod little end and the piston pin boss.

The oil pump pickup almost touches the bottom of the pan, reaching down into the pool of oil to pick up the layer closest to the cool metal of the deeply finned aluminum sump. Put another way, the oil pump pickup is sized to the sump. Since there are several sumps available for the Giulia engine, it's important to verify that you have the right combination if you're assembling an engine from pieces. The sumps of 101-series cars are narrow and deep; 105-series cars typically have the "hammerhead" sump with its large, baffled cooling surface.

Drilled passages in the block carry oil to the crankshaft's main bearings. Drilled passages in the crank carry the pressurized oil to the rod bearing journals.

Crankshaft

In the crankshaft, the drilled oil passages are sealed using soft-metal plugs. On the Giulietta, there never has been a tendency for the plugs to loosen; the plugs on later Alfas will fall out and cause a drop in oil pressure.

Pressurized oil is supplied by the oil pump, which is driven by a gear near the front of the crankshaft. The driven gear is on a shaft which also extends up and ends in a cup which is used to drive the distributor. The oil pump itself consists of a pair of gears which supply oil at a nominal 55 psi to the bearings.

The Alfa crank is legendary for its strength, in part because there are five main bearings (a bearing between each rod). Crankshaft failure is virtually unknown, even in engines which have raced long distances.

There is one way the crank will fail, and that is when there is a loss of lubrication resulting from oil which has been emulsified with coolant. This failure is caused when the head gasket O-rings fail, and coolant is forced into the oil passages after a hot engine is shut down. Potentially catastrophic, this failure can be identified early enough to avoid trouble simply by watching for a light-brown sludge on both the dipstick and the underside of the radiator cap.

At the front of the crankshaft, adjacent to the gear which drives the oil pump and distributor, is a sprocket which drives a short chain to the intermediate or half-speed sprocket. The half-speed sprocket drives a longer chain to the cams and is held in tension by a spring-loaded idler located in the head.

This idler should be tensioned occasionally. The official procedure is to rotate the engine backwards at least one revolution (put the car in second and push it backward), then loosen the tensioner lock bolt on the head and retighten it. I have never trusted the factory procedure because you have no assurance that the few turns you give the locknut in fact frees the tensioner so its spring will work against the chain. I prefer instead to remove the cam cover and use a large screwdriver to wedge the idler sprocket to its proper tension. Then, when I retighten the lock bolt, I can also test that the sprocket is locked in place without having to put blind force on the locknut. A warning: if someone does put too much force on the locknut, the tensioner will be wedged open and not release for adjustment. You can't check for this condition unless the cam cover is removed.

While contemporary engines, like that used in the MGA or Triumph TR2 used three main bearings, the Giulietta crank was amply supported by five main bearings.

The cam-drive chains are housed in an aluminum timing cover that bolts up to the front of the block. The water pump and tachometer drive are mounted to the front of this cover. Occasionally, one would like to remove this piece to ease access to the cam-drive chain or to replace the front oil seal around the crankshaft. In theory, by removing the pan and the head, it is possible to then remove the front timing cover. In practice, it is not a practical operation. Any repair requiring the removal of the cover should be made with the engine removed from the car.

The Head

I don't mean to slight the remainder of the Alfa engine. It is, after all, a five-main-bearing, wet-sleeved design which uses lightweight castings extensively, but it's the head design which has most distinguished Alfa over the years. So, that's where we should start in discussing the Giulietta engine.

The Giulietta head is a V-shaped aluminum casting which carries the combustion chamber, camshafts and valves. More happens in the head than in any other part of the engine. Its most important function is to control the passage of gasses through the engine. It does this using valves, which are opened at the appropriate time by a pair of chain-driven camshafts.

The combustion chamber is a hemispheric depression in the head where the two valves and a spark plug are located. The spark plug is placed virtually dead-center in the chamber's depression so that the flame front of the burning fuel can expand uniformly

This view from the intake side of the alloy cylinder head shows the ports, as well as the deep dish of the hemispheric combustion chambers, complete with the centrally positioned opening for the spark plug.

The intake valve (standing) of the all-aluminum engine can be differentiated from the exhaust valve (lying down) by its larger head diameter.

in all directions over the top of the piston. Because flame propagation is so uniform in the Alfa head, the tendency toward power-robbing spark knock (uneven burning of the gasses) is significantly reduced.

Incidentally, the Alfa combustion chamber is designed for power, but is exceptionally dirty as far as emissions are concerned. Its shape means that only the inertia of the incoming and exhausting gasses provide turbulence to maintain even atomization of fuel during the compression stroke. On modern emission-controlled engines, the combustion chamber is usually a wedge that "squishes" the charge around the chamber as the piston rises to compress it. The area exposed to combustion by the flat-topped piston and wedge-shaped combustion chamber is much smaller than the hemispheric configuration. It therefore produces fewer emissions. Fortunately, emissions control is not a matter of importance to the Giulietta (at this time, that is: retroactive emissions laws are not impossible). Rather than change the shape of the combustion chamber from the classic hemisphere, in 1969 Alfa simply modified its fuel system for the improved accuracy of fuel injection.

The head is sealed to the block with a metal-clad gasket. Some aftermarket gaskets use a fabric sandwiched between sheet copper, but the stock Alfa item is a fabric gasket with steel reinforcements around each combustion chamber opening.

The head gasket also seals the six oil passages for camshaft lubrication. The actual seal is provided by small O-rings that are placed in head-gasket openings during rebuild. These O-rings have proved to be the single most troublesome feature of the Alfa engine (including the V-6). Particularly on later Alfas, head-gasket sealing has become a major problem. Generally, the Giulietta does not share Alfa's legendary head-gasket sealing problems. I have had a single Giulia head-gasket failure, and that was a compression, rather than an oil leak.

Valves

The valve is basically a disc with a stem attached. When closed, the disc of the valve is seated against a steel insert in the top of the head's combustion chamber. When opened by the camshaft, the valve is held about nine mm off its seat so the intake or exhaust gasses can pass. Because the valve provides really a very narrow opening for high-speed gasses, a lot of fluid-dynamic science has been applied to the exact shape of the valve and its seat. Current practice uses three different planes ground around the circumference of the valve's head, only one of which matches the angle at which the seat is ground. The shape of the slope as the valve disc joins its stem is another aerodynamically important feature, though, in practice, much less important than the surfaces of the valve seat.

The valves do not work directly in the bare aluminum of the head. Instead, bronze valve guides are pressed into the head to assure a long-lasting surface for the valve stem to bear against. A very small amount of oil is permitted to leak onto the valve stem for lubrication. This oil is overflow from the camshaft bearings, which is caught in galleries near the camshaft follower cups for camshaft lobe lubrication.

Each valve is held in a normally closed position by a pair of springs. The small clearance between the valve and the camshaft base is adjusted using shims that are fitted over the tip of the valve's stem.

Camshafts

The camshafts are driven by a chain from the crankshaft and run in bearing surfaces machined into the aluminum of the head. What this means is that there are no camshaft bearing inserts as there are crankshaft bearing inserts. The load carried by the cam bearings is quite low, and their large surface provides ample capacity. The lobes of the camshafts bear on the stems of the valves, so that the valves are opened as the camshaft lobe rotates.

In stock Giulietta engines, the intake and exhaust camshafts have the same profile and so are interchangeable. This is not true of aftermarket high-

performance camshafts, so it is a good idea to keep track of which cam goes where if they're removed from the engine. The rotating camshaft has four lobes that open the intake or exhaust valves to admit or exhaust gas from the engine.

The profile of the cam has undergone much development over the life of the internal combustion engine and it is the most exotic part of an engine. Engine performance is affected not only by how wide the camshaft opens a valve, but also by how long the valve remains open.

In general terms, you can tell how "hot" a cam is by looking at it. If it is rounded, with a very gradual curvature toward the tip of the lobe, it is a mild camshaft which will produce low-end torque and not much high-speed power. If the lobe peaks sharply, the camshaft gives higher performance.

The intake and exhaust camshafts can be timed individually to the exact needs of the engine. This is a unique advantage of the twin-camshaft design which allows a great deal of experimentation to extract the maximum possible horsepower or torque from an individual engine. It does not amount to letting you grind your own, but adjustable cam timing comes very close to that.

Camshaft timing adjustment is provided by two mating discs on the sprocket of the camshaft that are held in place by a small through-bolt. One disc has one more hole than the other so that, as they rotate in relation to each other, only one hole can line up between the two. The advantage of this vernier arrangement is that it permits changing camshaft timing in 1.5-degree increments.

The clearance between the camshafts and the valve follower cups should be checked occasionally. The proper distance for the Giulietta is 0.018 to 0.019 inches for the intake and 0.020 inches for the exhaust. In practice, you can go slightly closer to get more overlap and a wider opening. Under any circumstances, 0.012 inches is the minimum clearance for any valve. The exhaust valve is much more critical in needing a wide clearance than the intake valve.

Always record valve clearances for reference. Over time, a valve clearance that is gradually closing up indicates a stretching valve head or a receding seat. Replace the particular valve and have the remaining valves inspected closely by a professional.

With the cam covers and timing chain removed, the pair of camshafts and the gears for driving them are clearly visible.

Valve Adjustment

Twin cams may be the best of all possible worlds for free-breathing, high-revving engines, but the compact design means that valve adjustment is tougher than twiddling the adjusting screws of a rocker-arm engine.

All modern four-cylinder Alfas use small "caps" which fit over the top of the valve stem and under the cam follower. Because the Alfa's spacers are located beneath the cam followers, its camshafts have to be removed to adjust the valves. While removing the cams is easy enough, putting them back, properly timed, can sometimes be a challenge. For this reason, an Alfa valve adjustment isn't something you should try on a whim. The only special tools needed are a feeler gauge set and micrometer—either SAE or metric. And, a source for adjusting caps, such as an Alfa dealer or an independent shop is also required. Valves are always adjusted on a dead-cold engine, so it is best to let it sit overnight.

The fronts of Alfa engines can get wonderfully grungy. Before you begin to dirty your hands, clean off the timing pointer and the crank pulley well enough to be able to see the timing marks stamped on it (Giuliettas have the timing marks on the flywheel, so they're always clean). You'll see several marks, but the one you want is stamped P, the Italian equivalent of Top Dead Center (TDC).

The complete oil filter assembly unbolts from the engine block. The paper filter element can then be replaced without spilling the dirty oil from the filter canister.

Cooling

In order to overcome the heat of the exhaust gasses which pass through it, the head is the first part of the engine to receive cooled water from the radiator. From the water pump (located just below the head on the front timing cover casting), cool water flows alongside the engine through a tube cast into the block. It is directed through four oval-shaped holes in the head toward the exhaust valve seats. Thus, the very hottest area of the engine gets the coolest water. After circulating the head, the water passes through the thermostatic housing on the intake manifold and returns to the radiator.

Oil Filter

The Giulietta's oil filter element is changed from beneath by removing a single (long) mounting bolt. The Giulia oil filter cartridge is especially difficult to change because of the hammerhead sump. Adapters are available to fit modern spin-on filters, but these detract from originality. When you change a stock Giulia oil filter, remove the entire housing where it attaches to the block (two nuts) and then dismantle the filter on the bench. Verify that the paper gasket is usable before you reassemble the unit to the block.

Intake Systems

Alfa has pretty well stuck with three basic fuel systems. For its sedans, a downdraft Solex carburetor is common. On the Giuliettas, this Solex was a single-throat unit; on the Giulias it was a dual-throat unit. The same system was used on Giulietta and Giulia Spiders and Coupes up to the Giulia Sprint GT which had two twin-throat Webers. The Weber setup (sometimes, Solex or Dellorto

Model	Fuel System
Giulietta Berlina	Solex 32BIC single downdraft
Giulietta Sprint, Spider	Solex 35APAIG dual downdraft
Giulietta Veloce	Weber 40DCO or 40DCO3 two dual side-draft
Giulia	Solex C32PAIA-7 dual downdraft
Giulia Veloce	Weber 40DCOE32 two dual side-draft
1750	Weber, Solex, Dellorto two dual side-draft (Europe) or SPICA (United States)
2.0-liter	Weber, Solex, Dellorto two dual side-draft (Europe) or SPICA (United States). Beginning in 1982, Bosch L-Jetronic

The Giulietta was introduced with a single downdraft Solex carburetor as seen on this early Giulietta TI.

Beginning in 1971 all Alfas bound for the United States were fitted with the SPICA fuel injection, as seen on this 1976 Alfetta GT.

Veloce versions of the Giulietta and Giulia, as well as SZ, SS, Duetto and Giulia Super models, were fitted with dual Webers, which are partially hidden beneath the neat alloy intake plenum.

The Normale exhaust manifold consisted of two pieces that paired cylinders 1 with 4 and 2 with 3.

units were substituted) was continued on the continent while SPICA fuel injection was used in the United States until 1982, when Bosch L-Jetronic was introduced.

Exhaust Systems

The Giulietta cars had a four-into-one exhaust manifold which swept back toward the bulkhead, while the Giulietta Veloce exhaust systems were virtual Abarth parts. None of the cars had baffled mufflers, but relied on careful tuning of the straight-through mufflers to manage the exhaust note.

The Veloce had mandrel-bent headers and separate exhaust paths for pairs 1/4 and 2/3. The Abarth mufflers

had dual inlets and exhausts. The difference between the Giulietta and later exhaust manifolds is the angle of the flange for the head pipe (no great challenge if you're fabricating something). If you're fabricating an exhaust system for a Giulietta, you should use only straight-through glasspack and resonator units for silencing.

The stock Giulia exhaust system is a pair of cast headers with a 1/4-2/3 design that was also carried on to the later 1750 and 2.0-liter engines. With the increasing requirements of emissions controls, the configuration of the exhaust manifold changed: in 1976 to permit air injection, and in 1981 to accommodate exhaust gas recirculation (EGR).

The exhaust manifold for the 1975–80 cars is very prone to cracking between cylinders 3 and 4.

▪ Electrical System

Ignition

The Giulietta ignition system is conventional, with a coil and distributor supplied by either Lucas or Magnetti Marelli (Veloce). Later systems, beginning with the Giulia, were Bosch, which were generally more robust. The distributor has an automatic advance provided by weights and springs.

In spite of the fact that aftermarket ignition systems are attractive, the stock Alfa ignition system is perfectly adequate for the Giulietta. On these cars, hard starting in extreme cold is more likely due to a poor ground connection for the battery (or a discharged battery) than an inadequate coil or distributor.

Most owners will want to adjust the gap of the distributor points. This is a very straightforward procedure, eased somewhat if the distributor rotor is removed (on some models it's screwed on, so take care not to drop the screw into the distributor). The distributor cap is held on by two blue-steel clips which are pried free with a screwdriver.

First, with the engine rotated so the points are closed, run an ignition file between the points (ignition off!) to clean them of deposits. Rotate the engine until the points are fully open and use a feeler gauge to measure the gap between the points. It should be between 0.014 and 0.016 inches.

If the gap is not within the specified tolerances, look closely at the points and identify the adjusting mechanism and locking screw. Loosen the screw slightly and move the stationary point to achieve the proper clearance.

Be careful in returning the rotor and cap to their original positions. Both are one-way fits and are not easily misinstalled. The most common error is to cock the distributor cap at an angle. If the cap is not seated correctly the rotor will break the cap when the engine is started.

Timing

Alfa's timing marks (which appear in Italian) are:

Model	Top Dead Center (TDC)	Fixed Advance	Maximum Advance	Injection Timing
Giulietta	P.M.S.	A.F.	A.M.	
All Others	P	F	M	I

Top Dead Center (TDC) is the point at which pistons 1 and 4 are at the top of their stroke. This is the reference point for timing the camshafts. Note that the TDC mark also comes up when pistons 2 and 3 are at the top of

Giuliettas used distributors from either Lucas or Magnetti Marelli (shown), while those used in Giulias were supplied by Bosch.

their stroke. To resolve the correct TDC setting, remove number 1 spark plug and look into the cylinder with the aid of a flashlight. You should see the piston very near to the bottom of the spark plug threads. Probe carefully with a screwdriver if you cannot see the piston clearly.

Fixed Advance is the point at which the points open, breaking the circuit to the coil and firing it. You can time an Alfa engine statically (with the engine not running) by attaching a twelve-volt lamp between the distributor terminal on the coil and a ground connection. First, draw a mark somewhere on the distributor body so you have some point of original reference. Loosen the distributor clamping nut at the base of the distributor just enough that you can rotate the complete distributor body by grasping its cap. With the engine on the fixed advance mark, turn on the ignition (don't start the car) and rotate the distributor very slightly in one direction. You should reach a point that the light turns on or off. If you don't after about a quarter-inch of rotation, turn the distributor in the opposite direction, using the mark you made on its body to keep track of where you started. Stop as soon as the lamp changes state (from on to off or off to on). Then, move the distributor back and forth in increasingly smaller increments until you reach the point that any motion at all causes the light to change state. Turn off the ignition and tighten the distributor clamping nut.

Maximum Advance is the preferred timing mark for Giulietta and Giulia engines, which are timed dynamically at 5,000 rpm. This assures that the timing is correct at maximum advance. You need a strobe timing light to do this: cheap neon lights will not work. The procedure is extremely dangerous, because it involves rotating the distributor (which is on the passenger's side of the engine) while looking at the timing marks (which are on the driver's side of the engine)—and with the engine turning at 5,000 rpm. This is a job for two people, one of whom should watch the mark with the strobe and have a loud, clear voice.

Injection Timing is set statically with the crankshaft approaching TDC on number 1 cylinder. This is the condition where the exhaust valve on cylinder number 1 is closing and the intake valve is about to open (overlap). Like ignition timing, you can get this 180° off, but injection timing is much less critical and the engine will still run (somewhat underpowered) if you are 180° off.

I've found that, since the injection pump toothed belt is inextensible, it's easiest to remove the crankshaft pulley after it has been brought to the I mark before TDC. Loop the belt onto the crankshaft sprocket, then work the belt over the sprocket on the pump pulley as you slide the crank pulley back onto the crankshaft. Double check that the marks on both the crank pulley and the injection pump still align, then replace the crank bolt and rebend the locking tab to secure it.

Generator/Alternator

The 750 Giuliettas had Lucas electrics; Veloces had Magnetti Marelli and Giulias (and everything since) had Bosch. Owners with Lucas electrics longed for Marelli pieces, and owners of either wanted Bosch. A universal truth lurks here: no matter which system is fitted to your Alfa, you'll yearn for another. By and large, the order of reliability is Bosch as the most reliable and Marelli as the least reliable.

The most significant problem with the generator on the Giulietta was that it was not mounted securely enough to the engine. The back of the Lucas generator was cantilevered off the mounting bolt. As the bolt loosened, it wore an oval hole in the alloy timing cover. The resulting motion hastened the failure of the mounting and required a new front timing cover to correct. Most early timing covers have since had a steel insert fitted, but generator mounting is something every early Giulietta owner should check regularly. This problem was solved in later models by the addition of a rear generator mount.

It's permissible to adjust the Lucas voltage regulator on Giuliettas. You'll need a shop manual, an ammeter and a voltmeter to do so. For Marelli and Bosch systems,

buy another regulator. Like the ignition system, the charging system on all Alfas is adequate for all but the most extremes of hot and cold. That presumes that you have a good battery—cheap ones fail faster than more expensive ones, typically.

You can fit an alternator to a Giulietta. Doing so, however, spoils its originality in a very visible way. Giuliettas are valuable enough now that this alteration is not wise.

Starter

Very early Giuliettas had a mechanical starter cable. A key-switch was introduced in 1957.

The Marelli starter on the Giulietta Veloce requires special care. When starting a Veloce, you must not hold the starter engaged for an extended period: get it going with a series of five-second bursts of the starter. If the starter is engaged for too long, the solder on the commutator connections will melt.

■ Engine Variations

750-Series

The original production version of Alfa's twin-cam engine appeared in 1954 and was phased out during 1959. It is identified by an engine number beginning with 1315 and a body numbered 14xx. The 750-series designation is stamped on the bulkhead plaque.

A 750-series engine has several identifying characteristics:

- A fuel pump mounted on the front of the head, and driven off the camshaft. In the case of the Veloce engine, the fuel pump opening is blanked off with a trapezoidal plate.
- Stamped-steel sump (Veloce has an alloy sump)
- 8mm valve stems and adjusting caps
- 57mm crankshaft journal diameter.

Compared to the later 101-series engine, the 750 is slightly more fragile because it has smaller-diameter bearing journals and lower oil-pump capacity.

750 Veloce

Over the years, a lot of Giuliettas became Veloces with the addition of two DCOE Weber carburetors. Real Veloces offered much more than that:

- An 8,000 rpm tach
- Longer-duration, higher-lift camshaft
- A specially prepared, milled head (for higher compression)
- Borgo forged (higher compression) pistons

The twin Webers and canted engine are obvious cues that a Veloce engine lurks under the hood of this 750 Spider.

- Lightweight Marelli starter
- Marelli distributor
- Stronger rods that have been shot-peened and polished
- Shims to increase valve spring pressure
- Alloy sump with surge baffles and windage tray
- Electric fuel pump located near the rear axle

To permit the side-draft Webers to clear the inner fender panel, the Veloce engine was canted slightly to the driver's side by fitting a longer motor mount. The earliest Sprint Veloce cars had aluminum panels and sliding-plexiglas door windows.

The Veloce engine was literally a factory hotrod. It redlined at about 7,000 rpm (factory specs were for 6,000 or 6,500 rpm depending on which book you read). It was not the most friendly car Alfa ever produced. You got underway with the engine at about 3,000 rpm (to keep it from stalling) and in very cold weather, you subtracted the ambient temperature from 100 to get the number of times you had to work the accelerator pump before trying to start it.

101 Series

In 1959 Alfas began appearing—unannounced—with new gearboxes and engines which were slightly different.

The most noticeable change was that the shift lever of the gearbox was made to telescope slightly when you pressed down on it to overcome the reverse gear lock-out. Moreover, on closer inspection under the car, it was clear that the transmission case was completely new, since it split longitudinally into two halves. The new four-speed Giulietta case was almost identical to the five-speed unit fitted to Alfa's 2000 range of cars introduced in 1958. It differed only in that the tail casting on the 2000 was longer to accommodate a fifth

gear. Quite a few Giuliettas were converted to five-speeds using the 2000 gearbox, although the conversion was fairly expensive.

The significant differences in the new engines were almost all dimensional. While the bore and stroke remained the same, the newer engines had larger main-bearing and valve stem-diameters. The camshaft lobe width was also increased to improve load-bearing capacity. A steel crank pulley was fitted and the generator mount strengthened. In addition, the fuel pump was relocated low on the engine where it could be driven off a cam on the shaft which drove both the distributor and the oil pump.

These new parts carried numbers beginning with 101, and the cars which use them are referred to as 101-type Alfas. According to factory records, the 101 designation had been introduced with the Giulietta Sprint Speciale in 1957. Practically, it became the standard designation of all Giuliettas in 1960.

Comparing the 750- and 101-series engines:

750	101
Aluminum generator and crank pulleys (probably replaced with steel pulleys by now)	Steel pulleys
Single generator mounting bolt through the front timing cover	Generator mounting bolt through the front timing cover and rear generator mount
Fuel pump mounted on the front of the head, and driven off the exhaust camshaft (Normale)	Fuel pump mounted on the front cover
In the case of the Veloce engine, the fuel pump opening is blanked off with a trapezoidal plate.	Fuel pump mounted on the intake side of the front timing cover
One-piece stamped-steel sump (Normale)	
(Veloce has an alloy sump)	Three-piece steel sump
8mm valve stems and adjusting caps	9mm valve stems and adjusting caps
57mm crankshaft journal diameter	59.9mm crankshaft journal diameter

At the time, the purpose of these increases was not fully appreciated. In fact, what had happened was that Alfa Romeo had created the basis for the Giulia engine.

101 Veloce

The performance figures for the Veloce were unchanged from the 750-series engine, in spite of the 101's more robust design.

105/116 Series

When the 105-series 1570 cc engine appeared in 1962, it produced 92 hp with a single Solex carburetor, compared to the 90 hp of the Giulietta Veloce. The new engine was much more tractable than a Giulietta Veloce. Aside from differences in bore and stroke, there were virtually no changes to the configuration of the engine. Perhaps the most notable change was an indentation in the camshaft cover to help clear the intake hose between the air cleaner and intake plenum on the Weber-carbureted Giulias.

Giulia Veloce

Alfa has always been sensitive to maintaining its performance image, and everyone hoped that it would only be a matter of time before a Weber-carbureted version of the Giulia spider would appear.

The wait was not long. A 105 Veloce engine did appear in 1963—in the Bertone-bodied Sprint Speciale—and it showed up the following year in the Spider, which became the Giulia Spider Veloce.

Veloce means fast, and the Giulia Spider Veloce was truly fast. Indeed, its top speed was five km/h greater than the legendary 8C2900B. Though Alfa has since applied the term Veloce to many of its models, the Giulia Spider Veloce remains, for the enthusiast, the last true Veloce.

In its test of September 1965 *Road & Track* compared the new Giulia Spider Veloce to both the Giulia Spider and the Giulietta Super Spider, the Weber-carbureted version. The test concentrated on the changes which produced the Veloce version. "The most obvious of these differences is additional power: the

There were few visible indicators to distinguish this 101 Veloce engine from its predecessors.

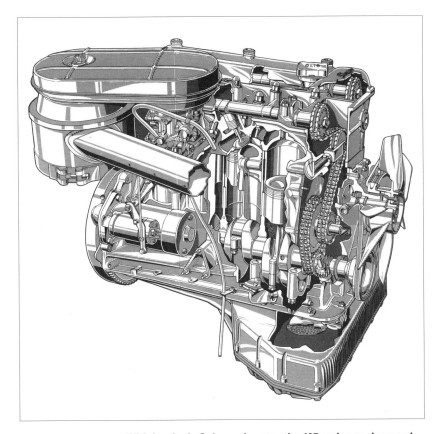

With its single Solex carburetor, the 105-series engine used in the Giulia made more horsepower than the Giulietta Veloce, and was much easier to drive at low rpms. This factory cutaway drawing shows the engine's key elements.

The 105 Veloce engine first appeared in the engine bay of the Giulia Sprint Speciale.

1750 and 2.0-Liter

If at any time, you asked an Alfa executive whether or not a larger displacement were envisioned, the answer would always be "no." Such is the mantra of the marketing types: I was assured at one time that there was no room in the V-6 engine design for three liters!

Without changing the stroke of the crankshaft, Alfa subsequently increased the displacement of its four-cylinder engine to 1779 and then 1962 cc. In order to achieve the larger displacement, the bore centers of the engine were modified, It would be nice to plot the horsepower increase from an original 1290 cc to 1962 cc, but unfortunately emissions regulations interfere with strict comparisons. For what it's worth:

1300 Super Spider's 103 bhp (risen to 108 in the 1570cc 1600) has reached 129 in the 1600 Veloce, bestowing a comparable and thoroughly welcome rise in torque from 86.8 @ 4,500 rpm to an estimated 105 @ 4,000.

"Owners of 1300s have all experienced stop-light-despair syndrome as they delicately fiddled their little jewels off the line, trying to maintain sporting aplomb as the hulks roared by. The 1600 Veloce has no such problem: its Weber-fed engine leaps eagerly up into the meaty high-revolution range, and even pulls well farther down the tachometer." While the Giulietta Veloce certainly had no torque, the Giulia Veloce had both torque and excellent top speed. *Road & Track* found 109 mph on tap, very close to the 110 mph claimed by the factory.

Model	Horsepower	Top Speed
Giulietta	80	102.5 mph (165 km/h)
Giulietta Veloce	90	112 mph (180 km/h)
Giulia	92	107 mph (172 km/h)
Giulia Veloce	From 109 to 125	112 mph (>180 km/h)
Duetto	From 109 to 125	115 mph (185 km/h)
1750 (Weber)	118 (SPICA: 135 SAE)	118 mph (190 km/h)
2000 (Weber)	132 (SPICA: 150 SAE)	121 mph (195 km/h)

United States-market 1750s were distinguished by their dual brake boosters, SPICA fuel injection and air injection.

The chart shows a nice progression of power that is completely misleading so far as my personal experience is concerned. It's indicative of the marketer's "thumb on the scale" that the Giulia Veloce is rated at "over 112 mph." Since I've seen more than that in my own Giulia Veloce, I tend to suspect that its official performance was downgraded to fit nicely into charts such as the one above. Further, personal experience suggests that in the real world a 1750 is every bit as fast as a 2000, if not actually slightly faster. Under any circumstance,

This turbocharged twin-cam engine awaited installation into a European-specification Alfa Romeo in 1981.

the weight of the cars increased as they approached their terminal configuration, and performance suffered significantly as a result.

Turbodelta

In 1979 Autodelta homologated 400 Alfetta coupes with a turbocharged engine. A KKK turbo unit bowing into dual Weber carburetors gave 150 hp at 5,500 rpm. In 1980, a Turbodelta driven by Pregliasco and Reisoli won the Danube rally and finished fifth overall in the European Rally Championship. Turbodeltas were further modified by the German distributor to use fuel injection for even more power. I know of one Turbodelta in the United States. Unfortunately it is in need of repairs after being stolen and crashed.

Of interest, if not especially appropriate for this book, is the GTV 2.6-liter V-8 also constructed for the German distributor. Twenty Alfetta coupes received Montreal engines tuned to give 200 hp at 6,500 rpm. Acceleration from 0–60 mph was on the order of seven seconds, and top speed was in the range of 150 mph.

In a similar vein, 200 Alfetta coupes were modified by Autodelta for delivery in South Africa. These coupes carried an injected 3.0-liter V-6 engine which developed 186 hp at 6,700 rpm. Such a car won the performance index in the 1983 Thousand Miles of Kyalami endurance race.

When I visited the Alfa factory for the long-lead introduction of the Milano, I saw racks of turbocharged engines, waiting for installation into production Alfas: the 1983–84 Giulietta 2.0-liter Turbodelta. This engine carried an Alfa Avio compressor and produced 170 hp at 5,000 rpm.

Alfa never offered a turbo option on its United States engines, and two aftermarket companies, Jafco and Shankle, stepped in to fill the void. The two installations took different routes, the Jafco system relied on the SPICA injection unit, and the Shankle switched to carburetion. I've had rides in both conversions, and there is no doubt that they added significant performance to an engine which sorely needed the increase.

Modular Motor

In an attempt to increase fuel economy without sacrificing performance, Alfa equipped some four-cylinder motors with an electronic engine control system that cut the fuel to alternating cylinders under coast-down and idle conditions. The engines were fitted to a fleet of Milano taxicabs, and seem to have performed quite well. I suspect that the tremendously negative press over the 8-6-4 Cadillac debacle dampened Alfa's enthusiasm for this approach.

Laminar Flow Head

Alfa avoided the four-valve head long after it had become common in the industry. Instead, it experimented with designs which were more exotic. The laminar flow head was an attempt to increase the efficiency of the intake cycle by controlling reversion. Extremely large intake ports were required to retain an adequate intake path area and still fit the set of horizontally mounted reed valves which shut under the back-pressure of reversion. The complexity of the design and likely warranty costs were prohibitive. Further, I suspect that the power gain was not dramatic enough to justify the production expense.

Twin Spark

In a world populated by sedans with four-valve engines, Alfa's four seemed an anachronism. Alfa would not be stampeded into offering a feature that it did not consider a solid advantage. The company concluded that the improved combustion offered by twin spark plugs offered more performance than the complexity of four valves. As a result, the twin-spark engine was introduced at the Geneva show in 1987. This head should not be confused with the dual-plug head fitted to the GTA and TZ2.

The new twin-spark-plug head helped the 2.0-liter engine develop 145 hp at 5,800 rpm, a satisfying increase over the 130 hp of the conventional model. As soon as the head appeared in Europe, American Alfisti were eager to fit the heads, and several installations were completed. The cost of the conversion and its uniqueness in the United States make this conversion of questionable value to all but the most dedicated.

The twin-spark head may have revitalized United States Alfa sales momentarily, but the basic engine was getting so old that it probably didn't offer a significant advantage in this market. The same would probably have been true for turbocharging. For that matter, the V-6 failed to turn Alfa around here, so a new head on an old block would have failed to change the outcome too.

Variable Valve Timing

Variable valve timing was pioneered by Alfa, and introduced in the United States with the 1980 model. Later this system was modified with the addition of a solenoid that helped control the moment at which the intake cam's timing changed.

I suspect that the variable valve timing innovation had more to do with meeting emission standards than improving performance. The twin-spark design may also have been heavily influenced by the same need, since a hemispheric head is quite polluting. For the high-revving GTA, twin spark plugs would help in gaining complete combustion, but that is much less likely an advantage in a street engine which lives a significant portion of its life under 3,000 rpm.

The object of this chapter was to give you a general idea of the engineering and technology that is behind your Alfa Romeo twin-cam engine. Should you want to tackle the mechanics of this engine yourself, the following chapter is a useful guide to engine removal and rebuilding.

The Twin-Spark Engine

Most of the differences between the single-plug engine and model 75 (Milano) four-cylinder twin-spark engines are in the design of the cylinder head. The angle between the intake and exhaust valves has been reduced from 80 degrees to 46 degrees, making a much more compact combustion chamber. With this change, the valves moved closer together, leaving no room for a central spark plug.

The cylinder head is also 20mm taller because the valves are more vertical. The cams are still chain-driven, but the dimensions of the intermediate sprocket are slightly different. The oil pump and pan are carried over from the Alfetta, with one distributor in the timing cover and the other on the front of the head, driven by the exhaust cam.

	Single-plug	Twin-spark
Valve angle	80 degrees	46 degrees
Valve stem	9mm diameter	8mm diameter
Valve seat	30 degrees	45 degrees
Intake valve	44mm diameter	44mm diamater
Exhaust valve	40mm diameter	38mm diameter

There are also some minor differences in the twin spark's short block. The cylinder head studs are longer to accommodate the taller head, and the connecting rods are 1mm shorter than in the single-plug engines. The cylinders and cylinder-to-cylinder spacing remain the same. The crankshaft is built without a pilot bushing, like the Alfetta, but is otherwise interchangeable with a spider crank.

More changes were made to fit the twin spark in the front-drive 164 and early 155 models. The block was shortened at the rear, and the timing cover modified to reduce the overall length of the engine. The gerotor oil pump, now located in the timing cover, is driven at crank speed. The cylinder head in the 164 is the same as that used in the 75, but the second distributor is moved from the timing cover to the rear of the exhaust cam. That mounting pad had been provided in the original design, but covered with a blanking plate when installed on the Milano engine. The distributors were replaced with individual coils in the 155 and the head redesigned to eliminate the distributor drives. In addition, the VVT cam drive was also eliminated.

The Milano TS is a direct replacement for the Alfetta engine and is fairly simple to install in a 105/115 spider or GTV. The oil pump and pan from a spider are direct replacements for the TS pump and pan. The crank needs to be machined for a pilot bushing, or replaced with a spider crank, and a conversion exhaust manifold is required. Such manifolds are available in tuned-length header form from AutoComponenti and E.B. Spares, or can be custom-fabricated. In a spider, the cam-driven distributor interferes with the radiator and the intake plenum with the hood. To avoid these problems, an eight-wire distributor is available from AutoComponenti to consolidate the ignition in one distributor in the timing cover. Another alternative is to install a direct-fire ignition (like Electromotive). The intake plenum can be replaced with a custom manifold or replaced with carburetors, using a conversion manifold from AH Motorsports.

—Jim Steck

Chapter 8

Tending to the Twin Cam

The Alfa Romeo twin overhead camshaft may not be a simple engine, but it is a beautifully designed unit that the reasonably handy home mechanic can feel safe working on. The following procedures are basic guidelines for a variety of projects from valve adjustment through complete engine removal. A fairly complete set of metric tools will be required and it is strongly recommended that eye protection be used.

A feeler gauge set and micrometer—either SAE or metric— are also necessary. You should also be sure to work under a vehicle only if the wheels are blocked *and* it is supported on sturdy jack stands.

WARNING—Never work under a vehicle supported exclusively by a jack, or cinder blocks.

The basic design of the all-alloy twin-cam engine received only minor changes from the original Giulietta of 1956 through 1985. This Giulia TI uses a single Solex carburetor and is a prime example of this classic engine.

▪ Valve Adjustment

Remove the Cam Cover

The newer the Alfa, the deeper the cam cover will
be buried under hoses and tubes. Carefully remove
everything that runs across the top of the engine, then
disconnect the breather hose from the front of the
camshaft cover.

The cam cover is a U-shaped aluminum casting
which is held on by eight fasteners. Six are decorative
nuts situated atop the cover. There are two bolts which
help clamp the front of the cover to the engine: remove
these with a 10mm wrench, being careful not to drop the
nuts and washers as you pull the bolts free. If your Alfa
is air conditioned, you'll also find an A/C hose bolted up
to the rear brace of the cam cover.

With the fasteners removed, loosen the cam cover
by tapping it from the side with the handle of a large
screwdriver or rubber mallet. Very carefully start to lift
it up. The sealing gasket will stay with the cover in most
cases. If this is not your day, some part of the gasket will
be stuck to the head and some other part to the cover.
Use a small knife to try to release the gasket from one or
the other. If you're successful, you can reuse the gasket. If
not, you'll have to buy a new one. These gaskets are prone
to leaking, and a damaged gasket will leak oil all over the
engine, including the exhaust manifolds. There are two
rubber half-circles at the back of the head. Make sure you
don't lose one while you're lifting up the cam cover.

Be sure to use a 10mm wrench to loosen the two additional
bolts that clamp the front of the cover to the engine. Forget
these two and you may damage the cam cover.

The first step to removing the cam covers is to use a 14mm
Allen wrench to loosen the six decorative nuts.

By carefully removing the cam cover, it may be possible to
save the gasket for reuse.

Record the Clearances

After you get the cam cover off, clean it up and set it aside. A word of caution: with the cam cover removed, there's a gaping hole where the cam chain runs. It's waiting to swallow washers, wrenches and curious rodents. If it succeeds, the engine has to come out of the car and be torn down to get to the offending intruder. There's no safe alternative, so drape a good size rag beneath the chain and over the hole.

Use a feeler gauge to measure the clearances between all the cam lobes and their followers. Put the car in second gear and push it to rotate the cams. Measure each clearance with the cam lobe pointing directly away from the follower. Clearances should range between 0.012 and 0.020 inches, larger for the exhaust valves and narrower for the intake. Write down each clearance, making sure you know which valve it's for. The easiest way is to draw two rows of four circles on a sheet of paper, with an arrow pointing to the front of the engine. Write the cam clearances inside the circles.

Each time you rotate the engine to measure another valve clearance, take a close look at the timing chain which runs between the cams. You're looking for the master link. You may have to turn the engine over by hand several times before you locate the link. Once you've found it, you can put a chalk mark on it to help keep track of where it goes as you continue to measure the valve clearances.

After you've written down all the valve clearances, rotate the engine until the master link is located anywhere between the two camshafts. Look at the back sides of the two frontmost camshaft bearings: you will see timing marks. There's a corresponding mark on each camshaft. Rotate the engine until the mark on one cam lines up perfectly with the one on its bearing cap. The mating marks have the same width, so they can line up perfectly. Without rotating anything, check out the alignment of the mark on the other cam and the TDC "P" stamped on the crankshaft pulley (or flywheel). If all threee marks are spot-on, you've got a well-maintained car. If they aren't you'll soon have a chance to set things right.

Remove the Cams

Rotate the engine so that it's exactly on TDC and the master link is accessible between the two cams. You may have to turn the engine over once or twice to get there.

If you peer carefully inside the engine below the timing chain, you'll see an idler sprocket assembly which tensions the chain. On the outside of the engine, there's a 14mm (9/16-inch) bolt which clamps the sprocket in place. Loosen the bolt about one-half turn, which is just enough so you can use a large screwdriver to slide the idler sprocket back about a half-inch or so. The sprocket is spring loaded, so hold it in place as you retighten the clamping bolt. The bolt bears on a wedge; if you tighten it too much, you'll distort the assembly and make idler sprocket adjustment difficult, so just get the bolt snug. Never unscrew the bolt from the engine. Get the sheet of paper with the valve clearances and write down whether the frontmost cam lobes are pointing at each other or away from each other. This will prevent putting the engine back 360 degrees out of time.

With the chain tension relieved, grab the chain somewhere between the two cams and give it an upward pull to get some slack so you can remove the master link. Put the protective rag in place and carefully wedge the open end of the clip with a screwdriver so it slides off the master link As you pull the master link free, parts of it will fall from the chain, so keep a hand under the link as you withdraw it. Put all the parts of the master link back together and store it in a safe place.

If the engine wasn't assembled properly the last time it was apart, you won't be able to get the master link between the cams with the engine on TDC. In that case, get the master link where you will be able to remove it safely, then with the chain still in place, very carefully return the engine to TDC by hand.

Use a length of mechanic's wire to tie the ends of the chain out of the way, then begin incrementally loosening the nuts which hold the cam bearing caps in place. Take about two turns from each nut, then move on until you have removed all of them with their washers. From here on out, it's important that everything goes back exactly as you removed, so put the bearing caps in a safe place where they won't get jumbled. Lift the cams from the engine and put them so you can also get them back the same way. While the stock cams are identical, the timing marks may not align properly if you exchange them.

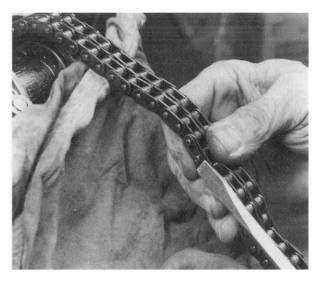

When removing the timing chain master link, be sure to have a large rag draped beneath the chain to prevent the clip or other hardware from falling into the engine.

Replace the Adjusting Caps

Pull the cam followers one by one. It's absolutely critical that they go back in their original bores. Turn the cam follower over: inside, you'll see the adjusting cap which is stuck to the follower by the surface tension of the engine's oil. If the adjusting cap (shim) isn't inside the follower, it's still on the stem of the valve.

Use your micrometer to measure the thickness of each cap. The anvil of the micrometer needs to be against the flat side of the cap, with the spindle inside the cap. After you've measured the cap, write its thickness next to the valve clearance on your sheet

Components of the valve assembly include the valve itself, inner and outer springs, the disc-shaped retainer and two "keepers" wedged between the retainer and the valve stem. The assembly is held together by valve spring pressure only.

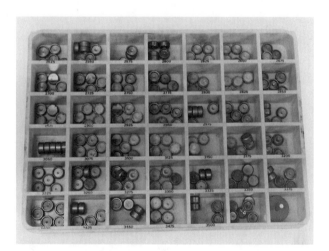

Adjusting caps (shims) are used between the valve stem and the valve foller to adjust the gap between the valve and its camshaft lobe. A full set of shims, shown here, is mandatory for a dealership, but an unlikely luxury for the typical Alfa owner.

of paper. You'll need to determine, using the valve clearances you've already measured, whether you need a thicker or thinner cap, and exactly how much. Remember that a thinner cap will give more clearance and a thicker one less clearance. Many Alfa shops will let you exchange caps when you're doing your own adjustments. The desired clearance is 0.021 inch exhaust and 0.019 inch intake (.550 and .500 mm).

With the new caps in place, replace the followers and the cams, remembering where the front lobes were pointing. Lubricate, then snug all the bearing caps down and check the valve clearances. You won't be able to rotate either cam a full 360 degrees: rotate it one way and then another to measure all four clearances. If you've made a mistake on the clearances, it's easy to correct it now.

Retime the Engine

OK, the crank's still on TDC, right? Rotate both cams so they are aligned with their timing marks and replace the chain and its master link. The open end of the master link clip points to the intake side of the engine. Now, loosen the tensioning sprocket bolt, and then rotate the engine backwards just enough to let the spring push the sprocket out as far as it will go. If you've been ham-handed with the sprocket bolt, you'll have to use a screwdriver to help wedge the sprocket out. Tighten the bolt so it's snug and turn the crank back to exactly TDC. With luck, both cam timing marks will now align. If they don't, recheck the crank position to verify you're on TDC.

CAUTION—The twin-cam Alfa Romeo engine is an interference engine. Piston and valve train damage may occur if camshafts are incorrectly timed. Confirm camshaft timing before attempting to start the engine.

The cam sprocket has a vernier adjustment. First, bend back the lock tab and loosen the 22mm nut at the front of the cam. With the engine on TDC, very carefully remove the cotter pin and 8mm castellated nut, then remove the bolt which locates the vernier flanges. Rotate the cam to bring it to its timing mark, then find the mating holes to return the bolt through the flanges without rotating the cam further. Adventurous types will recognize that the valve overlap can be changed at this point. Too-adventurous types will end up bending valves and breaking pistons. Resist temptation, tighten everything up, rotate the engine by hand at least four times, then recheck the cam timing against TDC.

Put everything back together. The engine should fire on only a few turns. If it won't start or if it backfires, you've got the cams 360 degrees out. The problem is most easily corrected by swapping the plug wires so No. 1 wire goes to cylinder No. 4, No. 2 to cylinder

No. 3 and so forth. This will completely confound the next person to work on your engine.

■ Engine Removal

Removing an engine can seem like a daunting task, but it doesn't need to be. You are basically disconnecting any wire, cable, pipe, hose, line or mechanical connection between the engine and transmission, and the body of the car. It will be a dirty job, but don't make it any dirtier than it needs to be. Clean the engine and engine compartment thoroughly before you start. Have plenty of rags and spill-absorbent material handy.

Always troubleshoot the engine before removing it. Try to determine, before you begin, those parts that will absolutely have to be rebuilt. The purpose of this step is to avoid rebuilding perfectly good parts: if oil pressure is good and the water pump doesn't leak, you can avoid disassembling both pumps.

Removal Guidelines

1. Never attempt a rebuild with the engine in the car.
2. Always remove the engine and transmission as a unit.
3. Don't just disconnect the battery: remove it.

4. Clean the engine thoroughly before you lay a hand on it. Cleaning it with a solvent and then washing it down with water also assures that it's cold enough to disassemble without warping a casting.
5. Always drain the engine and transmission of oil before removing them.
6. Label all wires left hanging in the engine bay.

WARNING—Use an appropriate jack for lifting the vehicle and an engine hoist rated for the appropriate weight for removing the engine and transmission assembly .

Removal Procedure

The guidelines above provide a basic overview of what is involved in engine removal and several tips to ease the project. Below you will find a step-by-step procedure for engine removal:

1. Disconnect the battery, remove it and store safely.
2. Drain the radiator and remove it, with its connecting upper and lower hoses. At the same time, if there is a

The engine and transmission (GTA Junior shown) should always be removed as a unit. Note the magnesium bell housing and oil pan.

functioning drain toward the rear driver's side of the block, open it to drain coolant from the block.

3. Before removing the engine, wash it down with a solvent and remove as much grime as possible with a stiff brush. Work at both the front and rear of the engine, where oil deposits are most tenacious.

Alfetta Notes

Most of the discussion in this chapter is for Alfas with solid rear axles. Engine removal from an Alfetta body is a bit easier because the oil pan is narrower and the casting bolted to the rear of the engine is shorter than a transmission. Further, you don't have to remove the shift lever from the body, and there's no steering link to drop out of the way.

1. To remove an engine from an Alfetta, jack the front of the car up so you can crawl under it comfortably. The front needs to stay in the air, so don't jack it up so high that you can't work around the engine comfortably. Put the car on jack stands, then crawl under and lower the rear engine support. Remove the large bolt that holds the support to the rear casting.

2. Release the three nuts that attach the driveshaft's rubber joint (donut) to the rear of the engine. You can reach them through the access hole in the bottom of the casting that replaces the transmission on other Alfas. If you can't reach one of the nuts because of the driveshaft, jack up the rear so the wheels just clear the ground, reach under and rotate the driveshaft, then lower the rear before crawling all the way back under the car. The rubber joint should stay with the driveshaft, but the odds are it will need replacing.

3. Move the lifting loop forward one set of headbolts.

4. As the engine is being lifted free from its two motor mounts, pause several times to crawl under and pry the rubber joint further along its attaching bolts. When the driveshaft is free of the casting, combine two large threaded hose clamps and place them around the outside of the rubber joint. Tighten the clamps to compress the joint to its installed diameter. This will ease its reassembly.

5. Alfettas and later spiders have electronic tachometers, so you don't have to worry about releasing the tach cable.

6. On reassembly, remember to remove the hose clamp assembly around the rubber joint.

4. Bend back the safety tab from the crankshaft pulley bolt. Put the car in first gear and have someone apply the brakes. Remove the (large) crankshaft pulley bolt, using a cheater bar if necessary. Leave the pulley on the crankshaft.

5. Some Alfa heads, most notably on the 2.0-liter, seem welded to their mounting studs. This is caused by water leaking into the tunnels for the studs and then corroding into an immovable crust. Loosen each head nut about one turn and flush penetrating oil beneath the nuts. You will want a very small movement of the head so you don't stress the chain or anything else bolted to the head. Therefore, don't unscrew the nuts more than one turn. With the spark plugs removed, rotate the engine so cylinders 1 and 4 are near the bottom of their stroke. Thread a quantity of rope into each cylinder (leave something hanging so you can get it out again.) Then, put the transmission in gear and push the car forward so the pistons compress the rope, popping the head free. In extreme cases, the head may still be hard to remove, but you've at least gained a running start.

6. Apply penetrating oil to nuts at the bottom of the exhaust manifold. These will usually be rusted and break upon removal.

7. The engine comes out with the transmission and its intake and exhaust manifolds attached. Rather than give an item-by-item list of things to disconnect, I'll suggest that you begin at the rear of the passenger side of the engine and simply disconnect everything connected to it, working slowly around the engine and ending with the speedometer cable attached to the transmission. This includes a braided ground strap running from the body to the starter area, and a mechanical tachometer drive at the front of the engine, if fitted. Disconnect the exhaust pipes at the exhaust manifold.

8. Jack up the front of the car and put it on jack stands. Disconnect one end of the steering link that runs beneath the engine and swing it out of the way.

9. Disconnect the speedometer cable from the transmission. There are two crossmembers running under the car: one also holds the rear of the transmission. Remove both crossmembers, then unbolt the driveshaft from the rear of the transmission. Also remove the exhaust hanger which attaches to the rear of the transmission.

10. Drain the oil from the engine. Lower the car to the ground.

11. Remove the transmission crossmember and the shift lever before trying to remove the engine/transmission assembly.

NOTE: With the transmission attached, the engine will balance level when suspended from the lifting loop between cylinders 2 and 3. You'll never get the engine out if it remains level: it needs to come out nearly vertically, with the transmission hanging down to clear the lower lip on the engine bulkhead.

---

12. With everything disconnected, move the lifting loop forward by one set of head bolts and jack up the rear of the car as far as you can manage. Put sturdy jack stands under the rear axle. Remove the shift lever as soon as the rear of the transmission drops low enough to allow access to the lever's pinch bolt.

13. As you lift the engine free, check frequently for things you forgot to disconnect: the leads to the alternator, the big wire to the starter, the choke cable, etc. The only thing which is likely to stall removal is the stub of the shift lever fouling against the underside of the bulkhead. With that exception, there should be no resistance to lifting the engine free. If there is, you've forgotten to disconnect something.

14. With the engine out of the car, remove the intake and exhaust manifolds, the alternator and starter motor.

15. If the car has SPICA fuel injection, remove the thermostatic actuator tube that runs between the injection pump and the intake manifold. Unbolt the lines to the injection pump and plug all openings with nonabsorbent material. To remove the lines at the pump, undo the two outside fittings before removing the two inside fittings. The SPICA injection pump lines are coiled and equal length. They come off and go back only one way, so they cannot really be confused (don't bend them). On the other hand, the relation between the four lines can be a puzzle, so mark them as you take them off so you know how they fit together. Also, keep track of where the clamps go to hold the lines to the engine.

16. Continue cleaning the engine until there is absolutely no dirt left. You can rebuild an engine while it is resting on the ground. The work surface should be hard, clean and easily rinsed off during the work. Clearly, an engine stand is preferable.

• • •

■ Engine Rebuild

A procedure such as rebuilding an engine is quite exacting and the following section is only a generalized guide to engine overhaul. It's roughly equivalent to a friend describing the procedure over the telephone or the Internet. He can't see all the unique things that have been done to your car. I'm sure he'd be impressed with the turbo you've installed between the cam covers, and the way those custom headers thread through the front suspension is really amazing! The moral: it's your responsibility if you have any parts left over, or the engine runs backwards. A corollary to the moral: when in doubt, don't.

Once the engine is removed from the car, the disassembly begins. The first step will be removing the engine accessories. With major accessories removed, the head can be separated from the engine block. Next the block can be disassembled, and the internal engine components will be measured and examined to establish what work and parts will be required for the rebuild. After disassembling the engine block, the cylinder head is taken apart and put through the same scrutiny of tolerances. Finally, with parts in hand, and machine work completed, the engine can be reassembled.

Dismantling the Engine

Before dismantling an engine, gather these new items:

- head gasket and its rubber O-rings
- main and rod bearings
- piston rings
- front and rear oil seals
- timing chain cover gasket
- all the blue-steel stamped locking tabs.

1. Remove the flywheel cover from beneath the transmission and then remove the transmission from the engine.

2. Remove any remaining linkages to the carburetor(s) or injection pump.

3. Remove the engine mounts and injection pump (if fitted). The injection pump is attached with four 10mm nuts, one of which is difficult to reach even with the engine out of the car. Withdraw the crank pulley at the same time you ease the timing belt off its pulley.

4. Remove the fuel pump if the car is carbureted. Pumps mounted on the front timing cover use two rods to connect with the lobe on the distributor drive shaft. These rods will probably slide out as you're removing the thick spacer beneath the pump itself.

5. Remove the 10mm nut that holds the distributor clamping plate to the timing cover. Pull the distributor out of the engine front timing cover.

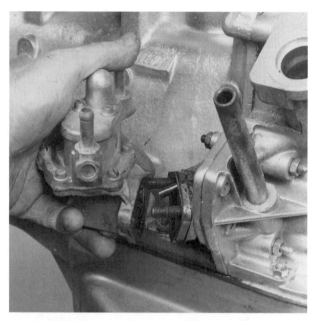

After loosening the nuts and pulling back the fuel pump body, the first pushrod must be removed, prior to loosening an additional three 10mm nuts which hold the balance of the fuel pump.

To remove the oil filter assembly, simply remove a pair of 17mm nuts.

6. Remove the spark plugs. Put them, the distributor and the secondary wires in a cardboard box.

7. Remove the alternator, any rubber hoses left connected to the engine and the dipstick.

8. Remove the oil filter. If you're working on a model with a replaceable element, remove the two 17mm nuts holding the assembly to the block. Discard the paper gasket. If you have a spin-on element, use an oil filter wrench.

9. Remove the thermostat cover and the thermostat. Discard its gasket and O-ring.

10. Remove oil pressure and coolant temperature sensors.

Removing the Head

1. Remove the two bolts at the front of the camshaft cover (if fitted) and then remove the six decorative bolts holding the cover to the head. For earlier cars, if you do not have a 14mm Allen wrench, use a Vise-Grip on a suitable bolt to get this done. Later cars have flats on the decorative bolts and invite the use of a crescent wrench.

2. The engine should turn freely. You may be able to rotate the crank by hand. Alternate methods are to use a screwdriver inserted into the teeth of the ring gear and pressed against a transmission mounting stud to lever the engine around, or loop a V-belt around the crank pulley and pull on one side of the belt to rotate the crank. Turn the crank until the master link on the timing chain is between the camshaft sprockets. The camshaft reference marks (journal to cap) should also be in alignment if the last guy to do the rebuild knew what he was doing. If the timing marks don't line up, don't worry, but remember to do it right on reassembly.

3. Loosen the chain tensioner setscrew about one turn, then push down on the top of the chain between the cams to put some slack in the chain. Retighten the setscrew even though the cams are out of time.

4. Drape a cloth under the chain so it covers completely the gulf inside the timing cover between the camshaft sprockets. Carefully remove the clip from the back side of the master link. Hold one hand under the chain while you remove the rearmost spacer of the link with your other hand, then continue withdrawing the master link. About half-way, the intermediate spacer should fall into your palm. If it doesn't, rotate the free ends of the chain until you can retrieve it. Continue withdrawing the master link. Reassemble the parts of the master link and store them in a safe place.

5. Remove the chain from its sprockets and let it slip down the timing cover into the engine.

Remove the head bolts by starting in a spiral pattern beginning at the center of the engine and working out toward both ends of the head equally.

Lifting the head is not as easy as the photo suggests. The head is not heavy, but it is a challenge to free it from its stud evenly.

6. If you haven't already loosened them, use a torque wrench to remove the cylinder head nuts. Start with the center two and spiral outwards towards each end of the head. Remove the lifting loop.

7. Lift off the head. If it's still stuck, just use a rubber mallet to hit the head and shock it free.

   OK, that didn't work. If the head won't come off, first check that you removed the two upside-down 14mm bolts which hold the front of the head to the timing-chain cover. You have to resist the temptation to wedge a screwdriver between the head and the block: you could destroy both. Continue soaking the crud around the head studs with penetrating oil and banging upwards on the head with a rubber mallet. Take a break now and then to let the oil do its job. If you can get the head free just a bit, use wood wedges to hold it up as you continue banging with the rubber hammer.

   That didn't work either? Hmm… You can fabricate an Alfa tool for head removal. Basically, this is a ½-inch-thick steel plate which is large enough to rest on the tops of the six head studs for cylinders 2 and 3. Inserts (possibly made from old ¾-inch spark plugs, but with internal as well as external threads) are first threaded into two spark plug wells. The plate is positioned over the eight studs, then bolts are inserted through the plate and threaded into the inserts. As the two bolts are tightened in sequence, the plate draws the head upwards along the studs.

Don't try to use bolts which thread directly into the spark plug threads. If the head is really stuck, you could strip the spark plug threads and end up with a ruined head that still won't come off.

Dismantling the Block

1. With the head removed, blow out the remaining water from the water jacket. Now would be a good time to remove any remaining pieces of the head gasket from the block surface. There's a mildly abrasive gasket-removing tool that fits on a ¼-inch drill, or you can use a soft-metal scraper to get the pieces off.

2. Properly, now is the time to fit liner clamps so the cylinders don't move in the block. If you plan to remove the cylinders, you may find this thought amusing, since some liners can prove harder to remove than the head itself. You have to be very careful not to cock the liners in their bores if you do try to remove them.

   On the other hand, if you're not interested in replacing the liners and want to leave them in place (so you don't have to replace the sealing O-ring at their base), then they'll probably fall out when you invert the engine. The simplest way to secure liners is to slip flat washers down the head studs and back each washer up with a length of PVC pipe, cut to a length so that the head nuts clamp the washers to the liners when the head nuts are tightened down (finger tight).

3. Turn the engine over and remove the oil pan and its gasket.

4. Remove the oil pump and its sealing ring. The pump slides out slightly sideways. Always remove the oil-pump blow-off spring and piston and verify that they move freely in the bore.

5. Remove the timing chain from its idler wheel and lay it out on a bench. Inspect the chain rollers for signs

With the engine inverted, remove the bolts from the perimeter of the pan, as well as the two nuts at the rear of the pan. Then the oil pan can be removed.

After removing three bolts, the oil pump can be worked out of the timing cover, following the axis of the timing cover.

of visible wear. Pull the chain out to its maximum length and mark where the ends are. Notice if it lies in a straight line. If it curves, it should be replaced. Then, press one end to compress it to its minimum length. The difference between minimum and maximum lengths shouldn't exceed the distance of one chain link. If it does, replace the chain.

6. Remove the crankshaft pulley by bending back the locking tab and unscrewing the large nut that holds it to the crankshaft. This nut may be tough to get off. Strike it squarely with a heavy hammer to help loosen it.

7. Now, start marking parts for reassembly. If this is your first time inside an engine, use a camera. Take plenty of pictures showing how things were before you took them apart.

   Connecting rods and their matching big-end caps are numbered from the factory. The rod stamped 1 should be in No. 1 cylinder and so on. If the rod has been replaced, it could be any possible number, or even be without a number. The important point is that all the identifying numbers should face the oil-filter side of the engine. There may also be marks on the opposite side of the rod, but what you're looking for is a single number between one and four that's stamped on the proper side of the rod.

   The goal is to be able to replace all the moving parts in the same orientation as they came from the engine. Rods are displaced slightly along the axis of the crankshaft so that the rod body is actually offset from the center line of the crankshaft journal. Two rods (2 and 4) are offset toward the center of the engine, while the others (1 and 3) are offset to the ends of the engine. Similarly, piston pins are also offset slightly in the pistons of newer engines, so the pistons can go in only one way. Some have an arrow pointing to the exhaust side of the engine, or some kind of identifying mark instead of the arrow.

   Making indelible marks on parts is a challenge. Don't use a file to inscribe Vs in the parts. That only gives cracks a place to start. You can use a center punch to number rods. A serious blow is required to mark the rod halves, and the only acceptable place to mark one is on the machined side of the rod in the area of the rod bolt.

   Once you get a piece off the engine, put it in a sturdy box in a way that will help you get it back together again in the right orientation. Valves get poked through a sheet of cardboard in the same order as they came out of the engine. Use small plastic cups to hold small parts, and write a clear description on the cup. Remember that all the fluids used in an engine are solvents, so whatever you write may be inadvertently obliterated by a dirty thumb. This is especially true if you use paper tags marked with a felt-tipped pen.

It is a given that you, or your next-door neighbor's cat, will spill everything at least once into a hopeless jumble.

8. Remove the rod bolts and then tap the caps lightly to loosen them from the crank journal. Remove the caps and slide out the bearing inserts. If the crank needs regrinding, you'll have to replace the bearings. Plan to replace the rod and main bearing inserts even after verifying that a regrind is not required. It's cheap insurance.

9. If you plan to replace the piston rings, push the pistons out the tops of the cylinders and reassemble

A breaker bar will give you the needed leverage to loosen the nuts from the rod bolts.

Once the oil pump has been removed, it's time to take off the front cover.

the bearing caps to the rods. If the engine had good compression and didn't burn oil before disassembly (what are you doing this for, then?) leave the pistons in their bores so you don't have to replace the rings.

10. Before unbolting the mains, check the crankshaft end play. You do this by pressing the crank as far to the rear as it can move in its bearings, and then as far to the front. The difference between all the way to the rear and to the front is end play. It should be between 0.003 and 0.010 inches. End play is set by a thrust bearing inserted between the face of the center crank journal and the crankcase. If end play is excessive you'll need new thrust bearing halves.

11. Next on the agenda is the removal of the front timing case cover. Begin by removing the 10mm nuts that attach the water pump. Tap the pump sideways to free it from its gasket. Slip the crank pulley off, if it's still on the crankshaft. Then, working carefully around the timing cover, remove its attaching nuts. If the cover doesn't come off easily, you've missed a nut. Remove its two gaskets and sealing ring.

12. The primary chain and two gears are removed as a single assembly. Keep the sprockets engaged with the chain. It's easy to forget the order of the front crank pulley, slinger, gear and sprocket, and the orientation of the gear. Make a drawing as you remove them from the crankshaft. Just in case you don't: the order is just as listed above, and the gear slips on so its teeth are nearest the sprocket. If you need to replace the long cam chain, also plan to replace the short one.

With the front cover off, now the timing chain and gears can be removed. Be sure to take pictures or draw diagrams to ensure proper assembly later.

13. Check for alignment marks positioning the clutch assembly and flywheel. If there aren't any, use a chisel to punch a single mark that spans the clutch pressure plate and flywheel so the two can be reassembled exactly as they came apart. Then, remove the clutch pressure plate and clutch driven plate.

With the flywheel still on the engine of this 1965 Giulia Spider Veloce engine, the clutch disc, pressure plate and release bearing are on the bench.

Look closely at each bearing as it is removed. If the crank journal is scored, the bearing surface will be deeply grooved. If a brown layer of metal shows on the bearing, then the bearing is quite worn and the crank journal should be checked for roundness. Never reuse rod or main bearings.

14. Use a chisel to mark the crankshaft/flywheel relationship. Bend back the locking tabs that capture the flywheel mounting bolts. Place a block of wood between a crank counterweight and the inside of the crankcase so the crank won't rotate. Then, unscrew the mounting bolts and lift the flywheel free of the crank. Two half-plates for the flywheel bolts will drop from behind the rear crank flange. Bend back the blue-metal locking tabs on the flywheel attaching bolts, remove the bolts and then pull off the flywheel.

15. The main bearings are secured by nuts that are held in place with spring-steel (Palmutter) locknuts. The rear bearing cap nuts are held by locking tabs. Remove the locknuts and bend the tabs back on the rear main bearing caps, then remove all the attaching nuts. Tap off each main bearing cap.

16. Note the marks on the caps and store them so you know they will go back exactly the same way. You'll get the bottom half of the center thrust bearing when you remove one of the center caps.

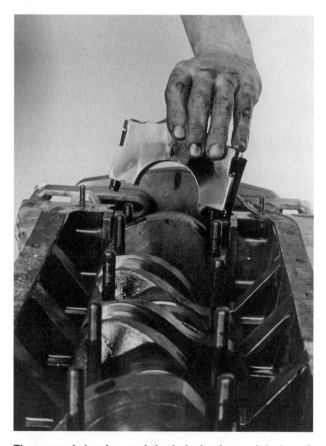

The rear main bearing cap is both the hardest and the last of the caps to be removed. After all other main caps are off, lift the nose of the crank slightly to start the rear cap upwards. After worrying it up about 0.5 inch, try to pry the two rubber seals free from either side of the cap.

17. You have to worry the rear main bearing cap off. There's really no safe place to pry against, and the two rubber inserts at the side of the cap tend to hold it tightly. The least elegant (and probably quickest) technique is to put a rag over the jaws of a Vise-Grip pliers and then clamp them over the rear cap with the handles pointing outboard. Give the pliers a tap with a hammer in the direction that will drive the cap free. Once you get the bearing started, it should come off fairly easily.

18. Grab the crankshaft by its ends and lift straight up. The other half of the thrust washer will fall away. Inspect the main bearing journals using the same techniques as the rod journals.

With the rear bearing cap finally removed, the crank will lift free.

Checks for Engine Rebuild

I'm presuming you've got to this part because you want to complete a rebuild yourself. If you're just going to cart the dismantled engine over to a rebuilder, there are still some things you should check.

First, talk to the rebuilder about Alfas. You may be surprised how little esteem some mechanics hold for the marque. I bought my '81 Spider from a gal who had sent it to a shop that quoted her $1,500 to fix what was wrong: presumably, a noise in the rear axle. She panicked and put it up for sale. I called the shop to ask what they would be repairing. I never found out: instead, I got an earful of what a piece of crap Alfas were. I bought the car sight unseen for $1,000, thanks to the shop and the vulnerability of the car's owner.

When the Alfa arrived, the driver of the transporter offered me $3,500 for the car before he unloaded it. On inspection (I turned the driver down) I could not find anything to fix.

In an infamous case, a friend took a gold mine of original Giulietta parts to a well-known Alfa shop for an engine rebuild. The engine he got back was filled with used parts, many of which were worn beyond re-use. Presumably, the mechanic kept the good stuff for himself, but that didn't keep him from charging $2,000 for the rebuild. The thing that tipped my friend off that something was wrong was the amount of RTV sealant that defined every gasketed surface.

Inspect the rebuild at frequent intervals. Ask to watch while the parts are being inspected, and tell the shop to call you before the head and pan are installed.

Pretend the shop you're contemplating is a restaurant. Imagine ham and eggs on your flywheel, with coffee served up in a piston. If you wouldn't eat there, you probably shouldn't have your engine rebuilt there. Ideally, the separate engine rebuilding room could double as an operating room in an emergency. That's the top end of the scale. The bottom is a dirt-floor shop with no lifts or engine stands, where automatic transmission internals are wiped clean with an oily rag, and parts for half-assembled engines litter the ground.

So you're committed to doing the work yourself. The genius of the Alfa engine design is that virtually all wear parts are replaceable. That gives you a lot of stuff to check.

Once the engine is apart, check each part for signs of wear or deterioration. Presumably, you've torn the engine down for a cause, so you should focus on repairing that fault. If a rod has gone through the block, spending a lot of time worrying about the condition of the alternator won't be productive. If the part produced no symptom before the engine came apart, you're probably safe in reusing it. Exceptions are rod and main bearings, piston rings and all gasket materials: these are always replaced whenever the engine is apart. Never, ever, tear down an engine without replacing the front and rear crankshaft oil seals, even if they didn't leak before.

In the 1960s, I could rebuild a Giulietta with parts from J.C. Whitney for a couple hundred dollars. At the turn of the century, these same parts cost nearly $1,000, and J.C. Whitney has long given up on Alfas. There may be a price point dictated by your wallet. Use common sense. If the engine has 20,000 miles on it from a reputable rebuild, you can assume that most of its parts are still good: if it has 200,000, you'll probably want to replace most of the wearing parts, which includes all bearings, chains, pistons and cylinders and gaskets.

Ultimately, diagnosing mechanical wear comes down to measurement with tools such as micrometers and dial gauges, which are not in the typical enthusiast's toolbox. At this point, you can decide to cart all the pieces to a reputable rebuilder who will tell you what to replace or keep, or go out and buy the tools, which you will then have to learn how to use before they will be of much use. Be warned: even micrometers can be misleading if not used properly (they are *not* more accurate the more you tighten them down).

Signs of deterioration are easily seen—if you know what to look for. Bend rubber parts to find cracks and to test for suppleness. Check metal parts for scoring, which is an obvious sign of wear. Bright patches suggest wearing surfaces, except on piston skirts, where the wear surface is usually darker. Discoloration suggests

The rod bearings are just some of the parts that must be replaced during an engine rebuild.

overheating. With the engine apart, if there is any question about the condition of a part, it is wise to replace it and false economy not to.

A careful engine overhaul can include a whole day of checks. Here's a short list of the most important ones:

Pistons

- The wrist pin is held in place by circlips. Make sure the grooves for the circlips are sound.

- The fit of the rings in their grooves is critical. First, clean the groove with the broken end of a ring. The gap between a new ring and its groove in the piston should not exceed 0.002 inch. Check this with a feeler gauge. If you can slip a 0.004-inch feeler between the ring and piston, you need fatter rings or a new piston/ring set.

- Put a piston in a cylinder and slide the top compression ring on top of it to make sure the ring is square in the groove. Let the piston drop down in the cylinder and then check the gap between the ends of the ring. It should not be less than 0.3 inch and should not exceed about 0.4 inch.

Rods

- Slip a piston pin into the rod's little end. If you can wiggle the pin in the bush, even slightly, have the bushes for all rods replaced by a qualified shop.

- If you're going to send the rods to a shop, have them magnafluxed and checked for trueness. Rods occasionally bend or twist slightly after a while, and it's good to know yours haven't. You may also want to have the rods shot-peened to relieve any internal stresses and improve durability.

Crankshaft

- Look at the crank journals. If they're deeply scored or even slightly blue, you're in need of a crank regrind.

- Draw your fingernail across the surface of the journal. If your fingernail catches on a score, then the journal has to be reground. If the journal passes that test, smooth the surface with a crocus cloth and then wipe the surface so it is perfectly clean. Reassemble the rod and cap around the crank with a piece of Plastigauge laid along the bearing axis. Without moving the rod on the journal, unbolt the cap and check the width of the Plastigauge against the scale printed on its wrapper. A value of 0.001–0.0025 inch is generally acceptable, but anything more than that should require a regrind.

- Measure the clearance of the main bearings in the same way. Usually, the rods go before the mains. Even if the rods check out fine, and the mains look new, it's still very much worth the effort to check the mains with Plastigauge.

- If the bearing journal is smooth and within the proper tolerance for clearance, I've found that measuring the journal for out-of-round with a micrometer is usually redundant. If you'll sleep better, go ahead and measure away.

- One common problem with the later Alfa engines is the loss of the oilway plugs on the crankshaft. It's important to check each of these carefully for any sign that they may be working loose (or missing). These plugs are staked in, and the force required to add another stake with a punch is considerable: bang away if you like. If you're going to race the engine, I'd recommend sending the crank off to a rebuilder who can tap the oilways and thread plugs in place of the staked-in slugs.

- A shop can check the crankshaft for bending (it does happen). If parts are already going to a shop, send the crank along and ask to have it checked for axial and radial trueness.

This set of stock Giulietta pistons and connecting rods has been prepared by Sperry Valve Works.

The forged crank is fully counterbalanced and provides a main bearing on either side of each rod bearing.

Oil Pump

- If you had good oil pressure before the tear-down, I'd leave the oil pump alone.

- If you didn't (and the crankshaft oilway plugs are OK), the first thing to check is the seating of the relief valve on its seat. Pull out the cotter pin from the end of the valve's cylinder and remove the valve. Check closely for signs of wear or dirt on its angled seating surface. You can use valve lapping compound to assure a good seal, but then flush the pump with solvent and clean the valve and its seat so they are absolutely clean before you put things back together.

- If oil pressure was low, you have to check the fit of the oil pump gears in their body. Remove the

sheet metal gear cover to make this check. The distance between a gear tooth and the pump body should not exceed 0.002 inch. Measure this with a wire gauge in several places around the inside circumference of the pump body. The distance between the gears and the surface of the pump body (end float) is checked by laying a straight edge across the pump face and slipping a feeler gauge between the straight edge and the pump gears. This gap should not exceed 0.016 inch.

- If any dimension exceeds the specification, get a new pump.

Dismantling the Head

Work on the head as a separate assembly. You'll need a specialized valve-removing tool which can reach down into the head casting to get the valves out. If you've never done a head before, it's better to send it out to a specialist shop.

You must use a proper fitting tool to drive valve guides in and out. You can make the tools easily on a lathe, but if you don't have the tools, don't try to replace the guides because you won't be able to get their depths correct or uniform.

Prepare a sheet of cardboard to hold the items to be removed. The cardboard should be placed so valve stems can be inserted through it, and items on it will not slide off if it is accidentally bumped. I number and glue eight small plastic cups to the cardboard to hold the valve follower cups and their adjusting shims.

1. First, measure the valve clearance for each valve and mark it near the cup where the follower and adjusting shim will be kept. Clearances on an assembled head are measured between the heel (smallest circumference) of the camshaft lobe and the top of the follower (with the adjusting shim fitted beneath it).

2. Remove the camshaft bearing caps. Loosen the caps incrementally so the cam rises away from the head without being bent. Place the caps on the cardboard and mark them so they can be reassembled to the proper bearing.

3. Lift off the camshafts. Usually, you won't want to remove the sprocket on the end of the camshaft because this will make retiming the cams harder. If you must remove the sprocket, remove the split pin and unscrew the castellated nut. Then, remove the nut that holds the sprocket to the camshaft. Pull off the sprocket and its mounting ring and pry the Woodruff key out of its groove in the camshaft.

4. Use a magnet to pull out each of the valve follower cups. The valve adjusting shim will usually be stuck to the inside of the cup. Keep the cup and shim together so they can be reinstalled in the same hole.

5. Before you remove the valves from the head, screw all the spark plugs back in. Turn the head so the combustion chambers are up and the head is level. Fill each combustion chamber completely with gasoline and come back in an hour or so. Some of the gasoline will have evaporated, and the level of gasoline should be equal in each chamber. If one chamber retains less fuel than the others, one of the valves for that chamber is leaking. You may be

The camshaft bearing nuts should be removed in several incremental steps. Begin at the center and work outward, just as when removing the head bolts.

able to verify which one by examining the inlet and exhaust passages for the leaking gasoline. A more exacting and faster test is to blow compressed air into the ports, watching for bubbles in the gasoline.

6. If there are leaks, you'll have to remove the valves. This will require an adapter for the typical C-clamp valve-removing tool, which can't reach deeply enough around the head casting to release the retainers. Buy a 1.5-inch length of lead plumbing pipe for an extension. Grind an access hole on one side to reach the retainers.

7. Always replace the intake valve stem oil seals.

8. Keep the spring lower seats together with any shims with the springs. I tie a length of string through the seat, shim (for the Giulietta Veloce) and spring to retain them as a set. The valve springs may be progressively wound. When you reassemble the springs in the head, the more tightly wound end goes next to the lower seat.

9. Remove all carbon deposits from the combustion chamber and valve heads, using a cup-type wire brush.

Checking the Head

1. Loosen the lock bolt and pull the chain tensioner unit from the head. A wedge will hang up on the tip of the lock bolt. Use a magnet to get it out of the head. Slip the tensioner shaft back into the head without the spring or wedge: it should work smoothly.

2. Whenever the head is off, always have it checked for flatness. If it is more than two or three thou off, I'd resurface it.

3. Look for cracks between the valve seats and spark plug holes. If there are any, have the head evaluated by a reputable shop. If any welding is attempted around the valve seats, they must first be removed. Heads can be heli-arced, but there should be some procedure after to normalize the stresses built up by the weld.

4. Try to rock the cams in their bearings like a teeter-totter. If you can, line-bore the cam bearings and have the head refaced.

5. Insert each valve into its guide so the head is about ¼ inch from the seat. If you can rock the valve back and forth even slightly because of excessive stem-to-guide clearance, then you'll need new guides. This is a job for a shop, and the valve seats have to be recut if new guides are fitted. If you're delivering the head to a shop, and it's a Giulia or later, warn them that the exhaust valves are sodium filled.

6. There's a danger when seats are recut or new seats are installed, and that is to recess them too far into the head. If the seats are set too far in, the valve stem will protrude too far to be accommodated by the available adjusting shims. You can correct this by grinding the tip of the valve, but this is a very dangerous step with sodium-filled exhaust valves. If the sodium contained in the stem is exposed to air, it bursts into flames.

7. The proper disposal for sodium-filled valves is to bury them. Depending on your degree of enthusiasm, a brief ceremony with a few close friends may be appropriate.

8. Check the free length of the valve springs. If the engine has covered 40,000 miles or more, you should consider replacing them. If the free lengths vary significantly, you should replace them all. The length of the outer valve spring is 43 to 44.5 mm for Giuliettas, 51.3 mm for Giulias and 46.5 to 47.3 mm for later cars. The inner springs are always a bit shorter.

9. Check the camshafts and journals for scoring. If the tops of the cam followers are scored pay close attention to the cam lobes. Scored or worn followers (with a concave working surface) have to be replaced. The cam can be slightly reground for improved performance or to clean up the lobes.

10. If you're considering regrinding the cam or replacing the stock cam with a more aggressive one, proceed with caution. Most enthusiasts want a fire-breathing steed under them, but few find it comfortable to live with the drawbacks. As I've stated so often in this book, an automotive advantage always invokes a disadvantage. A camshaft will give significantly improved performance, but a major power gain requires other modifications and a loss of driveability. By itself, a cam is a relatively ineffective way to increase horsepower. With an increase in compression ratio, larger intake and exhaust paths and adjustments to the ignition timing and carburetion to match, a stock Alfa engine can be made to breathe fire, indeed. But the losses include low-speed driveability (which is where we spend most of our life on the road), reliability and serviceability (the next mechanic won't have a clue to your changes).

Reassembly

Head

Reassemble the cam tensioner sprocket if you removed it from the head. Unscrew the lock bolt completely. Note that the cutout on the tensioner shaft and the edges of the wedge are beveled so they mate perfectly. Smear the wedge with a light coat of grease and stick it in place near the end of the tensioner shaft. Insert the shaft with its spring into the head, watching for the wedge to center itself in the lock bolt's threaded hole. When it is exactly centered, thread the lock bolt with your fingers so it captures the wedge lightly, then press the tensioner shaft a bit further into the head. The wedge should remain with the lock bolt, sliding along the cutout in the tensioner shaft. To test the assembly, tighten the lock bolt about 45 degrees with a wrench. If the wedge is not seated properly, turning the lock bolt will not clamp the shaft. Take it apart and do it over until you get it right.

If you had a shop install new guides, you should get the head back with the valves already assembled to it. If you haven't sent the head out, do the following:

- Make sure the valves are absolutely free of carbon deposits.

- If the valves passed the leak test with gasoline, I'd still lap them in. Buy a valve-lapping kit which includes a spring to fit under the valve head, a lapping tool with a rubber suction cup and two grades of lapping compound. The kit will come with instructions, so I won't repeat them here.

As seen from the exhaust side, the head is complete with valves, cam shafts and bearings.

- After installing the valves, tap the ends of the stems lightly with a soft hammer to assure that the keepers are seated.
- Reassemble the cams to the head. During reassembly, be sure to return any used parts to their original locations. Pay special attention to the orientation of the camshaft bearings.

At TDC, the intake and exhaust lobes of cylinder No. 1 should be pointing away from each other.

You can gain some performance by retiming the Alfa's cams for more overlap. Using the vernier adjustment on the cam sprockets, advance the intake cam so it opens earlier and retard the exhaust cam so it opens later. This will move the power band up at the cost of low-end torque. If you choose this no-cost improvement, always turn the engine over by hand to verify that the valves are not hitting the pistons.

Valve Adjustment

Before dismantling the head, you measured valve clearances. Now is the time to adjust shim thicknesses to correct any out-of-spec clearances. A micrometer is required to measure the working thickness of the shim: the spindle goes inside the shim, which rests on the anvil. A thicker shim means a smaller valve lash value.

I personally like my exhaust valves to run with 0.019-inch clearance and the intake valves with about 0.017-inch clearance. I'm willing to be off one or two thou in either direction. Purists will faint at this suggestion, because it messes up valve timing, but I've found the approach both safe and satisfactory: I've never dropped a valve. Factory specs are about 0.020 inch for exhaust

and 0.018 inch for intake, so I run my valves slightly tighter than is called for.

Once you get the engine back together and after it's run for a few hours, it's worthwhile to let it cool down and then recheck valve clearances. In theory, there's no way they could change, but you might be surprised. At the same time, verify the camshaft timing. Over the operating life of an engine, plan to check valve clearances once or twice a year depending on how far and fast you drive. Don't worry too much about variations of a few thousandths of an inch. What you need to watch for is an exhaust valve that returns a progressively smaller clearance with each check. When the clearance drops under 0.015 inch it's time to pull the head and replace the valve, because its stem is stretching and will eventually separate from the valve head, causing serious grief to the head and piston.

For many readers, the question will be where to get replacement shims. The large Alfa aftermarket stores can still supply the larger internal-diameter shims for the 101 and later engines, but the smaller 750 shims may be a challenge.

I have a collection of spare shims from dismantled engines, plus one of the factory shim assortments of thick shims. When I can't find a shim of the proper thickness, I grind the flat surface of one of the thick shims to give the proper dimension. This is not a desirable procedure, but in the absence of any other alternative, it will work. I wouldn't do this on a car that's going to be raced, but for an engine used on the street and not often over-revved, I've found it to be safe.

If shims are simply not available, they can be turned on a lathe from bar stock, machined to the proper outside diameter. Cut the inside diameter first, matching the inside radius to that of the tip of the valve stem. Then machine the outside radiuses. Use a cut-off to finish the shim and grind the surface to get the desired working dimension. Don't harden the shims; if they are hardened, they could shatter under heavy use.

Block

Even though you cleaned the outside of the engine before taking it apart, and cleaned parts as you removed them, now is the time to clean everything again so the engine goes back together as spotlessly as possible.

I'm astounded at enthusiasts who want to try an engine overhaul without having access to a torque wrench. Admittedly, an inexpensive beam-type torque wrench is not nearly so accurate as the ratchet type, but it is orders of magnitude more precise than a "good enough" effort from your bulging muscles.

The purpose of torque measurement is to moderate how much you stretch the bolt. Bolts are made to survive a certain amount of stretching without damage. Less torque runs the risk of having the fastener vibrate loose, and more torque puts you in danger of snapping the bolt or stripping its threads. Only a torque wrench will put you within the designed-in capabilities of the fastener.

1. With the engine upside-down, place the main bearing halves in the block. Double-check that they seat perfectly, and that any holes in the bearings correspond to oilways machined in the block. Pour clean engine oil over the bearing surfaces.

2. Use heavy grease to hold the crankshaft thrust washer in place in the block. The thrust washer half without a tang fits in the block. Be sure not to get the two halves confused.

3. Place the crankshaft on its bearings, then lubricate the remaining bearing halves and thrust washer half (with tang). Fit all the bearing caps except the rear main, being sure to return the bearing caps to the exact positions from which they were removed.

4. Lubricate the main bearing stud threads, and torque the nuts to 35 pound feet. Remember that a beam-type torque wrench is accurate only so long as it is moving. Back the nuts up with locknuts, tightened securely with a wrench.

5. The rear bearing cap installs easily by itself, but you cannot push the two "cigarette" oil seals into it when it is fully seated. To get the seals in place, lubricate them and position them at the sides of the rear main bearing cap before you begin placing the cap in the block. As the cap slides down on its bolts, the seals will be forced up. To counteract this, use a socket extension or similar blunt object to press down on the seals so they will seat just slightly ahead of the cap. Do this in stages: push down on the seals, then

In the view of the upside-down block, the sturdy cast-in supporting webs between the main bearings and the block's wall can be seen.

on the bearing cap. The job becomes progressively difficult as the cap nears its fully seated position, and no amount of hammering on the seals will move them once the rear cap is seated. Once properly installed, trim the cigarette seals so they are flush with the surface of the bearing cap and block.

It strikes me that freezing the seals should make this job easier. I've not heard of anyone trying this, but I can't think of any reason why it would not work. I'd suggest fitting the frozen seals so they're flush with the bearing cap ends, and then quickly slipping the cap in place. If the seals don't seat fully for some reason, don't hammer on them, for fear of cracking or breaking them. Start over.

6. Just before the cap is fully seated, lubricate the surfaces of the rear main bearing seal and fit it in place over the rear crank journal so that the lip of

the seal is to the inside. With the rear main bearing cap, the cigarette seals and the rear main seal in place, place the locking tabs on the rear main bearing cap studs, torque down the nuts and bend the locking tabs up to capture the nuts.

7. If you removed the rear cover plate, replace it, along with a new gasket.

8. Install the flywheel, aligning the marks you made on the flywheel and crankshaft end. Use a thread-locking compound and tighten the flywheel bolts to 82 pound feet. To do this, you'll need to wedge a block of wood between a crankshaft counterweight and the inside of the block.

NOTE: Alfetta engines have their flywheel at the other end of the car. Also note that the transmission input shaft pilot bush for crankshafts in Giuliettas, Giulias and 1750 engines does not exist in engines installed in Alfettas with a rear transaxle.

---

9. Rotate the engine block so the cylinders are upright.

10. If you removed the cylinders, clean the mating surface on the block carefully. Fit new rubber rings to the cylinder liners, lubricate all the machined surfaces of the liners and slip them into the block. The liners have a flat on their upper circumference, and these flats must mate between cylinders. Clamp the liners in place as described earlier during disassembly.

11. The connecting rods and pistons must be assembled so the offset of the rods and the orientation of the pistons are correct on assembly. Normally, this detail is handled by the number stamped on the side of the rod and cap. If in doubt: the centerlines of rods 2 and 3 are offset to the ends of the engine while the centerlines of rods 1 and 4 are offset to the center of the engine (outers point in, inners point out).

12. Check the directional marks on the piston so it's right, given the proper rod orientation. Slip the rod inside the piston, slide the wrist pin in place and then secure it with the snap rings. Using a tiny screwdriver, carefully rotate the snap rings in their seats just enough to assure they're properly seated.

13. Install new rings to the pistons. Rings usually come with installation directions. I install them with my fingers, but there are tools for doing the job. Stagger the ring ends in 120-degree increments around the circumference of the piston.

14. You cannot fit the piston/ring assembly into a cylinder without compressing the rings with a tool. The tool is usually a compressible spring steel cylinder. Lubricate the piston and rings liberally, then fit the tool around them. Remove any cylinder

clamping devices. Tighten the tool firmly around the top portion of the piston so the rings are compressed flush with the surface of the piston and some of the piston skirt extends below the tool. Place the assembly atop the cylinder, with the rod hanging down into the cylinder and the bottom of the piston skirt locating the piston in the cylinder.

15. Check the position of the crankshaft so that the rod won't hit the bearing journal as it's driven down the cylinder. Then, with the wooden end of a sturdy hammer, or any similar tool that won't damage the top of the piston, drive the piston into the cylinder with a single, decisive motion. If one of the rings hangs up on the top of the cylinder liner, remove the assembly, reclamp the rings into the piston and try again.

16. Torque the rod bolts to 35 pound feet. Reclamp the cylinders in place.

17. Now, it's time to assemble the front of the engine. Smear grease on the idler sprocket thrust washer and stick it to the front of the block. Then, assemble the primary sprocket, chain and idler sprocket as a unit and fit them in place. Next, slide the distributor drive gear in place, then the oil slinger.

18. Find the middle of the long timing chain and put it in place on the idler sprocket.

19. Always install the front oil seal before you put the front timing chain cover in place. Press the seal into the timing cover, with the lip of the seal pointing toward the engine. Place new gaskets on the front of the block and attach the front timing cover.

20. Slip the oil pump into place at the base of the front timing cover. Check the position of the off-center drive slot on the end of the distributor drive. With

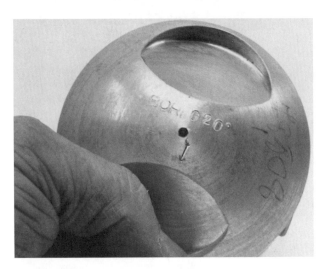

The piston top is marked with an arrow and should be installed with the arrow pointing forward.

the pump pressed home, and the engine on TDC, the slot should be parallel with the crankshaft (at a 45-degree angle for Bosch distributors) and offset toward the bottom. The orientation of the slot is not absolutely critical, since timing can be made to work by rotating the distributor and changing the spark plug wires around to accommodate an oil pump that is not installed in its original orientation.

21. If the fuel pump is mounted on the front timing cover, slip the long push-rod in place, then fit the gasket, spacer, gasket, shorter rod if needed, and the remainder of the pump.

22. If the water pump vanes are not corroded and its bearing sound, use a new gasket and then attach it to the front of the timing cover. The alternator adjusting link goes on at the same time.

23. Lubricate the sealing surface of the crank pulley and carefully slip it onto the nose of the crankshaft. Put a new lock washer in place and screw on the nut. Block the crank from turning with a piece of wood and torque the nut to about 140 pound feet. This amount of torque may not be possible on some engine stands, and it will certainly be impossible if you've assembled the engine on the floor of your garage. If necessary, leave the nut finger tight and plan to torque it after the engine is installed, but before the radiator is put in place.

24. If necessary, rotate the crank so pistons 1 and 4 are at the top of the stroke. Now would be a good time to brighten the timing marks. Giulietta timing marks are on the flywheel. On later engines, they're on the front timing cover and crank pulley.

25. Check the bottom surface of the block and front timing cover to assure that they are clean and smooth. Do the same for the mating surface of the oil pan, then bolt it to the block, working around the circumference and tightening the bolts incrementally.

26. On 2.0-liter engines, oil leaks at the head gasket are common. These leaks can be minimized by fitting roll pins into the six oil passages on the top of the block. Some gasket sets come with these pins, which should be installed if none are already in place. If pins are already there, don't disturb them.

27. Remove the cylinder liner clamps and verify that the top surface of the block and timing cover are absolutely clean of any gasket material. Slip a new head gasket in place, making sure that the water and oil passages to the head are not blocked. Coat the six rubber O-rings for the oil passages with non-hardening sealer and slip them in place around the roll pins.

The cam timing mark is located on the forward cam bearing. The mark on the cam must line up exactly with the mark on the bearing.

28. Rotate the camshafts so their timing marks are aligned, then slip the assembled head onto the block slowly, being careful not to smash the timing chain against the head gasket. Thread the timing chain around the tensioner and over the cam sprockets so the master link will be centered between them. Replace the head bolts so they are finger tight. The lifting link goes between the first two cylinders.

29. Connect the master link and retension the chain. I use a long screwdriver to pry against the tensioner and assure that the chain is adequately tight. When you work the chain up and down half way between the cams, it should allow only slight vertical movement.

30. Verify that the cams are still properly timed. If they are not, you'll need to rotate them using the vernier adjustment mechanism. Remove the castellated nut and bolt that goes through the sprocket, then loosen the mounting bolt on the front of the cam. Rotate the camshaft so its timing mark aligns with the mark on the front bearing cap. Find a hole in the vernier adjuster that will accept the bolt without further rotating the cam. The odds are that the hole won't be where you can get at it. Find the hole first using a small mirror and flashlight. Bend a length of small rod so you can run it through the appropriate vernier hole, then rotate the engine until the hole is accessible. Return the engine to TDC before timing the other cam.

31. With the chain properly tensioned and the cams properly timed, rotate the engine by hand two full turns and then recheck the camshaft timing. The engine should turn without significant resistance. If it does not, you should try to determine why and correct the condition.

32. Look around the shop for any parts that belong on the engine. Since you haven't torqued down the head yet, it's still possible to install something, even inside the engine, without destroying anything. At this stage, the pan and cam cover gaskets are reusable.

33. After you're fully satisfied that the engine is properly assembled, torque the head bolts to 55 pound feet. Retension the cam chain and recheck cam timing. Refit the cam cover, using a new gasket.

34. Attach any remaining components to the engine, including:

    - distributor

    - spark plugs

    - intake and exhaust manifolds. It's easy to get the copper exhaust manifold gaskets on backwards: check them carefully before bolting up the exhaust.

    - generator/alternator

    - oil pressure and temperature sensors/switches

    - thermostat and housing

    - bypass hose between thermostat housing and pump

    - oil filter and dipstick

    - engine mounts (if disassembled)

35. If the engine has SPICA fuel injection, install the injection pump and time it to the I mark on the crank pulley near TDC of No. 1 cylinder. Slide the crank pulley onto the crank at the same time you slip the toothed belt onto the pump pulley. Attach the cover for the toothed belt.

This completed Giulietta SS 101-series engine is ready for installation or for display.

■ The Final Steps

Reinstalling the Engine

Since you took it out, you're an expert on reinstalling the engine, so I can make this brief.

Reattach the clutch assembly and transmission. Install the clutch slave cylinder if fitted.

As a last act before lowering the complete engine/transmission into the car, chase the motor-mount threads on the chassis, and selectively fit the nuts and bolts which most easily thread on. The lower two studs are very hard to get to, and it helps if you can run the nut on with your fingers.

Start the two bottom motor mount nuts on their threads. As the mounts are lowered into the engine bay, they'll slip under the nuts and make the task of tightening the nuts easier.

You'll have the same difficulty getting the engine in as you did in getting it out. Thread the engine into the car almost vertically, being careful to clear the bulkhead with the transmission shift stub.

Put all the accessories on the engine before you put it into the car. This is especially true of a Weber-carbureted manifold, which is a pain to remove or install with the engine in place. If you've disconnected the exhaust manifold at the head, the engine will have to be properly tilted fore/aft before you can slip the manifold onto its studs. With the engine settled on its mounts in the engine bay, put a jack at the tail of the transmission and use it to tilt the engine so the exhaust manifold will slip on to its studs.

With the intake and exhaust manifolds attached, the side-to-side room in the engine bay is limited and you run a chance of snagging something as you lower the engine in place. Every once in awhile, stop and check around the engine to be sure you haven't captured a hose or wire inadvertently.

If you didn't remove the center console from inside the car to remove the shift lever, reattach the lever just before you rotate the transmission into its final position. This is also a good time to reattach the speedometer cable.

Don't forget the braided ground cable which bolts up near the starter.

The bolts which attach the exhaust pipes to the exhaust manifolds are tightened from underneath using a long socket extension. Have a friend hold the heads of the bolts from the top.

Breaking In

Break the engine in using standard nonsynthetic 20W50 motor oil. If you use synthetic oils, you're likely to glaze the cylinder walls or rings and you'll always burn oil. Before starting the engine, disconnect the coil wire and use the starter long enough to see oil pressure on the gauge.

There are no generally accepted rules for breaking in a rebuilt engine, even though the break-in period is a critical time in the life of the engine and the manufacturer's recommendations are well known. The critical factor is the amount of load on the engine, most notably the rings. Load is a combination of throttle opening and speed. I know respected mechanics who load the engine quickly from new, and others who follow a more leisurely course. The worst thing that can happen is to glaze the cylinder so the rings won't ever seat. This happens most often if the engine is run at a constant, relatively low load. So, the first rule is to avoid constant speeds and rates of acceleration during break-in.

Stay under 3,500 rpm for the first 100 miles or so, but progressively increase the loads on the engine upto the 100-mile mark. After that, a few brief full-throttle runs are appropriate. After about 2,000 miles the engine is broken in.

Rebuilding an engine yourself can bring a great deal of satisfaction, especially when your beautiful Giulietta or Giulia runs smoothly and powerfully and no longer uses oil.

The engine of this 1965 Giulia Spider Veloce was totally rebuilt during the car's restoration.

Chapter 9

Carburetion

The internal combustion engine will run on an incredibly poor mixture of air and fuel. Once, many years ago, I was working on a Fiat 1200 sedan. I had the manifold completely off, with the fuel line draped somewhere near the inlet to cylinder number 3. For some reason or other, I hit the starter. To my amazement, the engine caught and ran. Not just on one cylinder, but at least on two and perhaps three. I couldn't accelerate, of course, but the engine would have continued idling—except that the poor mixture caused the engine to backfire and that caught the car on fire ….

The early carburetors, including the Memini that powered the 6C1750, were hardly more sophisticated than the dribble of gas that had kept my Fiat engine running. The early Webers represented a new era of sophistication, since they provided two different-sized venturis to accommodate the wide range of fuel-delivery needs of the "modern" high-speed engines.

The reason carburetors need to be complex is that liquid fuel flows at a different rate than air. As the pressure differential increases, increasingly more fuel flows than air. The carburetor is a passive device that depends on the dynamics of fluid flow for its operation.

The air cleaner partially obscures the single Solex carburetor of a Giulia TI.

The uncorrected result would be to have a carburetor go progressively rich at higher speeds.

Solex Carburetors

The stock Giulietta Berlina intake consists of a single heated manifold carrying a single-throat Solex carburetor. The Sprint and Spider have one two-throat Solex carburetor. Giulietta Veloces have an abbreviated manifold which is really little more than a spacer for the two side-draft DCOE Weber carburetors.

Two slightly different dual-throat Solex carburetors are used on Giulietta and Giulia engines. The differences have to do with control of the secondary throttle plate and the two units are generally interchangeable. Several Weber downdraft carburetors also match the mounting studs of the Solex manifold. If you try to exchange a Weber downdraft, check to see that the throttle bellcrank is on the outboard side of the carburetor when the float bowl faces forward. The throttle shaft must point toward the engine, not run parallel to it.

In spite of the fact that carburetors invite adjustment, once set up none should ever need readjustment as long as nothing breaks and the jets are not clogged with dirt. The first rule, then, is to replace the fuel filter regularly.

Short of a catastrophic mechanical failure, then, carburetor repair is limited to dismantling the unit and cleaning it.

The most common carburetor fault is that it is defenseless against owners who are convinced that they can improve performance just by fiddling with its adjustments. The only external adjustments to a single carburetor affect idle only.

In general, the only change to a properly tuned carburetor which will improve performance is to fit larger venturi. Since Solex and Weber carburetor venturi are removable, they can be chucked in a lathe and enlarged (following approximately the same contour as the original). After that modification, rejetting is mandatory. The size of the main jet sets overall fuel delivery rate, while the size of the air correction jet controls the rate at which the mixture changes at higher speeds (say, over 3500 rpm). As a result, if a larger main jet is used, a proportionately larger air correction jet will also be necessary in order to maintain a consistent mixture over the rev range. If a leaner mixture is desired at high engine speeds, a larger air correction jet is required. If a richer mixture at high engine speeds is what you're after, a smaller air correction jet is what you need.

The most common catastrophic carburetor failure is a leaking float, which sinks to the bottom of the float bowl and never closes the fuel inlet needle valve. This causes the carburetor to flood with fuel. In theory, metal floats can be resoldered, but when you try to solder up

Installed in a Giulietta TI, the dual-throat Solex nestles beneath a cylindrical air cleaner.

a hole, the heated air inside the float bubbles the solder and a good job becomes impossible. It's much easier to get a new one. Plastic floats can be repaired with epoxy, but use as little as possible so as not to add weight to the float.

The next most common failure of the Solex carburetors is worn throttle-shaft bearing surfaces. The throttle shafts rotate in bearings that are machined into the pot metal casting. As the throttle shafts rotate, they will eventually wear these bearing surfaces oval. The symptom is an irregular idle which can't be corrected by adjustments. You can troubleshoot this condition by spraying WD-40 or starting fluid at the base of the carburetor with the engine idling. If engine speed increases, the shafts have worn the bearings and the carburetor should be replaced or repaired by a capable machinist.

28PBIC Solex

This carburetor is standard equipment on Giulietta Berlinas and offers a single 21mm venturi for the 53 hp engine. This carburetor is very simple and offers a cold-start circuit but not an accelerator pump. The cold-start device has two modes of operation: the choke pulled all the way out, and a half-way position. The Solex carburetors fitted to the cars in this book all used a separate fuel delivery circuit for cold-start enrichment instead of a butterfly at the top of the carburetor. This cold-start circuit carried its own metering jet. It is operated by a rotary valve that controls air flow into the starting circuit.

During a cold start, with the choke pulled out all the way, fuel from two small chambers is drawn into the engine for initial enrichment. Because these chambers are small, they are eventually exhausted of fuel if the

The standard Solex carburetor of the Giulietta mounts on a heated manifold and has two throats, the second of which opens at higher engine speeds.

cold-start device is left engaged. The result is that the mixture is leaned out automatically.

In the half-way position, the mixture is not as rich as the full-out position, but it is enriched continuously.

It is interesting to note that this Giulietta carburetor is similar to the Solex instrument fitted to Volkswagens and small Fiats of the same era. Although these units have a strong resemblance to the Giulietta's 28PBIC Solex, they are not identical.

32PAIAT Solex
This dual-throat carburetor was installed on the first 1,000 Giulietta Sprints. It had a 22mm primary venturi and a 23mm secondary venturi. In design, it was little different from the 35APAIG unit.

35APAIG Solex
This is a dual-throat unit featured on Giulietta TIs, Sprints (after the first 1,000) and Spiders. Both the primary and secondary venturi have 24mm bores, and the secondary throttle is operated mechanically by a cam off the primary throttle. A counterweighted throttle plate below the secondary throttle plate helps smooth the opening of the secondary venturi. The secondary does not have an idle circuit. A diaphragm-type accelerator pump is used.

The carburetor is assembled in three sections: the top cover, the body and a bottom casting which carries the throttle plates. There are two jetted circuits: idle and main. The Sprint and Spider use a 1.20mm main jet with a 1.50mm air correction jet, while the Giulietta TI has a 1.30mm main and 1.80mm air correction jet. The idle air jet is 1.00 mm for all Solexes covered here.

35PAIA Solex
This carburetor is standard equipment on the Giulia TI, Sprint and Spider. It is functionally identical to the 35APAIG except that it uses a vacuum-

controlled secondary throttle opener and deletes the counterweighted throttle plate. With this modification, the operation of the secondary venturi is more intimately associated with engine load.

Weber Carburetors
With the introduction of the Veloce versions of the Giulietta Sprint and Spider, Weber carburetors became standard equipment on certain new Alfa Romeos. They were also fitted to all Sprint Speciales, SZs, GTAs, Giulia Supers and Super TI models, as well as Duetto Spiders and GTVs through 1967 for North America. For Europe and other markets, Webers (and frequently Dellorto or Solex carburetors) were used well into the 1980s, and even into the early 1990s for the 1600 Junior.

40DCO3 and 40DCOE Weber
The 750 Alfa Veloces carried 40DCO3 Webers, while the 40DCOE was fitted to 101 models. They are functionally identical, though they differ in detail.

Probably there has never been a Giulietta owner who didn't covet the Veloce's dual-Weber setup. No doubt that the single Solex carburetor under-carburetes the Giulietta engine, but it does have the advantage of simplicity.

The single Solex does not necessarily have the advantage of economy, however, and certainly not of performance. In order to fit dual Webers to the Giulietta engine with Solex carburetor, both the Webers and their manifold are required. If you don't have the Weber manifold, you're in for a major search. You can use a SPICA fuel-injection manifold (not including the part that carries the throttle plates, of course) in conjunction with a Weber-adapter kit.

On the Giulietta, the lowest manifold mounting stud on the engine has to be replaced with a shorter one to

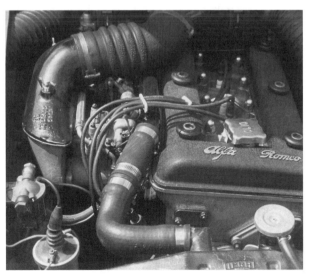

Beneath the plug wires, intake plenum and intake trunking lurk the 40DCO3 Webers of this 750 Spider Veloce.

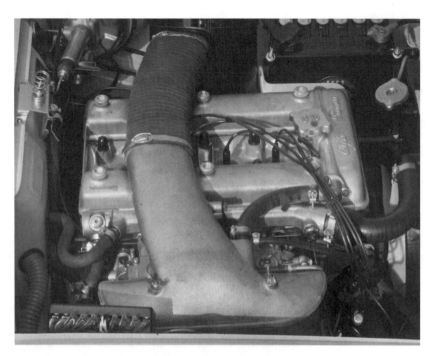

In the days before emissions controls, when most Americans thought of Alfa Romeo, they expected to see a large pair of Weber carburetors beneath the intake plenum of a car like this Giulia GT Veloce.

In Europe, Veloce models were often delivered with Dellorto carburetors in place of Webers. The Dellortos worked along exactly the same principles as the better known Webers.

adapt a Weber manifold. And—the engine should be tilted using Veloce motor mounts. Actually, the carbs will fit without tilting the engine if you don't have an air cleaner attached, but that is truly inviting long-term disaster.

If you fit the Weber carbs, you'll need different cams, at a minimum. The carbs alone free up the top revs so the engine feels as if it has a set of new lungs, but actual performance will not rise significantly unless you do more to the engine. The obvious choice is to use Veloce cams, but if you can't find a pair, Shankle (and a large number of other suppliers) offer aftermarket cams in a wide range of grinds. Don't go to the racing section and order yourself a set of hot GTA cams if you want to drive on the street. In general, you should order the mildest cams you think you can live with, not the hottest. You can learn to hate hot cams really quickly if you do a lot of city driving.

Having fitted new cams to your newly Weber-carbureted engine, you'll of course want to increase the compression ratio of the engine and then add a set of proper headers, then the rear axle ratio should be changed….

I've known Veloce owners who preferred to swap their dual Webers for the single Solex. They gain some tractability and the engine becomes slightly more convenient to maintain. If you do make the swap, pack up the Webers neatly and put them away. Avoid selling them, for a real Veloce Giulietta is a very rare and desirable piece.

▪ Adjusting Your Carburetors

This portion of the chapter provides you with basic information on how to make minor adjustments to your carburetors or to synchronize them in the case of dual Webers. No attempt has been made here to guide you in a carburetor rebuild or in fitting Webers or Dellortos to a car that started out with a single Solex.

Solex

For the most part, a healthy carburetor needs very little adjustment. More often, the ignition settings will be the culprits. However, though a carburetor is a precision instrument, there is no reason why the average home mechanic can't set the idle or mixture himself.

28PBIC Solex

The only adjustments to this carburetor are idle speed and idle mixture richness. The procedure for obtaining the proper idle adjustments is the same on this carburetor as on all other carburetors. Begin by adjusting the idle speed as nearly to specification as possible. Then, screw in the idle mixture adjustment until the engine begins to stall out. Back the idle mixture adjustment screw out until the engine reaches its highest speed, then readjust the idle speed screw for the desired idle speed.

If there is no change in engine speed as the idle mixture screw is adjusted, the idle speed is set too high and the engine is running off the main circuit. Lower the idle speed as much as possible and readjust the idle mixture screw to obtain the highest idle speed, then reset the idle speed.

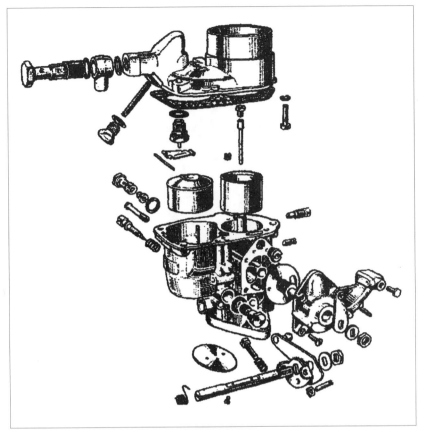

The 28PBIC Solex carburetor was fitted to the Giulietta.

Solex 28PBIC Carburetor

1. Choke circuit air intake
2. Choke circuit air jet
3. Choke valve
4. Choke control lever
5. Opening in the choke valve to admit extra fuel
6. Choke passage
7. Choke venturi
8. Emulsion holes
9. Emulsion tube
10. Main air correction jet
11. Float bowl vent
12. Idle mixture passage
13. Idle air correction jet
14. Idle jet
15. Choke reservoir
16. Air vent to the well
17. Choke reservoir
18. Float needle seat
19. Union with fuel filter
20. Filter
21. Float
22. Choke jet
23. Main jet carrier
24. Main jet
25. Idle mixture richness adusting screw
26. Idle circuit emulsion tube
27. Idle circuit opening
28. Throttle

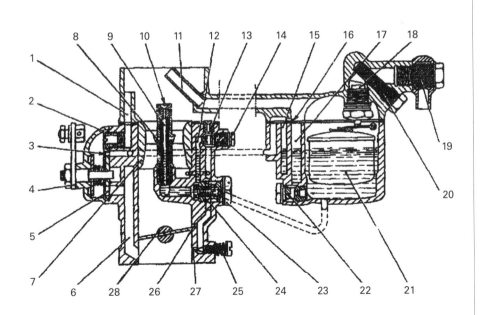

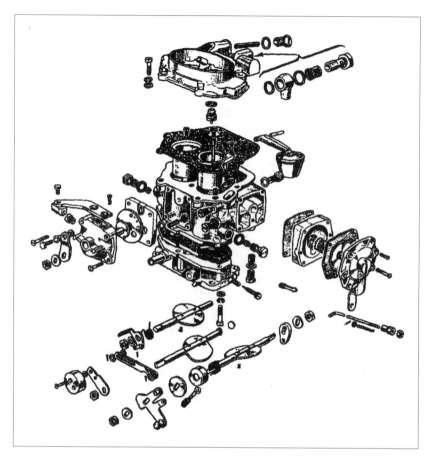

Except for the earliest cars, standard equipment for Giulietta
Sprints and Spiders included the Solex 35APAIG carburetor.

35APAIG Solex

Since the secondary throttle plate
is linked mechanically to the
primary, the only way to modify its
operation is to change the size of
the counterweight. A lighter weight
will cause the secondary to come
on earlier and a heavier one will
delay the operation. With the weight
removed, the secondary comes on in
a very decisive manner.

When used in racing applications,
the 35APAIG carburetor will lean
out and cause misfires on long right-
hand turns as fuel is centrifuged away
from the pickup hole to the main jet.
To correct this condition, remove the
main jet holder and drill a passage
into the float bowl near its bottom.
Some tuners press a pipe in place that
terminates in the center of the float
bowl to help assure fuel delivery.

Solex 35APAIG Carburetor

1. Main throttle
2. Secondary throttle
3. Secondary throttle control rod
4. Counterweighted throttle plate
5. Main emulsion tube
6. Secondary emulsion tube
7. Secondary fuel outlet
8. Balance hole
9. Accelerator pump control lever
10. Accelerator pump inlet (suction) valve
11. Accelerator pump pressure chamber
12. Accelerator pump diaphragm
13. Accelerator pump jet
14. Pump outlet
15. Secondary main jet
16. Primary main jet
17. Secondary air correction jet
18. Main air correction jet
19. Idle circuit air correction jet
20. Venturi
21. Idle mixture richness adjustment screw

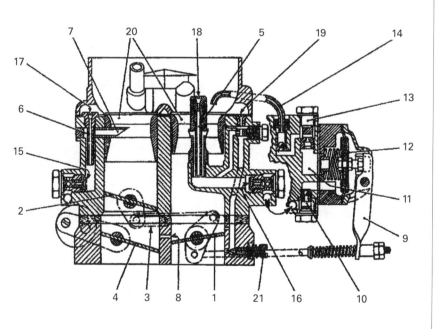

Balancing Webers

For best results, the two Weber carburetors on your Alfa Romeo should be adjusted to exactly the same specifications. The two Webers are connected by a balance screw that captures a tab linking the two carburetors, and works against a spring. In this procedure, this screw is adjusted to synchronize the two carburetors mechanically before adjusting idle speed and mixture richness. With the exception of this balance screw, all the adjustments in this procedure affect only the engine's idle quality.

Overall mixture strength, especially anything over idle, is controlled by the combination of jets and their associated emulsion tubes.

There are three adjusting screws referred to in this procedure. Identify them. All are held in adjustment by coil springs:

- A throttle stop screw blocks the throttle plates from closing all the way, and thereby controls the idle speed.

- A throttle shaft balance screw is used to adjust the mechanical link between the two carburetors. This screw is part of one throttle shaft assembly, and it presses against a tab which is part of the other throttle shaft. The tab is held against the screw by a coil spring.

- Each carburetor throat carries an idle mixture richness screw that adjusts the amount of fuel available at idle.

1. Let the engine warm up (if possible) and then shut it off. Remove the air cleaner assembly and disconnect the link at the bellcrank on the throttle shaft.

2. Remove the "hats" atop the carburetors by unscrewing the wing nuts. Unscrew the four main jets (two per carburetor). Verify that the main jets, emulsion tubes and air correction jets in both carburetors have the same values. The numbers are stamped on the parts. Return the jets and hats.

3. Back out the throttle stop screw until it no longer touches its seat on the carburetor body.

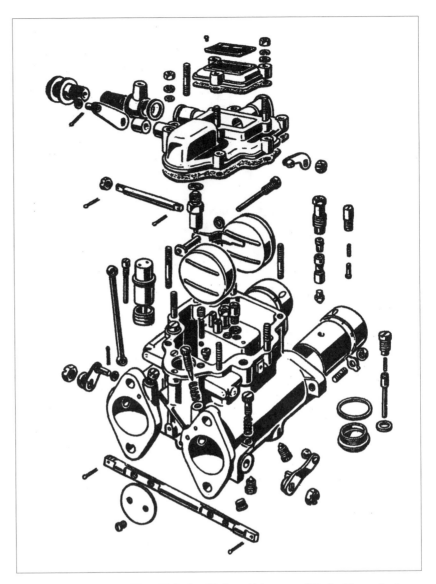

The 750 Series Giulietta Veloce was fitted with a pair of 40DCO3 Weber carburetors.

4. Turn the throttle shaft balance screw so you can see how it controls the adjustment between the two carburetors.

The carburetor's transition holes are covered by blanking screws, located on the axis of the throttle shaft near the base of the carburetor. If you remove one blanking screw from each carburetor, you will see the tip of the throttle plate, probably with the aid of a flashlight. As you watch the throttle plates through the transition holes, adjust the throttle shaft balance screw so that the throttle plates are mechanically synchronized. Verify that the plates for both carburetors uncover the same transition hole at the same time. Return the blanking screws and make sure they're tight.

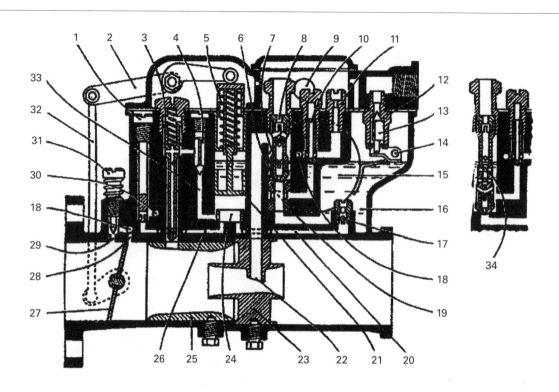

Weber 40DCO3 Carburetor

1. Pump drain screw
2. External pump operating lever
3. Pump jet
4. One-way needle valve
5. Piston return spring
6. Main jet
7. Well
8. Air correction jet
9. Ambient air balance port
10. Idle jet
11. Idle air screw
12. Needle valve housing
13. Needle valve
14. Float fulcrum screw
15. Float
16. Float bowl
17. Pump suction valve
18. Idle mixture passage
19. Idle communication passage
20. Pump suction tube
21. Pump piston
22. Jet Tube
23. Mixture metering device
24. Piston stroke blocking piece
25. Venturi
26. Pump drain pipe
27. Throttle
28. Progression port
29. Idle port
30. Pump drain
31. Screw for adjusting idle mixture richness
32. Pump rod
33. Pump inlet
34. Emulsion bowl

5. Use a mirror and flashlight to peer down the bores of both carburetors. Verify that the throttle plates are completely closed. If the plates are not fully closed, determine why and correct the condition (without bending anything!). The throttle plates must close completely on both carburetors with the throttle stop screw backed out.

6. Screw the throttle stop screw in until it just begins to rotate the throttle shafts, then reattach the accelerator pedal link at the bellcrank. If the length of this link needs to be adjusted, do so now. It should not change the idle speed when attached to the bellcrank.

7. Start the engine and let it settle to an idle. If it will not idle, readjust the throttle stop screw to get the lowest possible idle without killing the engine.

8. (Optional, but recommended) With a manometer such as the Unisyn, verify that both carburetors are drawing the same amount of air. If they are not, turn the throttle shaft balance screw until the flow rate is the same on both carburetors. If you don't have a sensitive instrument such as the Unisyn, leave this step out.

9. Stop the engine. Count the number of clockwise turns for each of the four idle mixture richness screws as you seat them lightly. Remember the smallest number. Note the orientation of the slots in the screw heads for each throat. From now on, all the screw slots must maintain this relationship.

10. Remember the smallest number of turns you counted while seating the idle mixture richness screws. Back out all four of them this number of turns.

11. Restart the engine and let it run until you are satisfied it is fully warm. If it won't idle, turn the throttle stop screw clockwise until it will.

12. In the following adjustment procedure, you're trying to hit the target idle speed by turning both the idle mixture adjustment screws and the idle stop screw the maximum number of turns counterclockwise. Turning the mixture screws should speed up the idle and turning the stop screw will slow down the idle.

13. Turn all the idle mixture richness screws 45 degrees counterclockwise. The engine speed should increase slightly. Rev the engine and let it return to idle to verify the engine idle speed. If the idle speed is too fast as a result of the mixture adjustment, turn the idle stop screw counterclockwise just enough to get the desired idle speed.

    If the engine dies after this initial 45-degree adjustment, you started with the idle mixture adjusting screws set too rich. Screw them all in one complete turn and recheck the idle speed. Then, repeat this step.

14. Repeat this process until you achieve the maximum idle speed with the least assistance from the idle stop screw. Since you're turning four mixture screws and the idle stop screw in small increments, this is a time-consuming procedure when done correctly.

    If the engine continues to speed up no matter how far out you turn the mixture screws, the throttle plates are open too far. Start over at step 3.

15. When you've achieved maximum idle speed, you've reached the idle mixture setting for maximum performance from closed throttle. Now, turn the idle mixture screws all clockwise about 45 degrees to lean out the mixture slightly.

    If you'd prefer economy, continue turning all the screws clockwise the same amount until the engine begins to stall, then turn them counterclockwise 45 degrees, or until you get a smooth idle.

16. Refit the air cleaner assembly and go for a drive.

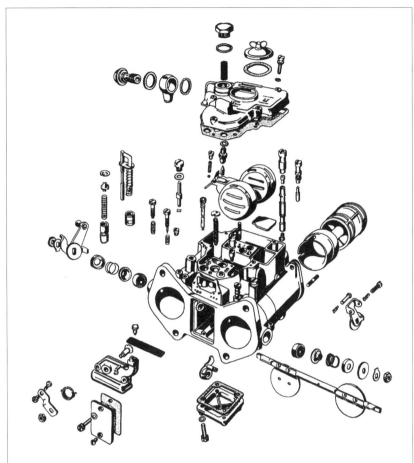

When the 101-series took over, Veloces received the slightly modified 40DCOE Weber carburetor.

Once adjusted, Weber carburetors should not go out of adjustment. If you're satisfied with the way the car runs, keep your hands off the carburetors.

With leaded fuel, you could verify overall mixture richness by reading the plugs. Since leaded fuel is no longer available, this test is of questionable value now.

One way to verify proper mixture strength is to momentarily enrich the mixture with propane gas. Use one of the small handyman propane torches available in hardware stores. With the engine running at idle, point the torch (no flame) at the intake inlet and open the valve one or two turns. If the carburetors are jetted correctly, the engine should speed up momentarily and then stall out. If the engine speeds up and does not stall, it is jetted too lean. If it stalls right away, it is probably jetted too rich.

Hopefully, this basic section on carburetors will be sufficient to give you both a better understanding of how they work and a good idea of how to accurately set the Solex or Webers fitted to your Alfa Romeo.

Chapter 10

SPICA Mechanical Fuel Injection

Fuel injection was first applied to internal combustion engines during World War II to give the Luftwaffe's aircraft superior altitude and maneuverability capabilities. In the mid-1950s, the Mercedes-Benz 300SL introduced direct fuel injection. This mechanical system was very high pressure because, like a diesel, it injected fuel directly into the cylinders near the peak of the compression stroke.

In the 1960s, smog was beginning to be recognized as a problem. Our legislators jumped in with laws which attempted first to restrict the unburned fuels (hydrocarbons, or HC) and carbon monoxide (CO) which dribbled out of every car's tailpipe.

American auto companies reacted to the legislated emission controls exactly as they had to legislated safety devices: they predicted doom, then did their best to make sure it happened. The first emission-control devices implemented were make-do and burdensome to the consumer.

Remember three-point seatbelts and five-mph bumpers? American emission-controlled engines of the early 1970s were simply leaned out to keep HC emissions low. Drivability and vehicle mileage suffered dramatically, but since temporary-solution engineering was used, the controls were easily removed. No doubt, had the emission controls proved widely unpopular,

Bosch's first commercial application of mechanical fuel injection was to the Mercedes-Benz 300SL, which entered production in 1954.

the government would have backed off on them. Instead, a large cottage industry sprung up to remove the emission controls. By allowing the public to switch, rather than fight, the net effect of the "de-smoggers" was to ensure that emission-control laws would stay on the books.

With the air-injection trunking removed, the view of the linkages of the SPICA injection system of this 1979 Sports Sedan is improved.

▪ Why SPICA?

The view from Europe was much more timid. European manufacturers were terrified of the new American laws. With no real inside information from the halls of Congress, importers quaked at rumors of 35-mph barrier tests and the banishment of over-polluting cars from the American market. Alfa was certainly convinced that, if it encouraged owners to disable emission controls, it would be kicked out of the lucrative American market.

It was in this atmosphere of fear that Alfa Romeo management chose to take the most comprehensive approach to engineering emission controls into its engines. While all American manufacturers and most importers simply bolted on "tamper-proof," leaned-out carburetors, beginning in 1969, all Alfas sold in the United States were equipped with a mechanical fuel injection system.

Fuel injection can deliver an almost ideal fuel/air mixture over the engine's operating range. As a result, it provides the best emission control without degrading drivability. In addition, it can be made to meet increasingly stricter emission controls with simple refinements. As a measure of Alfa's engineering skill, it was not until 1981 that it needed to use exhaust gas recirculation, many years after other manufacturers were forced to employ this performance-killing technique for reducing oxides of nitrogen.

The injection pump around which Alfa built its fuel injection system came from SPICA, a sister company to Alfa within the Finmeccanica group of nationalized companies. SPICA fuel injection pumps were used until 1982, when Bosch EFI was adopted.

The SPICA pump started out as a mystery to all. No other car imported into the United States used it. On top of its rarity, Alfa wouldn't say anything about how to tune it. "Field" repairs, even by Alfa-trained technicians, were forbidden. The stone-walling was due to Alfa's fears that any information it released about the pump would be used to disable its emission-control characteristics. So, if your SPICA pump went sour, you either sent it back for an expensive rebuild or simply threw the whole

Demystifying SPICA

It was not long before curious Alfa owners were tearing into the pumps. The technical editor of the Alfa Club, Joe Benson, finally published a series of descriptive articles in the club magazine which made the SPICA system much less intimidating. Now, it's just another thing the Alfa enthusiast loves to fiddle with. As long as you know what you're doing, the SPICA system is a piece of cake.

system out and fitted two Weber DCOE carburetors for about half the price of a rebuilt pump. SPICA pumps got a bad name and a lot of perfectly good ones were scrapped simply because Alfa owners didn't think they were worth the bother.

Anatomy of a SPICA

The SPICA pump is divided into two parts. The front part of the pump is a small four-cylinder compressor which is responsible for squirting the right amount of fuel at the right time. It's driven by a toothed belt off the crankshaft. The cylinders of the pump have a port which controls how much fuel is taken in. It's an arrangement similar to the way a two-stroke engine operates, except that the SPICA cylinders have helical ports and can rotate to change when the piston opens and closes the port.

A geared rack controls cylinder rotation, and the linkage for moving the rack is moved by a logic section in the rear half of the pump.

The logic section of the SPICA pump is nothing more than a speed-sensing governor and a set of levers

Although this SPICA pump is an eight-cylinder unit for a Montreal, all components are clearly revealed, including the compressor (far left) and the eight piston/cylinder units. A pump for a four-cylinder engine would have a similar compressor section, but only four piston/cylinder units.

which eventually push or pull on the rack. The levers are moved by mechanical sensors for coolant temperature, barometric pressure, engine speed and throttle angle. In addition, solenoids provide for cold-start enrichment and fuel cut-off to shut everything down. We'll describe each function in some detail.

A Bourdon tube connected to the cylinder head senses coolant temperature. As the liquid inside the tube is heated, it expands, extending a small plunger which presses on one of the levers of the logic section. An accordion-shaped capsule expands or contracts depending on barometric pressure. The capsule presses on another part of the logic section's linkage.

The engine-speed sensor in the logic section works like a governor. As the pump crankshaft turns, heavy steel balls press against a spring-loaded ramp. The faster the speed of the crank, the more energy the balls have to press outward. As the balls travel up the ramp, they force a three-dimensional cam to slide fore and aft inside the logic section. As engine speed changes, the three-dimensional cam moves forward and backward.

A long rod from the throttle linkage causes the same three-dimensional cam to rotate around its axis. Thus,

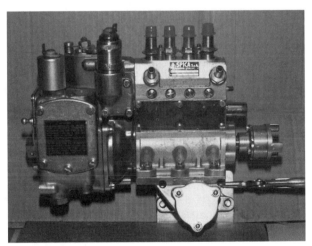

The logic section of the SPICA pump is on the left, while the actual fuel metering takes place in the right-hand portion of the unit.

as the throttle plates open and engine speed increases, the three-dimensional cam moves along, and also rotates about, its axis. Now, the surface of this three-dimensional cam is literally a "map" of the fuel delivery curve. A lever which rides on the surface of the cam is raised or lowered depending on both the rotation and the fore-and-aft motion of the three-dimensional cam. The cam itself is super-precise: some 3,000 plots are made on its surface to assure proper fuel delivery. The cold-start solenoid presses on the logic linkage to enrich the fuel delivery as long as the starter is engaged. An oil dashpot slows the solenoid's return to continue fuel enrichment for a short time after the starter disengages.

The logic unit is a mechanical calculator that uses moving levers and fulcrums to change the pump's capacity to deliver fuel.

The mechanical inputs that play a part in determining fuel quantity and timing include engine coolant temperature, throttle angle, barometric pressure and engine speed.

- Engine coolant temperature is input by the expansion of the thermostatic actuator.

- Throttle angle is sensed by the position of the long link extending from the bellcrank on the intake manifold.

- Barometric pressure is sensed by the expansion of a barometric capsule inside the pump.

- Engine speed is sensed by the centrifugal force of balls inside a spinning ramp.

All four mechanical inputs are part of a system of levers, the motion of which corresponds linearly to coolant temperature, throttle angle, barometric pressure and engine speed.

The end of one lever in the system rests on the surface of a three-dimensional cam. The four linear inputs are converted to a nonlinear response through the three-dimensional cam. The cam is rotated by the long link, and moves in and out according to the position of the balls inside the spinning ramp. That is, the three-dimensional cam interprets both throttle angle and engine speed. The result of linkage-cum-cam establishes the capacity of the pump to deliver an accurate charge of fuel to the engine.

From the manufacturer's standpoint, this arrangement is very versatile. For engines with different air/fuel needs, you don't have to change the basic linkage system: just changing the cam alters the fuel delivery profile.

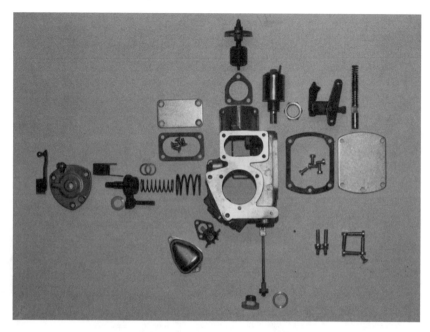

In the logic section, the bellcrank (far left) triggers the proper throttle opening.

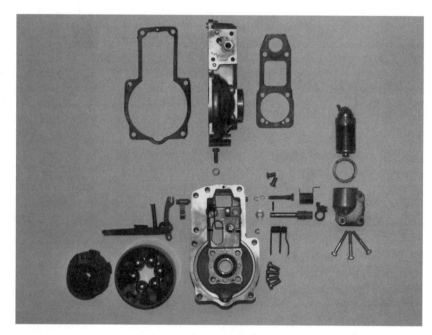

The major components of the logic section include the casing and spinning ramp.

The output of the logic system is the fore-aft movement of a rack that controls the capacity of the pump's cylinders in the front half of the SPICA unit, which is a variable-displacement pump. Each cylinder uses a helical opening in the cylinder wall. Movement of the rack moves the hole higher or lower along the cylinder wall. When the hole is located above the piston, fuel enters the cylinder. When the piston is higher

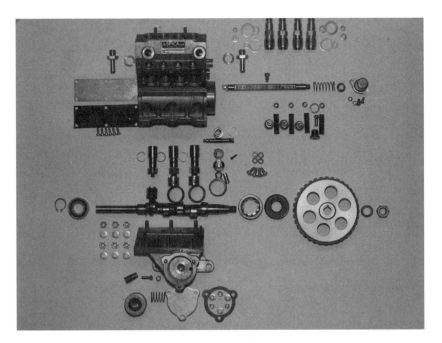

The rack (above right) controls the volume of fuel held by each of the pump's cylinders, while the cam (center) is responsible for the fuel delivery profile.

than the hole, the cylinder is closed and the piston compresses the fuel.

Fore and aft movement of the rack, then, changes the working length of the cylinder. Clearly, the mechanism in this pump uses extremely close tolerances, because there are no seals in the helical mechanism nor are there any rings to seal the piston. SPICA injection specialist Wes Ingram talks about getting the proper feel of an acceptable fit between the piston and cylinder, clearly not an exercise for the inexperienced.

The force of the compressed fuel opens a one-way check valve, sending the fuel charge into the lines and finally out the injector nozzle. With this arrangement, the volume of fuel inside the lines between the pump and injector must be absolutely equal, otherwise the timing of the charge to the cylinders would be unequal. That explains why there are coils in the fuel lines between the pump and the injectors.

Things to Know About the SPICA Pump

The short link and long link are two rods running from the bellcrank (a spool with a round springy-thingy wound around it) at the top of the intake manifold.

There are two fuel filters: one near the gas tank and another in the engine compartment. In addition, there are two fuel pumps: an electric pump beneath the engine and another bolted to the engine on the intake side which is properly called the fuel injection pump (the SPICA unit). At the rear of the fuel injection pump is a lever which connects to the long link. One edge of

the lever is cut away and a screw mounted on the pump itself points to the cut-out part of the lever. The screw should have a plastic nose-cone wired to it. If it doesn't, proceed anyway, but be a little more nervous about everything. The gap between the cut-out part of the lever and the screw is called the pump gap.

As already discussed, the front part is responsible for getting fuel up to the injectors; the rear part is for figuring out how much fuel to squirt. The front part, with the pulley on it, has four pipes running up to the fuel injectors on the intake manifold. The rear part of the pump has a bunch of things on top of it and a big bulge toward the end. One of the things on the rear part snakes upward past a bulge (where it is bolted to the underside of the manifold) and then to another bulge which is held against the intake manifold by two small nuts. This is the thermostatic actuator.

Depending on whether you have a 1750 or a 2.0-liter, there are one or two "cans" on top of the rear section and both have wires connected to them. The front one on 2.0-liter cars is the threaded fuel cut-off solenoid which is also used to adjust overall fuel mixture. The rear one (on both 1750 and 2.0-liter cars) is the cold-start solenoid.

On all models, there's a triangular plate held on with three screws. On some cars, there's a lever attached to the shaft sticking out of the plate; on others, there's just the shaft. Beneath the plate is the barometric capsule (you really don't need to know). If there's a lever, it should be in the "N" position, regardless. On 1750 models only, there's an adjusting screw with a locknut. This is for adjusting overall fuel mixture.

That's really all there is to the insides of the SPICA system. Unless something breaks, there's no need to open the pump, or even remove it from the engine. All tuning adjustments are made on the top of the pump and to the linkages which connect the pump to the throttle plates.

■ Adjusting the SPICA Unit

With a few tools and some patience, it is possible to adjust the mechanical fuel injection on your 1969 through 1981 Alfa Romeo. Be sure to approach the system cautiously and follow the directions below.

On the back of the fuel injection pump, next to the bellcrank, you should see a stop-screw locknut with a bullet-shaped plastic cover wired over it. If the plastic cover is missing, and the fuel injection system is obviously way out of tune, you might consider stopping right now. If the reference screw has been adjusted, you'll never be able to set the SPICA system up properly and the pump will have to be recalibrated. The lesson here is to avoid Alfas with missing plastic covers on the bellcrank stop screws. For those cars on which the screw has clearly been adjusted, I'll give a work-around at the end of this section.

The two screws sitting on top of the intake manifold shouldn't be adjusted, either. There's no way of telling if they have been fiddled with and, in fact, their obvious location almost invites adjustment. There's a factory tool used to set these two screws. If you're a perfectionist, have an Alfa mechanic set these for you, using the proper tool. One screw sets the closed-throttle stop and the other sets the wide-open-throttle stop. You can survive if these screws are misadjusted slightly, so presume that they're OK for the time being.

The first step in setting up a SPICA system is to verify that the rest of the engine is operating properly. It has to have good compression—at least 120 psi—and its ignition has to be properly timed.

Special Tools for SPICA Injection

Alfa supplied its dealers with a few special tools for the SPICA system. Initially, it was felt that these tools were mandatory for setting up the system. That conviction automatically eliminates virtually every Alfa owner on the planet. Over the years, enthusiasts have developed ways of tuning the system without the tools, and that is the bulk of the information I'm including here. However, for the record, the following special tools are used to set up the SPICA pump, following factory procedure:

Fuel Cut-Off Solenoid Wrench: To loosen the ring holding the fuel cut-off solenoid on 1971 and later SPICA pumps, you use this castellated wrench. While I'm sure there is a number for this tool, Alfa did not put it in their shop manual supplement because it didn't want nondealer types changing the setting from factory specifications. From the manufacturer's standpoint, there should never be a reason for loosening this ring; from the enthusiast's standpoint, if it can be fiddled with, it should be. There is probably not a single Alfa in the United States with a virgin setting for the fuel cut-off solenoid. Never try to loosen this ring with a chisel or screwdriver: you'll only destroy it. On some cars, I've had some luck using a medium-sized vise grip to rotate the ring and solenoid counterclockwise as a unit, after which the ring can be rotated by hand. It's best to bend up a tool using a two-inch muffler clamp. Grind the ends of the clamp so they fit in two of the castellations in the locking ring. It may be necessary to strengthen this tool by welding a large washer in place between the arms of the clamp. The washer must have an inside diameter adequate to clear the solenoid.

Idle Stop Adjustment Tool (A.4.0121): The two screws sitting proudly on top of the intake manifold casting shouldn't be adjusted, but most have been. They do not adjust idle speed, nor maximum throttle opening, since their settings can be overcome by changing the lengths of the short and long links. This tool sets the two screws to their factory specifications. If you're a perfectionist, have an Alfa mechanic set these for you, using the proper tool.

One screw sets the closed-throttle stop and the other sets the wide-open-throttle stop. If you don't have this tool, just be sure that the throttle plates close fully.

Thermostatic Actuator Tool (A.4.0120): The skinny tube running from the head to the injection pump reports engine coolant temperature. Beneath the tube, inside the SPICA pump, is an adjusting screw which compensates for wear and individual variations in the temperature sensing device. The tool verifies that the adjusting screw is set to factory specifications, and is probably the only tool you'll really wish you had. However, a bolt with a nut threaded on it is a workable substitute. The proper setting is 27 to 29 mm between the bottom face of the nut and the tip of the bolt, depending on model year (use 29 mm if in doubt).

Throttle Cable Tool (A.2.0181): An adjustable replacement for the throttle cable, this tool is necessary to set the baseline length of the entire throttle linkage to factory specifications. It is useful only if you also have tools C.6.0140, C.6.0141, C.6.0142 and C.6.0143.

Bellcrank Protractor (C.6.0140 and C.6.0141): This two-part tool fits on the rear of the SPICA pump and is used in conjunction with the throttle cable tool and the throttle shaft protractor tool to verify the lengths of the long and short links.

Throttle Shaft Protractor (C.6.0142 and C.6.0143): A two-part protractor used to verify the angle of the throttle plates.

Manometer (C.2.0011): This device verifies that each intake port is pulling the same amount of vacuum. The most resourceful will fabricate a manometer, or get one at a motorcycle store.

Idle Equalizer Adjustment Tool (A.2.0183): Useful only for 1971 and later cars, this tool adjusts the idle air bleed screw located atop the intake manifold. Useless: use a large screwdriver instead. You probably won't be able to tell a difference because the sealing O-ring has hardened and is not functional.

The Alfa crankshaft pulley has four timing marks: "F," "P," "M" and "I." If the engine is not running, the ignition points must just begin to open on the "F" mark. The "P" mark is top dead center. The "M" mark is for maximum-advance timing at 5,000 rpm, and has to be set using a strobe timing light, not the inexpensive neon types.

The "I" mark is the timing mark for the fuel injection. To check pump timing, make sure that the valves are closed on number 1 cylinder when bringing the "I" mark up to the crankshaft pointer. There is a timing mark on the pump pulley and a corresponding mark on the body of the pump. Both are very hard to find.

With the crank pulley on "I," the mark on the pump pulley must align with the mark on the pump body. To adjust this, you need to:

- Remove the crank pulley when the "I" mark is right...

- Rotate the pump pulley so it's on time, then...

- Simultaneously replace the toothed belt on the crank pulley and press the pulley onto the crank.

With all the marks aligned, slip the toothed belt onto the pump pulley. Late-model pump pulleys have a lip on them so you will also have to loosen the crankshaft pulley to get the toothed belt on. The crank pulley has a 1.5-inch nut held on by 150 pound feet of torque.

Start the engine and warm it up. Remove the air cleaner and slip the throttle cable off its bellcrank. Use a Unisyn or similar flow-measuring meter to verify that the throttle plates close uniformly. The factory manometer set plugs into the nipples for the idle-air hoses, but most carburetor synchronizing tools will work fine. There's an adjusting screw between throats 2 and 3 for synchronizing the front and rear throttle shafts. Adjust the short link on the throttle bellcrank to get the throttle plates to close.

If the engine doesn't run (yet), you can get pretty close simply by watching the motion of the linkage and the throttle plates carefully. All four throttle plates must close, otherwise the engine will backfire under deceleration.

Reconnect the throttle cable and, with the engine off, have a friend floor the accelerator to verify that the throttle plates open all the way. If the plates don't fully open, there's an adjustable stop under the accelerator

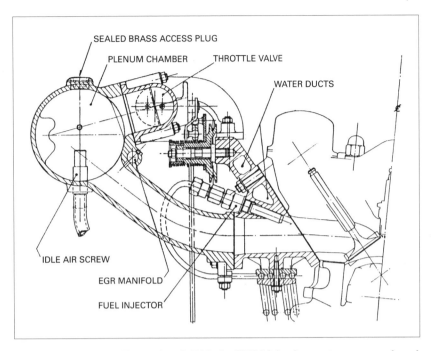

For 1980 and 1981, the SPICA injection system was equipped with just a single throttle. The inlet passages, throttle bellcrank and injector can be seen. The large alloy manifold was required to withstand the exhaust gas recirculation that was used as part of the emission-control equipment.

pedal and another on the firewall. You can also readjust the throttle cable length to help get wide-open-throttle, but then recheck to verify that the plates also close. A lot of low-performance SPICA complaints are solved just by getting the throttles to open wide.

The pump gap is the distance between the tip of the plastic-sealed stop screw and the pump bellcrank. The procedure for setting the pump gap depends on maintaining the engine at operating temperature. Work quickly. If you run into difficulty, start the engine and let it idle for a minute before shutting it off and continuing. The engine will idle with the long link disconnected between the throttle bellcrank and the pump bellcrank.

Setting the Gap

Let the engine warm up fully, then disconnect the long link from the throttle bellcrank to the pump. Measure the gap between the pump bellcrank and the stop screw. The bellcrank arm has an indentation in it, so use a narrow feeler gauge to measure from inside the indentation to the tip of the screw. The gap should be between 0.012 inches and 0.024 inches; the closer to 0.019 inches the better.

If it is not, quickly remove the two screws which hold the thermostatic actuator to the top of the pump and carefully pull it free, being careful not to kink the Bourdon tube. Directly under the tip of the actuator,

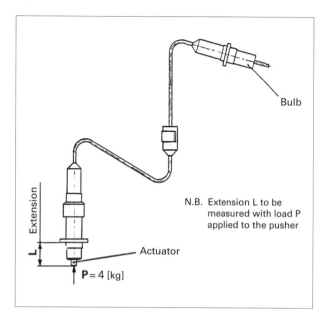

N.B. Extension L to be measured with load P applied to the pusher

P = 4 [kg]

The thermostatic actuator may require calibration. Failure of the actuator is typically caused by a loss of fluid. This can sometimes be overcome by pinching the bulb located midway along the Bourdon tube.

inside the pump, is an adjusting screw. Turning the screw clockwise will increase the pump gap, and turning it counterclockwise decreases the gap. Give the screw a turn in the desired direction and push the thermostatic actuator home, holding it firmly in place with a long screwdriver. Check the pump gap again and repeat the adjustment drill until you get the desired clearance.

You may not be able to get the pump gap within the specified distance. If you can't, use a mirror to look carefully at the tip of the thermostatic actuator. A pin should protrude from the tip of the actuator by at least 0.08 inches. If it doesn't, the actuator is bad and must be replaced. If the pin protrudes so far that you can't get a proper pump gap, you can cut several cardboard gaskets to shim the actuator away from the pump body.

When the pump gap is as close to 0.019 inches as you can get it, reattach the thermostatic actuator with its two screws. Check to see that the bulb in the middle of the Bourdon tube is firmly attached to a support beneath the intake manifold.

Lengthen or shorten the long link between the pump and throttle bellcrank so the pump gap is 0.045 inches with the link attached.

Setting the Fuel Mixture

While 1750 Alfas have a simple screw adjustment for mixture richness, 2.0-liter Alfas use the fuel cut-off solenoid as an adjustment. On the 2.0-liter cars, the fuel cut-off solenoid is held in place by a castellated ring which requires a special tool to loosen. Don't try

to chisel it loose. Instead, use a U-shaped tool made out of the top of a two-inch or larger muffler clamp (see Special Tools for SPICA Injection). Compress the ends of the clamp using a vise until they just fit over the solenoid and then grind the threaded tips of the clamp down so they engage two opposite castellations in the ring. Don't rotate the solenoid more than 1/8 turn while loosening the ring.

With the clamping ring loosened, start the engine, bring it to operating temperature and then place a large screwdriver or wedge at the throttle cable stop on the firewall so you get a solid, steady idle anywhere between 2,000 and 3,000 rpm. Slowly turn the adjusting screw (on 1750s) or the fuel cut-off solenoid (on 2.0-liters) until the engine speed peaks. Turning the adjustment too far in either direction will lower the engine speed. Once the highest speed is achieved, turn the 1750 screw 1/8 turn counterclockwise or the 2.0-liter solenoid 1/8 turn clockwise to lean the mixture slightly. Lock the adjustment in place and remove the wedge.

If you have access to an HC/CO emissions meter, adjust the fuel mixture to get one-percent CO at idle. On 1750 Alfas, idle air adjusters are located in two small boxes connected to the air cleaner. On 2.0-liter cars, a single large adjuster sits atop the intake manifold.

You can continue to make running fuel-mixture adjustments in 1/8-turn increments by checking your spark plugs. At highway speeds, push the clutch in and carefully shut the ignition off at the same time, then coast to a stop. Unscrew a spark plug and look at the color of the ceramic tip. You want a light cocoa brown, about the color of a chocolate milkshake. If the tip is too white, the fuel mixture is too lean. If it's too dark, the fuel mixture is too rich.

Plan B: When the Reference Screw Has Been Adjusted

If the reference screw has been adjusted previously, begin by acting as if it is okay. Set everything up just as described above, including a 0.019-inch pump gap.

The reference screw establishes a baseline to adjust the operation of the thermostatic actuator. Because this baseline reference is suspect, you need to find the best compromise between two adjustments: the screw under the thermostatic actuator and the rotation of the fuel cut-off solenoid.

A properly set-up SPICA system will fast-idle when cold. If it doesn't, the most likely cause is that the thermostatic actuator screw adjustment is set too lean. Therefore, over a few days, keep adjusting the thermostatic actuator screw until you get a fast idle on a cold engine. Screwing the adjustment in (clockwise) enriches the mixture. By the time you get a good fast idle when cold, you may be running very rich when hot.

Adjust the fuel cut-off solenoid to lean out the overall mixture when hot. This adjustment will change the effect of the thermostatic actuator, so continued juggling will be necessary.

If you keep at it, you may be able to get a decent-running engine and save yourself the cost of a recalibrated pump or a set of carburetors.

While the procedures described above abbreviate the official factory routine, they will set up most SPICA fuel injection systems so they run very well. Experience has proved the SPICA system to be both reliable and forgiving, which is quite a different impression Alfa enthusiasts had when the system first appeared.

Quick Tune-Up

The following will certainly offend those purists whose tool chest includes many of the special SPICA tools called out above. The more compulsive will rush to assure you that the kind of shade-tree techniques I suggest here are wholly inappropriate for the high-precision capabilities of the SPICA system. Even the procedure above will offend some because it fails to utilize the special tools Alfa provided for adjusting the SPICA pump.

I don't intend to sanctify the priestly class of mechanics that believe only they understand or are competent to work on the SPICA system. Nor do I wish to make the SPICA special tools objects of veneration which compete with the Holy Grail. The SPICA system is a mechanical contrivance. It is a bit complex, to be sure, but it is still man-made.

What follows is an abbreviated SPICA setup which I considered putting first in this chapter. However, had it started the chapter, most would not have bothered with the more complete procedure. Further, understanding the material above helps one appreciate exactly what's happening in the faster method.

When should you use this quick setup? When you've gone through the long procedure but something seems out of whack, or you just want to verify that everything is optimized. Remember, if it ain't broke, don't fix it.

It ain't broke if:

- You can start your car without playing footsie with the accelerator pedal. Most systems are set up to start with no pedal at all; some seem to start better with a little pedal. If you have to jiggle or move the pedal slowly to start the car, the system is a little sick.

- Your car doesn't backfire on deceleration.

- The exhaust is invisible most of the time and the engine idles smoothly at around 1,000 rpm.

- You get reasonable acceleration and gas mileage. Fiddling with the SPICA system to improve either is probably going to get you into more trouble than it's worth.

It *is* broke if:

- You can hardly start the car on cold mornings (it may start fine when warmed up).

- The car starts only after five minutes of cranking.

- It backfires on deceleration.

- Your exhaust is sooty black and you get about ten mpg.

- Idle speed is very uneven or extremely low or high.

- You smell gasoline on the oil dipstick.

- The little tube from the cylinder head to the injector pump is broken.

- The car won't start at all and there's no fuel visible if you loosen an injector fitting and crank the engine.

In virtually all of these cases, take the car to a reputable shop if you have any doubts about how to proceed.

The genius of the SPICA system is that it is very forgiving and a car can run very well even with a system that is out of adjustment. The procedure I'll describe depends on the fact that one adjustment of a component in the system will correct for the poor adjustment in another. The procedure I'll describe begins with a rough adjustment of the most critical settings (the pump gap and throttle plates) and then proceeds to refine the settings by testing. This approach has something legitimate to recommend it, because if it's followed, you will have tuned the car for the exact requirements of its individual needs, not to the generic factory setting.

If the Car Won't Start

Even if the car won't start, we have to presume that the engine is mechanically sound (no bent rods or dropped valves), the ignition timing is correct and the plugs are getting ample spark. Those may be large leaps of faith, but this isn't an encyclopedia of Alfa fix-its, either. Be absolutely sure there's fuel in the tank. Pour in a gallon if there's any doubt.

Here's what to check on the fuel delivery system: You hear the fuel pump whir from beneath the car (amidships) when you turn the ignition on. If it doesn't, there's an electrical problem getting battery voltage to the pump. Fuel should gush out vigorously toward the engine if you remove the front rubber hose at the fuel injection pump. If it doesn't and the pump whirrs, the fuel filter(s) are clogged. That's right; there are two: one near the fuel tank and the other one in the engine compartment. You may also find small in-line filters in the rubber hoses near the SPICA pump. With cylinder number 4 coming up on compression and the pointer at the "I" on the flywheel pulley, the two timing marks should line up on the SPICA pump and its pulley. The mark on the SPICA pulley is almost impossible to see, so be very careful here.

If you loosen slightly one of the injector fittings and then crank the engine, fuel should weep from the fitting. Retighten the fitting. Be sure there's a little slack in the cable which runs from the firewall to the bellcrank on the intake manifold. If there isn't, readjust the cable so you can press the accelerator pedal slightly before the bellcrank begins to move. This assures that the idle position is set mechanically by the SPICA linkages rather than by the accelerator linkage. If all these things are okay and the car won't start, you're probably in over your head, so quit now.

We have to presume now that the engine will run. Remove the air cleaner from the engine. Record where all the hoses attached to the air cleaner go.

Use a needle-nose pliers to carefully wedge the upper end of the short link running from the bellcrank to the throttle shafts. When it's free, pull up on the short length lightly to be sure that the throttle plates are closing completely, then see where the end of the link falls in relation to the pivot ball it snaps around. Adjust the short link (it screws on) if necessary so you can feel the plates as they just close. They should stay just closed when the link is reattached to the ball on the bellcrank. Don't worry right now if the front two and rear two sets don't close simultaneously, and don't try to cheat by making the link too short: just closed is the proper adjustment. Reattach the link.

Use a mirror and flashlight to check that all four of the throttle plates are closed. If they are not, very carefully adjust the joint between the two throttle shafts to get parallel operation so the front two and rear two throttle plates shut at the same time. Readjust the short link again so the throttle plates just close.

Check the Thermostatic Actuator

Clean the area around the thermostatic actuator at the injection pump. The unit is attached to the pump with two small machine screws. Use a magnetic screwdriver to remove the screws and their lock washers, then very carefully lift the end up so it just clears the pump, being careful not to kink the small hollow tube. Use a mirror to examine the end of the actuator. If you cannot see a shaft protruding about 1/16 inch from the body of the actuator, then the actuator has failed and must be replaced before proceeding.

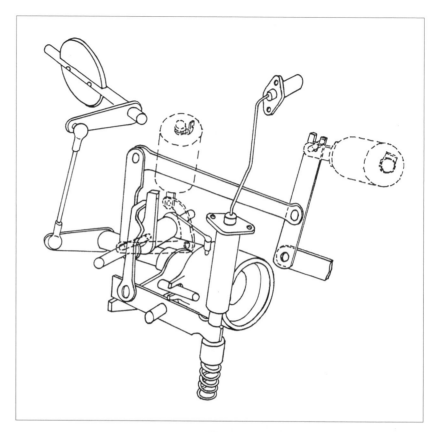

In this partial, exploded view of the logic section of the SPICA injection system, the bellcrank assembly triggering the throttle shaft is clearly visible.

A Shankle Sure-Start is an acceptable (and less expensive) replacement for the thermostatic actuator. Peer into the hole from which you removed the actuator: see the slotted screw? Keep it in mind. If you can't see a screw, peer some more with a flashlight. If you still can't see the screw, it may be covered with a protective cap. You can remove this cap by carefully piercing it with a sharp punch (dead center) and then prying carefully to work the seal free. If the projecting shaft at the tip of the actuator seems okay, replace the actuator into the injection pump and then tighten the screws so it seats against the pump. Be careful: you can snap the screws off very easily and if you do, the pump probably will have to come off the engine (you don't want to know how hard that is).

Check the Cold-Start Solenoid

Remove the connector to the rearmost solenoid (the only one on 1750s) and touch a twelve-volt lead to the terminal momentarily. You should be able to hear a click. If you can't, keep going, but don't get your hopes up. If there's no click, its plunger is sticking and might be freed by flushing the pump's insides with a solvent like diesel fuel (then changing the engine oil and filter).

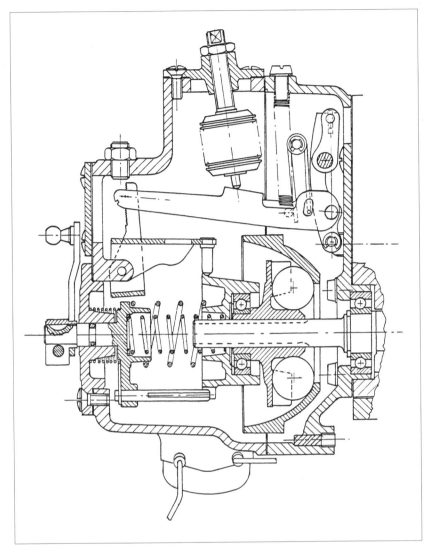

The logic section of the SPICA fuel injection unit controls the amount of fuel for each cylinder.

Adjust Mixture Richness

The main mixture adjustment remains to be made, but the engine should idle smoothly near normal speed. Use a needle-nose pliers to pinch off each of the four rubber hoses running from atop the manifold to the intake runners. Pinching off each hose should cause the engine speed to drop a little. If it does not, then there is either a leak in one or more of the hoses (probably a crack near either end at the nipple) or the throttle plates are not closing fully. A properly tuned SPICA system at idle breathes through the four rubber hoses, not the main throats.

With the engine at idle, place the palm of your hand over each intake throat to seal it off. If there is a drop in engine speed when you seal the intake, then that throttle plate is being held open. Re-inspect the closing of the throttle plates and try shortening the short link

a little to see if you can improve the adjustment. You can also tell if the throttles are not closing fully because the car will backfire on deceleration. Hold the top joint of the long link against its ball on the throttle bellcrank. Check the pump gap: it should now be about twice as wide, or 0.045 inch. Adjust the long link to get the pump gap, then snap the top joint on its ball. With pump gap now adjusted to your satisfaction (as directed earlier in this chapter), the throttle plates closing well, and both the short and long links set, you're ready to adjust the fuel mixture.

For the moment, we'll pretend that the engine was running rough as a cob, but you got the pump gap to satisfaction. Notice the position of the terminal on the top of the solenoid. This will be the pointer which lets you keep track of the turns you make from here out. Keeping track of the number of turns, unscrew the solenoid—using the tool described earlier—so it can be removed from the pump. At this time, you can clean up the castellated lock nut and assure that it threads easily along the entire body of the solenoid. Now, seat it lightly and screw it in ten turns. Seat the castellated lock nut against the pump body but do not tighten it. If you're working on a 1750, loosen the mixture-adjusting locknut on the top of the fuel injection pump.

Now, for both 1750 and 2.0-liter models, start the engine and when it's fully warm, insert a wedge into the throttle mechanism at the firewall so the engine runs steadily between 2,000 and 3,000 rpm. For a 2.0-liter, turning the fuel cut-off solenoid in, or clockwise, leans the mixture while turning it out counterclockwise richens the mixture. The opposite is true for the 1750 mixture screw: clockwise richens and counterclockwise leans. Adjust the mixture richness in one direction until the engine speed begins to slow. Turning the adjustment in the opposite direction will cause the engine to speed up, and continued turning will cause it to begin to slow down. Adjust the mixture so the engine runs at its highest speed. If the engine won't behave as described, then recheck all the adjustments you've made so far, including throttle plate seating and pump gap.

▪ In Summary

You'll note that there is really only a single critical SPICA adjustment: the pump gap on a hot engine with the long link disconnected. Everything else can be adjusted to compensate for variations in other adjustments. We've left the cold-start solenoid alone. That's clearly not appropriate for northern winter temperatures. Adjusting that solenoid, however, requires a very thin wrench. Fortunately, the cold-start solenoid most often creates problems, not from misadjustment, which is unlikely, but by sticking: listening for a click will indicate that it is not seized. As suggested before we began, there are several "essential" SPICA tools. I've not given any information about a dummy actuator: you use your own thermostatic actuator to set the pump gap. I've not mentioned the special tool used to set the throttle stops: you do that empirically by testing at idle for closed throttles. And, the actual mixture adjustment is made using engine speed as an indicator, so that tends to compensate for any minor misadjustments.

Since these settings are fairly gross, I'll now give you a technique for fine-tuning the thermostatic actuator setting for the actual needs of your engine. When properly adjusted, the thermostatic actuator should give a decently fast idle on a cold engine and a steady, proper idle speed (provided the ignition timing is correct) when warm. If you do not have a fast idle with a cold engine, you should turn the screw under the thermostatic actuator clockwise and then notice how it starts the next morning. Continue turning in increments each morning until the initial cold idle is between 1,500 and 2,000 rpm, then drops to the correct idle speed as the engine warms up.

Clearly, it's the warm idle speed which is more critical, but if you don't get a fast idle on a cold engine, then the screw isn't properly adjusted, no matter what the pump gap is or how far the thermostatic actuator shaft extends. Continue adjusting the screw over successive mornings until you have a recognizable fast idle cold and a steady idle at the proper speed—about 850 rpm is my preference—when warm. Then, re-adjust the main mixture after blocking the throttle partially open as described above. The adjustment to the main mixture should be very minor. Reattach the air filter and recheck all connections and fittings.

▪ Looking Ahead

We're in a transitional period where parts for the SPICA system are rare but still available, thanks primarily to Wes Ingram of Ingram Enterprises in Seattle, Washington. At some time in the future, replacement parts will become absolutely unavailable. I've done some future thinking about what proud owners of SPICA injected cars will do, say, in the year 2040.

It's clear that the map of the three-dimensional cam (it has about 3,000 discrete reference points) can be duplicated by a computer program. That raises the possibility of substituting a computer-controlled servo motor to operate the pump rack in place of the logic section of the SPICA pump. This solution is possible only if one knows each of the 3,000 data points of the original cam—or, has his own idea of what they should be. I suspect that such a system is not only feasible, but likely as the SPICA units wear out. The cam profile could be mapped fairly easily by using a computerized system which indexes over x-y coordinates and measures deflection as a z coordinate. This is not a solution if the pump section of the SPICA unit is faulty, of course.

The configuration I have in mind would be indistinguishable from the stock SPICA pump. Tachometric information would come from a Hall-effect sensor looking at the crankshaft speed of the injector pump. Throttle angle would be sensed by a potentiometer that replaces the bellcrank assembly at the rear of the pump. The thermostatic actuator would be replaced by a negative-coefficient sensor, with connecting wiring running down the tube of the original unit. The barometric sensor would be wholly electronic.

Inside the pump, there would be no linkage or three-dimensional cam. Instead there would be a single chip that would duplicate all the functions of the logic section. The chip would control a servo motor which properly positions the rack.

If the front section of the pump were worn out, the solution would be quite simple, and that is to replace the one-way valves at its top with solenoids. The solenoids would be activated in exactly the same way electronic fuel injection operates. The wires to the solenoids could be internal, in which case the solenoids would plug into the body of the pump adapter, or they could be hidden behind the solenoids to retain an "original" appearance.

All of this technology is currently available. Only the implementation—and the market—remains to be developed.

For now, though, there is no compelling reason to either modify the SPICA pump or logic section or to replace it with a pair of side-draft Weber carburetors. Although the SPICA injection is exclusive to Alfa Romeo and its inner workings were once a closely held secret, most of those secrets have long since been revealed. And if the SPICA is still too mysterious for you to want to tackle it on your own, there are several experts who can rebuild and recalibrate your fuel injection unit.

Chapter 11

Bosch Electronic Fuel Injection

There is no doubt that federal regulations in the United States have forced manufacturers to adopt increasingly stringent fuel delivery methods. The impetus comes in part from the need to reduce tailpipe emissions, but the requirement for self-analysis (On-Board Diagnostics, or OBD) has also mandated electronic controls. Alfa made the jump to Bosch electronic controls only after the SPICA system had been taken to its limits in the 1981 model year. In that year, Alfa needed exhaust gas recirculation to meet federal NOx requirements. The resulting layout, a single throttle plate with a large alloy intake plenum, reduced the engine's serviceability significantly. Introduced late in 1981 GTV-6 models and later that year for Spiders, Bosch L-Jetronic fuel injection was used into 1994 on Spiders, while the 164 and a small number of Commemorative Spiders (sold as leftovers into 1995) used Motronic fuel injection.

Bosch electronic fuel injection is a relatively low-pressure system that places the fuel injector nozzles, one per cylinder, directly into the intake ports in the cylinder head. This approach requires only enough pressure—about 35 psi—to atomize the fuel and is much easier to manufacture and maintain. Electronic fuel injection simply replaces the fluid dynamics of a carburetor, or the mechanical calculations of the SPICA system, with an electronically controlled system.

■ Anatomy of the Electronic Fuel Injection System

In an electronically controlled fuel injection system, the set of sensors that make up the system's inputs must have electric outputs, and the actuators that control fuel delivery must be electrically controlled. Data from the several input devices are used to calculate the amount of fuel that each injector delivers. In early Bosch systems, data was analog; in the Motronic system, it is almost wholly digital. The advantage of a digital system is that it is unambiguous, and the native language of computers.

The input/output arrangement of an electronic fuel injection system is frequently illustrated in a diagram:

SENSORS ⇨ CONTROL UNIT ⇨ ACTUATORS

In an electronic system, sensors may include:

- Engine temperature
- Air (ambient) temperature
- Engine speed
- Throttle angle
- Barometric pressure
- Manifold absolute pressure (barometrically corrected)
- Intake air mass or volume
- Exhaust gas oxygen content.

The engine control module (ECM) contains the electronics necessary to calculate the proper amount of fuel to be delivered. It expresses this as the duration (in milliseconds) that the injector is held open. This pulse width, or duty cycle, of the injector signal changes to meet engine needs. In this respect, the ultimate output of an electronic fuel injection system is a pulse-width

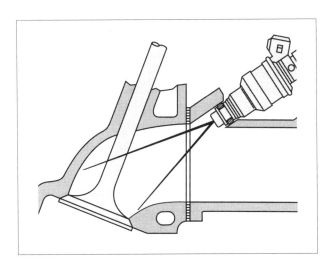

With L-Jetronic, mixture is intermittently injected onto the engine intake valve.

modulated signal to each injector. It is clear that if the technician has no way of monitoring this signal, he's really in the dark.

In the case of Motronic, the ECM supplies signals to other actuators, which may include:

- Fuel pump
- Idle speed correction servo motor
- Engine over-speed fuel or ignition cut-off
- Ignition timing controls
- Transmission controls.

The real reason for electronic fuel injection in the United States is to optimize economy and power while keeping emissions low. As already noted, a gasoline engine will run very well on only an approximately correct fuel mixture. Classic carburetion theory, reflected in Weber practice, is simply to throw as much fuel at the engine as it can handle without fouling the plugs. This approach has the additional virtue of using the fuel to help cool the valves. Such large amounts of fuel were used on the Alfetta 1.5-liter Type 159 engine that it returned a fuel "economy" of as little as 1.5 gallons per mile.

Along came the government and sat down beside her. As we said earlier, when you start pouring gasoline into an engine, some of it dribbles out the exhaust pipe as unburned hydrocarbons. These, of course, are a major contributor to smog. The point at which an engine burns virtually all the fuel it breathes is called stochiometry, and the stochiometric ratio is 14.7 parts air to one part fuel by weight. Until emissions controls came along, no one thought much of stochiometry, because it was almost impossible to obtain using a carburetor.

The intricacies of most emission-controlled engines in the 1970s defies belief. That is because emission-control devices were all "Band-Aids" to the basically inadequate carburetor. Alfa escaped the typical morass by the adoption of mechanical fuel injection in 1969, well ahead of the curve. By paying attention to the three-dimensional cam, emissions standards could be met without resorting to exhaust gas recirculation, air pumps or catalytic converters. It's worth noting that all these fixes were finally employed in the 1981 Spider; not even SPICA was adequate for the increasingly stringent emission controls.

Electronic fuel injection maintains a very simple approach: measure whatever you need about the engine to determine its fuel requirements and then deliver just that amount of fuel with ultimate precision.

Alfa has never been forthcoming about the nitty-gritty of its fuel injection systems. There's a good reason for this. The more information generally available, the

With the aid of Bosch fuel injection, the venerable Alfa twin cam survived into the 1994 model year, although the last examples were not sold until 1995. The spider shown dates from 1991.

more likely amateurs like you and me will try to fiddle with the system, trying to extract one extra horsepower with no concern for the increased emissions. This position was asserted to me on several occasions by ARI's service manager during the time that Joe Benson was taking us inside the SPICA system. Since the SPICA system appeared on no other automobile, Alfa had a lock, literally, on its technology.

That situation does not apply to the Bosch system. The workings of those systems are not only well known, but the subject of a very fine book by the late Charles Probst: *Bosch Fuel Injection & Engine Management*, published by Bentley Publishers. Virtually anything you'd want to know as a casual mechanic is contained in the book. What is not contained is the particular flavor of Bosch systems Alfa has adopted, and that is one thing I hope to provide in this section.

If you plan on doing much work with the Bosch injection, your best source of information will be *Bosch Fuel Injection & Engine Management* by Charles Probst.

■ The Bosch That Fueled Alfa

The two types of Bosch injection employed by Alfa Romeo are L-Jetronic and Motronic.

The L-Jetronic system was the first Bosch fuel delivery system used by Alfa and was first fitted to 1981 model year GTV-6 coupes. In late 1981 it appeared in Spiders—without any notice in the owner's manual. Virtually all of the Bosch-injected Spiders used the L-Jetronic system, although the 190 Commemorative Spiders received the Motronic system.

The air flow sensor on the L-Jetronic system is a spring-loaded vane door which measures air flow volume. The sensor includes a damping cavity to help smooth out the signal sent to the ECM.

A refinement of the L-Jetronic system was the LH-Jetronic, which was capable of measuring the mass of the intake air mass versus the volume measurement. This distinction is important, and now is the time to explain it.

A floating flap or vane door is moved by the incoming air velocity. Now, air velocity is only a gross measure for determining air/fuel mixture ratio. That is because the engine doesn't care about the volume of air it breathes, only how much oxygen it gets. If intake

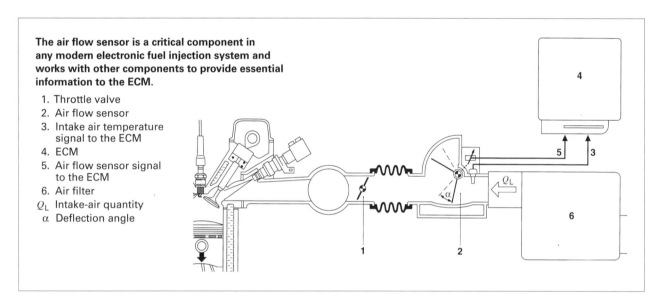

The air flow sensor is a critical component in any modern electronic fuel injection system and works with other components to provide essential information to the ECM.

1. Throttle valve
2. Air flow sensor
3. Intake air temperature signal to the ECM
4. ECM
5. Air flow sensor signal to the ECM
6. Air filter
Q_L Intake-air quantity
α Deflection angle

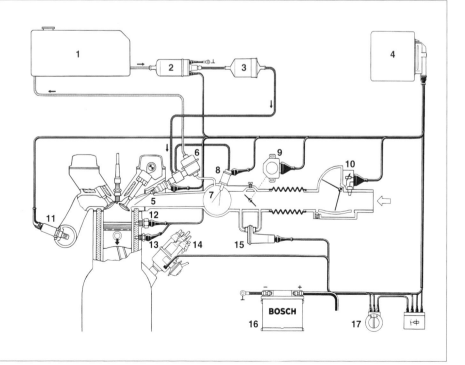

The schematic diagram of an L-Jetronic system with lambda closed-loop control shows the various key elements.

1. Fuel tank
2. Electric fuel pump
3. Fuel filter
4. ECM
5. Fuel injection valve (injector)
6. Fuel rail and fuel-pressure regulator
7. Intake manifold
8. Cold-start valve
9. Throttle-valve switch
10. Air flow sensor
11. Lambda sensor
12. Thermo-time switch
13. Engine temperature sensor
14. Ignition distributor
15. Auxiliary-air device
16. Battery
17. Ignition and starting switch

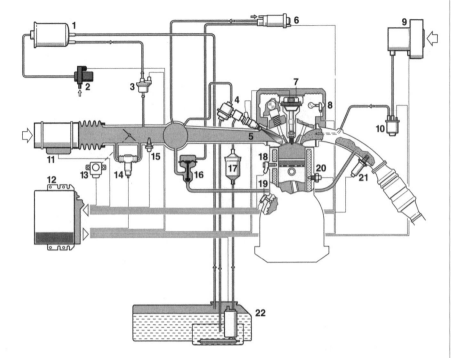

The diagram illustrates the many elements of Motronic with integrated diagnostics (OBD).

1. Carbon canister
2. Shut-off valve
3. Canister-purge valve
4. Fuel-pressure regulator
5. Injector
6. Pressure actuator
7. Ignition coil
8. Phase sensor
9. Secondary-air pump
10. Secondary-air valve
11. Air flow sensor
12. Control unit (ECM)
13. Throttle valve sensor
14. Idle actuator
15. Air temperature sensor
16. EGR valve
17. Fuel filter
18. Knock sensor
19. Engine speed sensor
20. Engine temperature sensor
21. Lambda oxygen sensor
22. Electric fuel pump

volume flow is measured, the amount of oxygen actually contained in the inlet charge can only be determined by collecting atmospheric temperature and pressure data. Therefore, a proper volume-flow system usually includes an air temperature sensor and barometric capsule.

As already noted, the fuel pump is operated by the vane door when the engine is running and the ignition switch in the "Start" position.

The other Bosch system used on Alfa Romeos sold in the United States is Motronic, which is a wholly digital system that combines fuel and ignition systems into a single control module. It was available on the Commemorative Edition Spider, which was sold just before Alfa Romeo's withdrawal from the United States, as well as on the 164, which is outside the scope of this book. (For more information about Motronic-injected Alfas, refer to Pat Braden's *Alfa Romeo Owner's Bible*, also published by Bentley Publishers.)

The Motronic system uses electronic sensors to replace the physically sensed vacuum and throttle signals which control the carburetor. In addition, inputs of engine operating temperature, engine speed and exhaust gas oxygen content help modify the basic fuel delivery and ignition timing in order to optimize economy and power while keeping emissions low. Because only a very few four-cylinder Alfas imported into the United States used Motronic, the bulk of this chapter will focus on L-Jetronic.

▪ How L-Jetronic Works

As with any electronic fuel-injection system, the actual quantity of fuel delivered and its timing is dependent on the information provided to the Electronic Control Module.

Seven sensors act as the eyes and ears of the ECM, telling it what the engine is actually doing. Those sensors monitor:

- oxygen content
- air flow
- air temperature
- coolant temperature
- throttle position
- engine rpm
- system voltage.

The ECM processes this information and uses it to decide how long the fuel injectors remain open: that is really the only "Output" of the system, since fuel-pressure control is handled mechanically. Other details, such as cold starting and idle-speed control, are handled outside the L-Jetronic system.

Since they are not directly controlled as ECM outputs, the following devices are not part of the system, but work with it:

- Idle-speed control
- Fuel-supply system (fuel pump and cold-start valve).

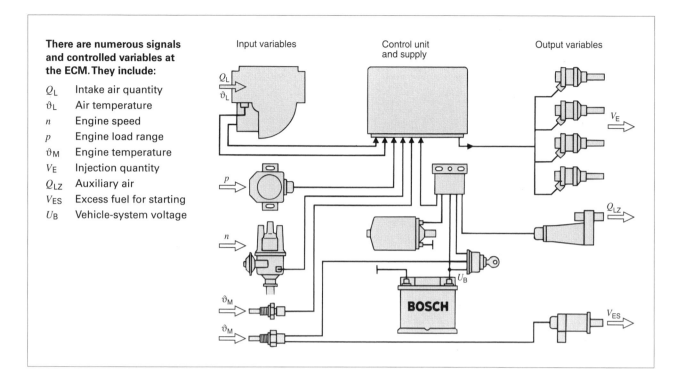

There are numerous signals and controlled variables at the ECM. They include:

Q_L	Intake air quantity
ϑ_L	Air temperature
n	Engine speed
p	Engine load range
ϑ_M	Engine temperature
V_E	Injection quantity
Q_{LZ}	Auxiliary air
V_{ES}	Excess fuel for starting
U_B	Vehicle-system voltage

Input variables

Control unit and supply

Output variables

Oxygen Sensor

The oxygen sensor is mounted in the exhaust stream and senses the amount of oxygen in the exhaust gas. A description of the oxygen sensor's construction is beyond the scope of this chapter, but in general terms it translates the oxygen content of the hot exhaust gasses into a weak voltage. The output of the oxygen sensor is roughly between 0.2 and 0.8 volt at pin 24 of the ECM harness connector. Pin 23 of the connector is the shielded ground for the sensor.

This sensor is a fragile device and should only be tested by someone with experience. The oxygen sensor can be destroyed if it is:

- Tested with an inexpensive VOM (i.e., sees voltage across its terminals)

- Dropped or shocked mechanically

- Contaminated with silicone sealant or antifreeze (blown head gasket).

The oxygen sensor output is the "policeman" of the entire L-Jetronic system. If it senses a too-rich mixture in the exhaust, it causes the ECM to shorten the duty cycle of the injectors. If the mixture is too lean, then the oxygen sensor causes the ECM to lengthen the injector's duty cycle. As long as the oxygen sensor is controlling the injector duty cycle, the system is said to be in closed loop. At wide-open throttle or when the engine is cold, the oxygen sensor is ignored and the system is said to be in open loop.

Air Flow Sensor

In addition to measuring the volume of air entering the engine, the air flow sensor also turns on the fuel pump. This can be verified by removing the inlet ducting and pushing the sensor flap open by hand with the ignition switch on. You should hear the fuel pump operate when the flap is opened. The fuel pump is also turned on by the ignition switch in the "crank" position.

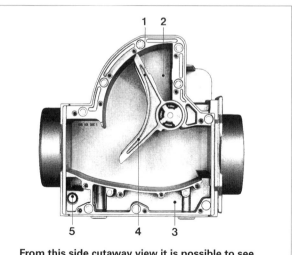

From this side cutaway view it is possible to see the following components of the air-flow sensor:

1. Compensation flap
2. Damping volume
3. Bypass
4. Sensor flap
5. Idle-mixture adjusting screw (bypass)

Air Temperature Sensor

As already discussed, the air temperature sensor helps the system decide on the mass of ingested oxygen. The sensor is located in the air flow sensor housing and is in parallel between pins 6 and 27 at the ECM. This sensor, like all the other Bosch temperature sensors, is a negative-temperature-coefficient (NTC) device, which means its voltage output is high when cold and low when hot. When probing pin 27, there should be a voltage drop as the air temperature sensor is warmed, admittedly not an easy test. As an easy way to estimate whether or not the sensor is working properly, at 20° C, there should be about 2.6 kΩ resistance and about 2.6 volts. At lower temperatures, resistance drops and voltage rises.

Coolant Temperature Sensor

This sensor is another NTC device located on the thermostat housing along with another temperature sensor which controls the cold-start solenoid (see below). The coolant temperature signal can be found at pin 13 of the ECM. Its calibration is different from the coolant temperature sensor. At 20° C, resistance is 2.2 to 2.7 kΩ and there should be around 3.44 volts. The coolant temperature sensor causes the ECM to enrich the fuel delivery when the engine is cold.

Throttle Switch

The throttle switch (Bosch calls it a throttle-valve switch, engine load-range switch or full-load switch, depending on where you look) is used to determine when the driver has floored the accelerator pedal and neared wide-open throttle (WOT). The sensor itself is a switch with slotted mounts for adjustment.

To test the throttle switch, unplug the connector and connect a test lamp across the switch terminals. Carefully examine the switch for terminal identification on the switch housing. With ignition on, the lamp should light (contacts close) when the throttle is rotated 55 to 60 degrees. With the engine running, jumper wires 3 and 18 at the connector momentarily: the engine speed should increase.

WOT is a special situation when the engine goes out of closed loop and the injectors fire simultaneously for maximum fuel delivery. WOT is signaled by the throttle switch, and pins 3 and 18 at the ECM harness should show continuity at WOT.

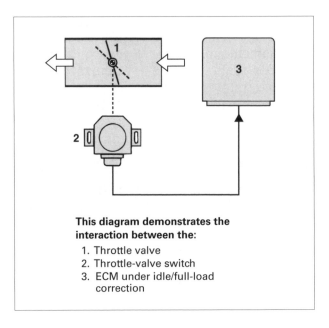

This diagram demonstrates the interaction between the:

1. Throttle valve
2. Throttle-valve switch
3. ECM under idle/full-load correction

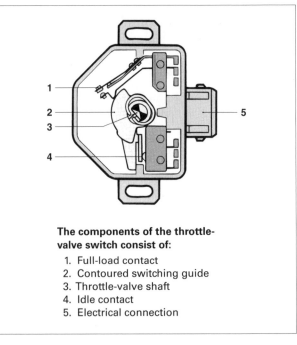

One of the system's key sensors is the engine temperature sensor:

1. Electrical connection
2. Housing
3. NTC resistor

The components of the throttle-valve switch consist of:

1. Full-load contact
2. Contoured switching guide
3. Throttle-valve shaft
4. Idle contact
5. Electrical connection

Engine RPM

Clearly, the ECM needs to know how fast the engine is going around, and it gets this information from the distributor. The signal at pin 1 of the ECM is a simple tachometer pulse which is converted within the ECM to meaningful data. When the rpm sensor signals higher engine speeds, the duty cycle of the injectors is increased to provide more fuel to the engine.

System Voltage

You may be surprised to see that system voltage (nominally 12 volts but actually about 13.5 volts and as high as about 14 volts when the battery is being charged) is an input to the ECM. Since this is an electronic system which depends on the accurate assessment of analog signals, system voltage becomes very critical if the ECM is to make the proper decisions.

To illustrate how important system voltage is, consider that the ECM is programmed to read the output of most sensors as a voltage value. The programmed value is based on nominal system voltage. If the system has fallen, say, to ten volts, then that is also the maximum output a sensor can reach, and the ECM will see an inaccurate signal.

One of the first things anyone should ever do when troubleshooting an electronic fuel system (not just L-Jetronic) is to measure system voltage at the ECM (not the battery: there may be corroded connections involved). To do this, back-probe the harness connector at the 1.5mm red wire. If you get less than 12.5 volts, then all bets are off, and if you get less than 10 volts, the system will not operate properly.

Grounds

Right about now you may be thinking "I thought we were talking about sensors, what is a ground doing in here?" True, a ground is not a sensor, but if the grounds are poor or broken, all the new sensors in the world won't do you any good. As a result, it is important to measure that the ECM is getting a good ground. Any black wire at the harness connector should give a ground with no more than 0.5 v. To verify that the battery is properly grounded, you may wish to do a voltage drop test:

1. Disconnect and ground the center lead to the distributor so the car will not start.

2. Connect one lead of a DVOM to the battery terminal.

3. Connect the other lead to the battery ground cable where it bolts to the body. Do not touch the

attaching bolt or body, just the connector itself. You may have to cut back some insulation to do this.

4. Turn on the lights and crank the engine momentarily.

5. The DVOM should show a voltage less than 0.5 v. If it shows more, the ground connection to the battery should be cleaned and the test rerun.

I need to belabor the point of checking for good grounds. A faulty ground connection is the cause of most fuel injection problems, industry-wide.

Cold Starts

Though the coolant temperature sensor contributes to the fuel richness when the engine is running, it does not provide a "choke" operation for cold starts. A completely separate system does this on L-Jetronic cars. It consists of a heated temperature sensor (the thermo-time switch) located on the thermostat, next to the coolant temperature sensor and an injector located on the plenum above the engine.

The cold-start injector is controlled by the thermo-time switch. The switch opens to disable the injector at coolant temperatures above 50° C. It is also heated to make it warm up faster and thus shut the cold-start injector off as quickly as possible to reduce hydrocarbon emissions.

If your L-Jetronic Alfa starts, but won't run when you let go of the ignition switch (or will start and run when hot but not cold), the likely cause is a failure in

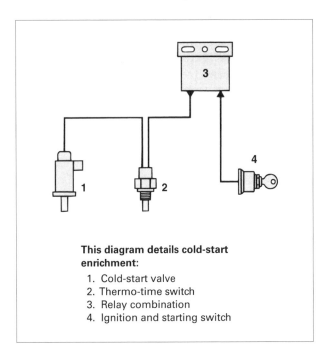

This diagram details cold-start enrichment:

1. Cold-start valve
2. Thermo-time switch
3. Relay combination
4. Ignition and starting switch

the circuitry which controls the cold-start injector. Since this circuit doesn't go through the ECM, you can futz with it a little more heroically without fear of frying a transistor.

1. With the ignition on, unplug the connector at the thermo-time switch and probe the terminal to locate twelve volts to the heater circuit.

2. With an ohmmeter, determine which wire carries the signal to the cold-start injector. Connect a jumper between the two wires at the thermo-time switch connector to bypass the sensor at its connector.

3. Remove the injector from the plenum and ground its body.

4. Turn the ignition key to the start position momentarily. The injector should spray gasoline if it is good.

5. If the injector doesn't spray fuel, replace the injector. If it does, you'll probably fix the problem by replacing the thermo-time switch.

Idle Speed Control

A cold engine needs some extra air and fuel to overcome the inertia of its moving parts and the thick oil in its sump, not to mention its propensity for incomplete combustion when cold. That is, a cold engine idles at a slower speed than it should. By adding extra air to the intake path, the L-Jetronic system forces a higher idle speed (mixture is enriched in part by the cold-start injector, then by the oxygen sensor when the system goes into closed loop).

The idle speed controller, or auxiliary air device, is nothing more than a thermostatically controlled air leak. Its thermostat is heated, like the thermo-time switch and for the same reason (emissions reduction).

Idle Speed Bypass Adjustment: Basic engine idle speed is controlled by "leaking" a little air past the throttle plate which, on the L-Jetronic system, should close completely. Idle speed is adjusted by a nut at the end of a U-shaped tube that runs along the throttle body.

Decel Valve

When coasting down on a closed throttle after a full-bore run, engine revs are high but there is maximum vacuum in the intake manifold. This is an upside-down condition (on acceleration, revs are high and manifold vacuum is almost nil) so some compensation is required to keep the engine from backfiring. The decel valve adds air and is operated by manifold pressure alone. It has no connections to the ECM.

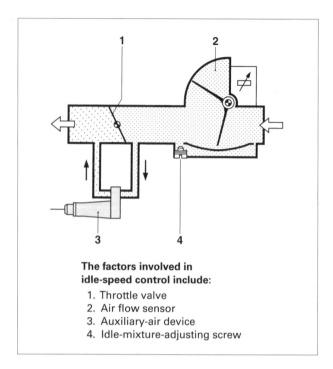

The factors involved in idle-speed control include:

1. Throttle valve
2. Air flow sensor
3. Auxiliary-air device
4. Idle-mixture-adjusting screw

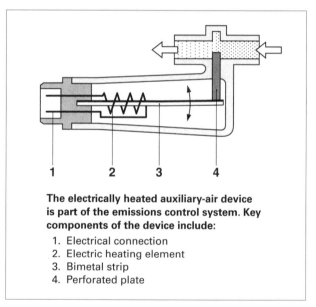

The electrically heated auxiliary-air device is part of the emissions control system. Key components of the device include:

1. Electrical connection
2. Electric heating element
3. Bimetal strip
4. Perforated plate

■ Beyond the Do-it-Yourselfer

Unlike Solex and Weber carburetors, and even the SPICA mechanical fuel injection system, the Bosch L-Jetronic and Motronic electronic fuel-injection systems are beyond the scope of most DIY mechanics. Not only are the electronics virtually impossible to diagnose empirically, expensive analysis equipment is required. So, without expensive electronic tools, the electronic fuel injection on your 1981 or later Alfa Romeo is best left to a well-equipped shop.

Chapter 12

Transmissions

Alfa's transmissions are legendary for smoothness and responsiveness. I need to add, up front, that they are also legendary for weak second-gear synchronizers. This failing is not unique to Alfa, fortunately, but a weak second-gear synchro is the one thing about an Alfa gearbox that you have to get used to.

Therefore, to the point: shifting between gears requires a slight pause in neutral. When you engage second, do so with a progressive pressure. Do not try to slam the shift lever from one gear to another. Double clutching is not necessary except to impress a companion with your driving skills.

The second-gear synchro on the 101 and subsequent gearboxes is identical to those that command all the other gears, so there is nothing inherent in the design that could cause it to fail prematurely. There are several reasons why the second gear-synchro goes bad:

- It is more frequently used than the other gears (especially around town).
- When it is used, the engine is usually developing near its maximum horsepower.
- It tends to be overworked by fast shifts (by the time you need to shift to third, you're either already at the next stop light or have already been beaten decisively).

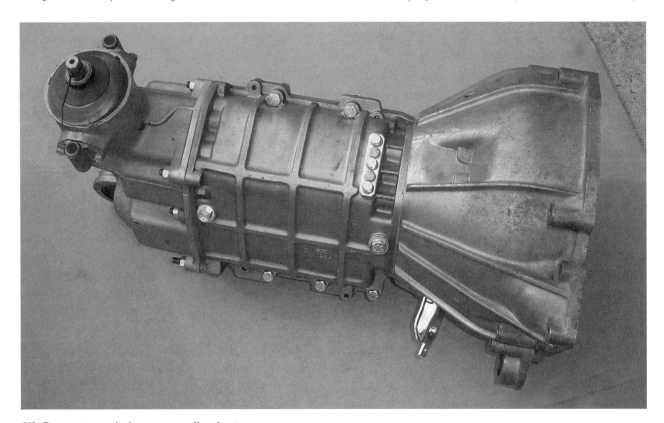

Alfa Romeo transmissions are usually a joy to use, offering short and smooth throws. This transmission is from a 105-series car.

There is an exotic procedure for reducing second-gear synchro wear, and that is to lighten the gears. This involves a complete disassembly of the transmission, drilling the webs of the gears to remove metal and then balancing them. Given the undrilled gearbox's success in race cars, it is hard for me to imagine the circumstances under which such a procedure would be indicated. Similarly, it's hard to imagine just how expensive the process might prove to be. In spite of my skepticism about the process, I'm sure there are some Alfa transmissions out there with drilled gears.

▪ Something About Synchronizers

My first Alfa didn't have synchronizers in its gearbox. When I moved the shift lever, I moved a gear on one shaft into mesh with a gear on another. In order to accomplish this, I had to make the two gears spin at the same speed. Shifting up was a matter of pausing slightly so one of the gears could slow down, and shifting down required blipping the throttle in neutral with the clutch out to speed up one gear so it matched the speed of the other.

The downshift procedure I've just described is called double clutching (for my British friends, double-declutching). Properly performed (you test your technique by shifting without the clutch), it will save wear on the synchros. Performed incorrectly, it is a counterproductive procedure in any modern car with a synchromesh transmission.

All modern cars have synchromesh transmissions. In this kind of transmission, the meshing gears are adjacent on the same shaft, and they are engaged by locking a freely rotating gear to the adjacent gear which is fixed to the shaft. The rotational speed of the two gears is adjusted by a clutch-like device which is engaged just before the gear itself. This device is the synchronizer, and its operation depends on some friction between the two gears to get their speeds to match. Unfortunately, the synchro itself makes clutchless shifting almost impossible, because it interferes with the speeds of the gears, so in practicing clutchless shifting on a synchronized transmission, you may destroy the gears long before the synchros.

▪ 750-Series Four-speed

The earliest Giulietta transmissions used three small springs and detent balls under each synchronizer ring to help gear engagement and ensure that the gear remained engaged. These early four-speed gearboxes were carried in a cylindrical transmission housing. The input and output shafts were placed in mesh and then drawn into the housing with a special puller. Reading the Giulietta shop manual's description of a 750-series gearbox teardown is depressing because of the number of special tools referenced. Without question, overhaul of a 750-series gearbox should be left to a professional technician who has some familiarity with the process and a lot of spare time. As a result, I'm not including a rebuild of it in this book.

If you own an Alfa with this early style gearbox, shift gears attentively.

▪ 101–105 Four-speed and Five-speed Transmissions

Introduced without notice in mid-1959 on Giuliettas, a new gearbox was easily identified because it split along the length of the unit. At the front of the housing was a bolted-on bellhousing that covered the flywheel and clutch assembly. The earlier 750-series transmission had

Components of the synchronizer assembly used on 101 and later series transmissions consist of (from left) a synchronizer ring surrounding the blocking mechanism responsible for expanding the synchronizer ring, the gearset, the shift sleeve (top right) and the hub. Alfa Romeo obtained a license from Porsche to manufacture its patented synchronizers, while the synchro rings themselves were supplied by Porsche.

an integral bellhousing. At the rear of the new transmission was a short extension housing which, beginning with the Giulia, carried fifth and reverse gears.

This gearbox was a modification of the five-speed gearbox introduced in the cast-iron 2.0-liter Alfa 2000 in 1958. It was not long before enthusiasts began to fit the internals from the larger Alfa's gearbox into the smaller. They quickly discovered that the task was relatively easy as long as the 2.0-liter's rear gearbox casting was used along with the fifth-speed gear set.

Operation

As noted above, a modern transmission works by connecting two adjacent gears rotating on a common shaft. The Alfa transmission consists of three shafts:

1. Input shaft
2. Lay shaft, sometimes called the counter shaft
3. Main shaft, also known as the output shaft.

The input shaft is driven by the clutch and ends with a gear that meshes with a gear on the layshaft.

The layshaft rotates beneath the input shaft and has a set of gears machined along its length. These gears mesh with freely rotating gears on the main shaft.

The front of the main shaft slips inside the rear of the input shaft, so it and the input shaft run on the same axis, above the layshaft, but independently of each other.

The main shaft carries gears which rotate independently of the shaft. Each of these gears meshes with a corresponding gear on the layshaft. Thus, all the gears on the main shaft rotate constantly, being driven by the gears on the layshaft. The gearsets (driving and driven) are of different proportions, so the speeds of the gears rotating around the main shaft are all different,

The original 750-series cars used the four-speed "tunnel case" gearbox.

The so-called "split-case" gearbox was much easier to work on than the 750-series tunnel-case unit. Initially, 101-series cars were fitted with this four-speed version of the split-case transmission.

The five-speed transmissions were quite similar to the four-speed versions of the split-case transmission. This transmission is 105-series and features mechanical clutch actuation. Later cars used hydraulic clutches.

representing the speeds of which the transmission is capable.

Shifts are accomplished by locking one of the free gears on the main shaft to the main shaft. When this happens, the power flow is from the input shaft, through a gear set to the layshaft and then through another gearset to the main shaft.

Gear Shifting

A sliding shift collar is used to lock the free gear to the main shaft. The shift collar has internal teeth that can mesh with teeth machined into both the splined and free gears. The collar is always engaged with the splined gear. As the collar slides toward the free gear, a synchronizer ring uses friction to match the speed of the free gear to the splined gear. As soon as the speeds of the two gears match, the shift collar can continue to engage the free gear so it is effectively locked to the main shaft.

The exact method of synchronization changed with the new gearbox. The new technique, borrowed from Porsche practice, does away with the detent springs and balls and toothed synchronizer gear. Instead, it uses two semi-circular expanding pieces that expand slightly beneath the synchronizer ring as the synchronizer begins to work. The added friction helps the synchronizer match the gear's speed as the collar moves to engage the gear. In this gearbox, the synchronizer ring has no teeth.

In the newer gearbox, the synchronizer ring only wears on one side. Since it is manufactured with two working faces, turning the synchro rings around is the equivalent of replacing them. Clearly, you can only do this once before buying new synchros. If you have a transmission apart, however, it is false economy not to replace all the synchronizers, bushes and bearings. The bushes between the gears and main shaft are machined to size: you don't just "drop them in."

The sliding shift collars are moved using selector forks which are attached to a set of three rails which you move using the shift lever. There's nothing in the transmission's basic design to keep more than one gear from being engaged at a time: indeed, some transmissions erupt in a hemorrhage of pieces when more than one gear is accidentally engaged. There is an elegant lock-out system used between the rails to assure that only one rail at a time is used to engage a gear. Movement of the rail for reverse gear also turns on the back-up light.

With the case split, the shafts and gears of this 105-series transmission can be seen clearly. The upper shaft is the input shaft, which features the gear sets and the synchronizers, with output from the right side, while the lower portion of the case holds the layshaft. The components are:

1. First gear
2. Second gear
3. Third gear
4. Fourth gear
5. Fifth gear
6. Reverse gear
7. Input shaft from clutch
8. Output shaft
9. Layshaft

The transmission selector forks are triggered by rails moved when the driver selects a gear. The third/fourth shifter fork is on the left and the first/second shifter fork is on the right.

If you understand the operation of the friction clutch which gets the gear rotating at the same speed as the shaft on which it rotates, then appreciate how the gear is locked to the shaft by the shift collar, you have conquered about 95 percent of the transmission's mystery. The layshaft is simply a device to communicate torque from the input shaft, through the gear to the output shaft. Probably the other five percent of the transmission's mystery is how the shift detent lock-out system works: this is a system of sliding balls and a rod which assures that only one gear is selected at a time.

The complexity of a transmission is not from its basic concept. How one gear shifts is a relatively straightforward thing to understand. It's just that, on the five-speed Giulia transmission, there are so many of them.

Lubricant

The 750 gearbox used synchronizers that required non-EP oil, commonly known as Shell Dentax. This lubricant was not widely available, and came only in 55-gallon drums. The average enthusiast had to beg some from a shop that did enough Alfa business to buy a whole drum. A work-around was to use 40- or 50-weight engine oil with a can of STP and/or molybdenum disulfide.

When the 101-style gearbox was introduced, it too worked with non-EP lubricant. This requirement was soon dropped, however, by changing the composition of the synchronizers. It is doubtful if any late-model non-EP synchros still survive, so you may assume that any 101-style gearbox you encounter will work with EP lubricant.

While understanding a transmission is not out of range of the average enthusiast, rebuilding one may very well be. Cleanness counts, and a press and lathe are required tools for a complete overhaul. If the bushes don't require replacement, you can take a transmission apart by renting a very large gear puller (a minimum 15-inch reach is required), but you won't know if the bushes are bad until after you have the transmission apart. That is, you may well find yourself with a

The major variations of transmissions to match the all-alloy twin-cam four are (top to bottom):
- 750-series tunnel case four-speed
- 101-series split-case four-speed
- 105-series split-case five-speed, mechanical clutch
- 105/115-series split-case five-speed, hydraulic clutch

disassembled transmission but lacking the lathe to put it back together again.

In point of fact, it's cheaper to buy a good used transmission than to rebuild one. You can use any Alfa transmission from the 101 Giulietta to the current spider, but the Giulia bellhousing must be used to mate to the engine.

▪ Alfetta Transaxle

In principle, the Alfetta transaxle is no different from the 101 gearbox. It's just mounted in a different place. However, there is added complexity because the ring and pinion is part of the assembly. Transaxle pinion depth is determined by the stack-up of the transmission main shaft components.

For those owners of 101-series and later twin-cam Alfas, including Alfetta, wishing to tackle the challenging task of a transmission rebuild, the next chapter is for you. However, the average owner will probably want to refer his transmission overhaul to an experienced shop.

The deDion rear end from an Alfetta shows the transaxle layout with deDion tube, half shafts, inboard brakes and front subframe.

Chapter 13

Rebuilding Transmissions and Transaxles

In general, you shouldn't attempt to overhaul a 101 or later transmission unless you have access to a lathe and a press, or a gear puller with long arms. The lathe is required to fit the gear bearings to the shaft, and the press is used to dismantle the main shaft.

The transmission is made up of a very large number of parts, and it's a challenge to work with the parts and not get them confused. When first opened, the transmission presents you with what appears to be miles and miles of gears: disassembled, it's amazing how many parts will fit into such a small case.

The transmission is its own best teacher: study it carefully as you take it apart to understand exactly how everything works. By the time you have it dismantled, you should be able to reassemble it blindfolded. If there are no broken gear teeth, an overhaul will probably consist of renewing the clutches, bearings and seals.

Be sure to work under a vehicle only if the wheels are blocked *and* it is supported on sturdy jack stands.

WARNING—Never work under a vehicle supported exclusively by a jack, or cinder blocks.

With the gearsets on the main shaft (foreground) and the input shaft (background), these assemblies appear very compact; dissasembled, they could easily fill a bench or a bucket with gears, synchro rings and bearings galore.

▪ Rebuilding Transmissions

Removing the Transmission (As Opposed to the Transaxle)

Unless you have a transmission jack and a clutch centering tool, don't try to remove the transmission from the car by itself. Remove the transmission and engine as a unit. This may seem excessive, but experience has shown that it's faster and easier in the long run.

If you do decide to remove only the transmission, you'll find that the bolts that hold the transmission to the engine are hard to get to. A couple of bolts require a long socket extension and a flexible coupling. On

reassembly, trying to engage splines in the clutch-driven plate while holding the transmission on the same axis as the crankshaft is the major challenge. If you're intent on removing the transmission only, you can do it with only the front end of the car jacked up. Otherwise, refer to the section on engine removal for the details.

You will forget to remove the speedometer cable, and will be reminded of it when the engine/transmission refuse to come free of the car. Hopefully, you will have proceeded with sufficient delicacy not to have stretched the outer cable beyond use.

The steep angle is needed to clear the transmission.

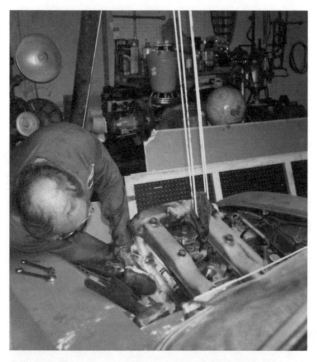

With ancillaries and all fasteners removed, the engine/transmission unit of a Giulia Berlina is tilted and lifted.

As the engine comes forward and up, the angle is increased.

If the lift angle is steep enough, the entire driveshaft will also pull free through the engine bay.

Disassembly

Once removed from the car, clean the exterior thoroughly and then place the gearbox on a clean workbench.

Fair warning: the following procedure is detailed enough to provide an overall introduction, but for the sake of readability and clarity it does not include the orientation of every spacer or washer involved. If you are going to disassemble a transmission, I'd recommend copying these pages and then, as you disassemble it, write in all the small details of spacer location, bearing orientation, etc. that I've glossed over. If this is the first time you've attempted a transmission teardown, plan on at least one extra reassembly to get things right. Copious notes will assure that you are almost right the first time.

Separated from the engine and clean, this Giulia Veloce transmission is ready for the bench.

1. Place a sturdy bolt through the output flange to keep it from turning, then unscrew the 1.25-inch nut which holds it in place. Remove the yoke.

2. Remove the O-ring and sliding covers around the shift lever.

3. Shift the box into third, then remove the nuts securing the rear cover and remove the cover.

4. Unscrew the bolt holding the fifth/reverse selector fork and slide out the shift shaft.

The fifth/reverse shift rail must be removed to allow removal of the corresponding shift fork.

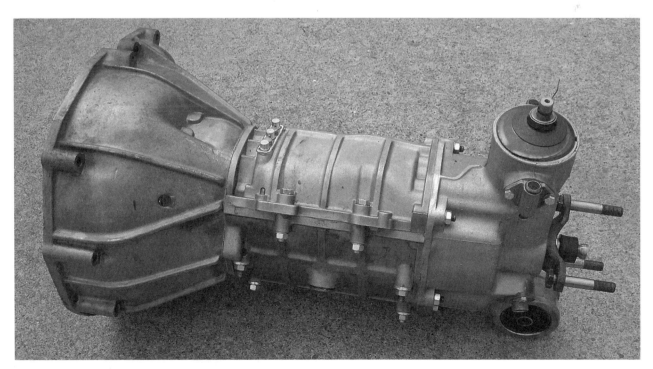

The first step before starting any transmission work is to get it as clean as possible. This five-speed unit is from a 1972 GTV.

5. At the front of the transmission, remove the back-up light switch and throwout bearing.

6. Remove the six nuts securing the clutch housing and remove it.

7. Remove the ten nuts and bolts holding the transmission halves and carefully separate them. Don't damage the mating faces of the halves, because these have to seal without a gasket.

8. Remove the reverse sliding gear.

9. Remove the plate that covers the shift detents. Take out the fifth/reverse detent plunger, spring and ball.

10. Loosen the shift fork setscrews. The shift interlock mechanism consists of three jellybean-shaped shafts that allow movement of only one rod at a time. One

With the transmission halves separated, you can see the reverse idler on the case. The pointer indicates where the long bolts go through the thin part of the case. Because of minimum surface area at that point, leakage often comes through here. O-rings installed under the washer can prevent oil seepage.

of the shift rods should slide out easily. Use two small screwdrivers to position the remaining jellybeans so the remaining shift rods can be pulled out.

11. If you're going to replace all the bearings, use a slide-puller to remove the outer race of the layshaft rear bearing from the end cover.

12. Lift the input and main shafts out of the case together, then pull the input shaft free. Remove the roller bearing cage (the inner race is the input shaft itself).

13. The input shaft ball bearing is held in place by a circlip. Use a puller to remove it after the circlip and shim are removed.

Main Shaft Disassembly

Even if all you want to do is replace the synchros, you'll have to dismantle the main shaft. You may use a press or a long-arm puller to strip the main shaft of its components. If you've gotten this far, it probably isn't necessary to indicate exactly where to place the half-plates for a press, or the jaws of a puller. Keep in mind that you should try to avoid pulling a bearing by its outer race, wherever possible. Whether you use a press or puller, you'll have to do this in several instances, so it will be necessary to inspect the bearings closely for wear. For this process, we'll use a puller.

There is a shoulder machined into the main shaft between second and third gears. Because of this, third gear comes off toward the front of the shaft and the remaining gears are removed to the rear of the shaft.

1. Working from the fifth gear end of the shaft, position the puller jaws so they capture the reverse gear. Pull off the rear bearing, fifth gear synchronizer hub and sleeve, and the reverse gear as a unit, then remove the key from its keyway on the shaft.

The input shaft (top) and main shaft (bottom) are removed together.

Fifth gear is being pulled. Notice that the puller is positioned on the synchro sleeve and not on the gear teeth.

2. Attach the puller arms so it captures first gear and remove the gear, bushing, bearing, spacer and the first/second synchronizer sleeve.

3. Use the puller to pull up the second gear just enough to be able to reach the first/second hub. Reposition the puller to remove the hub.

4. Remove the key from the keyway and then lift off the second gear.

5. From the other end of the main shaft, remove the circlip and lift off the third/fourth synchronizer assembly and spacer.

6. Use a puller to remove the third/fourth hub, then remove the key from its keyway.

7. Lift off the third gear assembly.

Here is fifth gear removed from the shaft and without its synchronizer ring.

Removing the synchro retainer from first gear.

Layshaft Disassembly

Compared to the main shaft, the layshaft is a simple matter to disassemble.

1. Hold the shaft in a soft-jaw vise and unscrew the nut that holds the fifth/reverse gears onto the shaft. Slide off the rear bearing and the fifth/reverse gears.

2. Use a puller to remove the middle ball bearing.

3. Remove the nut at the other end of the shaft, then use a puller to remove the front ball bearing.

Inspection

1. Disassemble each synchronizer unit and check for:
   - Worn, chipped or broken engaging teeth
   - Sleeves that slide freely on their hubs
   - No wear to the semi-circular elements, stops and synchronizer rings.

   Use a small amount of lapping compound to assure maximum contact between the synchronizer ring and the thrust surface on the gear. Lap sparingly, otherwise the friction surface will be too smooth to function properly. Clean all parts until they are perfectly compound-free, then reassemble the synchromesh units to keep things together.

2. Check the runout of the bare main shaft. It should not exceed .05 mm (.002 inch). The main shaft can be straightened in a press if a new one is not available.

3. Check the ball/roller bearings and their races for wear. A dull surface indicates excessive wear on roller bearings. Ball bearings should be washed in a solvent and spun by hand. Listen for clicks, indicating worn spots on the balls or races. If in doubt, replace the bearing.

This is the needle bearing between third and fourth gears. Notice that the edge of the bearing cage is worn off.

4. Check the fit of each freely rotating gear on its shaft. You should not detect any wobble. The bronze bushes are replaceable, but must be machined to fit.

5. Check the working surfaces of the forks and sleeves for shiny spots or discoloration that indicates wear. The end play between the forks and sleeves should be 0.0098–.0197 inch.

6. Reassemble the parts of the shift mechanism temporarily to verify their smooth operation. You can clean up working surfaces with a file. The detent balls should engage decisively. The free length of the detent springs is 0.6 inch.

Reassembly

It is easier to assemble the hubs and ball bearings if they are heated to about 300°F, otherwise they must be pressed on. You can install a cold ball bearing by hammering, using a brass drift against its inner race. Never hammer on the outside race, even with a drift.

Input Shaft

1. Press the bearing into place with its snap ring groove facing toward the clutch splines.

2. Put the shim and circlip in place and check for any clearance between the shim and circlip. If there is any, remove the circlip and replace the shim with one thick enough to give zero clearance.

Layshaft

1. Press the middle ball bearing into place.

2. Assemble the fifth/reverse gear and the rear roller bearing, then tighten the end nut to 57 pound feet.

3. Press the front ball bearing into place and torque its retaining nut to 57 pound feet.

Main Shaft

As noted above, the synchronizer hubs must be heated to at least 300°F in order to be able to slide them into place. It's also easier to slip the bearings into place if they're heated to the same temperature. Put them all in an oven while you clean and then lubricate all the parts for reassembly. Be especially careful to lubricate all bearing surfaces. Lubricate the ball and roller bearings after they have been installed.

From the front of the shaft:

1. Install third gear.

2. Replace the key in its keyway.

3. Press the third/fourth hub into place.

4. Install the circlip. If there is any play between the hub and circlip, insert a shim between the two to eliminate it.

5. Install the third/fourth gear synchronizer assembly.

From the rear of the shaft:

1. Install second gear with its synchronizer teeth facing the rear end of the shaft.

2. Replace the keys in their keyways.

3. Press the first/second gear hub into place

4. Install the first/second synchronizer assembly.

5. Install first gear, bushing and shims (which determine third and fourth gear spacing).

6. Install the intermediate bearing.

7. Install the reverse gear.

8. Install the fifth gear synchronizer hub and spacer.

9. Install the fifth gear synchronizer assembly.

10. Install the fifth gear and bushing.

11. Install the rear bearing.

12. Slip the speedometer gear in place and then the output flange.

13. Tighten the flange bolt to 87 pound feet.

14. Slip the input shaft into the main shaft, then engage the input/main and lay shafts so the gears mesh.

15. Place the entire assembly into the transmission case half that also carries the shift interlock mechanism, being careful that the retaining circlips on the bearings are seated properly in the case. The input and main shafts should turn freely and all bearings must be seated squarely in place.

16. With a caliper, check the distance between the outside faces of the fourth and third gear synchronizer teeth. This distance is set by the bushing between the first gear and the intermediate bearing inner race. The proper distance is 1.65 to 1.66 inches. If it is not, disassemble the shaft and replace the bushing to obtain the correct distance.

From the left, the main shaft holds fifth gear, its synchro and slider rings, reverse, main shaft support bearing and first gear.

17. With a feeler gauge, check the end play on the first, second and third speed gears. It should be less than 0.009 inch for first, and less than 0.008 for second and third. If it is greater, replace the appropriate shims as necessary.

18. Remove the nut which retains the output flange and remove the flange and speedometer gear.

19. Reinstall the reverse idler gear assembly.

20. Fit the shift forks and shift linkage, making sure that all parts move easily and positively.

21. Replace the housing centering ring in its groove around the input shaft bearing.

22. Put a thin bead of RTV sealant along the mating surfaces, then reinstall the other half of the transmission case and tighten its ten fasteners.

23. Install the fifth/reverse shift shaft and fork, detent ball, spring and holder.

24. Check that, in neutral, the fifth gear synchronizer ring is about ⅜ inch from fifth gear. Adjust this distance using the locking grooves in the fifth shift fork boss and washer.

25. Complete the reassembly of the shift mechanism and reinstall the rear housing.

26. Replace the speedometer gear and slip the output flange onto the main shaft. Tighten the flange bolt to 87 pound feet again.

27. Install a new front seal in the bell housing.

28. Install the bell housing, being careful not to cut the seal on the input shaft splines.

29. Shift the box into each gear to verify that they all work properly and smoothly.

■ Alfetta Transaxle

Operation

As discussed in the previous chapter, the Alfetta transaxle is very similar to the 101 gearbox. However, there is added complexity because the ring and pinion is part of the combined transmission/rear axle assembly. Transaxle pinion depth is determined by the stack-up of the transmission main shaft components.

Removal From the Car

It's possible to rebuild the transmission without removing the main alloy casting from the car. The main and lay shafts are carried in a center casting that can be removed from beneath the car. You have to remove the clutch and front casting before you can withdraw the gears and the center casting. If you attempt to do this (it does make transaxle rebuilds easier), I would strongly

As an alternative to dropping the entire rear transaxle and suspension assembly as was done with this 1979 Sport Sedan, the gears and center casting may be removed while the assembly remains in place on the car.

suggest draping plastic over the top of the unit to prevent dirt from the underside of the body falling into the transaxle components, especially during reassembly. It is also a good idea to pressure wash the undercarriage prior to this procedure.

Preliminary Steps

1. Drain the transaxle.

2. Jack the rear end of the car up as far as you can and put jack stands under the body at the rear jacking points. The rear suspension must hang free.

3. Unbolt the half shafts from the brake discs. This is one of the most problematic operations on the car. The bolts are probably frozen in place and a lot of torque is required to free them. If you blunder ahead, you'll end up with all the bolts neatly rounded off and still firmly in place. I have found it helpful to grind the face of a box-end wrench so the tapered portion of the wrench inner diameter is completely removed. This will assure maximum contact between the wrench and bolt head. Use a penetrant liberally and apply the emergency brake when loosening the bolts. If everything, including vise grips (as a futile last resort) fails, you'll have to grind the heads of the bolts off. Wire the loose driveshafts out of the way.

4. Remove the entire exhaust system, beginning at the downpipes.

5. Completely remove the rod that connects the gearshift lever to the transaxle input shaft.

6. Remove the complete driveshaft. It's easiest to loosen all the bolts, and then wait until the transaxle is tilted down, at which time the driveshaft may fall out (at least at one end).

7. Remove the speedometer cable.

8. Unplug the reverse lamp connector.

9. Remove the clutch hose and brake lines so they are free of the transaxle. Both systems will have to be bled on reassembly.

10. Disconnect the handbrake cable at the adjuster nut on the transaxle case and pull it free of the transaxle.

11. Unbolt the six bolts that mount the front transaxle crossmember to the body (three bolts each). Note that there is a heavy shim on one end of these mounts.

12. Place a jack under the center of the deDion tube and carefully raise it. This will force the front end of the transaxle down. Stop jacking when it's easy to reach the four bolts (two on each side) which attach the transmission front rubber mounts to the triangular sub-frame. Remove the four bolts and leave the jack in place.

13. Prop something very sturdy between one of the triangular side tubes and the body. A 4x4x10-inch block of wood works. Or, if you have a stamped-steel jack stand, I've found that the top section with the saddle will also work fine. Put the saddle on one of the side tubes and jam the square end against the body. Be warned: this creates a dangerous mouse trap; if the prop works loose, the triangular frame will slam upwards, powered by the considerable force of the rear springs. Anything in the way is likely to be crushed or severed.

WARNING — Trailing arms are being forced away from the body by jacking the deDion tube against the spring tension of the rear suspension. Be sure to use a suitable block, and that the block is securely wedged between the trailing arm and the body of the vehicle. Serious injury may result if the block becomes dislodged. The trailing arms will snap back against the body of the vehicle under spring tension of the rear suspension. If you are not comfortable performing this procedure, refer it to a qualified Alfa Romeo mechanic.

14. Reassure yourself that the prop is securely in place, then slowly lower the jack from the deDion tube.

15. At this point, with the front mounts of the transaxle free and adequate access to all the bolts on the unit, you can disassemble the clutch housing and front casting of the transaxle, then remove the center section and gearsets. For these instructions, follow steps 3-10 under Disassembly, just below.

16. If you've elected to remove the entire transaxle, then support the rear end of the unit with a floor jack and unscrew the nut on the rear mounting bolt. A bottle or screw jack is inadequate for this procedure: you need something that can support the transaxle and also move on wheels. Raise or lower the rear of the transaxle until the bolt comes free. You should be able to pry out the bolt with a flat-blade screwdriver.

17. The transmission is now free to fall to the ground. Of course, it won't: the front of it will catch on the triangular sub-member, or the rear mounting boss will foul against the rear deDion tube. You need to lower the rear of the unit slowly on a jack, moving it backwards slightly and then rotating it partially to one side to clear the triangular member. Be careful not to upset the prop that wedges the triangle down. The transaxle is very heavy and the prop is problematic: you will need help to get the unit safely on the ground. Remember that, if the transmission should fall, your reaction time will not be fast enough to get out of its way.

18. There may be some clearance problems dragging the transaxle from under the car. You may need to jack the back of the car up higher to clear the transaxle. You can't do this against the deDion tube now, because the front of its triangle is loose. Put a large piece of ½-inch plywood under the rear edge of the trunk pan to spread the pressure and then jack slowly and carefully. Jacking against the rear bumper will only harm it.

Over its production run, there were some minor changes made to the transaxle assembly. Of special note are the kinds of ball bearings used: some were sealed and others came apart. The procedure which follows is generalized, but appropriate for those competent enough to get into a transaxle's bowels.

Disassembly

1. Clean the exterior of the transaxle thoroughly. Any dirt on its outside will end up on its inside.

2. Remove the nut and washer that retain the shift selector lever, then remove the lever.

3. Remove the rubber dust cover from the clutch slave cylinder.

4. Remove the bolts that hold the clutch housing to the gearbox and pull the clutch assembly free from the input shaft.

5. Remove the throwout bearing and its lever from the bellhousing.

6. Remove the reverse lamp switch.

7. Remove the speedometer drive gear.

8. Remove the nuts that attach the front casting of the transaxle to its center casting.

9. Remove the entire front casting, along with the reverse sliding gear.

10. Use a soft-faced hammer to tap the center casting flange, which carries the transmission gear sets. As you pull it free, the gear train will pull free from the rear transaxle housing.

The transaxle internals, including main shaft, layshaft, shift rods and forks, slide right out of the housing.

At this point, make a thorough, preliminary inspection of all the components on both shafts. Check each gear set for chipped or worn teeth. The free gears should rotate smoothly on their shafts. You should not be able to "rock" them along the bearing axis. When in doubt, you should plan to replace a gear or bearing. Doing so now may forestall a second rebuild within a few miles.

11. It's easiest to work on this transaxle if the center flange is firmly supported. Don't just clamp the alloy casting in the jaws of the vise. Doing so will ruin the mating surface of the flange. Shape and drill a sturdy piece of sheet metal so it bolts up to the flange, then clamp the sheet metal in the vise.

Main Shaft Disassembly

The main shaft has the tapered pinion gear on its end.

In step 11 (above), you inspected the components along both the main and output shafts and determined which parts required repair or replacement (presumably, some components are damaged, otherwise you wouldn't have pulled the transaxle apart in the first place). We're at a significant decision point, and you need to

Here the gear shafts have been removed from the intermediate flange and the components removed in order.

determine now if you're over your head or not. Basically, this comes down to whether or not you're comfortable reading gear patterns. If you need to replace any of the components which determine stack-up on the main shaft (synchronizer hubs, bearings or spacers), you must measure the distance between the inside face of the center flange and the end of the pinion gear. This is a large but very precise measurement, normally made with a set of special tools that, of course, are not available to you.

Probably the best way to make this measurement is with a digital caliper. The nominal distance is 8.925 inches (226.7 mm). The problem is that a digital caliper is simply not accurate to a thousandth of an inch over almost nine inches. If you do use a digital caliper, then you should use a marking compound on reassembly and read the tooth pattern of the pinion gear on the ring gear. If you're not comfortable doing this, stop now and get help, or look for a rebuilt transmission.

Presuming that you're comfortable to proceed and are planning to reuse the pinion gear, pinion depth is adjusted by a shim that sits next to the double-row ball bearing (main shaft intermediate bearing) in the intermediate flange. If the pinion gear is replaced, then the value (in millimeters) stamped on the end of the pinion gear must be taken into account to get the proper pinion depth.

1. Remove the shift detent spring plugs, springs and balls from the edge of the center flange.

2. Slide the selector shaft for fifth/reverse gears free of the center flange. Rotate the gear selector assembly to allow the shaft to come free.

3. Unscrew the retaining bolts on the two remaining selector forks, then remove the shafts and forks.

4. Use a small screwdriver to remove the interlock pieces from the intermediate flange.

5. Engage two gears at the same time to lock the input shaft, then unscrew the nut on the input shaft.

6. Unscrew the nut from the end of the main shaft.

7. From the end of the main shaft, remove the components for reverse and fifth gears.

8. Slide the synchronizer sleeve so it engages fourth gear securely.

9. Tap the end of the main shaft with a soft hammer to free it from the intermediate flange. As it comes free, be careful to catch the intermediate ball bearing.

10. Set the main shaft on the bench and remove the ball bearing, shim that adjusts the pinion height, fourth gear and its bushing.

11. Remove the third/fourth synchronizer sleeve and hub.

12. Remove third gear and its bushing.

13. Remove second gear and its bushing.

14. Similarly, remove first and second gear assemblies.

15. Use a press or puller to remove the remaining bearing and shim.

Input Shaft Disassembly

1. Remove fifth and reverse gears.

2. Using a soft hammer, tap the input shaft free of the intermediate flange.

3. Remove the bearing.

Inspection

Component inspection is the same as for the earlier transmissions.

Reassembly

If the transmission has been disassembled, all components should be thoroughly cleaned before reassembly. During reassembly, lubricate all components liberally with 90 weight gear oil. Use grease on needle bearings to help retain them during reassembly.

Input Shaft

1. Install the intermediate bearing on the shaft

2. Install the input shaft in the intermediate flange.

3. Install fifth/reverse gears.

4. Install the shaft nut finger tight.

Main shaft

1. Press the main shaft into the bearing until the bearing is tight against the pinion gear.

2. Heat the spacer with a propane torch, but don't let it get so hot it begins to glow. Slip it onto the shaft so it seats squarely against the bearing.

3. Install first gear with the synchronizer teeth facing away from the pinion gear.

4. Install the first/second synchronizer hub and sleeve.

5. Install second gear and its bushing, then install third gear and its bushing.

6. Install the third/fourth synchronizer sleeve and hub.

7. Install the fourth speed bushing and gear, the pinion height adjusting spacer and the bearing that fits into the intermediate flange.

As the components come off of the main shaft and the pinion shaft (lower left) it is a good idea to lay out the parts in the order they were removed, trace them and label them. That way, when it's reassembly time, everything is positioned to go back on the shafts in the order it was removed. The differential can be seen at the bottom center and the synchro rings are at the bottom right.

8. Engage fourth gear, then tap the main shaft assembly into the intermediate flange.

9. Install the bushing and the needle bearing race.

10. Install fifth gear and its synchronizer assembly.

11. Install reverse gear.

12. Thread on a new nut, finger tight.

13. Engage both fourth and fifth gears so you can tighten the main shaft nut to 85 pound feet.

14. At this point, you must verify the pinion depth using a digital caliper. The target distance is 8.925 inches (226.7 mm), but the actual measurement must be the same as the one you recorded when dismantling the transaxle. If the distance is not correct, undo the nut on the main shaft, disassemble the fifth/reverse gear components and fit a replacement shim to correct the spacing.

15. Reassemble fifth/reverse components and tighten the main shaft nut again to 85 pound feet then stake it in place.

16. Tighten the input shaft nut to 74 pound feet and stake it in place.

17. Slide the shift interlock pieces into the intermediate flange.

18. Place the first/second and third/fourth shift forks onto their grooves in the synchronizer collars.

19. Install the shafts for third/fourth and first/second through their shift forks and then into the intermediate flange. You'll need to fiddle with the shafts and interlock mechanism to get everything in place.

20. Insert the gear selector rod with its locating spring into the intermediate flange. Check the assembly to be sure it will catch the shift rods which have been installed so far.

21. Install the fifth/reverse shaft into the intermediate flange. Rotate it as necessary to get it into place.

22. Install the three detent balls, springs and plugs. Check that the balls seat in the shaft grooves.

23. Put the three synchronizer sleeves in neutral. Move the shift forks on their shafts so the sleeves are equidistant from the gear faces on either side. Use a caliper to get them as equally spaced as possible, then lock the forks to their shafts with the lock bolt.

24. Check again that the gear selector mechanism works freely and that all three shift rods can be engaged easily.

25. Smear the transaxle intermediate flange mating surface with jointing compound and put it in place against the differential housing.

26. Smear the pinion gear with a marking compound such as white lead or Prussian blue, then temporarily bolt the intermediate flange in place so the pinion depth can be verified.

Setting Pinion Depth

At this point, it's necessary to verify pinion depth. With the intermediate flange bolted in place, rotate the transaxle main shaft so the pinion gear moves the ring gear and differential assembly at least two revolutions. Unbolt the intermediate flange and carefully remove it from the differential housing.

Look at the pattern of marking compound transferred to the teeth of the ring gear. The pattern should be centered on the working surfaces of the gear faces. Since side-to-side adjustment of the ring gear has not been disturbed, you can concentrate on the pinion depth setting. Experiment with shallower depths by placing brass shim stock between the mating surfaces of the intermediate flange and differential housing. Use the amount of shim stock to help determine the final thickness of the shim on the main shaft. If the pinion does not seat far enough into the teeth of the ring gear, then the main shaft shim itself will have to be replaced with a thicker one.

While this may seem a tedious procedure, anything less than a proper mesh between the ring and pinion gears will produce a noisy final drive with a very short life expectancy. If you are uncomfortable with this procedure, get professional assistance.

27. Install a new input shaft needle bearing and oil seal in the bell housing.

28. Put the throwout bearing guide sleeve in place.

29. Install the reverse sliding gear so it operates with the selector pin.

30. Install the front casting part way, then check the operation of the reverse gear. Finish the installation of the front casting.

- Tighten the case nuts in a diagonal sequence to 17 pound feet.

- Reinstall the speedometer drive pinion and the back-up lamp switch.

- Reinstall the clutch assembly.

- Reversing the instructions for removal of the transaxle, reinstall it in the car.

- Refill the transaxle with oil after installation.

Now it's time to try out your newly rebuilt transaxle. Make sure you're able to select all gears and that there is no undue noise from the gears. If properly performed, the rebuild should enable you to put many thousands of miles on the transaxle.

Chapter 14

Chassis

One premise of this book is that the primary attraction of the Giulietta, Giulia and successors is their brilliant, four-cylinder all-alloy engine. Clearly, for a lot of enthusiasts, bodywork offers another strong attraction. In point of fact, the feature which really kicked off the Giulietta was the svelte coupe bodywork that introduced the series. This gives us engines and bodies to love at first sight. Chassis are more of an acquired taste.

Cars with separate chassis and body are easy to understand. When you bought a chassis from Alfa, you got a ladder-shaped frame with everything needed to drive it to the bodybuilder. Since the Giulietta has a unit body, the distinction between what Pininfarina or Bertone wrought and the chassis itself is somewhat subtle. With unit construction, there is no frame. Unit-body cars are exoskeletal: the bodywork itself holds things together and resists the loads imposed on the car when it is being driven. Even the Giulietta's dash is a functional part of the structure.

■ Rust

It follows, then, that if the body rusts, the strength of the unit will be compromised, ultimately to the point that the car will be unserviceable. Since I spent the first 42 years of my life in Michigan, I know something about how Alfas rust. And, after almost 20 years in California, I can verify that rust is more of a subjective concern than an objective one. A California "rusted-out car" would

What looks like the beautifully painted body for a 1958 Spider Veloce is also the complete body/chassis unit. Because there is no separate chassis structure, the strength of the entire car is dependent upon having a sound and strong unibody.

have "some rust" in Michigan. I can assert from personal experience that the center tunnel of the Giulietta Spider provides enough beam strength by itself for the car to be fully functional. That means that the rocker panels, as well as the reinforcing members running beneath them, can be completely rusted away without undermining the Spider's serviceability—or restorability.

If you own a Giulietta or Giulia you may face a question of rust at one time or another. If you have an Alfetta, then you will most assuredly face the question. It's not that the cars were more rust-prone than some of their contemporaries. That's something which needs stressing: rust resistance was a developing science when these cars were being built.

It is true that at about the time the Alfetta models appeared, Alfa began using a grade of steel which was more rust-prone. There is firm evidence that these cars left the factory rusty. Certainly the salt-water air of the Atlantic crossing added to the problem, as did (many) months of sitting in the port, waiting to be sold. I believe that the majority of rust encountered on these cars began while they sat in the ports: in some instances, this amounted to more than a year of sitting in salt air.

I want to give three brief anecdotes about rust, which may help put the subject in its proper perspective.

The Blue Spider: At one time, I decided to try to determine the minimal level of serviceability for an Alfa. I threw an engine together from the most marginal parts I had in the garage, and installed it in a body which had rusted so badly it had neither rocker panels nor supporting pieces behind them. I drove this car only in the city, afraid to take it up to freeway speeds. A young neighbor finally convinced me to sell him the car. I cautioned him that it was an experiment in marginality, and he should treat it with great respect. Early one morning, I got a call from him. He was in the hospital. On the return leg of an approximately 250-mile trip in Michigan, he fell asleep at freeway speeds. The car had run off the road, did three end-to-end flips and landed in a field looking as if a giant had stepped on it amidships. He wanted to know if I'd sell him another Alfa.

Joe's Car: Joe Benson (author of the *Alfa Buyer's Guide*) owned a very fine 1750 Berlina which I obtained after he had pulled the engine and transmission from the car. I installed a Giulia Super engine and transmission in it, and used it for regular transportation for several years in Michigan. After that engine wore out, I installed a 750 Giulietta Berlina engine with a single-throat Solex carburetor. That conversion was dangerously slow, so another Giulia replacement was fitted and the car continued to be used. After many Michigan

winters, the car developed severe rust on the exterior panels, but was still structurally sound. I torched the exterior sheet metal from the car, beginning at about knee level, welded in scrap panels from a school bus, then painted the car a dark brown. It was not pretty, but still serviceable. Enough so, in fact, that I brought it to California with me. The car was finally parted out because I needed its space, not because it had stopped being serviceable.

Ron's Car: One of the fastest Alfas I've ever owned was the Giulia Veloce Spider I bought from Ron Crawford. He had put a lot of money into the car. The body was shiny and the interior neat and clean. This was still a high-mileage Michigan car, and it was subject to rust in the usual places. Most of these places had been corrected, so the car was cosmetically very attractive. However, it's the only Alfa I've ever retired because of rust. The critical failure was under the seats, where the trailing links for the rear suspension attach to the body. I've never seen this failure again on an Alfa, but I consider it a fatal one. While I can survive Alfas with no rocker panels, the thought of accelerating a Giulia Veloce and watching the rear axle assembly unwind itself back down the street behind me gave pause. A repair of this nature is problematic: welding in a simple sheet-metal insert would not be adequate to withstand the forces from the trailing link, and fabricating a satisfactory replacement section opened the possibility of inadvertently changing the rear suspension geometry. This was another Alfa I brought from Michigan to California, and it still sits, somewhat more disassembled, at Portello Works near San Diego.

The moral of these stories is that an Alfa has to be a lot more rusty than you've ever seen before it is truly done for.

On Giulietta Sprints and Spiders, you'll find rust in the following places:

- Over the rear-wheel arches
- Around the battery tray in the trunk
- Along the bottoms of the doors
- Along the rocker panels
- Where you rest your feet on the floor.

Later model Alfettas added rust:

- Around the front and rear glass
- At the front shock towers in the engine compartment.

This is far from an exhaustive list, but it will give you a start at being paranoid about your car's future.

How can you tell if the car is so rusted to be beyond hope? Consider how many cars have been rebuilt after catastrophic high-speed accidents: as long as the serial number is still stamped on the firewall, a car is restorable. Don't be put off by rust holes over the fender wells, along the rocker panels or the floorboards. I've already suggested one critical area that may decide for you: if the front anchor points of the trailing links have rusted away, a truly major restoration process is ahead. I don't mean this can't be saved, only that this is an area which usually doesn't rust, and by the time rust appears here, the remainder of the car has already been significantly weakened. Rust around the windshield frame is another area (on Alfetta coupes and sedans) which is probably terminal, simply because the complex bends in the area are so difficult to fabricate. If the doors on the car open differently when people are sitting in it, there is some evidence that the beam strength of the body is weak.

The value of the car has much more to do with its viability than any rust it may have. No car is ever rusted so badly that it can't be rebuilt: it's only a matter of money.

■ Suspension

According to *The Road & Track Illustrated Automotive Dictionary* compiled by John Dinkel and published by Bentley Publishers, suspension is defined as: "The various springs, shock, absorbers, and linkages used to suspend a car's frame, body, engine, and drivetrain above its wheels." To better understand how the suspension works on your car, below you'll find a quick glossary of suspension terms.

Contact Patch

A tire's contact patch with the ground (and hence, adhesion) is largest when it rolls vertical to the ground on all three axes. Logically, the purpose of a suspension should be to keep the tires always perpendicular to the ground, thus assuring the maximum contact patch. However, the forces of a turn typically reduce the size of the contact patch. To maintain the size of the patch during cornering, and to improve steering responsiveness, the suspension is tilted in several axes.

Caster

Caster is the vertical axis around which the steering pivots. If you tilt this axis so the tire contacts the ground to the rear of its axis (negative caster), the wheel will have a tendency to steer itself in a straight-ahead direction, like the wheels on an office chair. If

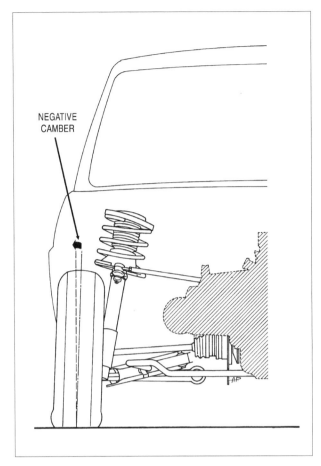

This diagram illustrates the slight outward tilt of a tire, which characterizes negative camber.

the contact point of the tire is ahead of the vertical axis (positive caster), steering becomes more responsive to the point of being "twitchy."

Camber

Camber is the lateral angle at which the tire contacts the ground. As the car's body rolls in a sharp turn, the bottom of the inside tire rolls inward, and the outside tire tends to lift. To counteract this effect, the bottoms of the tires are frequently displaced slightly outward (negative camber) so the tire remains more nearly vertical during hard cornering. This is a frequently noted characteristic of swing-axle rear suspensions, such as fitted to some Mercedes and BMW cars, as well as early Volkswagens and Porsches.

Toe

Toe is the angle between the front or rear wheels. Steering is more stable if the front wheels are splayed slightly outward (positive toe). Cars with independent

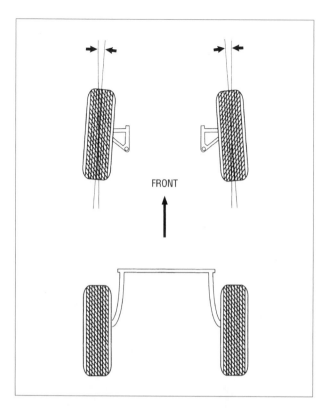

This illustration shows toe-in at the front wheels. Toe can be adjusted with independent suspension, but in the case of a solid axle or deDion system, toe is fixed.

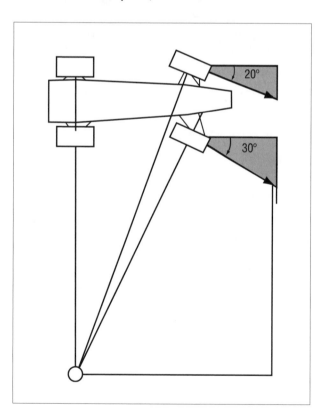

Your Alfa Romeo, like all other cars, has steering geometry that causes the outside wheel in a turn to describe a larger arc, as seen in this illustration.

rear suspension typically have some kind of toe adjustment for the rear axle. The deDion suspension is technically a solid rear axle, so there is no toe adjustment.

Ackerman

When the car turns, the outside wheels describe a larger arc than the inside wheels. That means that the inside wheels have to turn more than the outside wheels. Ackerman is built into all steering systems and is not adjustable.

Center of Gravity (cg)

The center of gravity is the location, somewhere inside the car (hopefully), that its mass balances in all axes. If you could jam a pin into the car, it's the point at which the car would sit level on the pin. It's desirable to have the center of gravity located as low and as near the center of the vehicle as possible.

Weight Distribution

For optimum handling, the weight of the car should be evenly distributed between the front and rear wheels. Conventional vehicles, with the engine and transmission in the front, are usually nose-heavy. The Alfetta corrects this by placing the transaxle at the rear of the car.

Oversteer

Oversteer is the tendency of the car to turn more than the driver commands through the steering wheel. An oversteering car wants to turn into the inside of a turn.

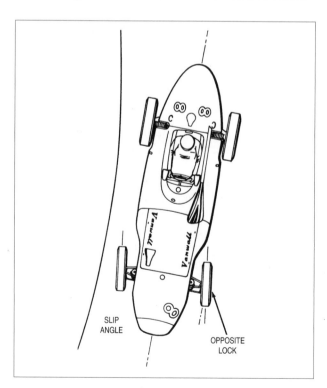

As the diagram indicates, oversteer can be corrected by applying opposite lock to counteract a car's tendency to turn into a corner more than is desired.

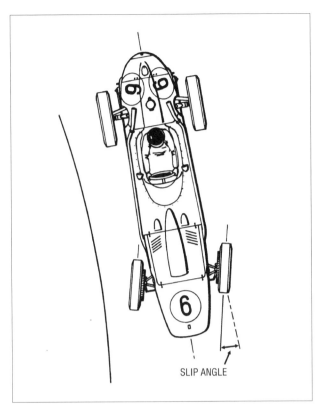

SLIP ANGLE

An understeering car is one that requires additional steering lock as a car navigates a constant radius turn.

Understeer

Understeer is the tendency of the car to turn less than the driver commands. An understeering car wants to turn toward the outside of a turn.

Polar Moment

The center of gravity depends on where all the heavy components of the vehicle are located. Some heavy parts, such as the engine, transmission and differential, are usually located near the ends of the car. Once put in motion (in a turn or spin), these parts tend to remain in motion, adversely affecting the ability of the car to change direction quickly. The most popular way of considering this phenomenon is to think of a barbell which has been twirled by a weightlifter: the inertial forces tending to keep the barbell moving are considerable. A barbell has a high polar moment of inertia. On the other hand, if the heavy parts were all located near the center of gravity, the barbell, or car, would be able to change direction more easily: in this case, we have a small polar moment. For most nimble handling, designers like to keep the heaviest parts of the car nearest its center, and ideally, nearest its center of gravity.

Roll Center

As a car turns, its body leans to the outside of the turn. The axis on which this happens is the car's roll center. Simply put, the lower the roll center, the more stable the car and the less likely it is to roll over. The roll center is determined by the geometry of the front and rear suspensions. The goal is to get the roll center as low as possible, and always below the car's center of gravity.

■ Giulietta

Alfa's suspensions have always been optimized for sporty driving. Even the most sedate of the Alfa sedans offers superior roadability, and under most circumstances, the suspensions are more competent than the drivers. This is in marked contrast to the American cars of the same era, which had an annoying tendency to be overwhelmed by the forces of normal driving.

The suspensions covered in this book depend on a rigid body structure for support. It's worth noting that this is exactly the opposite of the ladder-frame Alfas built before the war. These cars had rigid suspensions and supple frames, and the ride quality of these cars had more to do with the design of the frame than that of the suspension.

Giulietta suspensions favor ride comfort over outright cornering ability. The springs are soft enough that they can be worked to their limits under very hard cornering. Limit straps are used front and rear to control body roll and improve cornering ability. At the front, steel cable is used, while fabric straps are used at the rear. An anti-sway bar also helps maintain the composure of the front suspension. It's essential that the limit straps are in good condition if you drive your Giulietta hard.

None of what follows is especially technical. Suspensions are an intensely technical subject, and there are much better books on them than I could ever write. I hope this thought gives you pause: those enthusiasts who chase superior roadholding by lowering or otherwise modifying an Alfa suspension are throwing away decades of race-proven design. Whatever faults an Alfa suspension may have are minor compared to the results of well-intentioned amateurs. As with engine power, suspension performance is always a trade-off of virtues. Most race-worthy suspensions tend to be too harsh and limited in their travel for normal use. Unless you are one of the very few who plan to race an Alfa, you're much better off leaving the suspension alone.

Front Suspension

The front suspension on the Giulietta consists of two equilateral triangles, one situated atop the other. This layout is known as a double A-arm, or wishbone suspension. The bases of the triangles are attached to square-section sheet metal reinforcements on the body and the apexes of the triangles form the pivot points for the front wheels.

If the heights of the two triangles were equal, the suspension would be a regular parallelogram. The wheel would always be parallel to the bases of the triangles and, presumably, always perpendicular to the surface of the road. This assures maximum contact between the tire and road, and maximum traction. On the Alfa, the upper triangle describes a shorter arc than the bottom one. This geometry is used to help counteract the effect of body lean during hard cornering, and provide neutral steering. You can change camber with the adjusting shims placed at the anchor bolts on the body.

The pivot points on the front suspension all require lubrication, and are either bushes (inboard) or ball joints (outboard). The bushes wear gradually, providing a reduction in agility which is slow enough to be imperceptible to the owner. Rebuilding the front suspension is simply a matter of fitting new bushes and ball joints.

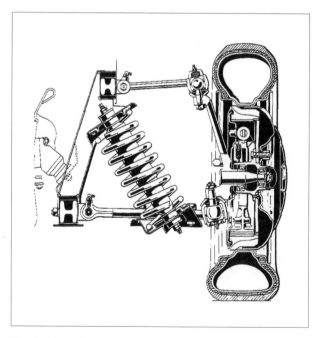

The Giulietta front suspension was a true dual-A-arm arrangement. A large forged spindle was used instead of a kingpin.

Rear Suspension

The coil-spring rear suspension of the Giulietta consists of two torque-reaction trailing arms and a triangular member which resists side forces. This layout is retained in slightly modified form throughout the Giulietta/Giulia/1750/2000 production run, testimony that it works quite well.

On the Giulietta, the rear suspension members are tubular, and the forward most pivot points are rubber bushes. Shock absorbers seat directly on the axle tubes.

There is empirical evidence that the setup does not adequately locate the rear axle under racing conditions. Occasionally, die-hard racers modify the rear suspension to accept a Panhard rod instead of the triangular member. The Panhard rod is attached to the chassis near one of the rear wheels and extends along the length of the rear axle, attaching near the point at which the trailing arm meets the axle. Heim joints on both ends assure sturdy side-to-side location. A Panhard rod changes the geometry of the rear suspension completely, and must never be used in conjunction with the stock triangular member.

An even more dramatic technique, used on the GTA cars, is a vertical sliding block situated between the differential housing itself and the chassis. This layout assures that there can be no side-to-side movement of the rear axle. A sliding block is impractical for street use because it requires constant cleaning and lubrication.

WARNING—If a Giulietta is going to be raced, you must box in the trailing arm attachment point at the rear axle. This helps resist side forces during cornering at racing speeds.

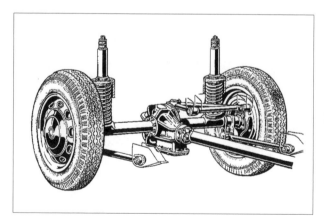

The Giulietta rear axle was located by tubular members, and the shock absorbers and springs sit right on the axle itself.

■ Giulia

While the Giulia spider retained the Giulietta front and rear suspensions, new layouts were introduced on the Giulia sedan and coupe. A similar layout was later used on the Duetto.

Front Suspension

Early reviews in the enthusiast press missed a significant point of the new Giulia sedan: its new front suspension. (The *Road & Track* review incorrectly called it "the same as the Giulietta…with unequal A- arms….")

The 105-series cars have a lower A-arm very similar to the 101-series suspension, but the upper elements are properly called transverse and trailing links. In a way, the upper A-arm of the Giulietta is rotated about 45 degrees for the Giulia, and the base of the triangle extends from the centerline of the wheel bearing to a point near the front headlight. This layout causes a small caster and toe change in addition to a camber change when cornering.

As proof that everything is a trade-off, the grease-eating bronze bushes of the Giulietta were replaced on the Giulia with "no-maintenance" sealed joints that were actually large rubber bushes. The initial idea of never having to lubricate the suspension is appealing, but Giulia owners soon learned that rubber is not a perfect material for a suspension. It is attacked by ozone and becomes brittle, causing the joint to seize. Neglected, frozen joints will tear the suspension from the Giulia body. Fortunately, the suspension gives ample warning before catastrophic failure by squeaking loudly when things begin to deteriorate. The hapless owner who ignores the squeaks, however, may find his front suspension missing after failing to negotiate a deep pothole.

A temporary repair to deteriorating rubber bushes is to inject brake fluid or automatic transmission fluid into the rubber with a hypodermic syringe to soften it. Since brake fluid is hydroscopic, its use is actually destructive. The only sure fix, of course, is to fit new parts.

On really rough roads, the new suspension design stresses the top trailing link's forward-most joint excessively. Owners who drive on rough roads find that they have to replace the joint frequently. The wear limit of the joint is indicated by a solid "clunk" when the suspension is working over a rough road. No repair to the joint is possible: it must be replaced when worn.

A popular modification to this suspension is to make the upper tubular link adjustable for additional negative camber. Cut the link at midpoint, shorten both tubes somewhat, then tap right- and left-hand threads in the inside diameter of the tubes. Kits are available for this, but you can fabricate an adjusting link from stock with right- and left-hand threads. Machine a hex on the link to ease adjustment, and use jam nuts to keep everything where it should be.

Rear Suspension

Although essentially the same as the Giulietta rear suspension (a solid rear axle), the location of the rear axle is much more robust on the Giulia. Instead of the Giulietta's small tubular triangle, a large, fabricated crossmember is used to locate the rear axle side-to-side. It bolts to sheet-metal subframes that run over the kick-up for the rear axle. The shocks are positioned outside the coil springs, which seat on the trailing arms.

Aside from cleaning and inspecting the rubber bushes which are part of the rear suspension, it's unlikely that anything will have to be done to the rear suspension for maintenance. Giulia springs tend not to sag: nonetheless, it's a good idea to measure the two rear coil springs to verify they have the same unloaded height.

The Giulia rear suspension was modified to be more robust. The rear axle is located by stamped trailing arms which support the coil springs.

Inspect very carefully the area where the rear suspension trailing arm attaches to the body. The area must be rust-free and perfectly sound. If the body shell is badly rusted, it is possible that the metal around the attaching point has been weakened. If there is any question about the strength of the area, replace the body's floor panel with new metal, welded in place.

If a Giulia spider is going to be raced, you must box in the trailing arm's attaching point at the rear axle. This helps resist side forces during cornering at racing speeds.

▪ Alfetta

1993 was the 100th anniversary of the deDion rear suspension. In spite of its age, it remains one of the best rear suspensions, both in theory and practice.

If you think of trying to throw a strike by rolling a bowling ball and then a BB down an alley, you'll also understand that the mass of the moving item also has a lot to do with how easily it changes direction. Big, heavy things bore on while light objects are easily deflected.

So we've got this wheel rolling down the road. When it hits a bump it's launched into the air. Suspension designers want it to change direction quickly so it can regain traction and continue to contribute to the car's acceleration, braking or steering. That means that the mass which moves with the wheel needs to be as light as possible.

The reason why independent rear suspension is so desirable is that it removes the considerable weight of a solid axle, complete with differential, from the mass which moves up and down with the wheel. As a result, independent suspensions help keep the tire in contact with the road and provide significantly improved control.

A hundred years ago, a Frenchman was trying to figure out how to keep the axles of steam-powered trucks from breaking under load. Rather than simply increase the beam strength of the axle, Albert deDion did away with the single load-bearing unit. That was not his only accomplishment: deDion was an automotive pioneer whose efforts touched almost every facet of the developing industry, and his engines were used in several vehicles.

To solve the fragile rear axle problem, deDion simply eliminated it. He first separated the truck's chain-drive sprocket and differential unit from the axle itself and mounted them directly to the body. That made the drive unit part of the truck's load, rather than part of the mass which moved with the wheels. In other words, he made the differential sprung, instead of unsprung weight. Then, deDion connected the differential to the wheels using jointed axle shafts. As a result, all the weight of the truck bore through leaf springs on compact stub-axle assemblies. He then added a dead axle to locate the rear wheels. The dead axle only had to be strong enough to keep the wheels pointed straight ahead under its load.

The wheels on a deDion axle are solidly located by the dead axle, so a deDion suspension is not independent, even though it uses half shafts.

Over the decades, as vehicle speeds rose, designers began to understand that the real genius of deDion's axle was not superior strength, or even reduced unsprung weight, but optimum wheel geometry. Independent suspensions can change camber, caster and even the effective wheelbase of the car as they move. While these changes are usually very small, they still work in arcs which peel the tire's tread away from the ground. The dead axle on a deDion suspension keeps the wheels parallel to each other at all times.

To go along with its deDion rear suspension, the Alfetta received a modified front suspension, complete with torsion bars (far lower right) to augment the coil spring.

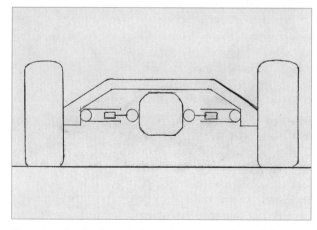

Though not actually an independent suspension, with the differential mounted to the body/chassis structure the deDion configuration offers low unsprung weight and excellent location of the wheels.

Alfa Romeo was a leader in the development of independent rear suspensions, having introduced a passenger car with fully independent suspension in 1935. In the same year an eight-cylinder Grand Prix Alfa featured a fully independent layout with a transverse leaf spring. In 1940, a prototype racer, the 512, used a deDion rear suspension, and the Type 159 Alfas used deDion rear suspensions when they won back-to-back world championships for Alfa in 1950–51.

When it was planning its new series of passenger cars for the late 1970s, Alfa revived the Type 159's deDion layout as well as the car's nickname, "Alfetta." Public relations ploys aside, the Alfetta passenger cars, along with the derivative GTV-6 and Milano, are among the few production models which have used the deDion layout.

The transaxle unit has been removed from this Alfetta; the deDion tube and coil spring assemblies can be seen clearly.

The rear hub mounts to an extension welded to the end of the deDion tube. If the hub looks naked, it's only because the disc brakes are mounted inboard.

On the Alfetta setup, the transmission and differential are combined in a transaxle which is attached to the body at three points. Rubber mounts are used to isolate gear noise. The deDion tube itself is the rear member of a large welded triangular structure. The front legs of the triangle are tapered tubes, which are beautiful but very expensive items to fabricate. The tip of the triangle is attached to a body cross member by a single large bolt. The rear is suspended by coil springs and damped by tubular shock absorbers. A Watts link locates the deDion tube laterally.

The deDion rear suspension provides a very comfortable ride and great roadholding. Simply put, the layout in the Alfetta lives up to its considerable potential.

In practical terms, the Alfetta's rear setup is a dream to work on, and it is clear that serviceability was high on the engineers' priorities. By unbolting the front crossmember and jacking up the deDion tube, you can lower the nose of the transaxle and remove the complete clutch assembly as well as the entire transmission internals, including the pinion gear. Clutch replacement or a transmission overhaul on these Alfas is a piece of cake.

The downside of the Alfetta setup has nothing to do with the deDion tube, but a lot to do with the decision to locate the transmission at the back of the car with the differential. Because the driveshaft is bolted to the flywheel and turns at engine speed, the Alfetta driveshaft is very sensitive to balance and shock. Alfa uses three rubber "donuts" along the Alfetta driveshaft to act as universal joints and reduce the shock of sudden clutch engagement. These donuts have to be replaced at regular intervals, and the more the car is hot-rodded the faster they fail. While taking it easy isn't the central idea of Alfetta ownership, it does protect the pocketbook from $100 donuts.

■ Other Chassis Components

Clutch

The clutch is a device which connects or disconnects engine power from the drivetrain. When you push the left pedal, you overcome spring pressure which clamps a fabric-faced disc (called the driven plate) between a heavy metal disc (called the driving plate) and the flywheel. The driving plate is bolted to the flywheel; the driven plate is splined to the transmission. When the clutch pedal is released, heavy springs in the driving plate clamp the driven plate to the flywheel, transmitting power from the flywheel to the transmission.

The advantage of this arrangement is that the fabric-driven plate can slip without (immediately) burning up from friction. Its ability to slip allows you to transition between clutch in and out gradually.

American clutches are built with a robust idiot factor and can be slipped almost without harm. All early European cars (including Giulia) presume that the driver will use his brakes, and not the clutch, to hold the car on a hill while waiting for traffic. As a result, Alfa clutches are significantly more prone to failure than is American custom. This doesn't mean they are fragile: but they do have a limit to the abuse they'll take.

There are two kinds of clutches: those fitted to Giuliettas and Giulias used wound steel springs to get the clamping force. On these clutches, you can increase the clamping pressure by fitting stronger springs to

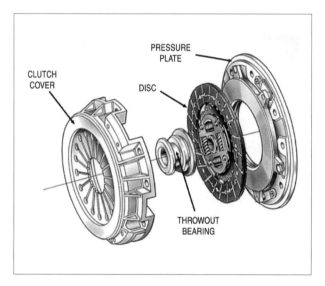

A basic clutch assembly consists of a clutch cover, throwout bearing, disc and pressure plate and serves to transmit power from the engine to the transmission.

This is the center universal joint for the Giulietta driveshaft.

the driving plate. You can also lengthen driven plate life by using a harder fabric. Fitting anything different from stock will involve trade-offs: you can end up with a clutch which requires two feet to release, or a lining which slips easily or has a short service life and virtually no transition between "on" and "off."

Later-model Alfas use a dished spring-steel plate instead of the multiple coil springs used on the Giulia. The flywheel diameter is larger on 1750 and newer Alfas, so the flywheels and clutches are not interchangeable to the Giulia unless a lot of other parts are swapped, including bellhousings and starters. The two-liter flywheel is not only larger, but it uses a different bolt mounting pattern to the crank and cannot be fitted (well, practically anyway) to the Giluia.

Driveshaft

Attached to the output shaft of the Giulia transmission is a large rubber donut which acts not only as a shock absorber for the remainer of the drivetrain but also as a universal joint. The Giulia donut has proved to be completely reliable, unlike the similar donuts which have sullied the reputation of the Alfetta cars. They are all identical in design, but much less reliable in the newer cars. The Giulia donuts last just fine.

The driveshaft is splined about half-way down the car, and the spline has a grease fitting which needs occasional ministration. Just ahead of the spline, there is a conventional universal joint and a rubber-supported steady bearing for the driveshaft. At the rear of the driveshaft is another conventional universal joint. Both universal joints may require occasional lubrication (later permanently lubricated joints may have been fitted).

All driveshafts require balancing. The Alfetta driveshaft is actually a part of the engine's reciprocating mass and so its balance is critical. The Giulia driveshaft is not nearly so critical in its balance requirements. Even so, if removed, it should be marked so it can be replaced in exactly the same rotational orientation to the transmission output shaft and the companion flange on the rear axle.

The ball-and-socket joint which centers the output flange of the transmission with the driveshaft should occasionally be lubricated with heavy grease. If it is not maintained, the joint can wear and cause vibration.

Differential

In practical terms, Alfa rear ends never go bad. None of the many Alfas I've owned have developed differential problems, nor even had an outboard wheel bearing fail badly. That is fortunate, for setting up a rear end properly is beyond the capabilities of most Alfa owners.

The procedure requires special tools—and a lot of experience reading the gear pattern which is the final test of the setup.

If you have a bad differential unit, I strongly suggest replacing it with a used unit. Get the whole axle assembly, with, if you can, the brakes attached. Check

This differential housing is from a 1971 Alfa 1750 Spider. As it sits, the opening for the right axle tube is toward the camera and the bottom of the unit is to the right.

The ring gear is mounted on the differential carrier and takes its drive from the pinion gear, which is turned by the driveshaft.

the outboard seals for leaking, fit new brake parts if needed and you've done about all you should.

Otherwise, let someone repair the differential who makes his living doing it. Because so much power is transmitted, setting up the mesh of the pinion to the ring gear is a very exacting art and clearly beyond the average hobbyist. The pinion is moved in and out using shims, and the ring gear is located side-to-side with other shims to provide an exact engagement where maximum pressure is developed at the sturdiest part of the gear. Both the ring and pinion gear faces are curved, and it is usual to have the center axis of the pinion fall somewhat below the axis of the ring gear.

The ring gear does not drive the axle shafts directly. Attached to it is a set of gears which allow the two rear wheels to turn at different speeds, a feature necessary for turning a corner without spinning one wheel (the outer wheel turns more times than the inner). This unit is called a differential which, itself, consists of two ring gears and two pinion gears. The pinion gears mesh with the ring gears and limit the rate at which the two ring gears turn in relation to each other. The net result is not two-wheel drive, as many may think. Actually, only one rear wheel controls the power which the Giulia puts on the road. As long as both wheels have equal traction, then the power is divided equally between the two. But the standard differential plays us false as soon as one wheel loses traction, as in snow or mud: then, the wheel without traction receives all the power. That is exactly the opposite of what is wanted.

Limited-slip differentials were used on only a few racing Giulias, so a detailed examination here is a bit out of place. To simplify the operation of a limited-slip differential, a clutch pack is used to simulate traction for both wheels. Under normal-traction conditions, the clutches slip, allowing normal differential action. When one wheel loses traction, however, the clutch pack attached to its axle resists the axle's spinning and thereby simulates enough traction to coax some power from the car's differential.

You cannot tell from looking at a rear axle whether or not your Giulia is equipped with a limited-slip differential. The only way to check is to jack up one rear wheel and try to turn it with the handbrake off and the transmission in neutral. If the wheel spins freely, you do not have a limited-slip differential.

My Giulia Super is fitted with a limited-slip differential from a later-model Alfa. The unit's more recent manufacture is revealed by the fact that both right and left wheel studs have conventional left-hand threads. On Giulias, the driver-side studs are right-threaded.

▪ Brakes

Giulietta and Giulia Drum Brakes

The Giulietta was famous for its large, finned Alfin front drums. If anything, these cars were over-braked, and it's with some dismay that I read of new owners wanting to replace these with disc brakes. It is possible for the front drums to wear beyond their service limit, and it isn't advisable to try to press-fit new steel inserts. If a drum is excessively worn, it's better to find a serviceable original than to replace the drums with disc brakes. Originally, the linings were riveted to the brake shoes; later replacement brake shoes will have bonded linings.

The Giulietta had terrific brakes for its day. The big aluminum drums were finned for cooling.

Early 1600 Sprints featured three brake shoes acting inside a big, finned alloy brake drum.

A few of the first Giulia 1600 Sprints were fitted with three-shoe brakes. These cars had rear drum brakes like the Giulietta. The three-shoe brakes are full floating, so movement of one of the three brake adjusters affects the position of all shoes.

I have never been able to remember a clever way to determine which way to turn the star-wheel adjuster used on Alfa drum brakes. Since the drums are only held on with two (or three, in the case of the three-shoe units) taper-headed screws, I've always found it easier to remove the drums to remind myself of how the adjusters work.

Rear drum brakes use a small square-headed adjuster which some person, surely, in the car's history will have mangled with a pair of pliers. The adjuster for the rear brake has a standard thread: screw it in to reduce shoe-to-drum clearance.

Disc Brakes

Most Giulias in the United States have four-wheel disc brakes. Front disc brakes were first introduced on the Giulia TI in 1964. The Giulia Super carried four-wheel disc brakes. Disc brakes for the Giulia were initially

The rear drums fitted to Giuliettas and early Giulias used two brake shoes within a drum with longitudinal cooling fins running around the drum's diameter.

Dunlops, and later ATEs. Parts for both are common with several other cars and a large parts store catering to foreign cars should be able to supply enough rubber to rebuild a cylinder. The Giulia Sprint Speciale and Giulia Spider Veloce carried Girling three-piston calipers.

The rear Dunlop disc brake design makes the internal combustion engine look intuitively simple. It is a maze of linkages. Essentially, the rear unit requires occasional adjustment of the pullrod that connects the two actuating levers, a point not covered in any of the repair manuals. If you have a car with Dunlop brakes, studying the linkage of the rear unit will yield a pleasant afternoon of hilarious disbelief. Fortunately, they work just fine.

ATE disc brakes use two pistons per caliper (they are not the cheap, "floating caliper" design). If the car sits for a long time, it's quite likely that a piston will freeze in its cylinder, reducing the braking effectiveness of the car slightly.

This rear axle assembly is fitted with Dunlop disc brakes.

This Giulia Super brake vacuum booster has been bypassed. This is not a desirable modification, but will keep the car on the road—albeit with higher pedal pressure—until the booster can be rebuilt or replaced.

Vacuum Booster

Beginning with the Giulia, Alfa adopted power-boosted brakes. A large diaphragm with manifold vacuum on one side is used to add pressure to the brake's hydraulic system when the brake pedal is depressed. These boosters leak occasionally, drawing brake fluid into the intake manifold and causing the car to appear to burn oil.

The vacuum-operated brake booster on Giulias and 1750s is the most likely part of the brake system to fail. The fact that there is virtually no information about the booster is evidence that Alfa would just as soon you leave it alone. Have the booster rebuilt by a competent shop.

If the booster is broken or leaking, it is quite possible to run the Giulia brake system unboosted in relative safety. Brake effort will increase noticeably, but not beyond the ability to lock up the wheels. Reconnect the lines (a female adapter is required) to eliminate the booster from the hydraulic system. Be sure to bleed the entire system thoroughly when you're through. Plug the vacuum line to the intake manifold.

Alfetta Brakes

Alfa Romeo has always been known for its excellent brakes. The large, helically finned drums of the Giulietta set the standard for drum brakes for many years, and the four-wheel disc brakes which graced most Giulia models were several years ahead of their time. When Alfa introduced the deDion rear suspension on the Alfetta in 1975, enthusiasts were pleased, not only with a sophisticated transaxle rear suspension, but also with inboard rear brakes which kept unsprung weight to an absolute minimum.

They were pleased, that is, until they tried to do a brake job. While the front brakes of the deDion cars were a snap, the rears offered a few innovations for which enthusiasts were not quite prepared. One of the first difficulties is accessibility. The transaxle, to which the brakes are attached, is bolted up to the unit body and the rear brake pads are removed in an almost vertical direction, so there is very little extra clearance to ease pad removal. In addition, before inserting new pads, the rear brake pistons have to be retracted using screw adjustments. And, once installed, the new pads must be readjusted for wear using the same screws.

Part of the reason for this necessary maintenance is that the mechanical handbrake assembly on the cars works on the inboard pistons, so the outboard pistons have to be held very close to the discs in order for the assembly to clamp successfully. The other reason is that the very small movement of the pads for handbrake operation is dwarfed by the total wear allowed by the pads. Hence, some adjustment mechanism is needed to keep the face of the pads close enough to the disk for the parking brake to operate at all.

Alfetta brakes are sensitive enough that you can tell pad wear simply by noticing how much free travel there is in the brake pedal before the brakes are actually applied. When everything is new, the pedal is quite high. As the pads wear, the pedal develops free play. With completely worn pads, the pedal will go almost to the floor before the brakes are applied.

A similar symptom applies to handbrake adjustment. With fresh pads, properly set, the handbrake operates within five clicks. As the rear pads wear, the handbrake takes hold with an increasingly greater number of clicks. Thus, the Alfa brakes are sensitive enough that, if you know what to look for, you'll know exactly how much pad wear you have.

While there is a handbrake cable length adjustment at the transaxle, the real solution to keeping good handbrake action is to readjust the clearance between the pads and disks to the approximately 0.005 inch. clearance specified by the shop manual. Since this is a regular maintenance operation, every Alfa owner should know how to do it, and that procedure will be covered later in this chapter. Even with Alfa's exotic rear suspension and inboard brakes, replacing brake pads is easy enough that every owner should be able to swap out a pair of pads on a Saturday morning.

▪ Steering

Rack-and-pinion steering is renowned for its great feel and precision. Because of that, many people believe that Alfas have rack-and-pinion steering. Not so: two different boxes were used for the Giulietta and Giulia, one with Burman recirculating ball design and the other with ZF worm and sector. Both offer some adjustment for wear and neither is especially better than the other.

For these models, the steering box operates one wheel directly and controls a track rod to another bellcrank arrangement on the opposite side of the car. The design means that the tie rods to each wheel have equal length, and also makes right-hand-drive conversion slightly more convenient.

The Alfetta introduced rack-and-pinion steering. This type of steering typically allows for less play in the mechanism than the recirculating ball or worm/sector styles, and is generally considered to have a better feel. Since no one has ever complained of inferior steering

Made of aluminum, this recirculating ball steering box was used in 750-series Alfas.

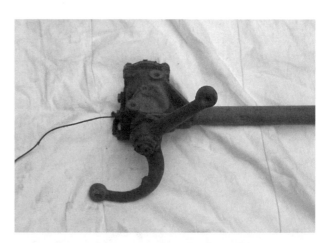

This 101-series steering box was made of steel.

The 105/115-series gearbox had a shorter shaft than the earlier units.

Rack and pinion steering was introduced on the Alfetta and offered better road feel and less play, although steering effort became greater.

characteristics on the earlier cars, the distinction is purely theoretical on Alfas.

Alfetta sedans and coupes tend to have much heavier steering than earlier Alfas. You can ease steering effort slightly by running higher pressures in the front tires and/or fitting a larger-diameter steering wheel. A more heroic conversion is to replace the standard rack-and-pinion unit with the power unit from a Milano. This also involves fitting a power steering pump, and invites the likelihood of a leaking rack, a common failure on the Milano. But, if you must have lighter steering on your Alfetta, the Milano unit is an alternative.

■ Understanding Your Alfa

With a basic understanding of the underpinnings of your Alfa, even if you don't plan on performing your own work, you will have a greater comfort level when it comes to identifying problems and arranging for brake, steering or suspension work. And if you do plan on performing your own brake work, the following chapter will be very helpful.

Chapter 15

Tending to Brakes

The average do-it-yourself mechanic should have little difficulty in changing the brake linings on his or her Giulietta, Giulia, 1750 or 2000. The combination of the basic description of the braking system in the prior chapter and the following procedure should make it possible to renew the braking capabilities of your Alfa safely and easily.

■ Giulia, 1750 and 2000 Front Brakes

The front pads are easiest so we'll start there. Before you jack up the car, loosen all the lug nuts on the front wheels about one turn each. Then, jack up the car and support it on jack stands so the front wheels are off the ground. Remove the road wheels.

Take a close look at the shiny surface of the disk rotor. It's going to be scored, so don't panic. If it is really heavily scored (say, marks a sixteenth of an inch deep) you should have the surface refinished by a brake shop. If you're in doubt, button everything up and drive to a shop you can trust for a knowledgeable evaluation.

Next, check the brake fluid reservoir. If it is near the full mark, remove and discard about half of the fluid. You can drain fluid using either a turkey baster (your wife won't want it back) or by opening one of the bleeders. If the reservoir is about one third down or

From 1965, all Alfa Romeos, be they Spiders or Berlinas, had four-wheel disc brakes, as did this 1967 GTV.

The left front rotor on this GTV 2000 shows minimal scoring and will not need to be resurfaced at this time. In this photograph, the mount for an aftermarket anti-sway bar is clearly visible.

A pair of pliers will help you grab the pin and pull it from the rear of the caliper.

Prepare for changing the pads by checking the fluid level in the master cylinder (arrow). If the level is high, remove some of the brake fluid to prevent spillage when you wedge the pistons back in their bores.

Once the cross-spring is out, the pads can be removed.

Use a small punch to drive out the pins that retain the cross-spring and pads.

Because there is no need to turn the brake discs, new pads may be inserted, followed by the cross-spring and the pins.

more, you can drape a couple of shop rags around the base of the reservoir to catch brake fluid which will spill over when the brake pistons are wedged all the way back in their bores.

Two large pins hold a cross-shaped spring against the ends of the brake pads. The pins are held in place by expanding spring collars. Look carefully at how the cross-spring fits around the pins on two ends and presses against the pads with the other ends. Remember the orientation so you can put it back properly. (A photo or quick diagram will come in very handy later.) With a small hammer and a drift, drive the pins out, working from the small end. A blunted nail makes a fine drift. As the first pin pops out, the cross-spring may come flying, so be ready for it and make sure you are wearing eye protection.

With both pins and the cross-spring removed, carefully force the largest screwdriver you have between the disk and one pad, forcing the piston back into its bore but being careful not to damage the disk. The piston will have to go almost completely home in order to fit a new pad.

■ Giulia, 1750 and 2000 Rear Brakes

The rear pads are held in place in approximately the same way as the front pads, except that the retaining pins themselves are held in place with a kind of hairpin clip that you can pull out with a pair of needle-nose pliers. Use a small mirror to look down on the pads so you can see what's required. With the clips removed, you can remove the retaining pins by pressing a screwdriver against their bent ends. There's a cross-spring beneath these pins too, but the spring is smaller and will launch itself against the underside of the body, so it won't go very far.

Don't try to pry the rear pads to force the pistons back into their bores. The pistons are held in place by screw adjustments. On each caliper, the outboard piston is held in place by a screw which has a 5mm in-hex head and that screw is retained by a locknut which is loosened with a 17mm socket. The adjusting screw and locknut may be concealed beneath a plastic cap which itself has a 17mm hex head on it. On most Alfettas, this plastic cap is long gone, but if you can't seem to find the adjusting screw, it is probably covered by a cap. The inboard piston is held in place by a 7mm hex-headed screw which has no locknut.

Three of these adjusting screws have the same kinds of threads: the inboard 7mm hex screw on the driver's side is reverse-threaded. In order to back out three screws then, turn them clockwise; the remaining screw is backed out by turning it counterclockwise.

Once the hairpin clips are removed, the pad-retaining pins can be driven out with a small punch.

With both pins out, the pads can be withdrawn.

Channel-lock pliers work well for extracting the pads.

Only a few turns will be required to release the pistons enough to withdraw the pads. However, quite a few turns are needed to get enough room to fit the new pads.

With the new pads installed and the springs and pins back in place, run the adjuster screws in so the pads clear the disks by about 0.005 inch. Tromp on the brake pedal a couple of times to verify that you have brakes. As you tighten the locknut on the adjusting screw, you'll find that the screw turns with the locknut. For that reason, it's necessary to hold the adjusting screw with an Allen wrench while tightening the locknut. A hollow-headed ratchet is perfect for this job. If you don't have one, however, clamp a 17mm socket in the jaws of a Vise-Grip pliers and stick the Allen wrench through the socket.

Button everything up and make sure you top up the brake fluid reservoir. Recheck the front wheel lugnuts. Then take a short, careful drive and apply the brakes lightly to seat them.

Now, we can make a final adjustment to the rear brakes. Jack the rear of the car up and support it on jack stands. Loosen the 17mm locknut on both calipers and set the inboard and outboard pistons on each caliper so there is about 0.005-inch clearance between the pads and disks. Some Alfa owners like to set the pads so they just brush against the disk: you make this kind of adjustment by ear, not feel.

Go in and pull up on the handbrake. If you can get any more than five clicks travel, you'll need to adjust the cable length. Near the differential housing on the passenger's side of the transaxle, up on top, you'll find the adjusting bolt. Loosen the locknut on the end of the handbrake cable, hold the inner cable itself with a

pair of pliers (not on the threads, please) and turn the adjusting nut clockwise to shorten the cable's effective length. Try the handbrake again, then keep adjusting until you get between three to five clicks to full parking brake application. Tighten the locknut and you're done.

As the rear pads wear, you'll find that you've got so much handbrake travel that the parking brake is useless. That's when you readjust the rear brake pistons to regain the 0.005-inch clearance between the pads and disks. If you adjust the handbrake cable instead, you'll only end up readjusting it again when you fit new rear pads.

▪ Alfetta Brake Replacement

While replacing the front pads on an Alfetta is very straightforward and quite similar to the procedure on earlier models, replacing the rear pads is quite another matter. The rear brakes on the Alfetta transaxle are inboard, meaning that they sit right next to the transaxle itself. The advantage of this is that the brake mechanism is sprung, rather than unsprung weight.

The rear brake pads are retained with an L-shaped pin, and a spring clip holds that pin in place. To remove the pads, you'll need a mirror and a good trouble light. Place the mirror on top of the caliper and move the light around to identify just how the pads are retained. Pull the spring clips free, then wedge the retaining pins out with a screwdriver. The pads come straight up, toward

With the transaxle out of the car, changing Alfetta rear brakes is a breeze. However, when the transaxle is where it belongs, the task can be trying simply because you're on your back under the car.

Since the rotors look good with only minimal scoring, new pads are installed and the wheels can go back on.

the underside of the body. Before removing them, work them in the caliper to press the piston as far back as possible. You can use a screwdriver from underneath to retract the piston once it's started back in its bore. With the piston pushed home, quickly remove one pad and insert a new one in its place. Repeat the procedure for the remaining three pads.

■ Drum Brakes

For the most part, Alfa Romeo drum brakes are pretty straightforward. Beneath the beautifully finned alloy brake drums you'll find an extremely effective system that rivals some disc brake setups.

There are three basic configurations of drum brakes used on Giulietta and Giulia cars. In the earliest configuration, as used on all Giuliettas, including the earliest SS and SZ models, the front brakes use a pair of cylinders (two leading-shoe) and are fitted with beautifully machined finned drums that are side-specific. The left drum is marked "S" for *sinistra* (left in Italian) and the right is marked "D" for *destra* (right in Italian). The rear brakes that go with this first configuration have a single wheel cylinder and are of the one leading-shoe, one trailing-shoe variety. The cast, finned drum can be used on either side of the car.

The second variety, as used on Giulias (except the SS) on 1962, 1963 and some 1964 models consists of three leading-shoes (and three cylinders) up front inside machined, finned drums that are also side-specific and wider than those used on the earlier cars. The rear brakes are of the single leading-shoe type with steel web shoes and cast, finned drums suitable for use on either side of the car.

The final variety of drum brakes were fitted to early Giulia SS models as well as to most Giulietta SS and Giulietta SZ cars. Up front, the three leading-shoe configuration is fitted inside the handed, machined and finned drums. To increase braking capacity, wider shoes are fitted to the rear of these cars, which requires an offset backing plate to maintain the same axle housing and also to accommodate the handed, machined, finned drums used up front on earlier Giuliettas. These rear brakes use a single cylinder and one leading and one trailing shoe. Later Giulia SS and Spider Veloce models use this rear brake mated to disc front brakes.

Regardless of whether they are equipped with two or three shoe brakes, the front shoes float, meaning that the entire shoe moves outward when the brakes are activated. In addition, the angle of the shoe to the drum is adjustable to keep the lining surface and the drum surface parallel. According to Alfa restorer Bill Gillham,

"adjusting Alfa front brakes can take half a day, but when they're right they're terrific."

The drums come off by a pair of flat-head screws and tapping the sides of the drum with a soft-face dead-blow mallet. Be sure to use anti-seize compound on the screws or they will be reluctant to come out. Wearing safety glasses, lift the top shoe free of the cylinders and over the hub, then relax the tension on the springs and pull the other shoe free. Be sure to clamp or wire the cylinders so they don't come apart with the shoes off.

The front brakes of this 101 Giulietta Spider use two shoes and two cylinders. It is very much like other drum brakes, except that the adjuster is operated from the rear of the backing plate.

Alfa Romeo drums come off with the removal of two screws and light tapping with a mallet. This drum is on a 1963 Giulia Sprint and hides three shoe brakes.

To install new shoes, link them together with the two long springs and guide them into position. It can help if you have someone to keep tension on the springs while you lower the assembly onto the backing plate. The springs will probably work loose a few times, but eventually, the shoes will slot into place.

The process is more complicated with the three-shoe front brakes, and although the job can be done solo, there is no substitute for a second pair of hands. Again, link the shoes together on the bench or floor and maintain the tension while you install them on the backing plate.

This rear 101 Giulietta brakes setup, like all postwar Alfa rear drums, uses two shoes.

Multiple hands can be very helpful when installing new shoes on three-shoe Alfa brakes.

To adjust the shoes, with the drums on, back off the adjusters until the drums turn freely, and tighten them until the shoes just brush the drum. After a test drive, you may want to make a minor readjustment. After a test drive, pull the drum again and check the shiny or dull spots on the shoe to determine if the wear is even. If it isn't even, you can work to ensure that the shoes are square to the drum by adjusting a small setscrew on the back of the drum backing plate to control the angle of the shoes.

If you ever put the same brake shoes back on, ensure that they are returned to the position from which they were removed.

▪ Brake Rebuild

You can rebuild a brake master cylinder with very little effort. On the other hand, if you make a mistake, you can also kill yourself, passengers and bystanders, not to mention picket fences and fireplugs.

Working on the brakes is closer to working on an airplane than anything else you can do on a car. In both cases, you probably won't be able interrupt your trip and hop out to fix what's suddenly gone wrong.

Having (hopefully) made the point, we return to the fact that brakes are essentially easy to repair, and repair kits are easily obtained.

The most likely problem you'll encounter in restoring the brake system is a frozen wheel piston. Sometimes, you can free it by forcing it back into its cylinder and

With the pads out of the caliper, the inside piston can be seen within its cylinder. If one is frozen and you can't free it up easily, take it to a shop.

then using brake pressure to move it along the cylinder. If the piston is well and truly stuck, you'll have to take it to a shop to have it fixed. Don't try to hone a disk brake wheel cylinder or sand its piston, but replacing the sealing rubber on a disk brake is an easy job. Never separate the halves of a disk brake caliper.

Freeing a Stuck Piston

You'll occasionally find a stuck piston. Frequently, a piston can be freed just by exercising it in and out of its cylinder. Wedge the piston back a bit with a screwdriver, then apply the brakes just enough to force the piston out again. After several "ins and outs" you may find that the piston moves freely in its bore. If it doesn't, you'll have to remove the piston from the caliper, a job better left to a brake shop. If you try to remove the piston itself for cleaning, you'll have to bleed the brakes. Never try to replace a pad on a caliper with a stuck piston and never use sandpaper on the piston or its bore. Have the caliper repaired properly because your life may very well depend on it.

Check the rubber dust boot around the piston: if it is torn, you'll probably want to replace it. You remove the seal with a very small screwdriver or pick, working around the seal's outer diameter and being careful not to scratch the piston. Clean everything scrupulously with new brake fluid before installing a new dust seal.

With the piston retracted, you can simply slide the brake pad out of the caliper. To install a new pad, you may have to press the piston further back in its bore. In this case, put the old pad back in place as a spacer. If you try to wedge directly on the piston itself with a screwdriver or pry bar, you run a risk of damaging the dust seal.

With one new pad installed, pry back the opposing piston and replace its pad with a new one. Returning

the cross-spring and pins is a snap. Feel like a pro? Now you're ready to tackle the rear pads.

When bleeding an Alfa's brakes, begin with the wheel furthest from the master cylinder (rear wheel on the passenger's side) and end with the wheel closest to the master cylinder. Brake fluid is a thin oil and can be harmful if it gets in your eyes. Wear goggles and be careful.

After performing any work on the hydraulic system, it's important to check all corners for leaks. Also check the pedal for proper feel. If it feels spongy, you should probably bleed the system again. And, if the brake pedal sinks under constant firm pressure, you need to check again for leaks. If you have any doubt about the braking system after performing this work, be sure to have the car examined by a competent shop.

A C-clamp is a great tool for retracting the piston within the caliper. With the pad in place, simply tighten the clamp and the piston retreats into its bore.

Chapter 16

Racing

This chapter is for the racers, boy and man, girl and woman.

Of course, the whole image of Alfa is that it is a fast car that, off the showroom floor, is quite capable of sustaining racing stresses routinely. There is a lot of truth in the image. As you will note throughout this chapter, precious few modifications are made to the basic design in order to prepare an Alfa as a winning race car. This is quite a different situation from the "stock" cars which circulate American tracks: those cars have almost nothing in common, mechanically, with the sedans we see on the streets.

Much of the challenge of racing is creating your own version of the perfect car. There isn't a competitor alive who doesn't believe that, given time and money, he'll be able to arrive at the perfect balance of tuning which will give him unique advantage. There's anecdotal evidence that undiscovered horsepower still lurks in the Giulia's classic four-cylinder engine. What makes this prospect so enticing is that advantages have been found in unlikely places: when everyone else was porting out the intake and exhaust passages to make them larger, Alfa discovered that a 3mm *reduction* in port diameter gave a horsepower increase.

I want to begin this chapter by emphasizing that, in spite of all the specificity, I offer a very gross approximation of the changes necessary to make a car competitive. As romantic as it may sound, the fact

Although most Alfa Romeos needed some preparation for racing, the Giulia-based TZ (center) and GTA (left and right) were essentially turn-key race cars. Carlo Chiti (center in sweater) discusses test findings with his drivers.

Anyone contemplating going racing will have to start with safety equipment such as a protective helmet, driver's suit and a full roll bar as seen on this Giulietta Spider at Willow Springs Raceway.

remains that every car is individual, and the changes made to one are frequently both subtle and non-reproducible in other cars. This is especially true in the selection and inflation of tires. The diligent competitor will find that inflation differences of only one pound will make a dramatic difference in lap times. One change frequently depends on another for maximum effectiveness: "hot" camshafts or big carburetors by themselves may degrade, rather than improve performance: it is only when they are used together that the benefit is realized.

▪ Sources of Information

The rulebook of your sanctioning body is one of the very best places to start before you lay a wrench on your Alfa. You'll quickly learn that rules govern the possible modifications depending on the class in which you'll be competing. By and large, these rules were established to keep competition as equal as possible. If it were not for these rules, racing would simply come down to the competitors throwing their checkbooks on the table. Knowing what the rules allow is clearly essential. Your primary source of information is the rulebook from the sanctioning body under which you'll race.

The Giulia owner is fortunate in that Alfa has already led the way in making modifications to the car. The Veloce, GTA and TZ cars are rolling factory tuning manuals. The GTA is covered in detail in Chapter 3, and the tuning information included in that chapter

should be studied carefully in order to understand how Alfa approached improving its basic car for racing.

Fortunately for the beginning racer, there is a large body of conventional wisdom about making an Alfa go fast. And, because the Giulia has been around so long, there is a lot of information available about making it go faster. As expensive as racing is, this body of conventional wisdom helps eliminate fruitless branches of exploration and thus helps keep costs in line. The best way to find out what works and what doesn't is to haunt the pits at race events, talking to as many Giulia drivers and technicians as possible. The information you pick up will be the most current, letting you take advantage of the latest improvements in tires, tuning or skulduggery.

On the other hand, there are a lot of self-proclaimed experts out there. As an author of technical materials, I've run into many flavors of experts, from the overbearing to the subtle. I've learned the hard way not to confront personal opinions, even when I think them wrong. In the absence of facts, every theory is credible. There is a dearth of information about some systems, especially those that are of greatest interest to racers. However, if everything about performance were known, racing would be no fun at all. It's unfortunate just how few successful racers take the time to write about it.

Treat race preparation as an advanced-level degree in your particular car. Not in all cars: just yours. It's frustrating just how little learned on one car is transferable to another. What you've learned on your first car colors your perceptions of the next. Unfortunately, many times the early lessons don't apply to later situations. I'm not talking general principles here: rather, the fine details of extracting 10/10ths from your steed.

Listen to everyone. If a majority seems to feel something is true, it usually, but not always, is. Pay special attention to those who have proved their experience by winning races. Then, decide for yourself and act accordingly.

The Alfa club has always been a nuts-and-bolts group. When the club began there was very little information about the marque itself and virtually no technical information about the Giulietta. One of the original members was Paul Tenney, who served as the first technical editor of the club. Working with factory information supplied by Don Black, the chief

The TZ is essentially a rolling factory tuning manual. This TZ2 is seen at Carlo Chiti's Autodelta facility in 1964.

Because the GTA (GTA Junior shown) is so much more closely based on the production road cars than was the TZ, much more of the tuning information is directly applicable to the average solid-axle Giulia or Giulietta.

engineer for ARI, Paul compiled all the relevant racing information into a collection that was published by the club as the Competition Advisory Service (CAS). More on Paul at the end of this chapter.

The introduction to the CAS best describes the scope of the document: "The facts are all here. If not, they just don't exist or were not recommended or proven. The experimentation has been done for you." The CAS was reissued by the club in 1971 and is currently available from Ricambi in California (626-281-7933). Many of the part numbers listed in the CAS are no longer available, especially part numbers ending in 99, which were exclusive ARI fabrications. As a result, the CAS is frequently of more historic than practical interest, but it does clearly indicate just what kinds of things need to be done to wring the most performance out of your Alfa.

▪ Factory-Recommended Modifications

Any discussion of factory-recommended competition modifications must include the Competition Advisory Service. The CAS recommended extensive balancing, including dynamic balance of the camshaft drive sprockets (with lock bolt included, of course). The intake and exhaust sets of valves were also balanced to match the weight of the lightest valve (note, however, that you don't try to make the intake and exhaust valves the same weight: the exhaust valve is sodium-cooled and any machining on it to lighten it is potentially very dangerous). The introductory section of the CAS included a multi-page reprint on blueprinting, which is simply the meticulous setting of all engine dimensions to exact factory specifications.

Head

In the GTA, Alfa improved the performance of the Giulia engine by increasing volumetric efficiency and upgrading its ignition system. The increase in volumetric efficiency was obtained by fitting larger valves and higher-lift, longer-duration camshafts. Twin-plug heads permitted larger valve diameters and also assured that the fuel charge was evenly and fully burned.

NOTE: In the following sections, Alfa Romeo part numbers ending in .99 are not official Alfa Romeo numbers, but refer to unique parts available only through the old New Jersey-based Alfa Romeo International (ARI) distributorship which is now a part of the Florida-based ARDONA organization.

The "stock" GTA head was 10532.01.053.00. ARI supplied a prepared head, part number 10532.01.053.99, with the following modifications:

- Head thickness was reduced by an amount determined in conjunction with piston selection.

- Intake ports were reduced to 29 mm with a 3mm aluminum pipe driven into the port 25 mm (up to the beginning of the lower radius). They were tapered to match the inlet port diameter just in front of the valve guide and epoxied in place. The smaller ports increase the velocity of the intake charge. Matching reducers were fabricated for the intake manifold.

- A sealing groove measuring 0.8 x 0.8 mm was machined in a radius of 85.5 mm around each combustion chamber. An "early" cylinder head gasket, without mastic, was used: 10100.01.508.00.

- Water-passage size was reduced to lower water-flow velocity and improve cooling (two 6.5mm-diameter holes replaced each of the oval ports for intake-valve cooling on cylinders 2 and 3), and the ten water

New GTA heads are not available, but specialists, like Sperry Valve, can offer cylinder heads in various stages of tune.

holes which surrounded the combustion chambers were sealed.

- Intake guides were cut off flush with the port and interior clearance was knurled to 0.001 inch (exhaust guides were not modified).

- An oil breather cap was used (part 10511.01.037.00 or 10532.01.037.00) with a carb-side internal diameter machined to 45.5 mm.

- Air horns (652.08.001) were used inside a cold-air plenum (10532.08.204.00).

With this setup, two Weber 45DCOE carburetors were used with the following jetting:

Venturi	36
Main	150
Air	150
Idle	F1255
Pump	35
Float level	48
Emulsion tube	F16
Auxiliary venturi	4.5

Following the instructions in the CAS, the cylinder head was milled to increase the compression ratio. For type 101 and 105 single-plug heads, the head was milled 1.8 mm for an overall height of 110.2 mm. As noted above, with a milled head, a sealing groove had to be machined around the combustion chamber. For the Giulia 1600 engine, the groove was 85.5 mm diameter, 0.8 mm wide and 0.8 mm deep. For the 1300cc engine, the groove had an 81 mm diameter. The thicker "early-type" head gasket was specified.

The groove caused the thicker head gasket to be embossed for an extra sealing surface, guarding against head gasket failure.

The valve guides were cut flush with the port surface. The valves were machined to take a safety ring, and special outer valve springs (10511.03.313.03) were used with spring pocket 10511.03.302.03.

The inlet ports were polished and smoothed to match the 45DCOE bore and air horns were fitted to the carburetors. Road-racing jetting was:

In lieu of the GTA pistons and liners, a variety of companies offer special liners, high-compression pistons, rings and wrist pins for racing applications. This set uses forged JE pistons and is available through Sperry Valve.

	1600	1750
Venturi	36	36
Auxiliary venturi	4.5	4.5
Main jet	150	150
Air correction jet	150	160
Emulsion tube	F16	F16
Pump jet	35	35
Idle jet	55F8	55F12
Air idle jet	90	90
Starter jet	65F5	65F5
Float valve	150	150
Float level	27–28 mm	27–28 mm
Float weight	26 gr	26 gr
Pump stroke	11 mm	11 mm

The throttle butterflies were rotated so their notch was opposite the progression holes. The first (lowest) progression hole had a diameter of 1.0 mm, the second, 1.2 mm and the third, 0.9 mm.

On GTAm cars with Lucas sliding-plate fuel injection, the control cam for the fuel delivery unit was Lucas part number 10541.04.03/b. The guillotine throttle unit was part 10551.01.060.99.

Block

If two-ring pistons were used on the GTA, the block height was reduced 0.8 mm and a corresponding

The Alfa crank is very strong. However, for racing applications, the swaged-in oil plugs should be removed and replaced with threaded plugs.

amount was removed from the bottom of the cylinder liner.

The GTAm used a monosleeve design, in which the four individual cylinder sleeves were replaced by a single casting for additional strength. Some of these monosleeve assemblies found their way into other racing Alfas.

The CAS recommended milling a groove into the top of each sleeve to match the groove in the cylinder head. The resulting compression ratio was 10.8 if pistons 10511.02.300.07 were used and the block was not milled. The compression ratio could be raised to 11.5 if the same pistons were machined (using drawing 10511.02.300.09) with the block milled 1.0 mm and the sleeve height reduced 1.0 mm by machining its lower mating surface.

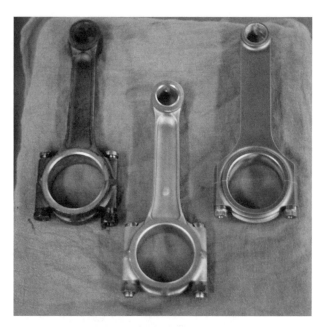

From left to right: a stock rod, one that's been polished to remove any surface roughness, and a Carrillo rod suited for the most severe racing applications.

Alfa experimented with turbocharging back in 1967 when it developed the GTA SA twin-turbo engine as an alternative to race-preparing a normally aspirated GTA engine. Notice the large sump.

Electrics

The generator was strengthened against centrifugation by epoxying the commutator and windings and then dynamically balancing it. Lightweight prepared GTA generators were part 10532.05.050.00.

Exhaust

Racing headers were available from Alfa, as well as from most aftermarket Alfa stores. The official Alfa headers were:

101-series	10121.01.071.00 and .072.00
105-series	10516.01.071.00 and .072.001750
Group 5	10500.30.002.98 (an equal-length, ARI part)

The CAS recommended the following additional changes to the block:

Steel flywheel	10532.02.040.00
Rods	105.12.02.020.00 (standard on some cars)
Reinforced rear main bearing cap	10500.01.017.02
Oil pump	Nine-tooth gear (standard on some cars)
Oil pan(except 105 series)	Stock Type 121 double-bottom 105
Wider sump	10500.01.211.03
Six-quart capacity	10514.01.211.03
Seven-quart capacity	10514.32.211.00
Seven-quart (magnesium)	10514.32.211.02
Ten-quart (magnesium) remote oil filter	10511.06.300.01
Oil cooler adapter	10516.01.014.00
Recuperator	10532.06.405.00 (meets FIA/SCCA regs.)
Ignition	Fixed advance = 18° Maximum advance = 52° at 7,000 rpm.

Equal-length exhaust headers, such as these from Sperry Valve, help to extract more power and can help to broaden the power band of the engine.

A lighter-than-stock flywheel, such as this Sperry Valve Works aluminum flywheel, will help the engine to rev more quickly. The downside is that it decreases engine braking and makes the car less suitable for the street.

Clutch

- The lightweight TZ clutch disc 10511.12.032.02 and pressure plate 10511.12.031.02 were used unless the stronger disc 10516.12.032.01 and plate 10516.12.035.00 were needed.
- A stock plate could be made stronger using springs 10516.12.031.01/11. These springs required a reinforcing ring on the spring cups.
- The clutch throwout bearing was 10532.12.042.00.

Transmission

- A magnesium bellhousing was part number 10532.13.012.00.
- Heavy-duty shift forks were available:

| First and second gears | 10514.13.503.10 |
| Third and fourth gears | 10514.13.504.11. |

- A heavy-duty rear transmission mount was 1365.15402.
- Shell Dentax 90 oil was used.

Driveline

- The front driveshaft donut was reinforced using covers 10516.15.032.01 and 10516.15.032.02 and spacer 10516.15.318.00.
- The dynamic balance of the driveshaft was confirmed.

Rear Axle and Differential

A ZF "Lok-O-Matic" limited-slip differential 10510.17.043 was used with axle shafts 10514.17.300.00, which were stronger than the original components.

The 101-series rear torque mounting brackets on the axle tubes were strengthened by making them box sections. Steel plates were welded between the stamped-steel flanges front and rear, making certain that the front plate didn't obstruct the trailing link. *Boxing the torque mounting brackets is an extremely important modification, and no Alfa should be raced without it.*

On 105-series cars, the rubber silentblocks in the trailing link were replaced with Heim spherical bearings. Rear stabilizer bars were added if not already in use. Stock 1750 bars were acceptable, but for more roll resistance you could select diameters of:

- 16 mm as used on the GTA (10532.25.600.00)
- 18 mm (10532.25.600.02)
- 20 mm (10532.25.600.03).

A variety of rear springs was available from Alfa, and virtually all Alfa specialty shops offer aftermarket springs.

Front Suspension

Stock front springs can be cut from ¾ to two coils, depending on the desired ride height. The GTA used Koni shock absorbers 80-1551, or Alfa part 10532.21.070.99 (ARI number). Front roll bars of 1¹⁄₁₆ inches diameter were suggested.

Shankle Engineering offered a complete line of roll bars, as does Ricambi and several other Alfa shops. If the car is lowered, knuckle extensions 10532.21.118.01 and idler arm 10532.24.020.00 (with arm 10532.24.201.00 and center tie rod 10532.24.401.01) should be used.

Rear Suspension

The stock solid rear axle has proved as good as, and a lot less bother than, the exotic (and expensive) independent rear suspension of the TZ. The rear axle's lateral location can be improved by using the sliding

The TZ rear axle assembly is very light, but expensive. It is a much cheaper proposition to simply work with the solid rear axle.

block modification made to the GTA, or (at much less expense) by fitting a Panhard rod. If a Panhard rod is used, the upper triangular locating link must be disconnected and new upper links fabricated to maintain the rear axle's geometry.

Brakes

If racing brake materials are used, remember that the brakes must be warmed up before they become effective. It is very dangerous to drive on the street with racing brakes because they will not stop the car on initial application.

▪ Adding Lightness

Alfa spends a lot of effort lightening its cars, beginning with an all-alloy engine. You can follow the factory lead only to the extent that the rules allow. Remove the floor mats, heater, seats, trim, and everything else not absolutely necessary to keep your car running. Since glass is very heavy, coupes may be fitted with Plexiglas side and rear windows (check the rules).

In summary, if you plan to race a Giulia, this chapter is a good peek at successful Alfa racing practice.

I want to emphasize that uninformed or half-way modification efforts are not likely to be successful. If you're reading this chapter with $100 handy to spend for modifying an engine, forget it. The absolutely cheapest way to gain a guaranteed and immediate significant increase in power is to fit a nitrous oxide system. Curiously, I know of only one Alfa modified for NOx (by Stewart Sandeman Jr).

If you're looking for really cheap horsepower, put your money in the bank and simply remove the plastic fan attached to the water pump with a 10mm box-end wrench (six bolts). You'll gain horsepower—and an engine that can overheat in traffic. No one said racers have an easy life.

In short, there are many ways to turn your Alfa Romeo into a race car. Many of them are very expensive and every one of these changes will have a consequence. Just as removing the fan will free up horsepower and render the car unsuitable for driving in traffic, lowering the suspension will make the ride harsher and reduce ground clearance. Before you start making changes, know exactly what you'd like to achieve and always rely on specialists with proven expertise in race-preparing Alfas.

Alfa restorer Tom Sahines races his 1959 750 Giulietta Veloce at Sears Point. Although he currently vintage races it with CSRG, it has always been a race car and is a former SCCA national champion.

A Tuning Guru Talks

Paul Tenney was one of the true Alfa gurus in the United States. In addition to being the original technical editor of the AROC magazine, he was part of Carlo Chiti's team at Sebring. I'd like to retell a story about Paul's skill with Alfas.

In 1960 or 1961 Paul and I attended the national Alfa club convention in the basement of Bill Knauz' Alfa dealership in Lake Forest, IL. I think this was the first time I had met Paul. To my surprise, Paul flipped me the keys to his Alfa and told me to take it for a drive.

Simply put, it was the fastest Alfa I had ever driven, by a very large margin. I was astounded at how fast a Giulietta could be. When I returned, I commented that I had never driven a faster Veloce.

"You'd better go back and pop the hood, Pat," was all he said. A single two-throat Solex carburetor stared back at me.

In preparing this book, I asked Paul to contribute something about performance modifications. His reply should be taken to heart seriously by anyone thinking about modifications. I'm including it here in its entirety:

April 3, 1997

I'm in the final stages of a total powertrain restoration/preservation process on an extremely fine specimen of a 1969 1750 Spider. The body is receiving a bare-metal-up renovation and basecoat/clearcoat refinishing by a national-class, award-winning coachwork restorer. Your request for some assistance with your new book is timely for me since I've, once again, become deeply involved with the nuts and bolts and decision-making involved in "doing" an Alfa in minute detail, professionally and correctly with regard to the design intent of the product and to the use I intend for it.

I think it best that I share with you some preliminary, experienced, and highly-opinionated views of what you are proposing in terms of a "race-preparation" or "improved performance" chapter in the new book. I'll start with some general, probably arguable, but sincerely held fundamental personal opinions.

I saw my first 1300 Veloce Giulietta Spider 40 years ago this month, and began professionally maintaining and modifying them in May 1957. I've had some time to accumulate some experience and attitudes about Alfas during these 40 years which included, at last count, personal ownership of 72 different examples.

When contemplating irreversible metal-removing "improvements" to any part of any Alfa we have to remember that the supply of the affected components is absolutely finite despite the existence of a (sadly) large fleet of abused, neglected—and often already-botched Alfa derelicts. True Alfisti should be devoting themselves to projects of restoration and preservation instead of attempting inevitably destructive "improvements" on the still-extant functional fleet.

A properly set-up, totally stock Alfa (all systems in absolute conformance with factory specifications for the model) will, in most cases, perform at least as well as one which has received amateur "improvements" and will most certainly outlast it.

I'm reminded of a "prominent" Alfa technician from Chicago who ran at the Joe Marchetti Fall Vintage race at Road America a couple of years ago. After buying and installing almost $5K in special "racing" parts on his 2.0-liter Spider, he was 5 seconds slower per lap than he had been the previous year running in "stock" form. I discovered he did not have the faintest idea of how to use a dwell meter for setting his ignition, and he had no concept of the suspension geometry changes caused by his "special racing" lowered front spindles. He hadn't even gotten adjustable camber links! It was a personal humiliation for him and for the assembled Alfisti.

You have to start in order to race and you have to finish in order to win.

I firmly believe that anyone who has to learn how to properly prepare ("improve the performance") of any motor vehicle from any book has absolutely no business attempting to do the work themselves. This is particularly true of well-intentioned, but misguided, persons who are susceptible to the belief that enthusiasm + limited funds + the "right" book + inexperience + inadequate tooling = a "do-able" and successful "improvement" in performance and reliability.

The last four decades of experience with the Alfa DOHC inline-four has produced several domestic professional specialists in making well-conceived, well-informed, well-proven modifications to the Alfa, all supported by good, sound R&D and documentation. Some names that come readily to mind would include Dennis Black, John Shankle, Ron Neal and Paul Spruell. There are many others now active of equal competence, thanks to the resurgence of interest in "vintage racing." Unfortunately, there is also a large cohort of self-anointed "experts" who are practicing expensive extraction dentistry on the gullible "wanna-go-faster" types.

I honestly think your overhaul/repair chapters in the "Owner's Bible" are superbly done and that your "Hot Set-Up" listing on page 251 is excellent. I'm not sure that Chapter 8 of the Giulia book [*Alfa Romeo All-Alloy Twin Cam Companion: 1954-1994*] needs much more than some deletions of the specific part numbers that are now obsolete and unavailable. Chapter 11 of the "Bible" is extremely well-done and provides the appropriate theoretical and technical guidance to the novice about what can be done.

You and I have discussed the prevailing level of knowledge—coupled with curiosity—extant in those who now profess to be "Alfisti." Given the technical evolution of automobiles in the last decade or two, we now have many people in Alfas who know nothing at all about automotive technology. Only a very small minority of new or used car dealerships even engage in what we used to call "repairs." Valves aren't ground, engines aren't overhauled, electrical systems are obsolete (replaced by "electronics"), etc. Everything now is "R&R it with new, or sub-contractor-rebuilt, modules. My own top-of-the-line valve/valve seat machine was acquired in virtually new condition from a Cadillac dealer who'd used it only twice in the year before I bought it. It's cheaper to "farm-out" such specialty work, if it's going to be done at all.

Your own comments reflect that the most critical area of engine power improvement comes from the cylinder head. For the Alfa, the most pragmatic, cost-and-performance-effective approach to this critical (and so-easily abused component) is to unbolt it and send it to a specialist shop: Sperry Valve Works, specifically. Period.

I use this recommendation as an example of a concern I have about giving "do it yourself" instruction. Telling someone what can or should be done and suggesting how and where to obtain the necessary services is very helpful and productive. Telling an inexperienced novice how to attempt the work themselves simply offers encouragement from an authoritative source for them to inevitably mess things up. I find absolutely no fault with the sections in the "Bible" relating to tune-up, maintenance and repair procedures because your descriptions and photos and cautions are so well done. But none of this relates to irreversible removal of metal from extremely critical components. All of the relevant measurements and admonitions will not suffice at home the absence of expertise, experience, proper tooling and impeccable workmanship.

So, DON'T mess with the cylinder head; send it to Sperry. As far as the rest of the engine is concerned, check with your local "racing machine shop" who'll have scads of small-block Chevy engines lying around in various states of disassembly. Talk to them about any crankshaft, flywheel, con-rod work. Take the specification manual for your engine with you so they've got some correct numbers to work with. Plan on magnafluxing all ferrous rotating and reciprocating parts, balancing, etc. They'll suggest what to do to make everything "right" by the book. If you've bought Carrillo rods and special pistons, let Sperry know what pistons you're using and make sure the rods and pistons pass all inspections in the specification book and are properly balanced.

The ONLY engine work you have to do is covered in the "Bible," plus ordering whatever you feel you must buy and running the parts around to the appropriate professionals who will actually DO the modifying. If a specific operation is NOT covered in the "Bible" DON'T DO IT YOURSELF.

It might be useful to suggest contemplation about what the intended use of the "modified" Alfa is to be. I subscribe to the maxim "Less is More", particularly with

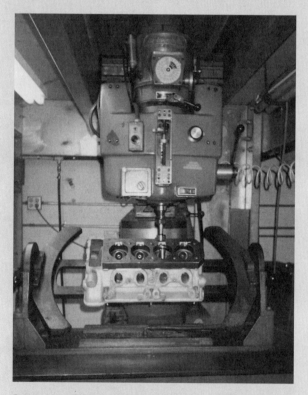

Sperry Valve Works prepares a valve seat. Note the heavy steel plate bolted to the head to prevent warping during the machining process.

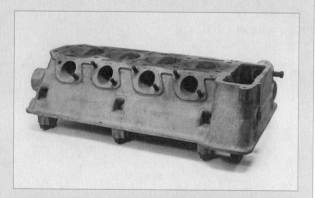

Experienced Alfa technicians, race prep shops and racers agree that a cylinder head is best left to the professionals.

regard to mechanical "improvements" to a well-proven durable design like the Alfa.

I started with Alfa before there was a "corporate presence" in the USA and, as I now recall it, the ONLY "performance" parts available were the famous "Mondial" pistons! It was not until the arrival of Arturo Reitz, Don Black and the 105's that any "enhancements" were available and those were carefully limited by FIA and SCCA regulations.

I remember the first Conrero-prepared Giulietta Veloce (owned by a member of the old Fox Valley Racing Team) had to run as an F-Modified against purpose-built racers. The average Alfa now running in "vintage races" would have been totally "illegal" under FIA and SCCA regulations in effect until Alfas became essentially extinct in such events as SCCA Nationals and the Trans-Am series.

Yes, removing the plastic fan blades from the water pump pulley is worth about 7 net HP. It's hard to get 7 HP from internal mods. Yes, going to single-row timing chains is worth about another net 7 HP, and you don't even need to machine off the unused sprocket teeth (although it's tidier to do so), and chain-life is quite acceptable. That's 14 HP on the dyno so far. Gutting the generator (or just dropping off the field wire (or putting a switch in the circuit) picks up another 4 or 5 HP on generator-equipped models (old trick!). I don't know if the same holds true on alternators. The point here is that there is + 20 HP (real) available from extremely simple and inexpensive (and totally reversible) things that have absolutely no influence on durability. Look how expensive and complex it is to get the same net gain from extensive internal modifications.

The combustion chamber can produce only "X" amount of power; the secret is to reduce power losses occurring after combustion.

Don't fuss with the ports on the head; just match manifold flanges and gaskets to enhance flow. The cast headers are virtually as efficient as the tubular ones now available, are more durable but a bit heavier. Use an aircraft "Gel-Cell" battery; it saves weight and there's no potential for spillage or corrosion. Forget the GTAM-style fender flares and too-large tires; frontal area goes up as does CD, not to mention the fact that frictional losses from tires are usually greater than any handling improvements.

Marketing is simply an interface between the gullible and greedy. Beware the arithmetic game. "These cams will give you ant extra 15 HP" + "This exhaust system will gain a lot in power" + etc. First thing you know the math adds up to 200 HP. I see this all the time in the "music business" and other areas. Unfortunately, Alfa owners seem to include an unfortunate preponderance of "boy racers" who manifest an insatiable appetite for "go-faster" stuff whether it is hardware or decalomania.

Alfas have never been "fast" cars. They have always been "quick" cars and have demanded conscientious maintenance and skillful drivers to succeed in racing competition. My own experiences are that one must truly drive "on the edge of the envelope," but in so doing you can experience an addictive epiphany of self-discovery. It is similar to negotiating (successfully) a field of moguls when skiing, doing a nice clean acrobatic sequence or playing a really up-tempo jazz chorus flawlessly. "Bragging rights" about your equipment or displaying esoteric decals has nothing to do with it.

My advice is to use this chapter as the definitive guide to what CAN be done (sensibly and realistically) and as a "wish-list" to discuss with a professional preparer. The information included is relevant, realistic and probably says all that needs to be said about performance modifications in general.

I'll conclude for now with these suggestions to the prospective "improver":

- Get your Alfa set up in absolute conformance with the factory specifications, including suspension, by a competent professional technician. Aftermarket steering wheels, shifter knobs, license plate frames and decals are OK.

- Learn to drive correctly from a professional school such as Skip Barber, Jim Russell, etc.

- Find a proper venue and drive the hell out of the stock Alfa.

- Then decide if you want to spend lots of money on "improvements" that will immediately depreciate the usefulness and market value of your Alfa.

It's now 5:00 a.m. on Friday 4 March and I'd better get to bed. I'm quite sure this letter isn't what you were hoping for but I do appreciate the stimulus and opportunity to ventilate. Pulling an "all-nighter" at the old IBM is sort of reminiscent of hand-typing and doing the "camera-readies" for Joe Paluch in the old days of the "Alfa Owner" back when I was young and passionate about such things.

I guess as we get "older" we start thinking more about restoration and preservation of those things that have been so valuable to us and increasingly intolerant of neglect and irremediable alterations so thoughtlessly undertaken. In my life, Alfa has been, and remains, an indefinable magical lure and reward. I know it will always be so.

Chapter 17

Restoration

This chapter deals with the generalities of a restoration. Specific details regarding engine and transmission rebuild are given in Chapters 8 and 13. Additional mechanical information regarding the engine, transmission, fuel systems and chassis is included in a variety of other chapters. Information about work on smaller assemblies and accessories is included here.

The emphasis of this chapter may surprise those who are looking for instructions on using an English wheel or where to find original sources for period-correct parts. My experience is that the reasons for collecting and restoring cars are overwhelmingly emotional, and the skills necessary for most restorations almost incidental. In recognition of this, I want to begin a nominally mechanical chapter with a discussion that has more to do with the hunt than the feast. The reason I think this approach is important is that aborted restorations destroy a lot of cars. Hopefully, a little counseling here may save a few Alfas for posterity.

If it weren't for its rarity and its desirability, this 1962 101-series Giulietta Sprint Speciale might not have been a candidate for restoration. Like so many projects, it languished for years and was close to being discarded on several occasions.

Alfa owners are very interested in the restoration process. Restoration was, by far, the single most-requested category of the persons responding to a survey almost two decades ago by the American Alfa club. This was especially significant in view of the fact that *Road & Track* had just finished a three-part series on the restoration of a Duetto.

On the other hand, not surprisingly, since the approach used in the *Road & Track* article was to remove major assemblies and have them "done" by competent restorers. Restoration of this kind amounts to project management, and is quite different from doing it yourself. Project management is an approach that has

much to recommend it. For those owners with little mechanical skill who still want to feel they've restored a car, delegation of the major work makes a lot of sense.

An overestimation of one's skills has ruined more cars—very valuable cars—than any other single cause. The surest way to destroy a car is to present it to a starry-eyed new owner who sees himself, only several weeks hence, standing with a 100-point car while all sorts of nubile females throw themselves on him and/or his car.

It happened to my 1900 Zagato. After several years of enjoying it, I concluded the time had come to sell it and buy another kind of Alfa. The purchaser, a law

The starting point for *Road & Track*'s three-part restoration project was Art Director Richard Baron's Duetto Spider.

Baron's approach of managing the restoration project and using different shops for various components and services resulted in an extremely attractive and usable Duetto Spider.

student and enthusiast, decided on a "total" restoration. He proceeded to dismantle it, portioning out the body to be done by a friend with a body shop, and saving the engine for another burst of energy.

The car remained disassembled for at least 15 years. I've corresponded with a subsequent owner, who never knew the car carried an (originally fitted) accelerometer, nor has he seen any trace of its (original) unique markings which I had carefully photographed to go with the car so it could be restored to its original condition. Over the years, valuable information about the car was lost.

Thus, my first observation regarding restoration is to be very circumspect about the likelihood of a "total" effort's success, given your skills and resources.

Very few people are capable of "total" restorations, emotionally, physically or financially. The tragedy—for many valuable Alfa Romeos—is that many people imagine that they *are* capable of completing such a project themselves.

■ Budget

Putting dollar figures to anything is hazardous, simply because books can't reflect changes in the marketplace. The following figures are ballpark, and you need to do a lot of research before you decide they represent what the market currently bears.

The first thing one should do before buying a car to restore is to make a budget. In making a budget, you need to add to the cost of the car, all the items which will have to be purchased for its restoration. These will include the following.

Engine Rebuild

The costs will include about $1,800 in labor alone for someone else to do it if there are no major broken parts. If you do it yourself, you may be able to do it for half that. Remember that a piston/liner set is about $500, bearings about $100, a gasket set another $100 and exhaust valves around $200 the set. Add to this the labor of grinding a crank and doing a valve job (around $300) and you have already logged an additional $1,100 just to rework an engine with no broken parts. If you need a water pump, oil pump, starter, alternator or distributor replaced/rebuilt, you'll exceed the $3,500 mark easily. As a rule, Veloce, SS or SZ engines will tend to be more expensive to rebuild.

The Braden 1900 Zagato (seen with a BMW 328, 6C Alfa Romeo and a Frazer-Nash) was sold to a well-intentioned would-be restorer. Like so many candidates for restoration, it remained apart for many years and changed hands several times.

Transmission Rebuild

Bearings are expensive, and if you have a transmission down, you should probably replace the bearings and the synchros. Use approximately $1,000 as a ballpark figure.

Driveline

Lord knows. They're durable, and I've never had an Alfa with a bad ring/pinion. You'll want to replace the donuts, no doubt, and the brakes, including a rebuild of the hydraulics. You'll also probably need to replace the emergency brake cable. Set aside a couple hundred bucks unless you're redoing an Alfetta, in which case the three donuts themselves will run nearly $300.

Count on between $4,500 and $6,000 as a basic estimate of what you need to put into your engine and transmission before it's ready—like these Veloce components—to reinstall in your Alfa.

Interior

Plan on at least $200 a seat plus a minimum of another hundred or more for the interior panels if you shop around. Carpet is extra, say another $200 unless you go for originality, in which case it's going to be over $500.

Bodywork

Preparing and painting a body will take up a large portion of your budget. A friend might be willing to do it for $500 plus paint, and you could do it yourself for less than that, providing Aunt Margaret buys you the compressor for Christmas and Uncle Joe throws in a decent spray gun…. Professional preparation and paint—assuming there is minimal body damage—can easily exceed $5,000 for a decent job.

I'm sure it's possible to take issue that the prices I've quoted are too low: I don't think anyone will say they're too high. Forget wiring harnesses ($800 for an original spider harness), a windshield, rechroming (gosh, what a silly restoration that is). For the sake of argument,

let's settle on $12,000 to $17,000 for a somewhat decent restoration of a sound car, assuming you're simply looking for a nice driver.

Now, what is it you're going to restore? Let's say a Giulia Super. Price one. Price a restored one. They go from $3,500 to about $8,000. Forget the top price for now, just take some middle ground, say around $6,000.

Now comes the tricky part. If you buy a running car with all the parts there, in somewhat good condition, you're going to spend the better part of $5,000.

Already, it's cheaper to go out and buy a restored one that you can drive today.

Put another way, anything spent to restore your car beyond the average price of a restored car is money you are simply throwing away. If you wish, you may consider the difference the cost of pride…or vanity. I know of several cars in which the owners have invested about twice the actual value of the car. The amount you invest in a car becomes a problem only when you have to sell it.

I have always sold cars to raise money. I may have fallen in love with another car—perhaps stumbled across a "once in a lifetime" opportunity—or had a need for cash. Either way, the car to which I had attached so much emotion suddenly became a commodity, no more or less. You're never more aware of the market value than when you need to sell an oddball car and are trying to establish a fair price for it. All those astronomical prices you see advertised for cars like yours become grotesque jokes, because the only offers you get are about half the "market" value. It is at just such a time that you realize the folly of investing more in a car's restoration than it is "worth."

There's another angle to mention. I have a friend who has a very rare car—one of ten—in which he has put $40,000 in a virtually perfect restoration. In fact, the car is probably worth the price. The problem is that it is a race car, and he can't bring himself to fling his very rare and very expensive car around a track. As it sits, the car is useless, too valuable to race, and illegal for the road. He has it up for sale and can't find a buyer. From a cash-flow standpoint, he's made an expensive mistake.

Even an excellent unrestored 1967 Giulia Super won't bring much more than $10,000, which is still well under the cost of restoration.

Racing a car like this 1964 TZ means being prepared to risk the value of a nice suburban house.

Enjoyment, not profit, was the motivation behind the Braden fleet of Alfas, which consisted of (from left to right) a 2.0-liter Berlina, a 1750 GTV, a GTV-6, a 1974 Spider, a 1981 Spider, a 1976 Alfetta and a 1979 Sport Sedan.

How do we get into such messes?

The first error is believing that, no matter how much you put into a car, if you just wait long enough, the market will rise to your price. This idea is a good rationalization, but the fact is that the market is unpredictable, and, unless you're talking about decades rather than years, the idea is patently false.

My personal experience is that no car should be considered an investment. You can play with 'em, but don't expect them to earn money for you, ever. The few cars I've owned which did turn out to be good investments are now out of my price range by an order of ten.

Now, I have a number of cars which will never be worth what I'll put into them to fix them up (notice, I did not use the word restore). I own them because I like owning them. They are costly luxuries, but I feel good having them. They have come close to breaking my bank, but somehow I manage to keep them, work on them and enjoy them.

Vanity has a lot to do with my ownership of Alfas. I think that vanity is probably the only defensible reason for owning some cars, most certainly those built by Alfa Romeo. Practically, you're better off with a Chevrolet. Vanity aside, I also enjoy working around the engineering that the car represents. I think Alfa engines are neat, and the people who designed them have a classic sense which I appreciate.

■ Motivation

There are quite a few reasons why people enjoy automobile restoration. Below you will find several of the primary reasons.

Craftsmanship

A garage full of machine tools allows this enthusiast to create a new Type 35 Bugatti with only a rusted rear spring shackle to begin with. Never mind that the block is cracked: he'll cast up a new one in his back-yard foundry. It's never quite clear what this craftsman does during the day to earn a living, but every evening finds him in his shop, buried in the details of a restoration. Never congratulate him on his work: he's left tool marks on one web of the new crank and is thinking of tearing the engine down to file them smooth. Of course, that will mean rebalancing everything….

The craftsman needs order and a goal: restoration allows him to practice the first while reaching the second.

Unrequited Youth

The perennial youth loves startling the neighbors with midnight runs around the block with the mufflers off. So much the better if he's having a party and can scare the wits out of a passenger as well. As he stands by the car, the engine crackling as it cools, you realize the cloth helmet and scarf are the emotional diapers of this boy-racer. The fact that he's spent a ton restoring the car cannot disguise that his knowledge of it is limited to operating the major controls. The boy-racer selects his car and restores it only to intensify the sense of youth and daring he needs to project.

Nostalgia

The restorer bent on nostalgia recaptures safe and enjoyable experiences through his car. His friends avoid mentioning the marque, for even the slightest opportunity sends the nostalgia buff into interminable stories about his experiences 30 years ago in a car just like the one he has now…. The car is transportation for this enthusiast, but only metaphorically. It is a time machine. The real car may not run, but it still sits, shining in his mind's eye, on the showroom floor. All the better if Tazio Nuvolari was passing by when he first drove it away. In recapturing the past, the nostalgic enthusiast enjoys life without danger, for he already knows how it is all going to turn out. A subset of this group owns cars which were too expensive when new.

Consumption

For some, the restoration of a car is an opportunity for conspicuous consumption, a ceremony with origins lost in the mists of time. If this man is a bore, it is because he cannot stop complaining about how many thousands of dollars he has spent finding just the right hides to complete the restoration of the trunk. While the consummate model of this type wears a Rolex President watch, his net worth is really irrelevant: appearance is all, and the car must be as conspicuous as possible. For this enthusiast, a car undergoing restoration is infinitely more desirable than a completed car, for it offers a continuing source of anecdotes punctuated by dollar signs. It is inevitable that this class form clubs where they can swap stories and impress young ladies. There are sexual overtones to the type, embracing virility and conquest.

Stupidity

Some people wander into restoration by accident, which also describes the product of their efforts. Sad to say, there are persons who don't know better. They've read a magazine or two, then buy the first old car to come along, join a club and put a set of Taiwan Tools on their Christmas list. A dismantled car may be an intermediate stage of the condition: the terminal stage is signaled when the body comes off for a plastic Testa Rossa replica and the engine is exchanged for a Chevy V-8.

While the categories are perhaps overdrawn, they still represent the universe of those who restore cars. The secret is to know where you fit. To be able to identify why we want to restore a car makes the whole process more efficient and manageable. For many people, the car itself is only an incidental part of the experience. Since we have been trained through advertising to fall in love with cars, it's not too surprising that a restoration can become a profoundly emotional experience. There should be some attempt to match the emotional need and the object of the affections. This may be a unique approach, but it is worth considering.

▪ Originality

The goal of most restorations is to return the car to its original condition, or as nearly so as is feasible. In the last several years, it has become proper to retain the patina on older, presentable cars rather than to give them a restoration that includes all new surfaces. An unrestored 8C2900 Touring roadster is currently available at $14 million; in restored condition, it would be worth significantly less.

A car such as this 1938 Mille Miglia 8C2900 with spider body by Touring is likely to be worth more in good original condition than if it were perfectly restored.

Alfa did not chrome-plate any of its fasteners on the modern cars (exception: early Giuliettas had chrome plated head nuts), nor were the aluminum camshaft covers ever polished to a chrome-like finish. While there is some tendency to want to over-restore a car by adding chromed and polished pieces, there is a very subtle line between a restoration which is dazzling and one which looks like it was managed by a bordello decorator. As these cars get older and more rare, it will be progressively harder to determine exactly what was original: to that end, when in doubt, keep a part finished as you found it.

As older Alfas wear out, there's a tendency to want to improve the car by installing a newer engine or transmission. Clearly, the result of this tendency will produce a world in which there are no original 750-series cars extant. As Giuliettas and Giulias become more rare, their originality becomes more precious. I read with concern posts on the Internet from Giulietta owners who want the added power (and reliability) of a larger engine. If they want these features, then they should buy Giulias or later cars which provide them. The Giulietta is a unique car of delicate temperament. To spoil its character with a more powerful engine is indefensible. Most importantly, it robs our progeny of an appreciation of what these cars really were. A real parallel can be found in the 6C1500 and 6C1750 Turismo cars, which are of great interest now simply because they have been so undervalued by intervening generations.

I have several Alfa friends who can remember details with astounding accuracy. Over the last several years, Dave Mericle and I have been looking for an absolutely original Giulietta at the Monterey event. We have yet

to find one that matches our memories of originality. The search has sharpened both our appreciations of the meaning of originality.

In my own case, I have come to believe that the term has no practical meaning. My faith in ultimate originality was shattered by Dave's discovery of a 750 Giulietta with vent windows on the door, a configuration that had always belonged to the long-wheelbase 101 floor pan. In 1957, Alfa produced a long-wheelbase 750 with vent windows. So much for the "rules."

Where does this leave the dedicated restorer? In a kind of purgatory 'twixt heaven and hell. You'll need all the resources you can find.

■ A Word About "Fakes"

I have encountered only one Alfa that came from a "chop shop." The front and rear of this Alfetta Sprint were two different cars. I have certainly examined a number of Alfas which have shown traces of major body damage and looked good from a few feet away, but the kinds of cars I'm talking about here do not necessarily have anything to do with resuscitated wrecks, though donor cars are usually involved in their creation.

Whenever there is so much value in an item, ersatz copies are bound to appear. This issue is not limited to automobiles, the same large questions having been raised about furniture, jewelry and most other objects of art. The issue may start in philosophy, but quickly boils down to money: how much is it worth if it isn't "real"? I'm fully aware that a fake Rembrandt is less valuable than a real Rembrandt. It is less clear that Stokowski's interpretation of Stravinsky (for *Fantasia*) is "real" Stravinsky. Finally, I'm not at all sure that these kinds of distinctions really carry over to an automobile: what proportions do aesthetic and purely mechanical values take in the equation?

In an age in which 99 percent of all the cars we know are mass-produced, any variation from the original in a collector car is seen as a fault. That, historically, has never been the case. Take my old 8C2300, as a prime example. Simon Moore has determined that it left Alfa as a long-chassis closed coupe. At some time around World War II, it was rebodied as a cabriolet, the configuration I enjoyed as its owner. After I traded the car off, the cabriolet body was removed and sold

Very few Giulietta TI models came into the United States and far fewer still were restored to absolutely original specifications and standards. This 1956 Berlina retains its original 1300cc engine, single carburetor and column-shift four-speed transmission.

to Italy for installation on a Hispano-Suiza. My car's chassis was shortened and a replica Zagato body was installed, making it a Spider. It remained in that style for several years before being sold to France, where the Zagato body was removed and a Monza body fitted. In other words, a car that left the factory as a long-chassis coupe is now a short-chassis two-seat racer.

I need to emphasize that the story of my 8C is not at all unique. In the early 1960s, I became friends with a restorer who made some of his income by buying SS Mercedes sedans, removing the body and frame and fitting the running gear to SSKL replicas that he made from scratch.

The examples I've given so far only suggest the nature of the problem, because the drivetrain of the cars in question remained largely original. However, we're now in the realm of the perpetual hammer that has had both the head and handle replaced, but remains "original" in the estimation of its proud owner.

There is no unarguable point at which a car loses its "originality" and becomes a "fake." The distinction is purely subjective and must include more than just the mechanical components. We have many instances of changes in bodywork to create more desirable models. This appears to be largely acceptable so long as the mechanicals remain original. In California, there was once a small industry devoted to cutting the tops off Daytona Ferraris. No one argues that these cars are not real Ferraris, they're just not real Daytona Spiders.

Just as long-wheelbase 8C Alfas often became short-wheelbase spiders and Monzas, Castagna dropheads such as this example on the 6C1750 chassis were sometimes converted to Zagato-style spiders. In the Giulietta and Giulia realm, "Normale" models can become Veloces, and SZ or TZ replicas have been fabricated.

Inevitably, some of the "fakes" will migrate to become "real Daytona Spiders." The same was certainly true of the ersatz SSKLs and will probably be true of my 8C2300 "Monza."

This is the case of the Giulietta round-tail SZ that was recently shown at a famous auction. The car appeared to be genuine, yet closer inspection, side-by-side with a known original, revealed that the car had been rebodied, and carried a few inappropriate parts. When it was discovered that the car was not completely original, the auction company agreed to the car's return. Clearly in this case, the body made the difference between "real" and "fake." Fair warning: there seem to be a number of SZs that are recently rebodied production cars.

In fact, however, a "new" body is not always "fake." Several years ago, a prominent Alfista decided to have his 1900SSZ renewed. At considerable expense, he returned the car to Italy, where it received a new replica body from Galbiatti. I think no one would argue that this car is not a real Zagato. Galbiatti is the de facto successor to the Zagato brothers' business, and has done a number of Zagato rebodies. In very broad terms, is a Zagato, when rebodied by a Zagato surrogate, still a Zagato? Probably, yes.

At virtually the same time that the ersatz Giulietta round-tail SZ appeared, a prominent museum sold a 1900CSS Zagato lookalike that had been constructed (at considerable expense, to be sure) on a cast-iron 2.0-liter chassis. The museum believed the car to be genuine. At first, identifying this car as a copy was made more difficult by the fact that Zagato never created two identical 1900CSSs anyway. To the considerable credit of the museum, it willingly returned the buyer's money.

If the bodywork is not an absolute measure of originality, what of cars with nonoriginal major mechanical parts? There are plenty of them around, and some are accepted as wholly original. The 8C2900 is the best example of this. The model is prone to cracking the large top engine casting which makes up the cylinders and head. For a number of years, there were no spare parts and several otherwise complete 8C2900s stayed in the shop for want of one or two head/block castings. Finally, some were made up in England and these cars were back on the road.

Curiously, there are almost wholly remade Alfas that are accepted as "real," and they are not at the low end of the market. The Alfa 8C2900 Boticella roadster has a patina that makes it look completely original, yet nether body nor engine is original to the car. The body is a new fabrication, following the lines of the original, and the engine is from a 3.2-liter grand prix Alfa. The value of this car in 2001 was approximately $3 million.

The most challenging example of all is an 8C2900B Spider, one of many collectibles in a Missouri barn that burned to the ground. During the fire, the engine melted, the body was completely vaporized and the frame was seriously deformed. The owner had the remains of the chassis buried by a bulldozer, and for years the car was considered destroyed. Recently, an enthusiast gained access to the car's grave and unearthed it. The frame was bent into an L-shape and one seriously damaged wheel was still attached to the front suspension member. Literally everything on this car was remanufactured; only the serial number is original. Again, the value of this car is in the millions, rather than the hundred thousands.

We're back to the perpetual hammer. Neither body nor major mechanicals alone determine the absolute originality of a car. Indeed, completely original mechanical and body parts together do not confer authenticity if the mixture is not completely original. Serial numbers identify specific cars, but certainly do not assure their originality. Finally, no car that has been raced can be completely original; modification is one of the inevitable results of racing.

Originality, as we apply it to some collectibles, is a largely subjective matter. For the most part, Ford Mustang or Corvette owners have no such conundrum, but life is not that easy for the person who aspires to own a hand-built collector car. It follows, then, that the value of a nonoriginal car is also largely subjective, and depends entirely on what you see, sitting on four wheels, right now.

■ Resources

Some years back I was a judge at an Alfa concours. While examining a Giulietta Spider, I commented that the piping on the seats was not original. The owner was furious at my remark, and protested loudly enough that he could be heard all over the field. No wonder: he had spent a lot of money on his restoration-to-original, and no one was going to tell him that he had been mistaken. In point of fact, he was not, and I was wrong in this case. Whom can you trust?

Certainly an old fuddy-duddy Alfa enthusiast was not to be trusted. Human memories are occasionally in error. The most accurate source of originality information is a contemporary sales brochure. Manufacturers take special care to assure that the cars they supply to illustrate their brochures represent real production, and every ad agency worth its salt has a product specialist whose only responsibility is to backstop the manufacturer and verify that even the most minor details are correct.

Pristine originality is hard to find with Alfas as they become older. Few people are also around who can remember what constitutes pristine and correct. Fine details are frequently lost with time. It is a fact that 8C2300 and 8C2600 Monza Alfas were distinguished from the production 8Cs by a gear-driven magneto on the exhaust side of the crankcase. The standard configuration was a distributor mounted atop the head. That means that a true Monza has a different crankcase from the standard 8C. At Monterey last year, I did not see a single "Monza" with the proper ignition: all had head-mounted distributors. Even so, these cars are fabulously valuable in spite of the fact that they are not absolutely original. I would not want to hazard a half-price offer to an 8C owner for this nonoriginal feature

The 8C2900 Boticella has been largely remade, but is still valued upwards of $3 million.

unless I was quite sure there was adequate running room behind me.

You can argue originality issues with Chevrolets or Fords that rolled off the assembly lines by the thousands in well-established production configurations. Alfa, on the other hand, is a small shop with a low production volume and high capacity to produce prototypes. There are ample examples of production-line changes which have confounded Alfisti; the most significant unannounced switch was the change from the 750 to the 101 Giulietta.

Sales Brochures

Eight years of writing Toyota sales brochures has taught me that even the most meticulously prepared documents will contain errors. It was a nightmare when a tire size or an engine specification had a typo. On other occasions, errors in photography resulted from using prototype vehicles. Whenever the lead time for the brochure extends past the time the production car will be ready for sale to the public, you have to use prototypes. These pre-production cars are correct in overall configuration, but always differ in detail from the final product. The differences are usually made up by retouching the wheels and interior trim, especially the radio.

In the 1950s, however, the sales brochure was more of a creative interpretation than a measure of fact. Even American manufacturers stretched and lowered their car illustrations in ads and brochures to make them more attractive. When more fakery than a retouched photograph was desired (they didn't have Photoshop back then), renderings were used to give the cars dream-like proportions. The all-time champ of this genre was a Renault Dauphine ad which actually made the car look wider than it was tall.

Shop Manuals

Probably the most useful of the workshop manuals for the Giulia is the Intereurope manual, while the Autobooks manual is a close second. Chilton also publishes an Alfa repair manual.

All of these books are written to the individual publisher's standard format, and there is some tendency for them to include "boilerplate" passages which are common to all repair books in their line. This is not an especially bad practice, but it does mean that the boilerplate sections will ignore any peculiarities of your specific model, and it is my intention to include those items here.

In my estimation, the Giulietta manual remains the best single work for Alfa engine repair from 1956 to the present. If you can obtain it, along with the 101-series supplement, you'll have the official "factory line" on repairing an engine.

Parts Manuals

The parts manual is valuable even if you can't order pieces from the factory. Every shop manual, no matter how exhaustive, will fail to cover just that operation which hangs you up in puzzlement. The most common conundrum you'll encounter in mechanical restoration is trying to remember how something should go back together. Even if you're lucky enough to have a blow-apart illustration (that's a distinct advantage of having a parts manual for your car), you may be sure that the parts illustration you're critically interested in will have been smudged by someone else's greasy thumb, or printed so reduced in size that even a magnifying glass will not help you to distinguish between a rubber O-ring and spring-steel washer.

If you do not have a parts manual, the absolutely best defense against confusion is to make a lot of drawings during disassembly and store them where you'll be able to find them again when it comes time to put things back together. Be especially careful to make drawings which clarify potential reversals: does the master link go on the inside or outside of the chain; does the oil slinger go on the shaft before or after the gear; just exactly how did that window-winder come apart?

▪ Value

Inherent to this entire discussion is the essential value of the vehicle. During the 1990s, enthusiasts watched the value of collector cars rise and then fall, so it's within all our memories that prices can go down as well as up. Some cars are demonstrably good investments, occasionally returning more than the stock market can manage, even long-term. If I could have only three of the Alfas back which have passed through my hands, I'd have well over a million dollars worth of Alfa in 2001 (trending upward, no less). And, if I could have one or two that I could have owned but didn't, I'd easily have had another million in cars.

Even with this background, I can assert that very few people ever realize a profit from investing in a car. Glance through the pages of *Keith Martin's Sports Car Market* magazine: they're filled with cars going for a small percentage of their investment. A really good restoration, regardless of the make of the car, begins at about $20,000 and can quickly exceed $100,000 if you don't keep a firm grip on your senses (and wallet). Since this is more than the value of most of the models covered in this book, it's clear that forces other than monetary spur the urge to restore.

The only defensible reason to restore a car is because you love it. All the funds you pour into it should be justified on that basis alone.

■ "Rare" Alfas

One mirage lures many restorers ever onward: the suspicion that the Alfa they own is really a very rare model. Posts on the Internet are filled with queries from owners who have found some unique feature or other on their car, and want to know its significance. Behind every such query lurks the hope that, somehow, the happy owner has inadvertently acquired a factory prototype—very rare to be sure—for which someone, perhaps the factory itself, will pay fabulous sums.

I have two Alfetta sedans with the ZF 3hp automatic transmission. There were only about 170 of these cars sold in 1978, so I'm pleased to have cornered a truly significant percentage of the Alfamatics in the United States. Both of my sedans have lived productive lives, and both carry changes which were the results of past owners' requirements. However, there are original trim detail differences between the two cars, even though their serial numbers indicate that they probably came off the production line within a few weeks of each other. The most notable difference is the width of the chrome trim strip on the rocker panel: one is much wider than the other. It is truly no great matter, but I'm sure that at some time in the future, someone will receive a letter inquiring whether or not his ex-Braden Alfetta automatic sedan with the narrow chrome strip on the rocker panels is really a valuable factory prototype....

For those who hope that theirs is truly a unique Alfa, I have a story which will only kindle the fire. A decade ago, my friend Jim Weber told me of a 2600 parts coupe in the possession of Martin Swig. I bought the

Any car bought as a nonrunner can be full of surprises. When received this 1962 Giulietta Sprint Speciale featured a very rusty body and in the words of the owner, "arrived on a flatbed with all the parts in boxes stuffed into the body shell (somewhat like as a turkey comes with all the bits in a bag stuffed in the body cavity)."

parts car, which was complete but a little crushed on the passenger's rear fender. The remarkable thing about this car was its paint job: a lacework of multiple colors gave it a psychedelic appearance. The fact that the car came out of San Francisco made me suspect that it was probably owned by a wealthy Beatles groupie. I never was curious enough to follow up on this hunch, and never regarded the car as anything more than a potential donor for my other 2600. Both cars changed ownership several times before they finally left my back yard and went to enthusiast William Hall. He was determined to verify the provenance of the car with the psychedelic paint job. Based on a police report obtained by one of the interim owners, it appears that this car was owned, not by a Beatles' hanger-on, but by John Lennon himself. Hall intends to restore the car to its psychedelic state, and will have saved a valuable piece of culture for his efforts. So much for parts cars with funny paint jobs.

■ Selecting the Specific Vehicle

Pretty obviously, for the ham-handed, a pre-war Alfa is not the car of choice, especially if funds are short. The Alfetta is currently the most economical and reasonable Alfa to restore (newer ones aren't an economically sound project), and now is the time to talk about the things to look for in selecting a car to restore.

There's an inverse relation between your abilities and the condition of the car. If your mechanical abilities are poor, a good car must be selected. If you're really good (as oppposed to wanting to be good), then you can save a little money and buy a car in truly poor condition.

It has been a hard lesson for me to learn, but always try to buy a car that is running. With a running car, no matter if it runs poorly, you will be able to check the steering, clutch, transmission, rear end and brakes. Be willing to spend several hours to get the car running (if only for a quick ride) so the running gear can be checked.

The danger of buying a nonrunner is the lack of opportunity to check for proper operation of critical parts. Consider the car with a dead battery and leaking sump (the gasket at the bottom of the two-piece sump is leaking and it won't hold oil). You take a chance and buy the car nonrunning. After fitting a new battery and pouring oil into the engine, the car starts and reveals: no oil pressure, excessive oil burning and a seized water pump. Pressing on, since you'll have to rebuild the engine anyway, a short drive reveals a loud rear end, a tendency to steer to the left and a refusal to select any gear but first. You get the idea.

Even a running car can hide expensive faults. My 2.0-liter fuel-injected spider only revealed a leaking fuel injection pump after an engine rebuild (I couldn't detect the leak for all the smoke, before). A replacement pump costs more than $700.

The biggest danger of purchasing a nonrunner is missing parts. For that reason, a disassembled car is a "no-no" under virtually all circumstances. Beware the car that is "90-percent complete." That missing ten percent represents 200 pounds of metal for a 2,000-pound car, almost the weight of a bare engine. Moreover, you can bet the missing parts will be the most expensive or hard to find, otherwise they'd still be there.

Quick Checks

Engine

You check the health of a running engine by wiping your finger around the inside of the tail pipe. If you get a black, oily goo on your finger, the car burns oil. Black smoke out the tailpipe means an excessively rich mixture, an indication that the carburetor or fuel injection is bad. White smoke is an indication of water in the fuel, probably from a blown head gasket.

Check both the oil dipstick and inside mouth of the radiator filler for a chocolate-malt-looking substance which is a giveaway for a blown head gasket. This is a common problem for 1969 and newer cars, less common for earlier ones. Depending on the severity of the leak, the consequences of a leaking head gasket can be minimal or catastrophic. Only a tear-down can verify the degree of damage. Signs that the leak has created a major problem include low oil pressure and smoking exhaust.

On a Giulia, try to wobble the generator on its lower mount. This is a weak area of the engine's design. If there is a rear mount, it falls off, and the single remaining bolt eats its way through the aluminum mounting boss.

Beware of fake Veloces. Twin Webers do not a Veloce make. The real thing had a special aluminum sump (finned), high-compression forged pistons, shot-peened and polished rods, special cams and a milled head. If an early Giulietta has Weber carbs, the body identification plate should read 750E (coupe) or 750F (spider). Later 101-series Giuliettas and Giulias can best be identified by looking up the serial numbers in Luigi Fusi's book. The two-volume d'Amico/Tabucchi book is another guide. Hint: most original Veloces had a separate cold-air intake in the driver's-side grille, next to the turn indicator light. Looking into the grille, there should be a sheet-metal separation toward the smaller end of the ellipse. Also,

the wire to the electric fuel pump at the rear of the car should be wrapped as part of the wiring harness.

Emission controls are serious business nowadays in some states, and will eventually be in all States. Emission pieces are very expensive to replace, so don't buy an Alfa with aftermarket carburetors, or one which is missing an air pump, even if the removed parts are thrown in as part of the deal. A bad SPICA fuel injection pump is going to cost upwards of $750 to repair, and a faulty Bosch installation could easily double that price.

Transmission

The transmission can only be tested during a drive. Any noise from the transmission probably indicates significant trouble. You test for transmission noise with a running engine and the transmission in neutral by pushing in the clutch. If the noise goes away with the clutch depressed, the bearing on the input shaft (probably) is bad, and you'll have to rebuild the transmission. If the noise increases with the clutch depressed, the throwout bearing is bad, and will require replacement.

Few used Alfa transmissions will shift into second gear without some clash. Learn to live with it, and don't rebuild a transmission just to fix the second-gear synchro.

All Giulia transmissions have a shift lever with a telescoping, press-for-reverse feature and are housed in a two-piece case that is split longitudinally. The same transmission, but with four instead of five forward speeds, also comes in Giulietta spiders with a fixed vent window (long wheelbase).

A car-speed-sensitive vibration or noise during a test drive indicates an out-of-balance driveshaft (can be fixed) or a bent one (requires replacement). The same phenomenon can also indicate an out-of-balance tire, bent rim (look at them to see), binding brake or bent axle shaft. Giulia donuts (rubber joint just behind the transmission) do not give trouble, but Alfetta donuts require regular replacement unless the car has an automatic transaxle.

A grinding sound from the rear that changes character as the car turns a corner or transitions from acceleration to deceleration indicates a bad rear end. Bad rears are uncommon on Alfas, and this will probably indicate very high mileage or abuse.

The wear pattern of the front tires will indicate the need for alignment, and might indicate worn suspension or steering parts. Generally, any nonsymmetrical wear across the tread indicates a problem.

Body

Virtually all spiders and most coupes will have been hit in the nose, and probably also in the rear. You can detect plastic body filler with a magnet. Try the magnet first on the hood panel to see how much pull it exerts on solid metal, then touch the magnet to the tip of the car's nose and pull up. If you feel significantly less resistance, you know a layer of plastic lurks under the paint. Work around the car, testing for plastic filler in the fenders and bumper-attachment areas. Look carefully at the symmetry of the nose, especially around the scallops for the headlamps. If one headlamp sits differently from the other, the bodywork is bad and you should probably not buy the car. The original Alfa sheet metal was fairly wave-free. Look along the side of the body: if the door doesn't align with the rest of the body or there are significant dimples in the sheet metal you know the car has been hit and poorly repaired.

Most body inspection will be to find hidden damage, either from an accident or rust. Rust does in more Alfas than any other single cause, probably, though the owner's gross stupidity is also a leading culprit. Of the two, at least rust is repairable.

Prior to the invention of plastic filler material, all surface body repairs were made using lead. The metal was cleaned and hot lead was ladled over the rough section, then ground down and sanded smooth. This technique is still optimum, but very expensive. Modern body repair involves smearing plastic over the damaged section and sanding it smooth to body contours. A careful plastic repair is undetectable unless you use a magnet. Since plastic or fiberglass fillers are non-magnetic, any unaccountable loss of magnetic attraction along the body indicates that there's plastic underneath. The ideal tool is a magnetic paint gauge that is calibrated to show paint thickness in mils. (A standard paint coat is about 3 mils thick.)

During their long lives, most Alfas will have sustained some body damage, particularly around the nose. Until all paint and primer is removed, the true condition of this spider nose won't be known.

If the repair's presentable, you shouldn't worry too much. What you need to look most carefully for is rust damage. There's a long discussion about rust at the beginning of Chapter 9.

Broken curved glass will be expensive for Giuliettas and Giulias. Be cautious of buying a car with a broken windshield unless you know where to get a replacement.

Interior

The interior of any car is probably going to be redone, so torn seats, mats and headlining are relatively routine items. The seats should be original, though, so don't get stuck with Triumph TR3 seats in a Giulia.

Giulietta and Giulia Sprint seats were rather fragile and tended to break around the hinge for the seat back. During restoration, you should have the seat checked for cracks in the metal support for the seat cushion near the hinge.

■ Shopping for a Restorable Alfa

Clearly, the way you use the above information is to attach a price to any fault. The sum of all the faults has to be added to the purchase price of the car to estimate the total investment you'll have in a restored car.

There are a few things to keep in mind before you even begin looking. The first is that the Alfa is a car that inspires hard driving. The examples you're going to look at have probably been thrashed much more than a different marque. If the steering seems imprecise, the engine smokes or stutters, or the driveline clunks or grinds, the chances are the Alfa has simply been beat to death. Look elsewhere. You should never buy an Alfa on a whim. Do some research first by talking to someone who is knowledgeable about the cars.

What Year?

There are no favorite years for Alfas. The 1750 model may prove to be slightly less prone to leak its head gasket, but the age of those cars means you should be very careful before buying one. If you buy a car with SPICA mechanical fuel injection you may have to service it at a specialist shop, since some franchised dealers won't work on the SPICA cars any more. The 1974 model year had a small advantage in power over surrounding years, thanks to an optimum fuel delivery curve. I recommend against purchasing an '80–81 spider with the single butterfly intake plenum simply because they're so hard to work on. Generally, buy an Alfa with Bosch EFI if you can afford it, because that's the current configuration and the one which is most trouble-free.

How Much?

Keith Martin's Sports Car Market magazine (P.O. box 16130, Portland, OR 97292-9915) lists Alfas for sale and contains a quarterly price guide. Considering the cost of a car, a subscription to this is small potatoes, especially if it keeps you from buying a junker at an exorbitant price. The national Alfa club (10 Raskin Road, Morristown, NJ 07960-2824) also has a monthly magazine which lists Alfas for sale. *Hemmings Motor News* (P. O. Box 100, Bennington, VT 05201) is another popular source for used Alfas. In all three magazines, both vehicle condition and asking prices will be marginally higher than you can find on the local market. The premium will be well worth it for a truly good car.

The best source of current pricing in your local area is the weekly free-ads publication such as *Recycler, Tradin' Times* or *Photo Buys*. Prices in these publications will not be inflated by the cost of running the ad, and you may truly find some exceptional bargains lurking in them. Prices on spiders vary widely, simply because they are an emotional car. For example, in a recent issue of *Keith Martin's Sports Car Market* magazine, a 1971 spider was advertised for $2,000. Next to it was another '71 spider for $12,000. If you can understand that either car could be a very good deal, then you're ready to start shopping wisely.

Although any price guide would soon be outdated, here are some basic guidelines for some of the most desirable models with the exception of the limited production and racing models. The Sprint and Spider Veloce examples will top the list, often commanding a 50-percent premium over their Solex-carbureted brethren. Of the mid-1960s models, the Duettos will often top the price charts, with early SPICA-injected 1980 and '81 models costing the least amount. With the later spiders, Graduates tend to pull lower prices, while Quadrifoglios go for higher figures.

There are a lot of desirable Alfas not listed here, including the TZ, Giulia TI Super and the Junior

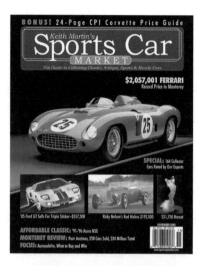

Keith Martin's Sports Car Market is a good place to look for auction results and want ads if you wish to buy an Alfa Romeo or other interesting collectible.

Hemmings Motor News has long been a primary source of collector cars for sale and should be part of the arsenal of tools you use when looking for an old Alfa or other collectible.

Zagatos. Generally, these rarer cars tend to create markets of their own. I can't stress too strongly the need to do extensive market research before buying one of these more rare cars.

Now that you've decided which model of Alfa Romeo to restore, it's time to make your plan and either send the car to a reputable shop—assuming your checkbook is big enough—or to tackle it yourself. The next chapter is dedicated to the Alfa owner who plans on a hands-on restoration.

Chapter 18

The Restoration Begins

By this time in the restoration process we have established a budget, a type of car to restore and a particular example of that type. In fact, at this stage, we'll assume that the car has been purchased and is sitting somewhat forlornly in the garage, ready for its restoration. We'll also assume that you're planning on doing much of the work yourself, even if your role is more that of a general contractor than the engine builder or body man.

■ First Steps

A first step is to set aside a storage area for parts. If you put the parts in cardboard boxes, label the boxes using a marker which is indelibly clear, the boxes may be filled with heavy parts for a long time, moved by myriads of greasy hands and rained upon at least twice.

Moreover, you can plan that at least one box filled with both heavy major components and all the fasteners to the entire car, will break as you're moving it, spilling irreplaceable parts in inaccessible corners of your garage.

To find them, turn out all the lights, and look with a flashlight, placed at arms-length so its beam just skims the floor and casts the longest shadow possible. As a last resort to find a small, irreplaceable metal part, vacuum the floor and then sift through the debris in the vacuum's bag with a magnet.

The completed body shell of a Giulietta Spider Veloce awaits paint at the shop of Alfa Romeo body restorer Bill Gillham.

To identify parts, get some parts tags, or labels to go on plastic bags or small containers containing smaller parts. The worst thing is to label small components with masking tape: the surface is too smooth to take an indelible mark, and the tape is too fragile to withstand much handling.

A handy storage technique, if you have a baby, is to save glass baby food jars for fastener storage. Just be careful not to store the jars where they will break. Paper egg cartons (the styrofoam kind melt in the presence of oil-based solvents) are handy containers for separating small parts.

Invariably during a restoration, I lose a box of small parts, mostly fasteners. Typically, I keep tripping over it, or moving it out of the way until the day before I need it. One way around this inevitability is to use the bolts to reassemble (loosely) the components they go with.

Some bolts and nuts should be used only as matched pairs: head nuts, bearing retaining nuts, rod bolts and the flywheel bolts are less damaged if they are replaced on the same threads from which they were removed.

Consider that the car itself is the largest single item you'll have to store. For this reason, keep the car as whole as possible and in running condition for as long as possible. You will loose fewer parts, feel better about the progress of the restoration and be able to manipulate the car most easily. It should be rollable at all times: plan to do brake, suspension and rear axle work at a time when you know you can complete the job within a couple of weekends.

Resist the temptation to take everything apart at once. The odds are, if you do disassemble the car completely, you will never see it together again.

There are alternatives to total disassembly, and I highly recommend them. For instance, you don't have to remove the engine to do a color change on the body. With the engine in the car, just spray what is convenient, around the top of the engine bay. When the engine is pulled (later), finish up the paint job. Similarly, if you have the engine out, paint the engine compartment and then finish the rest of the body once the engine is back together and in the car.

There is one instance in which total disassembly of the entire car is the only approach: if you're building a 100-point car for concours. Show standards require the virtual remanufacture of the car. The only way to do this is to take everything apart, fix everything at once, have all the chrome and paint done and then reassemble the car, touching up the paint as you go. The outlay for this approach is severe economically, physically and emotionally. Most amateurs are not up to it, and that means you and me.

The incremental approach gives you bite-size projects and keeps the car more or less salable at all times. A partially complete car brings a much lower sale price than one that is complete—even if it doesn't run.

For restoration purposes, a car is divided into several major categories, and your storage should reflect them:

- Engine
- Transmission
- Rear axle
- Front suspension
- Rear suspension
- Exterior body trim
- Major body panels
- Interior parts.

That is, keep the engine parts separate from the transmission parts.

Parts cleaning is one of the most time-consuming elements of restoration. Clean the item before it's disassembled, clean each part as it is disassembled and clean it again just before reassembly. (There's an important exception to this rule, however. If you know you're going to take months to get to a part, leave it dirty to reduce the danger of rust.)

I find that nuts and bolts are the hardest things to clean properly. Any dirt on a bolt will get wiped on the (clean) part it's fitted to, dirtying an otherwise clean surface.

Gunk, though popular, is a relatively weak solvent. Practically, lacquer thinner is the strongest solvent you should use in your garage, but be careful because its fumes are toxic. Industrial-strength solvents (like trichloroethelyne) have limited availability and are really dangerous. The best approach is to take really dirty major assemblies to a rebuilder to have them cleaned.

Bead blasting leaves a lovely finish but there is a danger that grit will inevitably get into critical parts and (possibly) ruin them. Use Gunk and a brush for internal mechanical parts.

I paint my cleaned engines with chrome aluminum. It's a very bright paint and makes the block look absolutely new. A can of aerosol flat-black is good for touching up the radiator and miscellaneous bits. A can of bright red paint is handy to highlight things like the fuel pump top stamping on a Giulietta, but that is a nonstandard trim if you're going after total authenticity in your restoration. Armor-All will do wonders for the interior plastic, and make rubber parts pretty, too.

One of the hardest decisions in restoration is drawing the line between replacement and repair. I try to repair everything and replace nothing. I think one of the pleasures of restoration is making broken parts work again. Occasionally I fabricate pieces, or adapt other parts to fit if I cannot make the original parts work again.

The decision becomes critical over an extensive restoration. You simply cannot replace everything with new parts unless you want a $40,000 investment in a car that's worth $7,000. There are some parts I never replace on an Alfa. Fortunately, I've never had to rebuild a water pump, an oil pump or a rear end. I've never replaced wrist pin bushes. Now, these are all critical items, and you must make sure they are serviceable before deciding not to rebuild them. My point is, however, if you rebuild each item as a matter of course, the cost of your restoration will skyrocket. Why rebuild a servicable transmission? If you need more convincing, just price the cost of replacing all the rubber on an Alfa.

One of the purposes of inspecting a car before you buy it is to identify what doesn't need rebuilding. The consideration is part of the budgeting process, and should guide you as the car comes apart.

You should begin the restoration by fixing the most needed item first. This is probably going to be either the engine or the body.

■ Tools

Before launching into the actual process—we'll do the body first—I want to say something about tools.

The actual number of essential tools for rebuilding an Alfa is very small. Many "required" tools, such as valve spring compressors, are eliminated if you have a machine shop do your valves (few amateurs have a valve grinder). Body work consists of almost 100-percent expendable materials (compressor and gun excepted). Some tools, such as the large gear puller required to disassemble the transmission, should be rented.

Now, I have a garage full of tools. In point of fact, I use very few of them and frequently, to take a ring compressor as an example, can do without them (the bottom of the cylinder barrel is beveled). So far as usual hand tools are concerned, a set of box-end/open-end wrenches and a socket set is just about all you'll need. I will say that a hacksaw is essential to remove rusted bolts, and a snap-ring pliers has no

substitute. My suggestion is not to celebrate an approaching restoration by purchasing $1,000 worth of Snap-on tools.

■ Body Restoration

As a result of the original inspection when you bought the car, you should have a good idea how much body work will be required.

Body work is hard physical labor. Initial body work (bending panels back to their original shape) can be downright brutal. Final body work is ultimately subtle. If you have an adventurous spirit, and can stand one fender looking significantly different from its mate, then there's no reason not to attempt body work.

A basic set of mechanics' tools is essential to most restorations. Any reasonably handy home mechanic should already have most of the required tools to embark on the restoration of any Alfa Romeo.

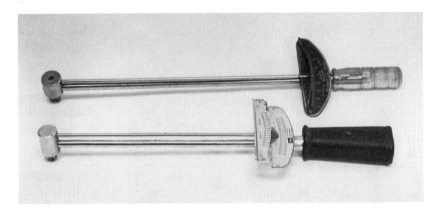

A torque wrench is also very useful to have when embarking on a restoration. The longer wrench measures pound feet; the smaller pound inches. These are relatively inaccurate beam-type wrenches. For maximum accuracy, take the reading only when the wrench is moving.

The first step is to wash the car with a strong detergent and remove any external trim.

The first step in beginning body work is to wash the car with a strong detergent. This removes any grease which would otherwise be sanded into the paint as you work.

At this point, you should remove any trim that could be scratched as you grind away rusted areas.

Chrome strips and badges are usually attached with nuts on an Alfa: lesser cars just stick them on with a glue. You must reach behind the panel on which the trim is located and unscrew its attaching nuts, which are on the order of four to seven millimeters, flat-to-flat. This is not an easy job, for some of the attaching nuts can only be undone after removing other panels to reach them.

This spider wheel well is severely rusted and will require new metal. Any attempt to fill this damage with body filler will result in a moisture trap which will eventually cause the plastic to lift as the corrosion continues.

In most instances, you'll find that the attaching nuts have rusted solid and you'll break the slender threaded studs on the badges. Avoid remorse: sharpen a putty knife, slip it behind the badge and give the knife a sharp blow with a hammer. You'll have anticipated what happens most often without having to remove a panel. Reattach the badge using contact cement after the restoration.

The chrome strips under the door of the Giulietta/Giulia Spider are held on by a bolt at either end and spring steel clips along the length. The grille pieces are bolted on, as is the chrome strip on the hood. Most other model Alfas follow this same pattern. Generally, a close inspection of the chrome strip will reveal how it is attached. A slip of paper can be used to probe behind the strip to find where the attaching bolts are located.

Polish the trim pieces after you remove them. Use 0000 steel wool coated in a good automotive paste or liquid wax to clean them up if they are not badly pitted. Though it is expensive, rechroming is the only acceptable repair for a badly tarnished or pitted chrome-plated part. Remember that some Alfa bumpers (the Giulia Super comes to mind) are stainless steel, not chrome.

The next step is to grind away all the rusted areas so there is nothing but shiny metal left. With plastic fillers, this is an easy step to slight, for plastic will bond to virtually anything. However, if you try to bond plastic filler to a rusted section, water vapor will eventually come between the porous metal and the plastic and pop the filler free. Be absolutely ruthless in removing rust.

The most frequently rusted exterior panels on an Alfa are the rocker panels and the rear wheel arches. The rocker panels can be removed by using a slender chisel to pop the spot welds holding the panels to the body. Typically, the lower attaching points of the rocker panels will already have rusted away, so a few deft pops along the flange below the door sill will be enough to free the rockers.

The outside rocker panels are not a structural part of the body. Behind each, however, is a strengthening member which runs along the underside of the car, tying the front and rear wheel arches together. These two side members and the central transmission tunnel are the only sources of fore-aft rigidity in the body.

Whatever rebuilding is to be done to the undercarriage should be done now. There is no reason why the substructure of a unit-body car such as Alfa cannot be rebuilt by welding new metal in. Try to spread the heat evenly around the body when welding, otherwise you may have to rewarp the body to get the doors to close properly. My suggestion is to use box- or c-section sheet metal to replace rusted components. Braze, rather than weld, wherever feasible and don't create any joint that will trap water.

I use a seven-inch grinding wheel to remove rusted sections. An 80-grit disk will work quickly on steel, and leave a surface which is roughened enough to encourage a close bond with a filler. As you grind away, you will be uncovering, something like an archaeologist, the history of your car. All its various colors may still be preserved in layers, and strata of plastic filler attest to old and forgotten accidents.

Whenever you use a grinding wheel, no matter how coarse the grit, strive for gradual transitions in surfaces, not craters. After all the rust has been removed, take a close look to see that the body panels line up the way they should. Now is the time to correct such basic misalignments. I corrected mine by measuring the misalignment very carefully and then jumping on the nose of the car twice.

Doors, hood and trunk lids can be aligned by loosening the bolts which attach their hinges and shifting the panel slightly. Trial and error is the only way to achieve good panel alignment. You will be able to shim some hinges with washers to raise a panel to its proper height.

Body Preparation

You may need to do some very basic panel beating to bring a fender or door closer to its original surface. The goal is to add as little plastic filler as possible to the body, so you must take some time to get the basic sheet metal as straight as you can.

I've never been very subtle in my approach to panel beating. I've found that a well-placed kick with a soft-soled shoe will work wonders on dented hoods and trunk lids. If more finesse is required, the heel of your hand can be used, provided you inspect the area first to be certain you're not going to impale your hand on a bolt or bit of sheet metal.

For those dented panels you can't kick from behind, a plumber's helper can do wonders. A door panel with a large dent may be helped by pressing a plumber's helper carefully in the center of the dent and then pulling quickly to pop the panel back to its original contour.

As a last resort, use a dent puller, which is a slide hammer attached to a sheet metal screw. The metal is

The outer rocker panel of this 1973 Spider is totally rusted away. Rust can also be seen in the structural member behind the rocker area and in front of the wheel well.

pierced with the tip of the screw, which is threaded in to form a secure attachment to the metal. Then, the slide hammer is used to pull the metal out. What usually happens is that a little dimple of metal is pulled out, with the remaining dent still pretty much untouched. Quite a few holes are required to do anything significant to the panel with a dent puller. One advantage of a puller is that the multitude of holes it leaves act as a sieve to catch plastic filler and help form a secure physical bond between the filler and metal.

An alternate approach, if you have an arc welder, is to weld short stubs of rod to the panel and then pull on the rods to pop the metal into place. Grind off the rod after the basic contour has been achieved and smooth everything out with filler.

Metal is literally plastic: if you stretch it, you will end up with more metal than you began with. Metal-shrinking techniques are beyond the scope of an amateur restoration. For that reason, be just a bit

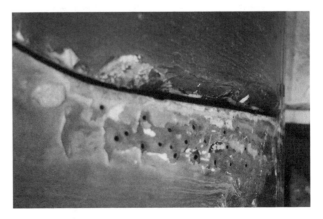

What looks like devastating damage is really the work of a dent puller. With the panel pulled back into a shape approximating its original state, the holes now need to be filled.

careful how much force you use to get a panel back to its original shape. The proper technique is to use just enough force, applied over as large an area as possible, to encourage the metal to "remember" its original contour. That's the reason I prefer a shoe to a hammer for removing dents. The hammer will leave you with a lot of dimples and stressed metal where a shoe will just kind of nudge things back to their general contour, which you will then complete in plastic.

If you're very ambitious, you might want to try cutting off damaged sections with a metal-cutting saw. This allows you to bang on them a little more conveniently. Once their original shape is restored, you tack-weld the part back on to the body.

Generally, any work with an oxyacetylene torch on a body is very risky for an amateur. As the metal heats up, it becomes very plastic, indeed, and forgets its original set. Usually, when a torch is used, lots of wet rags are used to surround the area and reduce the danger of warping the metal. Rather than resort to a torch, use mechanical means to fasten sheet-metal parts (pop-rivets are fine for unstressed panels) and cover the repair with plastic.

You may want to give in to a temptation to remove some trim pieces at this point and fill the holes with plastic. You have to understand that plastic only works well when it is thin and well-supported. Don't try to fill in a parking lamp mounting hole with a glob of plastic. It will fall out, eventually. The proper procedure is to depress the area immediately surrounding the hole (kicking is OK but a ball-peen hammer is better) and then pop-rivet a piece of aluminum behind the hole. Fill the depression with plastic. Never try to butt plastic against metal; only gradual transitions between plastic and steel maintain good bonds.

The first application of plastic filler should approximate the final contour you need. You will probably spread two to three more layers of plastic over the first layer, sanding each until it is almost gone. A grinding wheel may be used to correct gross surface deformities in the plastic on the first pass, but subsequent layers of filler should be sanded either with an orbital sander or a sanding block.

You'll need all the help you can get to make a decent repair using plastic filler. Don't pretend you're an Italian artisan skilled in the trade. Use straight edges and every other indicator you can think of to restore the body to its original contour.

I have found that the most helpful technique is to use light at a very narrow angle along a panel. Move the car so the sun shines tangentially to a panel, highlighting high spots and shadowing depressions. Use a trouble light at night to identify surface irregularities. Remember that the plastic, after it is sanded, is a dull surface that does not show irregularities. Paint, on the other hand is merciless, but it's too late to correct a wavy surface after it's been painted.

Body plastic comes in cans, accompanied by a little tube of hardener. There isn't any technique of judging the proper ratio of hardener to filler that is consistent, and experience is the only true guide. The ratio is not especially critical, providing you don't try to mix the whole can at once. To control the proportions of filler to hardener, always try to make the same-sized batch every time. Scoop out enough filler onto a piece of cardboard to make a couple of good-sized pancakes. For that amount, squeeze out a teaspoon of hardener. Mix the two with a spreader, trying not to trap bubbles of air in the mixing process. Don't try for a perfect mixture of hardener throughout the plastic: it will be further mixed as you apply it to the body. Just make sure there is a little bit of hardener throughout your lump of filler. You'll have from three to about ten minutes to work with the batch before it begins setting up.

If you haven't added enough hardener, the plastic will not harden. After about 20 minutes, just scrape it off and start over. On the other hand, if you've added too much hardener, the spreader will start to create a sandy surface as you smear the material: stop, throw the rest of the batch away and take a break while the filler you've applied hardens. Then, make a new batch using slightly less hardener and continue.

Paint Preparation

In general, it's no longer possible for an amateur to paint a car. A number of paints, including urethanes and catalyzed paints, are extremely toxic. By federal mandate, lacquer can only be used for restorations, and spraying paint in the open air is illegal in most areas. You can do all the preparation you want, but if you try to paint a car yourself, results can range from legal action to incapacitation.

At this point in the restoration, the major bodywork has been completed: some trim and all rust is removed, the body straightened where necessary, filled with plastic to restore the original contours and sanded smooth. The work to this point has required physical labor, rather rough at first, but becoming increasingly subtle as the final contours are achieved.

What one fails to realize in an actual restoration is that most of the work has been accomplished at this point. It is somewhat incredible: the body is spotted with islands of plastic in a sea of colors, much like a topographical map but in fact the color history of the car, displayed as the most subtle irregularities are sanded smooth.

This is the time for inspection and correction. The work that remains is physically easy and surprisingly quick. But the unprimered car is really the last opportunity to repair surface irregularities.

I've mentioned using a trouble light to evaluate the body surface. Hold it close to the body so its tangential light shows all irregularities, and then fix every one. This checking can be done in the evenings after work.

At this point, this Sprint has had body rust and damage repaired and filled and is ready for final priming and paint.

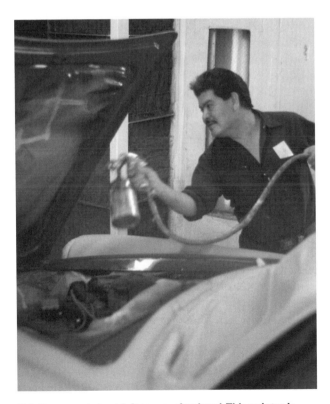

Painting a car is best left to a professional. This painter is not working with a modern two-stage paint which would require a respirator.

Spotting putty, "green stuff," is used to fill small pits which result from air bubbles in the plastic or the old paint. After all the sanding is finished, wash the car with soap and water.

Now the car is ready to be primed and block sanded after the primer has dried. Then it will be time for your Alfa to be given its color coats. Once again, block sanding will be required. As cited earlier, painting is no longer a task that can be done at home for reasons of both personal and environmental safety. This is the point where for best results you'll want to send the car to a body shop with a good spray booth. Once you see the finished result, you'll be glad that you didn't try to spray the car in your home garage.

■ Interior Restoration

There are many portions of interior restoration that the intrepid home restorer can easily undertake. However, some interior items should not be attempted by the average enthusiast. You should not try to remove the windshield from a coupe without professional aid. Similarly, I feel that headliner replacement, which involves glass removal, is not an appropriate project for the typical owner.

Seats

Replacement seat covers are available for many models, but I advise against trying to do anything more than slipping them over already existing upholstery. Upholstery, like painting, is a job which requires daily honing, and the occasional amateur is probably only going to botch it.

Nevertheless, there is a great deal of satisfaction in doing your own upholstery. If you use a reinforced plastic material, make certain that it is worth working on. There is no such thing as a cheap, good plastic: those two terms are mutually exclusive. The proper material is also probably the most expensive, backed with a deeply woven fabric and supple to the hand. Further, a durable thread is essential: mom's spare spool of black cotton thread won't work here.

A heavy-duty sewing machine is required to stitch upholstery material. You very carefully take the old material off the frame: what you take off becomes the pattern for what you put back on. Further: how you take it off is the pattern for how you put it back on. Note how the fabric is attached to the underside of the seats, and what hardware is used to attach it. You should obtain new hardware to use when you recover the seat.

It's possible that the foam material beneath the covers is crumbly: in that case, you can form new

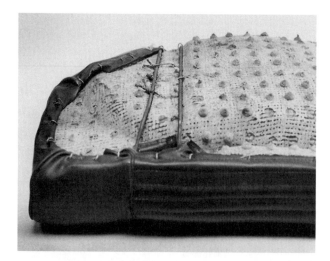

For many Alfas you can buy new seat cover kits and install the new materials yourself. The first step is to note how the covers are attached to the seat bottom or back.

Using pliers, remove the clips that secure the upholstery to the seat cushion.

material from a block of new foam using an electric carving knife. The trick is to cut the material without deforming it while cutting.

If you are lucky enough to be able to stand around an upholsterer for an hour or so (and, perhaps, ask a few questions), you will be able to approach the job with greater confidence. That failing, there are several books on the subject.

Side Panels and Headliner

Door panels are very easy to refinish on the Giulia because they are essentially two-dimensional. In fact, you can make door panels from scratch using a good quality brown fiberboard and the old panel as a pattern.

On the other hand, a headliner requires removal of the glass, and should be left to a professional.

Convertible Top

Although not exactly a part of the interior, installing a soft top uses the same techniques as for interior materials. You can buy inexpensive aftermarket convertible tops from several sources. Replacing a top is a major undertaking, no question about it, but the essentials are quite straightforward. The top is glued or clamped in place: you remove it by carefully pulling it free of glue or (carefully) unclamping it by removing screws or nuts.

You should not worry about getting a top drum-tight. Rather, be concerned that you install it evenly from side to side and front to back. As the top weathers, it will tighten up, but no amount of weathering or waiting will square up a top that has been put down crooked.

A good source for Alfa tops is Caribou Canvas (26804 Vista Terrace, Lake Forest, CA 92630). Complete installation instructions come with every aftermarket top, so I can afford to be brief here. You'll need a tube of trim cement, a pop-riveter and precious few hand tools.

You learn how a top goes on by taking the old one off. Note where it's glued to the top bows and how. There is no substitute for careful notes and a series of photographs or sketches as you remove the old top canopy. When you begin to fit the new top, begin with the front bow. Square the new top material very carefully and glue it in place at the front. Then, with the top partially erect, attach the rear of the top to the body using the clamping strip and its studs along the rear deck. After those two positions have been fixed, you can proceed to install the remainder of the top, running up and forward over the side windows.

Floor Mats

There is no substitute for the original rubber floor matting with the embossed Alfa logo. There is commercial ribbed rubber matting which can be cut to fit, but that is not really acceptable for a concours restoration. Most restored Alfas seen at national meets have replaced the rubber matting with standard fabric carpeting, properly bound all round with material which matches the upholstery.

Re-Originals (12618 Craigwood Lane, Cypress, TX 77429) is a popular source of original trim for Alfas. The pieces tend to be expensive, but if you feel there's no substitute for originality, then there's no substitute for Re-Originals.

Dash

The dash, which here is taken to include the instruments and electrical switches, is perhaps more of a challenge than the casual enthusiast should attempt. It's not so much getting the physical piece out: it's failing to scratch up the whole interior in the process, and then remembering where all those dangling wires go when you try to put it back in. It's instructive that no shop manual I know of deals with removal and replacement of the dash. I have removed the dash on a Giulia Super, as well as my 2.0-liter Spider, which is essentially the same as the Duetto. After having it completely free and attached only by a few wires (unlabeled) I decided that anything I needed to do would be as easily accomplished with the dash in situ as continuing its removal, and thus returned it to its proper position.

Be aware that the dash of the 750/101-series cars is an integral part of the body structure and is not removable.

Instruments should be rebuilt by a reputable shop. VDO has an office in Winchester, Virginia, if you can't find anyone to do it locally. In addition, California is home to West Valley Instruments and New York has Nisonger.

Wiring

Some Italian marques are notorious for poor wiring. Alfa is not. The Giulia is notorious for parking its fuse block out where its contacts are sure to fail, but the actual wires themselves are quite sturdy. The fact has not deterred owners from hanging a veritable Christmas tree beneath the dash to accommodate CBs, radios, amplifiers, several generations of burglar alarms and miscellaneous auxiliary lights and horns.

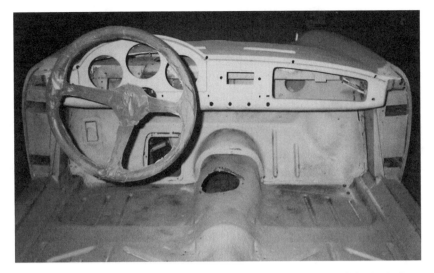

Because the 750- and 101-series dash is part of the body, it gets refinished in the same color as the body itself.

These Giulietta instruments are restored and ready to be returned to the dashboard.

A new wiring harness has been installed and electrical fixtures can now be connected.

▪ Accessory Restoration

I've made separate chapters on the engine and transmission and their restoration because they are large enough topics to warrant separate treatment. However, the accessories such as fuel pump, starter and generator are addressed here.

Fuel Pump

The mechanical fuel pump fitted to the Giulia is virtually trouble-free. You can dismantle it by removing the stamped-metal top that exposes the one-way valves. The top is spring-loaded, and held on by two screws, so be careful not to lose anything. The pump diaphragm itself is sandwiched between the two lower halves of the pump body. Rebuild kits are available, and the work is very straightforward.

The Giulia fuel pump is driven by two pushrods, and operated off a cam on the oil pump drive to the distributor. If you take the pump off and then reinstall it, only to discover it won't work, you have probably dropped the shorter of the two rods that is held in the fuel pump housing.

Some owners prefer electric fuel pumps. If you do fit an electric pump to the Giulia, verify that the fuel delivery pressure doesn't exceed about 3.5 psi: higher pressures can overcome the carburetor's float needle valve and cause flooding.

Although generators give little trouble, it never hurts to have one rebuilt when it's out of the car. This one has a worn mounting; you can tell because the unit doesn't sit parallel.

If you're dealing with a SPICA-injected Alfa, then you'll have (at least) two fuel pumps: an electric one amidships and one bolted up to the engine, which is the injection pump. The electrical one, responsible for delivering fuel at over 35 psi, is common for many cars. I've found that the pump for a fuel-injected Datsun Z-car looks like an exact replacement. You can rebuild a broken electrical pump; a common cause of failure is that the brushes hang up on their holders. The injection pump itself should not be rebuilt by an amateur (this means you). Send it to Wes Ingram (309 Cloverdale, #D-5, Seattle, WA 98108) along with about $700 for a rebuilt one.

Generator

The generator itself is a Lucas, Marelli or Bosch unit and virtually trouble-free. What you get on your car will depend a lot on sheer luck. Both Lucas and Marelli are denigrated by the bulk of Alfa owners, and there are a few who even hate Bosch. Of the three systems, in my estimation the most reliable is Bosch, followed by Lucas and then Marelli. Giulietta Veloces were equipped with Marelli electrics, while Giuliettas carried Lucas units. Bosch was introduced on the Giulia. The date of manufacture is stamped on most generators, and may indicate when your car was assembled.

On Giuliettas, the bottom generator mount is a stamped steel yoke which fits snugly against a boss on the aluminum front timing chain cover. If the long mounting bolt loosens, the boss can become worn to an oval: under extreme wear, the bolt can actually wear its way through the boss. Preventive maintenance—regularly tightening the bolt—is the only real insurance against wear. If the boss is worn, press-fit a steel bush to renew the mounting hole. Giulia and later cars added a rear support to the generator, which eliminated the wear problem.

A failure to charge, even with a good generator and regulator, indicates a slipping v-belt. If the red charging light stays on and gets brighter when the engine revs, the number 3 fuse in the fuse block is not making a good connection or is blown.

Starter

Like the generator, the starter is a Lucas, Marelli or Bosch unit. The number of teeth on the starter ring gear changed in about 1971. If you're replacing a starter, you need to verify that the starter engages properly with the ring gear. For the most part they should prove reliable. If the starter does fail, any number of auto electric repair shops should be able to rebuild it.

Carburetors

Solex carburetors on Alfas may be replaced by any of several Weber carburetors which are members of the DFT/DGAV family, since the mounting holes are identical. Refer to the author's book on Weber carburetors (H.P. Books, Tucson, 1987) for conversion information. The proper Weber for 750 Giulietta Veloces is the DCO model, while the 101 Giulietta and Giulia used DCOE Webers. Some European Alfas used Solex or Dellorto side-draft carburetors.

Two manufacturers supply bolt-on replacements for the Weber 40DCOE: Dellorto and Mikuni. Both are well-made and work as well as the Webers, though they look different enough that they're unacceptable for a concours where originality is judged.

During a restoration, there is an almost irresistible urge to throw away the single Solex carburetor in favor of a pair of Webers (or facsimile). I've swapped Solexes and Webers on an Alfa several times. Webers, because of their larger total venturi area, certainly make a more responsive engine, though they will not, by themselves, give much added power nor change fuel economy. The Solex-to-Weber conversion requires a new motor mount, manifold and air cleaner setup, different radiator top hose and a lot of work. Unless all these items fall easily to hand, the conversion is probably not worth the effort. To make the conversion truly worthwhile, you also need different pistons, the Veloce camshafts and a proper 1-4 / 2-3 header exhaust manifold. For more information about carburetors refer to Chapter 9.

■ The Point of It All

Even if you send out much of the work of a restoration, it is not for the faint of heart. A restoration will always take much longer and cost far more than you ever imagined. But if you persevere when the project seems endless and don't rush, the results can be very satisfying. At one time, you had a rolling collection of parts. When the restoration process is over, it is very likely that you have a gleaming red Alfa Romeo that sounds wonderful, is a joy to drive and attracts much attention. And just as importantly, you played a significant role in bringing a fascinating Italian sports car back to life.

This Alfa Romeo Giulietta Sprint Zagato is nearing completion of a comprehensive restoration to a very high standard.

Postlogue

In the mid-1990s, Alfa enthusiasts viewed the purchase of Alfa Romeo by Fiat with trepidation. That concern was relieved when Fiat proved, through the Alfas it produced, that it did not intend to cheapen the Alfa heritage as it had done with the Lancia Beta. That Fiat learned a lesson with Lancia is a fact for which Alfa enthusiasts must be forever grateful.

At the end of this history, I want to emphasize just how many times the fortunes of Alfa have changed, and how little those transitions have affected the essential character of the marque.

Try to imagine yourself in Italy just after the Great War. A.L.F.A. is almost ten years old, with an established line-up of mechanically reliable and somewhat sporting cars. It is purchased by Niccola Romeo, a well-known entrepreneur who is actually much more interested in railroads and earth moving equipment than automobiles. For the next decade or so, Romeo's direction of the company results in the hiring of Vittorio Jano, who gives him the P2 championship car, as well as a series of superb sport cars which still set standards of craftsmanship and engineering brilliance.

The Depression comes along. Rather than put Alfa Romeo out of business, the Italian government takes over the company. Mussolini is an important decision-maker in this change of fortune, for he has been enamored of Jano's masterpiece designs. Still, in the depths of the Depression, there is serious talk of ceasing automobile production. In just over another decade, near the end of the Second World War, the Alfa factory is leveled in a pair of bombing raids. Much of the staff has secreted itself, a few cars and parts in the mountains north of Milano. Within months of the end of the war, pre-war parts are being assembled as 1946 models. Soon, the Marshall Plan infuses new life into the company. In spite of a brilliant start with the 1900, Giulietta and Giulia models, a long series of weak governments and a firmly established bureaucracy combine to mis-manage the company past bankruptcy, to the point that it becomes a national scandal. For years, Alfa survives only because its closure would probably bring down the national government. Control passes to Fiat.

Through it all, the character of Alfa Romeo has survived intact: an engineering-driven producer of enthusiast automobiles. Perhaps this Alfa tradition is now so firmly established that it is truly an "Italian jewel," not subject to modification. For Fiat to fail in preserving the Alfa tradition, it must achieve something that a malingering bankruptcy, a dreary scandal, a Great Depression and two brutal World Wars could not accomplish.

Great Alfa Designers and Engineers

Since the its first beginnings as A.L.F.A, the company long known as Alfa Romeo has been known as a company of engineering insight and excellence. During that period, hundreds of designers and engineers have put pencil to paper for the great Milanese marque. Among those many were several handfuls of men who determined the entire cars or product lines coming from their drawing boards. Whether self-trained, apprenticed at an early age or holding engineering or other technical degrees, these few are closely associated with Alfa Romeo. This gallery of Alfa's engineering luminaries must include Giuseppe Merosi, Luigi Fusi, Vittorio Jano, Luigi Bazzi, Giuseppe Busso, Gioacchino Colombo, Bruno Trevisan, Wifredo Ricart, Orazio Satta Puliga and Rudolf Hruska. Many other worthies are omitted, despite their significant contributions. But, those men highlighted here are the ones whose thought processes shaped the mechanical layouts and functions of Alfa Romeo automobiles at a time when a given car was largely the work of one man. In the case of Hruska, he was capable, not only of designing an entire car, but also the factory in which to build it.

In the Fifties, Engineers Livio Nicolis (left), Orazio Satta Puliga (center) and Giuseppe Busso (right) worked together at Alfa Romeo.

Giuseppe Merosi

Giuseppe Merosi was born in Piacenza, Italy, on December 12, 1872. His father owned a small candle-making company and was affluent enough to send his son to the local technical school where Merosi earned his degree as a surveyor (*Geometra*).

Between 1891 and 1895, he seems to have been employed by the Italian department of public thoroughfares. By 1895, Merosi had formed a partnership with Vittorio Bassi, making bicycles and learning about design and fabrication. In 1898, he secured a job as a designer for sewing machine and motorcycle manufacturer Orio and Marchand. Merosi spent 1905 as a designer at Fiat, and the following year became the head engineer at Bianchi.

In 1909, Merosi accepted the job as A.L.F.A.'s chief engineer, a position he held until 1924. In 1923, Merosi began work on a new 2.0-liter Grand Prix car. Driver Ugo Sivocci was killed during testing and Merosi was demoted to Romeo's railroad empire. Merosi resigned officially in 1926 and took a temporary position at Mathis in Germany, but returned to Italy in 1928 to design motorcycles for Frera. In 1936, he was appointed the chief designer for Isotta Fraschini's line of trucks, but by late 1939, he was out of work. Hat in hand, Merosi asked for a job at Alfa. At 68, Merosi became a draftsman. By the end of the war, he had completely disappeared from notice. The only record we have of him after 1941 is that *Geometra* Merosi died at 84, in 1956.

A very young Giuseppe Merosi (in front passenger seat, number 1 at right) is with his colleagues at Orio and Marchand in that company's Marchand automobile dating from 1899.

Luigi Fusi

Luigi Fusi was born on June 6, 1906, and was only eight when his father went to work for A.L.F.A. At 14, the younger Fusi joined the firm as a draftsman-apprentice to Giuseppe Merosi. Fusi's apprenticeship at Alfa included work on Merosi's masterpiece six-cylinder RL series cars. It also included the disastrous 1923 Merosi design for the GPR race car.

Merosi's subsequent departure must have shaken the 17-year-old Fusi, whom Vittorio Jano selected as one of a five-man team to redesign the GPR. Fusi was involved in all of the great Jano designs, including the six- and eight-cylinder passenger cars and the supercharged eight-, twelve- and sixteen-cylinder Grand Prix cars of the Thirties.

Fusi was there for Jano's firing in 1937; for the devastation of World War II; the assassination of Alfa President Ugo Gobatto; and the ascension of Orazio Satta Puliga to the direction of the design department in 1946. Fusi was named chief of the Drawings Control Service in 1955, and later proposed a museum on the site of the original Portello plant, although he was disappointed when the archives and museum were located at the new Arese site.

With the museum established and the archives safe, Fusi retired into a consultancy with Alfa and turned to writing. His seminal 1965 book, *Alfa Romeo: All the Cars Since 1910*, set the standard for Alfa Romeo history. He subsequently worked on a variety of other fine Alfa Romeo books. Fusi passed away on December 27, 1996, after a long, debilitating illness.

Vittorio Jano

Jano was born to a middle-class family in San Giorgio Canavese in the Piemont (Piedmont) region near Turin on April 22, 1891. In 1909 he graduated from the Professional Operations Institute of San Maurizio. Despite his training in management and organization, that same year, Jano joined the Turin-based Ceirano company as a designer, a position he held until November 1911 when he joined Fiat's technical office. His drive and ability were soon recognized and in 1913 he was promoted to "construction designer." In May, 1920, he was again promoted to a group head position with five or six designers reporting to him—primarily designing production Fiats.

Jano eventually transferred to a group responsible for the development of Fiat racing cars, and during the 1923 season, Fiat's eight-cylinder supercharged Grand Prix car was a dominant player. Subsequently, he was recruited by Alfa Romeo and joined the company on September 27, 1923. Alfa won the Grand Prix championship in its first year with his P2. Subsequently, his 6C and 8C

As draftsman, Luigi Fusi played a significant role in all of the great Alfa Romeo designs of the 1920s and 1930s. Later he took the lead in establishing the Alfa Romeo museum and writing the definitive history of Alfa Romeo.

Vittorio Jano seems well pleased with himself in this photograph, which was probably taken when he was at the height of his success with Alfa Romeo.

defined the high-performance passenger car of the pre-war era. On the competition side, in an effort to keep up with the German Grand Prix cars, Jano designed a new V-12. When it failed to turn the German tide, he was fired.

By February 1938, Jano had found a place at Lancia. He was instrumental in the development of the Ardea and, after the war, the Aurelia. Jano was technical director of Lancia until he retired in 1955 and was retained as a consultant until 1958.

In 1965, with no medical evidence to support the theory, Jano determined that he had a malignant tumor. On March 13, in what Ferrari called "an act of courage," Vittorio Jano took his own life.

During his Lancia days, Jano (left, wearing suit) confers with Lancia Mechanics and driver Alberto Ascari.

Luigi Bazzi

Luigi Bazzi was born in Novara in 1892. His first job was with Fiat as a fitter and engineer in their racing department. When Fiat's 1923 GP car blew up in the French GP due to an unprotected supercharger intake, Bazzi became the scapegoat. He then joined Ferrari (who had left Fiat for Alfa in 1921) and became his best friend. In 1933, when Scuderia Ferrari became the official Alfa race team, Bazzi served as the technical director of the Scuderia. Bazzi remained with Ferrari for the rest of his working days, up through 1963. He died in Modena in 1986, at age 94.

Luigi Bazzi (left) with Aurelio Lampredi at the Ferrari factory in 1951.

Giuseppe Busso

Giuseppe Busso was born in 1913 and joined Fiat as a stress engineer in 1937. In 1939, he moved to Alfa and became Satta's protégé, being assigned to improve some of Ricart's designs. That made the pecking order Satta, Busso, and then Colombo. Initially, Colombo and Busso must have gotten along well. They traded places in 1945, with Busso going to Ferrari as its technical director and Colombo returning to Alfa. At Ferrari, Busso continued the development of Colombo's V-12 engine, but he rejoined Alfa within

a few years as Satta's superior. A "problem" developed between Busso and Colombo when Colombo became Busso's superior in 1951. The pecking order had now become Colombo, Buso and then Satta, a twist only the Italians could conceive. Fortunately for Busso, Colombo moved on to Maserati. Satta survived, eventually to became Busso's superior once more.

Busso's contributions to Alfa have been considerable. He was the chassis designer for the 1900, Giulietta, Giulia and Alfetta cars, and also contributed to the development of the Giulietta engine. He is currently retired and lives near the Arese plant, where he has been writing a series of history books for the factory.

Gioacchino Colombo

Gioacchino Colombo was born on January 9, 1903, in Legnano, Italy, and took an apprenticeship as a draftsman at Mssrs. Franco Tosi in Legano, designing diesel engines and steam turbines. In 1923, he won a competition sponsored by Alfa Romeo and in January 1924 began work as a draftsman in the special design department. Elevated to technical director of both the racing and production car departments in 1928, Colombo had become Jano's most trusted designer.

When Ferrari proposed a small Alfa to compete in voiturette 1.5-liter races Jano sent Colombo to Modena, where he worked on the type 158's supercharged eight-cylinder engine. When Alfa brought the Scuderia Ferrari operation in-house during 1938, Colombo became Alfa's chief engineer under Ricart. Charged with creating a new 3.0-liter Grand Prix car, Colombo developed the Tipo 308.

After Jano's firing, Bruno Trevisan turned to Colombo, and a pair of eight-cylinder blocks and heads from the 158 became the basis for the Type 316, a sixteen-cylinder GP engine. The potent sixteen-cylinder engine, fitted to Jano's "failed" twelve-cylinder chassis, proved the most serious competition for the Germans. When Mussolini's regime began to collapse in 1943, Colombo found himself on the wrong political side and was fired from Alfa. He returned to work with Ferrari, where he began the development of the Type 125 V-12 engine, the first modern oversquare Grand Prix power plant.

After the war Colombo returned to Alfa. But, under Satta, he was quickly reduced to occasional and menial design efforts. If he was underappreciated at Alfa, Colombo was honored by Ferrari, who brought him back as the first technical director in 1948, only to fire him in 1951. After a brief stint back at Alfa, Colombo moved to Maserati where he designed the successful 2.0-liter A6G engine, including the A6GCS, A6GCM, and the 250F Grand Prix car. He next accepted the challenge of designing a post-war Grand Prix Bugatti. His Type 251 mid-engine, four-wheel-drive Grand Prix car of 1956 was filled with innovation but was never properly developed.

After Bugatti, Colombo worked under contract with Abarth and MV Augusta. Then, in 1964, he joined Meccanica Verghera, another motorcycle firm. Always overshadowed, Gioacchino Colombo died on April 24, 1987.

Giuseppe Busso (left) was a key chassis engineer working on the Giulietta and Giulia cars, and also was involved with the Giulietta engine. Here Busso and the great Italian racing enthusiast Gianni Lurani are deep in conversation.

Engineer Gioacchino Colombo spent several stints at Alfa Romeo both before and after World War II.

Bruno Trevisan

Bruno Trevisan was born at Pavia di Udine on August 24, 1891, and served as officer in the Italian air force in World War I. In 1919, he joined Fiat as an aeronautical engineer and came to Alfa in October 1934.

Trevisan's first assignment was to upgrade Alfa's 6C2300 passenger car into what would become the 6C2500. He was promoted to chief engineer in 1937. In 1938, Trevisan helped design the S10 four-door sedan with fully independent suspension and a 3.5-liter, 60-degree, sohc V-12 engine. In the same year, Trevisan also developed the S11, a less-expensive car with a 90-degree V-8 of 2.2 liters, again with a single camshaft per cylinder. Neither car made it past the prototype stage.

Milan was bombed in October 1942, but Alfa's Portello factory was untouched. Alfa's president Ugo Gobbato moved Trevisan's group to Alfa's aero-engine factory at Armeno in the Lake Orta area. On June 18, 1943, partisans wrecked Armeno, and Trevisan's group returned to Milan. Portello was lightly bombed in September 1943, and was razed soon after by retreating Germans, with more bombing to follow. By this time, most of the actual manufacturing facilities had been scattered in the north, and management had moved north of Milan. In spite of the disaster all around them, Ricart's group held together.

On April 28, 1945, three days after the liberation of Italy, Ugo Gobatto was gunned down by assassins as he walked to work. On November 15, 1945, Bruno Trevisan died in an automobile accident which is believed to have been part of the same retribution which ended Gobbato's life.

Wifredo Ricart

Wifredo Pelayo Ricart y Medina was born in Barcelona on May 15, 1897, to a prominent Spanish family. Ricart was an accomplished manager and engineer by the time he arrived at Alfa in 1936, having run his own car manufacturing companies in Spain since 1920.

In 1937, racing activities were moved from Scuderia Ferrari to Alfa Corse. Ferrari continued as an Alfa Corse employee for a year, but Ricart's handling of the transition offended Ferrari's considerable ego. The brilliance of Ricart's Type 512, with its mid-mounted flat twelve—created as an alternate to "Ferrari's own" 158, only deepened the rift.

During the war, Ricart designed the 28-cylinder, 2,500 hp, 50-liter Type 1101 aero engine for Alfa. At less than 45 inches in diameter, it was 10 inches smaller than competing aero powerplants. Wartime pressures challenged all of Ricart's management skills as the design team was packed off to Lake Orta and the Grand Prix cars were hidden nearby.

Also during the war, Ricart designed the 6C2000 Gazelle, a futuristic sedan powered by an aluminum-alloy 2.0-liter, six-cylinder engine with twin overhead camshafts and an alloy crankcase carrying seven main bearings for the forged crankshaft. The Gazelle, which was fitted with a rear-mounted transaxle, was shelved in favor of a facelifted pre-war 6C2500.

In 1945, Ricart fulfilled his contract to Alfa Romeo. He returned to Spain where, in 1950, he designed the Pegaso and put Spain back in the car business. He died on August 19, 1974.

Orazio Satta Puliga

Satta was born in Turin on October 6, 1910, and received his degree in aeronautical engineering at the Turin Poytechnic in 1935. After a short stint in the military, he returned to teach aeronautical engineering at the Polytechnic until hired on at Alfa in 1939.

Satta worked in the design department, and after the war he was promoted to the overall management of design for the company. One reflection of his training, no doubt, is the use of unit-body construction,

Wifredo Ricart tests the Alfa 158 monoposto that had been developed at Scuderia Ferrari.

pioneered at Alfa with the 1900-series cars and continued with the Giulietta and Giulia lines. His unique vision allowed him to concentrate on the car as a whole, rather than treating it as a collection of distinct elements. He continued to rise in the organization: in 1951 he was central director and in 1969 he became assistant general director of the company.

Friendly and outgoing, he knew all of his subordinates by name and inspired great loyalty. Certainly he won the heart of Luigi Fusi, who could not have created his museum at Arese without Satta's enthusiastic and unflagging support. In 1972, he left active employment with the company and died after a protracted illness in March 1974.

Rudolf Hruska

Hruska was born in Vienna on July 2, 1915. His mother died when he was five and when his father remarried he went to live with relatives. At 23, he earned a degree in mechanical engineering from the Technische Hochschule in Vienna and took a job working on the design of truck tooling for Maqiros AG in Ulm. After a chance meeting with Karl Rabe, and Hruska was invited to Stuttgart and joined Ferdinand Porsche's group to work on a new "People's Car." Hruska's role was to furnish the factory with machine tools and it was during this time that he learned how an automobile should be mass-produced.

After the war—during which he worked on Tiger tank production—he was assigned the task of raising enough money to ransom Porsche from the French authorities. Eventually, an arrangement was made with Piero Dusio and his new Cisitalia company. In return, Porsche would design a Cisitalia Grand Prix car and Hruska would be Porsche's resident engineer at Cisitalia.

In 1950, Hruska was asked to apply his mass-production experience to the Alfa Romeo 1900. Subsequently, Hruska stayed on to help put the new Giulietta into production, and it was Hruska who suggested commissioning Bertone to design the coupe that became the Giulietta Sprint. When Giovanni Luraghi left Finmeccanica in 1956, Hruska was promoted to assistant managing director of Alfa. In 1959, he went to Fiat subsidiary Simca and in 1964 was put in charge of all Fiat sports cars. Three years later, Luraghi had returned to Alfa, and he turned to Hruska to put the new project BETA into production. Hruska completed plans for both the car (AlfaSud) and the factory in six months and was rewarded by being placed in charge of all design and experimental work in 1974. He held that position until his retirement in 1980. Active as a consulting engineer into his seventies, he died in December 1994.

Orazio Satta Puliga led all of Alfa Romeo engineering design following World War II and was ultimately responsible for the 1900, Giulietta and Giulia lines.

Rudolf Hruska was a skilled engineer, but his real talent was in the area of mass production.

Alfa Romeo Models

Model	Years Produced	Engine Type	Displ.	Transmission/ Drive	Chassis	Designer	Qty
Ur-Alfa	1907–1909	2-cycle / 2-stroke	N/A	3-spd / rear wheels	separate	Pedretti / Gulner	1
20/30	1910–1920	4-cyl / side-valve	4084 cc	3-spd / rear wheels	separate	Merosi	804
15/20	1910–1920	4-cyl / side-valve	2413 cc	3-spd / rear wheels	separate	Merosi	330
40/60	1913–1915	4-cyl / ohv	6082 cc	3-spd / rear wheels	separate	Merosi	27
Tipo G1	1920	6-cyl / side-valve	6597 cc	3-spd / rear wheels	separate	Merosi	52
RLN	1922–1928	6-cyl / ohv	2916 cc	4-spd / rear wheels	separate	Merosi	1,315
RLS	1922–1928	6-cyl / ohv	2996 cc	4-spd / rear wheels	separate	Merosi	939
RM	1922–1928	4-cyl / ohv	1944 cc	4-spd / rear wheels	separate	Merosi	371
RMS	1922–1928	4-cyl / ohv	1996 cc	4-spd / rear wheels	separate	Merosi	129
P1/GPR	1923–1924	6-cyl / dohc	1991 cc	4-spd / rear wheels	separate	Merosi	3
6C1500	1927–1930	4-cyl / ohc & dohc	1487 cc	4-spd / rear wheels	separate	Jano	1,108
6C1750	1929–1933	6-cyl / dohc	1752 cc	4-spd / rear wheels	separate	Jano	2,579
8C2300	1931-1934	8-cyl / dohc	2336 cc[1]	4-spd / rear wheels	separate	Jano	194
P2	1924–1925	8-cyl / dohc	1987 cc	4-spd / rear wheels	separate	Jano	13
Tipo A (P2)	1931	6-cyl / dohc X 2	3504 cc	4-spd / rear wheels	separate	Jano	3 est
Tipo B (P3)	1932–1935	8-cyl / dohc	2654 cc	4-spd / rear wheels	separate	Jano	14 est
8C2900	1936–1937	8-cyl / dohc	2905 cc	4-spd / rear wheels	separate	Jano	36
6C1900	1933	6-cyl / dohc	1917 cc	4-spd / rear wheels	separate	Jano	197
6C2300	1934–1937	6-cyl / dohc	2309 cc	4-spd / rear wheels	separate	Jano	1,606
6C2500	1939–1950	6-cyl / dohc	2443 cc	4-spd / rear wheels	separate	Jano	2,599
Tipo 158	1938–1940	8-cyl / dohc	1479 cc	4-spd / rear wheels	separate	Colombo	6
Tipo 512	1940	Flat 12 / dohc	1490 cc	4-spd / rear wheels	separate	Ricart	3
6C2000 Gazelle	1945	6-cyl / dohc	1954 cc	4-spd / rear wheels	unibody	Ricart	6
6CM3000	1950	6-cyl / dohc	3495 cc	4-spd / rear wheels	separate	Colombo	11 est
Tipo 159	1951	8-cyl / dohc	1479 cc	4-spd / rear wheels	separate	Colombo / Satta	4 est
1900	1951–1958	4-cyl / dohc	1884 cc	4-spd / rear wheels	unibody	Satta	21,092
Giulietta	1955–1963	4-cyl / dohc	1290 cc	4-spd / rear wheels	unibody	Satta	163,291
2000	1958–1962	4-cyl / dohc	1975 cc	5-spd / rear wheels	unibody	Satta	6,947 est
Giulia	1962–1979	4-cyl / dohc	1570 cc	5-spd / rear wheels	unibody	Satta	650,987
2600	1962–1968	6-cyl / dohc	2584 cc	5-spd / rear wheels	unibody	Satta	11,346
Duetto Spider	1966–1967	4-cyl / dohc	1570 cc	5-spd / rear wheels	unibody	Satta	6,325
Tipo 33 Stradale	1967–1969	V-8 / dohc	1995 cc	6-spd / rear wheels	tubular fr	Satta	18
1750	1967–1971	4-cyl / dohc	1779 cc	5-spd / rear wheels	unibody	Satta	154,069
Montreal	1972–1976	V-8 / dohc	2593 cc	5-spd / rear wheels	unibody	Satta	3,925
2000	1972–1995	4-cyl / dohc	1962 cc	5-spd / rear wheels	unibody	Satta	217,176
Alfasud	1972–1980	Flat-4 / sohc	1186 cc	4-spd / front wheels	unibody	Hruska	1,028,258
Alfetta	1972–1986	4-cyl / dohc	1962 cc	5-spd / rear wheels	unibody	Surace / Chirico	760,541

Model	Years Produced	Engine Type	Displ.	Transmission/ Drive	Chassis	Designer	Qty
Alfasud Sprint	1976–1989	Flat-4 / sohc	1286 cc	4-spd / front wheels	unibody	Hruska	490,180
Nuova Giulietta	1977–1985	4-cyl / dohc[2]	1351 cc 1560 cc 1779 cc	5-spd / front wheels	unibody	Surace / Chirico	348,145
Alfetta GTV V-6	1980–1984	V-6 / sohc	2492 cc	5-spd / rear wheels	unibody	Surace / Chirico	22,381
Alfa 6	1979–1987	V-6 / sohc[3]	2492 cc 1997 cc	5-spd / rear wheels[4]	unibody	Surace / Chirico	15,237
Arna L	1983–1986	Flat-4 / dohc	1186 cc 1350 cc 1490 cc	4-spd / front wheels	unibody	Nissan / Alfa	46,231
Alfa 33	1983–1994	Flat-4 / sohc[5]	1350 cc 1490 cc	4-spd / FWD; AWD option	unibody	Chirico / Bossaglia	1,102,070
Alfa 90	1984–1987	4-cyl / dohc[6]	1779 cc 1997 cc	5-spd / rear wheels	unibody	Surace / Chirico	49,516
Alfa 90 V-6	1985–1987	V-6 / sohc	2492 cc	5-spd / rear wheels	unibody	Surace / Chirico	6,912
Alfa 75	1985–1988	4-cyl / dohc[6]	1560 cc 1779 cc 1997 cc	5-spd / rear wheels	unibody	Surace / Chirico	355,135
Alfa 75/Milano	1985–1992	V-6 / sohc	2492 cc 2959 cc	5-spd / rear wheels	unibody	Surace / Chirico	9,526
Alfa 164	1987–1997	4-cyl / dohc or V-6 / sohc[7]	1962 cc 2959 cc	5-spd / front wheels[4]	unibody	Surace / Chirico	273,407
Alfa 33 1.7 16-valve	1990–1992	Flat-4 / sohc	1712 cc	4-spd / front wheels	unibody	Chirico / Bossaglia	157,600
Alfa 155	1992–1997	4-cyl / dohc[8]	1598 cc	5-spd / front wheels	unibody	DiSilva	190,118
Alfa 145	1994–2000	Flat-4 / sohc[9]	1351 cc 1596 cc 1712 cc	5-spd / front wheels	unibody	DiSilva	128,904
Alfa 146	1996–1999	4-cyl / dohc[10]	1351 cc 1596 cc 1712 cc	5-spd / front wheels	unibody	DiSilva	83,417
GTV Coupe	1995–2000	4-cyl / dohc[11]	1996 cc	5-spd / front wheels	unibody	DiSilva	14,322
Spider	1995–2000	4-cyl / dohc	1747 cc 1970 cc	5-spd / front wheels	unibody	DiSilva	12,311
Alfa 156	1997–2000	4-cyl / dohc[12]	1598 cc 1747 cc	5-spd / front wheels[4]	unibody	DiSilva	365,486
Alfa 166	1998–2000	V-6 / sohc[13]	1970 cc	5-spd / front wheels[4]	unibody	DiSilva	59,167
Alfa 147	2000–	4-cyl / dohc[14]	1598 cc	5-spd / front wheels[4]	unibody	DiSilva/ Zapatinas	13,358

Please note that the above chart is not meant to be a comprehensive listing of all Alfa Romeo models. Some sub-models, limited production cars and racing cars have been omitted in the interest of brevity.

1 Total includes six examples of 8C2600 Monzas.

2 Other engines include 2.0-liter Turbodiesel and 2.0-liter Turbodelta.

3 A 2.5-liter Turbodiesel was also offered.

4 Automatic also available.

5 The 33 was also available with a Turbodiesel.

6 Also offered with a 2.4-liter Turbodiesel.

7 Other engines include 2.0-liter V-6 turbo, 24-valve 3.0-liter V-6, 2.0-liter turbo four and 2.5-liter Turbodiesel. Note that the 2.0-liter is a twin-spark engine.

8 Base engine; options included 1.8-liter and 2.0-liter four-cylinders, as well as diesel and V-6 engines.

9 The 145 was also available with a 2.0-liter twin-spark 16V inline four and a 1929cc Turbodiesel; later twin-spark engines displace 1.4, 1.6 and 1.8 liters.

10 The 146 was also available with 1370cc, 1598cc, 1747cc and 1970cc twin-spark 16V inline fours and a 1910cc Turbodiesel.

11 V-6 in 2.0-liter, 3.0-liter or 2.0-liter turbo are optional.

12 For the 156, 1.6-liter and 1.8-liter twin-spark fours were available, as were 2.5-liter V-6 and 1.9-liter and 2.4-liter Turbodiesels.

13 In addition to the 16-valve 2.0-liter, other engines included 2.0-liter turbo V-6, 2.5-liter and 3.0-liter V-6s and 2.4-liter, inline five Turbodiesel.

14 The 147 was also available with a 1.9-liter Turbodiesel.

Index

For a more extensive listing of
Alfa models, please see Appendix 2:
Alfa Romeo Models on page 270.

A

WARNING

Your common sense, good judgment and general alertness are crucial to safe and successful service work. Before attempting any work on your Alfa Romeo, read the warnings and cautions on page v and the copyright page at the front of this book. Review these warnings and cautions each time you prepare to work on your car. Please also read any warnings and cautions that accompany the procedures in the book.

WARNING

Your common sense, good judgment and general alertness are crucial to safe and successful service work. Before attempting any work on your Alfa Romeo, read the warnings and cautions on page v and the copyright page at the front of this book. Review these warnings and cautions each time you prepare to work on your car. Please also read any warnings and cautions that accompany the procedures in the book.

WARNING

Your common sense, good judgment and general alertness are crucial to safe and successful service work. Before attempting any work on your Alfa Romeo, read the warnings and cautions on page v and the copyright page at the front of this book. Review these warnings and cautions each time you prepare to work on your car. Please also read any warnings and cautions that accompany the procedures in the book.

Art Credits

All photos or illustrations are either by or courtesy of Pat Braden except as noted below.

Courtesy Alfa Romeo Incorporated: 18 (left), 19, 37, 45 (bottom), 85 (top), 107, 109, 125 (bottom)

Photo by Mark April, courtesy Sperry Valve Works: 228, 229 (top), 230 (bottom), 231 (top)

Courtesy Bentley Publishers: 77 (top), 176 (bottom)

Photo by Margaret Black: 283

Courtesy Robert Bosch AG: 175, 177 (top, bottom), 178, 179 (top, bottom), 180 (all), 181, 182 (top, bottom)

Courtesy David Burgess-Wise: 96 (top)

Photo by John Clinard: 188, 195, 215, 220 (right)

Photo by Paul Davidson: 91 (bottom), 126 (top)

Courtesy Fiat Automobili Archivio Storico Alfa Romeo: 2 (bottom), 3 (top, bottom), 5, 7 (top), 14 (bottom), 30, 35 (bottom), 39 (top,), 40, 42 (middle), 49, 50 (top, bottom), 51, 52, 56, 57 (top), 60 (top, bottom), 61, 62 (bottom), 63, 64, 68 (top, bottom), 77 (bottom), 79 (bottom), 89 (bottom), 91 (top), 92 (top), 93, 94, 96 (bottom), 98 (top), 102, 103 (top, bottom), 104, 105 (top), 106, 108 (top), 113, 114, 157 (top, bottom), 158 (top, bottom), 159, 160, 161, 165 (top), 169, 170, 172, 173, 206 (left, right), 207, 225, 227 (top), 230 (top right), 231 (bottom), 234 (right), 242, 244, 264, 265 (top), 268, 269 (top, bottom)

Courtesy Wicker Francis: 191 (top, right), 192 (all), 193 (bottom left, bottom right)

Photo by Bill Gillham: 201, 239 (bottom), 249, 251, 254 (top), 259 (middle, bottom)

Photo by David Gooley: 59, 68 (middle), 90 (top), 101, 108 (bottom), 110, 226, 257 (top)

Photo by Michael Harris: 197 (top, bottom), 198

Courtesy Hemmings Motor News: 250 (bottom)

Courtesy David Kayser, Chelsea Motoring Literature: 10, 16, 17 (top), 32, 38 (top), 46, 58 (bottom), 62 (top), 80

Photo by Thomas Lesko: 140 (top left), 191 (top left)

Courtesy Ludvigsen Library: 4 (top, bottom), 12, 13 (middle, bottom), 29, 53, 55, 73 (top), 90 (bottom), 263, 265 (bottom), 266 (top, bottom), 267 (top, bottom)

Courtesy Dave McLellan: 208 (right)

Courtesy Simon Moore and Parkside Publications: 9

Courtesy Craig Morningstar: 13 (top left, top right), 15 (top, bottom), 17 (bottom), 18 (right), 20, 21, 22, 23 (top, bottom)

Photo by John Ortakales: 193 (top left), 211 (top, bottom)

Photo by Hans Quennet: 165 (bottom), 166 (top, bottom), 167

Courtesy Road & Track: 203, 204 (all), 205, 210 (top)

Courtesy Richard Baron, Road & Track: 238 (top, bottom)

Photo by Tom Sahines: 183, 186 (top, bottom), 189, 191 (bottom), 192 (bottom left), 194

Photo by Steve Snyder: 232

Courtesy Keith Martin's Sports Car Market: 250 (top)

Photo by Jonathan A. Stein: 2 (top), 8 (bottom), 28, 34, 35 (top), 36 (top), 38 (bottom), 39 (bottom), 41 (top, bottom), 42 (top), 43 (bottom), 44 (top, bottom), 45 (top), 47, 48 (top, bottom), 54 (top, bottom), 58 top, 65, 66, 70 (top, bottom), 71, 74, 75 (top, bottom), 76, 78, 79 (top), 81 (top, bottom), 82 (top, bottom), 83, 85 (bottom), 86, 88, 98 (bottom), 100, 105 (middle), 111, 115 (bottom), 121 (top left, top right, bottom left), 124, 125 (top), 150, 151, 154, 155 (bottom), 163, 164, 176 (top), 185 (all), 212 (all), 214 (all), 217, 218 (all), 219 (all), 220 (left), 221 (top, bottom), 222 (all), 223, 227 (bottom), 237, 240 (top, bottom), 243, 247, 255 (top)

Photo by Dave Trendler: 57 (bottom)

Photo by Jim Weber: 99 (top)

Cover Artwork

Front cover: All photos by Jonathan A. Stein: 1960 Giulietta SS engine (right), 1960 Giulietta Spider Veloce, 1962 Giulia Sprint of Jim Itin, 1967 Giulia Super of Lee Weinstein, 1967 Giulia GTV of Joel Ortega, 1987 Spider Quadrifoglio of Douglas Bechtel (top to bottom). Drawing of the Giulia engine in background courtesy Fiat Automobili Archivio Storico Alfa Romeo.

Back cover: Author photo courtesy Pat Braden. Photos by Jonathan A. Stein: 1956 Giulietta Berlina TI of Jim Allen, 1965 Giulia Spider Veloce of Felix Chiu, engine in 1976 Alfetta GT of Wilson Werhan, 1965 Giulia GTC of Gene Boyer and 1991 Spider of Michael Marzullo. Photo of all-alloy engines courtesy Fiat Automobili Archivio Storico Alfa Romeo.

In production of this book every effort was made to locate and obtain permission from the original artists of the included artwork.

Acknowledgments

Bentley Publishers would like to thank many people who worked very hard to make sure that this book could be completed and published despite the loss of Pat Braden.

Most important of all contributors was Cheryl Braden who wanted to ensure that Pat's final book would see publication and would be a book in which he could have taken pride. Pat's long-time friend Jim Weber also contributed much time and energy to the project.

As editor, I would like to thank Jim Allen, Russ Baer, Jane Barrett of *Road & Track*, Felix Chiu, John Clinard, Paul Davidson, Wicker Francis, Bill Gillham, Michael Harris, David Kayser, Tom Lesko, The Ludvigsen Library, Craig Morningstar, Michelle Muller, John Orkateles, Hans Quennet, Elvira Ruocco of Alfa Romeo, Tom Sahines, Sperry Valve Works, Henry Wessells and everyone who helped in any way.

Before Pat Braden's death, he expressed a desire to recognize: Jim Allen, Richard Ballentine, Joe Benson, Michael Bentley, Don Black, Ed Bond, Don Bruno, Antonio Cerlenizza, Ron Crawford, Fred diMatteo, Luigi Fusi, Pat and Glenna Garrett, Joost Gompels, Ed Hancock, Malcolm Harris, Keith Hellon, John Hoard, Nick Holt, Peter Hull, Bill Knauz, Phil Lampman, Vojta Mashek, Dave Mericle, Norm Miller, Simon Moore, Craig Morningstar, Tim Parker, Gary Patitz, Franco Perugia, Paul Pfanner, Bill Pringle, Stu and Carole Sandeman, John Shankle, Roy Slater, Chuck Stoddard, Martin Swig, Paul Tenney, Roby and Rob Thalmann, Dave Trendler, Dick van der Feen, Neil Verweij, Andrew Watry, Jim Weber, Henry Wessells and Tom Zat.

Unfortunately, with a project as big and as far-reaching as this book, it's impossible to acknowledge everyone who made a substantive contribution. For those who are not mentioned, we apologize.

— Jonathan A. Stein, January 2004

About the Author

Pat Braden came by his interest in automobiles naturally. The son of an automobile factory worker in Flint, Michigan, Pat was born in 1934. Pat was an accomplished author, internationally recognized for his knowledge and love of automobiles. He held bachelor's and master's degrees, and had completed the coursework for his Ph.D.

While living in Ann Arbor, Michigan, Pat first began to collect and to write about cars, helping to found the Alfa Romeo Owners Club of America and regularly contributing to many related publications. Pat took his family to Europe for several years in the late 1960s while working for the United Serviceman's Organization in Naples, Italy, and Rota, Spain. It was here that Pat became fluent in both Italian and Spanish. Upon their return to Michigan they lived in Dexter, finally buying a small farm where they remained until wife Marie died in 1978.

Pat moved to California in 1979 and was made an honorary life member of the Alfa Owners club the same year. He married Cheryl Lee in 1980. It was here that Pat's prolific career as a writer was established. He authored seven books (*The Ferrari 365 GTB/4 Daytona, Abarth, Weber Carburetors, Toyota Performance Handbook, Alfa Romeo Giulia, Alfa Romeo Owner's Bible*) as well as the *Alfa Romeo All-Alloy Twin Cam Companion*. He wrote countless magazine and journal articles about an amazing variety of automotive subjects and served as editor for four magazines. He self-published a pocket history of Alfa Romeo entitled *From Portello to Arese*.

Pat was an avid collector who had owned scores of exotic automobiles and motorcycles during his lifetime,

Pat Braden (left) with Alfa guru Paul Tenney (center) and Don Black (right), retired Chief Engineer of ARI, enjoying the Monterey Historic Races in 1991.

including over 50 vintage and modern Alfa Romeos, Fiats, Lancias, a Maserati, a Moretti, BMWs, Mercedes, Abarths, Ducatis and a BSA. At his death he owned 40 cars and motorcycles. He also collected cameras (he was an accomplished photographer), clocks and computers. His expansive automotive library is widely known.

The professional positions Pat held during his 40-plus-year career were wide-ranging and demonstrated his immense talent. These included corrections work, teaching, writing, technical editing, marketing and advertising, creative direction, management and administration. At the time of his death in August 2002 he was writing training materials for Hyundai.

Pat was the proud father of five children, born over a period of 34 years. Four children (Mark, 45; Leslie, 43; Kay, 20; and Patty, 11), one grandchild (Sarah) and wife Cheryl survive him.

Selected Books and Repair Information From Bentley Publishers

Driving

The Unfair Advantage *Mark Donohue*
ISBN 0-8376-0073-1(hc); 0-8376-0069-3(pb)

Going Faster! Mastering the Art of Race Driving *The Skip Barber Racing School*
ISBN 0-8376-0227-0

Driving Forces: The Grand Prix Racing World Caught in the Maelstrom of the Third Reich *Peter Stevenson*
ISBN 0-8376-0217-3

A French Kiss With Death: Steve McQueen and the Making of *Le Mans* *Michael Keyser* ISBN 0-8376-0234-3

Sports Car and Competition Driving *Paul Frère* with foreword by *Phil Hill*
ISBN 0-8376-0202-5

The Technique of Motor Racing *Piero Taruffi* ISBN 0-8376-0228-9

Engineering/Reference

Supercharged! Design, Testing, and Installation of Supercharger Systems *Corky Bell* ISBN 0-8376-0168-1

Maximum Boost: Designing, Testing, and Installing Turbocharger Systems *Corky Bell* ISBN 0-8376-0160-6

Bosch Fuel Injection and Engine Management *Charles O. Probst, SAE*
ISBN 0-8376-0300-5

Road & Track Illustrated Automotive Dictionary *John Dinkel*
ISBN 0-8376-0143-6

Alfa Romeo

Alfa Romeo Owners Bible™
Pat Braden ISBN 0-8376-0707-8

Audi

Audi A4 Service Manual: 1996–2001, 1.8L turbo, 2.8L, including Avant and quattro *Bentley Publishers*
ISBN 0-8376-0371-4

Audi A4 1996–2001, S4 2000–2002: Official Factory Repair Manual on CD-ROM *Audi of America*
ISBN 0-8376-1072-9

Audi A6 Sedan 1998–2004, Avant, including allroad quattro, S6 Avant, RS6: Official Factory Repair Manual on CD-ROM *Audi of America*
ISBN 0-8376-1076-1

BMW

BMW 3 Series Enthusiast's Companion™ *Jeremy Walton*
ISBN 0-8376-0220-3

BMW 6 Series Enthusiast's Companion™ *Jeremy Walton*
ISBN 0-8376-0193-2

Unbeatable BMW: Eighty Years of Engineering and Motorsport Success *Jeremy Walton* ISBN 0-8376-0206-8

The BMW Enthusiast's Companion *BMW Car Club of America*
ISBN 0-8376-0321-8

BMW 3 Series (E46) Service Manual: 1999–2001, 323i, 325i, 325xi, 328i, 330i, 330xi Sedan, Coupe, Convertible, Sport Wagon *Bentley Publishers*
ISBN 0-8376-0320-X

BMW 3 Series (E36) Service Manual: 1992–1998, 318i/is/iC, 323is/iC, 325i/is/ iC, 328i/is/iC, M3 *Bentley Publishers*
ISBN 0-8376-0326-9

BMW 5 Series Service Manual: 1997–2002 525i, 528i, 530i, 540i, Sedan, Sport Wagon *Bentley Publishers*
ISBN 0-8376-0317-X

BMW 5 Series Service Manual: 1989–1995 525i, 530i, 535i, 540i, including Touring *Bentley Publishers* ISBN 0-8376-0319-6

BMW 7 Series Service Manual: 1988–1994, 735i, 735iL, 740i, 740iL, 750iL *Bentley Publishers*
ISBN 0-8376-0328-5

Chevrolet

Zora Arkus-Duntov: The Legend Behind Corvette *Jerry Burton*
ISBN 0-8376-0858-9

Corvette from the Inside: The 50-Year Development History *Dave McLellan*
ISBN 0-8376-0859-7

Corvette by the Numbers: The Essential Corvette Parts Reference 1955–1982 *Alan Colvin* ISBN 0-8376-0288-2

Chevrolet by the Numbers: The Essential Chevrolet Parts Reference 1965–1969 *Alan Colvin* ISBN 0-8376-0956-9

Corvette Fuel Injection & Electronic Engine Management: 1982–2001 *Charles O. Probst, SAE*
ISBN 0-8376-0861-9

Ford

The Official Ford Mustang 5.0 Technical Reference & Performance Handbook: 1979–1993 *Al Kirschenbaum* ISBN 0-8376-0210-6

Ford F-Series Pickup Owner's Bible™ *Moses Ludel* ISBN 0-8376-0152-5

Ford Fuel Injection and Electronic Engine Control: 1988–1993 *Charles O. Probst, SAE* ISBN 0-8376-0301-3

Jeep

Jeep CJ Rebuilder's Manual: 1946–1971 *Moses Ludel* ISBN 0-8376-1037-0

Jeep CJ Rebuilder's Manual: 1972–1986 *Moses Ludel* ISBN 0-8376-0151-7

Jeep Owner's Bible™ *Moses Ludel* ISBN 0-8376-0154-1

Mercedes-Benz

Mercedes-Benz E-Class Owner's Bible™ 1986–1995
Bentley Publishers ISBN 0-8376-0230-0

Porsche

Porsche: Excellence Was Expected *Karl Ludvigsen* ISBN 0-8376-0235-1

Porsche 911 (964) Enthusiast's Companion: Carrera 2, Carrera 4 and Turbo, 1989–1994 *Adrian Streather* ISBN 0-8376-0293-9

Porsche Carrera 964 and 965, 1989–1994 Technician's Handbook: Without Guesswork™ *Bentley Publishers*
ISBN 0-8376-0292-0

Porsche 911 Carrera Service Manual: 1984–1989 *Bentley Publishers*
ISBN 0-8376-0291-2

Porsche 911 SC Coupe, Targa, and Cabriolet Service Manual: 1978–1983 *Bentley Publishers* ISBN 0-8376-0290-4

Volkswagen

Volkswagen Sport Tuning for Street and Competition *Per Schroeder*
ISBN 0-8376-0161-4

New Beetle Service Manual: 1998–2002 1.8L turbo, 1.9L TDI diesel, 2.0L gasoline *Bentley Publishers*
ISBN 0-8376-0376-5

Golf, GTI, Jetta 1999–2004, Jetta Wagon 2001–2004: Official Factory Repair Manual on CD-ROM *Volkswagen of America* ISBN 0-8376-1081-8

Passat Service Manual: 1998–2004, 1.8L turbo, 2.8L V6, 4.0L W8, including wagon and 4motion *Bentley Publishers* ISBN 0-8376-0369-X

Passat 1998–2004: Official Factory Repair Manual on CD-ROM *Volkswagen of America* ISBN 0-8376-1084-2

Jetta, Golf, GTI, Cabrio Service Manual: 1999–2003, 1.8L turbo, 1.9L TDI diesel, 2.0L gasoline, 2.8L VR6 *Bentley Publishers* ISBN 0-8376-0323-4

Super Beetle, Beetle and Karmann Ghia Official Service Manual: Type 1, 1970–1979 *Volkswagen of America* ISBN 0-8376-0096-0